Greetings from Colorado Springs

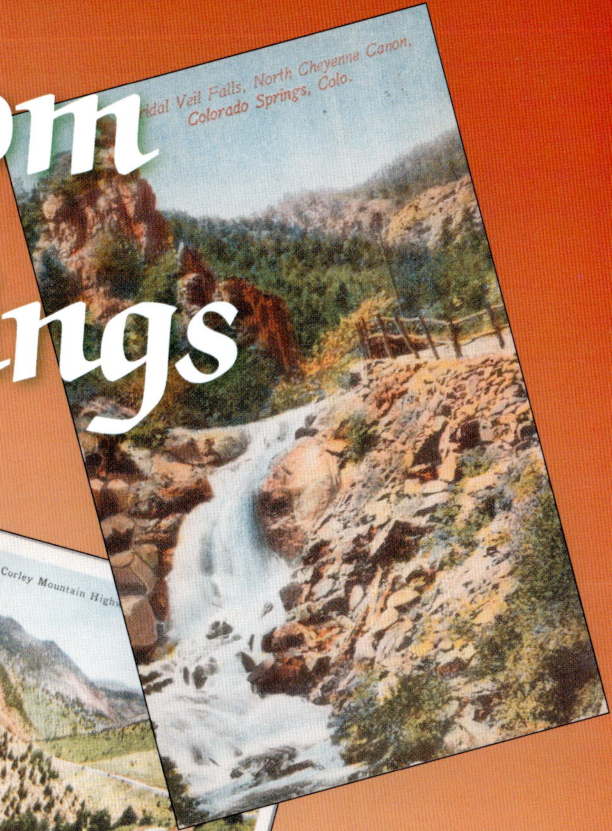

Mary L. Martin
& Nathaniel Wolfgang-Price

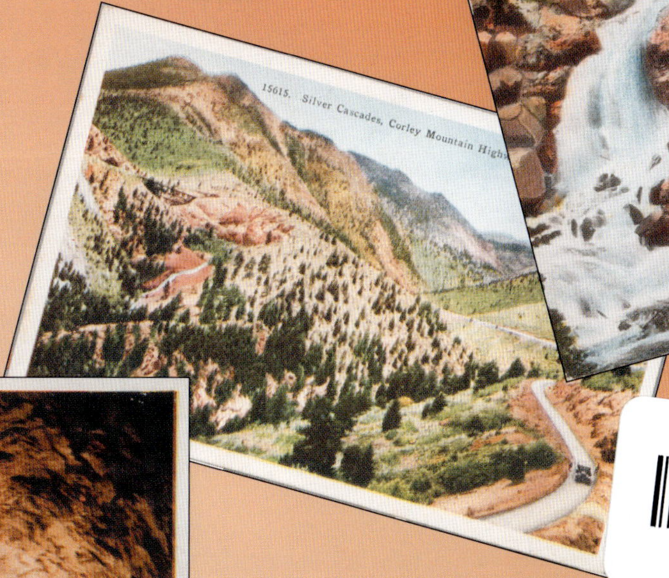

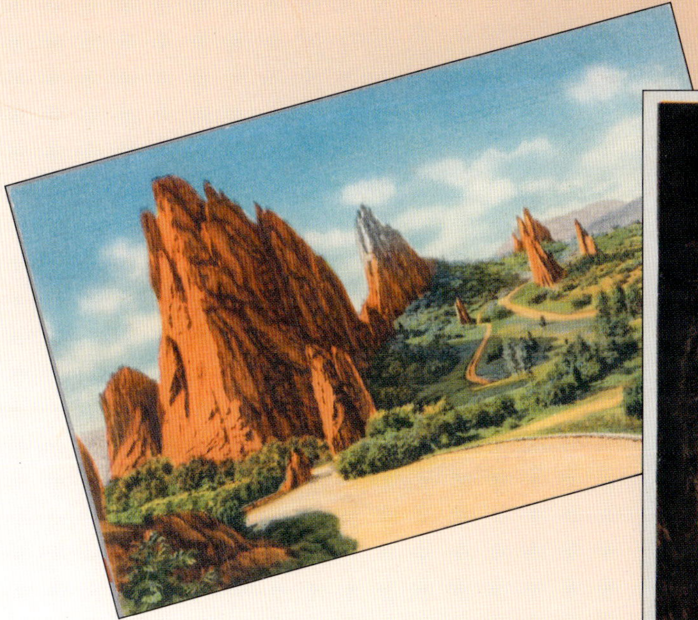

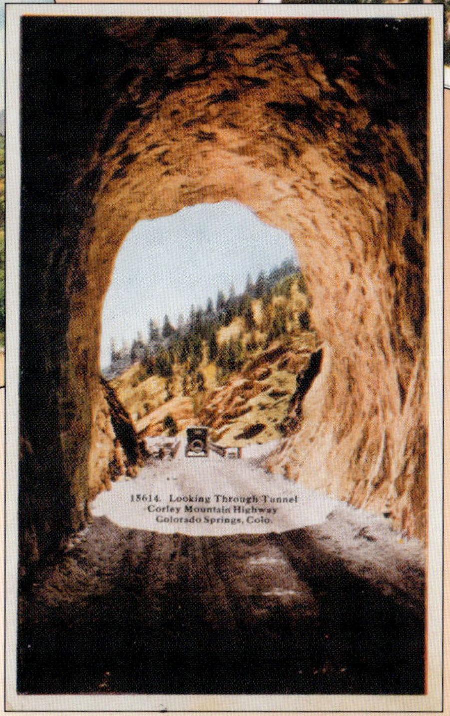

Schiffer® Publishing Ltd
4880 Lower Valley Road Atglen, Pennsylvania 19310

Other Schiffer Books by Mary L. Martin

Bathing Beauties of the Roaring '20s. Mary L. Martin & Tina Skinner.
Greetings from New Orleans: A History in Postcards. Mary L. Martin & Tina Skinner
Hawaiian Fish. Mary L. Martin
Hollywood Homes: Postcard Views of Early Stars' Estates. Mary L. Martin, Tina Skinner, & Tammy Ward
Miami Memories: A Midcentury Journey. Mary L. Martin, Tina Skinner, & Nathaniel Wolfgang-Price
Midget Exhibit: Images from the Heyday of Dwarf Display. Mary L. Martin & Tina Skinner
Naughty Victorians and Edwardians: Early Images of Bathing Beauties. Mary L. Martin & Tina Skinner
Cape Cod Memories: An Illustrated History in Postcards. Karen Choppa & Mary L. Martin
Geisha Women of Japan's Flower & Willow World. Tina Skinner, Mary L. Martin, & Wes Ponder
Greetings from Havre de Grace. David Craig & Mary L. Martin
Hawaii Remembered: Postcards from Paradise. Tina Skinner, Mary L. Martin, & Nathanial Wolfgang-Price
Historic Christmas Art: Santas, Angels, Poinsettia, Holly, Nativity, Children, and More Royalty-free Images on CD. Mary L. Martin & Tina Skinner
Historic Holiday Art: New Year, Valentines, St. Patrick's Day, Easter, July 4th, Halloween, & Thanksgiving. Mary L. Martin & Tina Skinner
Lighthouse Views. Mary Martin Postcards & Tina Skinner
Memories of Memphis: A History in Postcards. Mary L. Martin & Ginny Parfitt

Other Schiffer Books on Related Subjects

Advertising Postcards. Robert Reed
Art Deco Architecture: Miami Beach Poscards. Paul Clemence
Birds of Cape Cod & the Islands in Postcards. Roger S. Everett
Cape May Postcards.
Card Photographs: A Guide to Their History and Value. Lou W. McCulloch
Greetings from Ohio: Vintage Postcards 1900-1960s. Robert Reed.
Miami Beach Postcards.
Mies van der Rohe's Farnsworth House Postcard Book. Paul Clemence
Newport News: A Vintage Postcard Tour. Harold Cones & John Bryant

Library of Congress Control Number: 2006933128

Designed by Mark David Bowyer
Type set in Zapf Chancery Bd BT / Korinna BT

ISBN: 0-7643-2575-2
Printed in China

Published by Schiffer Publishing Ltd.
4880 Lower Valley Road
Atglen, PA 19310
Phone: (610) 593-1777; Fax: (610) 593-2002
E-mail: Info@schifferbooks.com

For the largest selection of fine reference books on this and related subjects, please visit our web site at **www.schifferbooks.com**
We are always looking for people to write books on new and related subjects. If you have an idea for a book please contact us at the above address.

This book may be purchased from the publisher.
Include $3.95 for shipping.
Please try your bookstore first.
You may write for a free catalog.

In Europe, Schiffer books are distributed by
Bushwood Books
6 Marksbury Ave.
Kew Gardens
Surrey TW9 4JF England
Phone: 44 (0) 20 8392-8585; Fax: 44 (0) 20 8392-9876
E-mail: info@bushwoodbooks.co.uk
Website: www.bushwoodbooks.co.uk
Free postage in the U.K., Europe; air mail at cost.

Contents

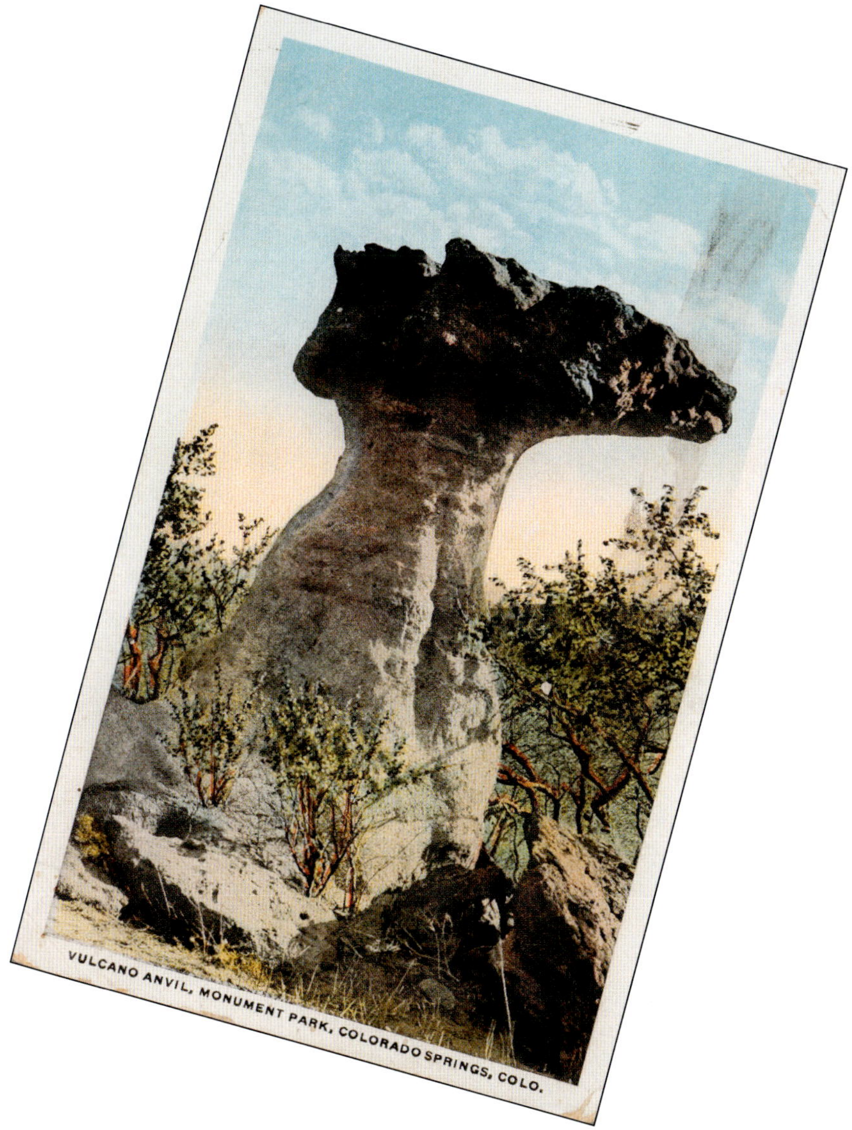

Preface

Historic Images Through Postcards

Postcards are said to be the most popular collectible history has ever known. The urge to horde them sprang up with the birth of this means of communication at the turn of the twentieth century and has endured great changes in the printing industry. Today, postcard shows take place every weekend somewhere in the country, or the world, and millions of pieces of ephemera lie in wait for those who collect obscure topics or town views.

Postcards once served as the email of their day. They were the fastest, most popular means of communication beginning in the 1890s in the United States. These timely cards provided a way to send scenes through the mail along with brief messages – a way to enchant friends and family with the places travelers visited, to send local sights, or to share favorite topics of imagery. They even provided the latest breaking news, as images of fires, floods, shipwrecks, and festivals were often available in postcard form within hours of an event. Moreover, mail was delivered to most urban homes in the United States at least twice a day. So someone might send a morning postcard inviting a friend to dinner that evening, and receive an RSVP in time to shop for food.

The messages shared and the beautiful scenes combine to create the timeless appeal of postcards as a collectible. Most importantly, history is recorded by the pictures of the times, moments in time reflecting an alluring past.

Dating Postcards

Pioneer Era (1893-1898): Most pioneer cards in today's collections begin with cards placed on sale at the Columbian Exposition in Chicago on May 1, 1893. These were illustrations on government printed postal cards and privately printed souvenir cards. The government cards had the printed one-cent stamp, while souvenir cards required a two-cent adhesive postage stamp to be applied. Writing was not permitted on the address side of the card.

Private Mailing Card Era (1898-1901): On May 19, 1898, private printers were granted permission, by an Act of Congress, to print and sell cards that bore the inscription "Private Mailing Card." A one-cent adhesive stamp was required. A dozen or more American printers began to take postcards seriously. Writing was still not permitted on the back.

Post Card Era – Undivided Back (1901-1907): New U.S. postal regulations on December 24, 1901, stipulated that the words "Post Card" should be printed at the top of the address side of privately printed cards. Government-issued cards were to be designated as "Postal Cards." Writing was still not permitted on the address side. In this era, private citizens began to take black and white photographs and have them printed on paper with post card backs.

Early Divided Back Era (1907-1914): Postcards with a divided back were permitted in Britain in 1902, but not in the U.S. until March 1, 1907. The address was to be written on the right side; the left side was for writing messages. Many millions of cards were published in this era. Up to this point, most postcards were printed in Germany, which was far ahead of the United States in the use of lithographic processes. With the advent of World War I, the supply of postcards for American consumption switched from Germany to England and the United States.

White Border Era (1915-1930): Most United States postcards were printed during this period. To save ink, publishers left a clear border around the view, thus these postcards are referred to as "White Border" cards. The relatively high cost of labor, along with inexperience and changes in public taste, resulted in the production of poor quality cards during this period. Furthermore, strong competition in a narrowing market caused many publishers to go out of business.

Linen Era (1930-1944): New printing processes allowed printing of postcards with high rag content that created a textured finish. These cheap cards allowed the use of gaudy dyes for coloring.

Photochrome Era (1945 to date): "Chrome" postcards began to dominate the scene soon after the Union Oil Company placed them in its western service stations in 1939. Mike Roberts pioneered these with his "WESCO" cards soon after World War II. Three-dimensional postcards also appeared in this era.

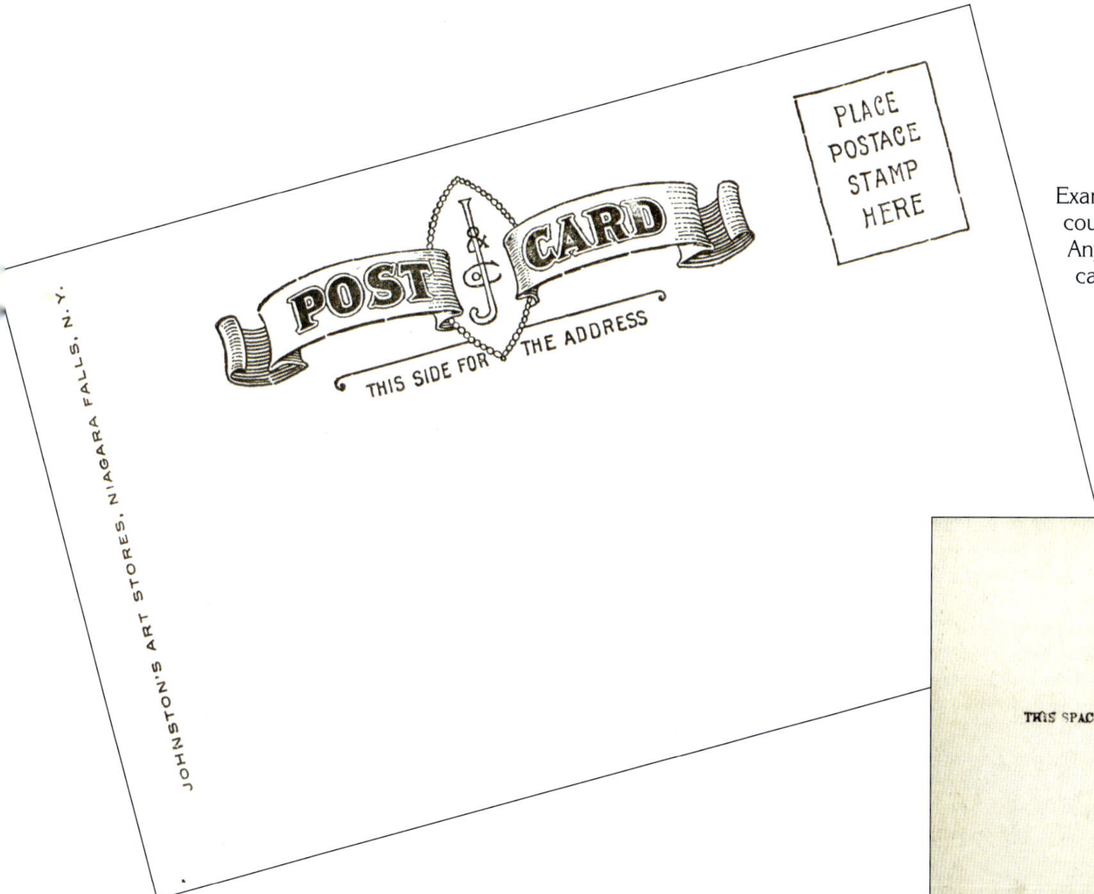

Example of a postcard with an undivided back. Senders could only write the address on this side of the card. Any message needed to be written on the front of the card along with the picture.

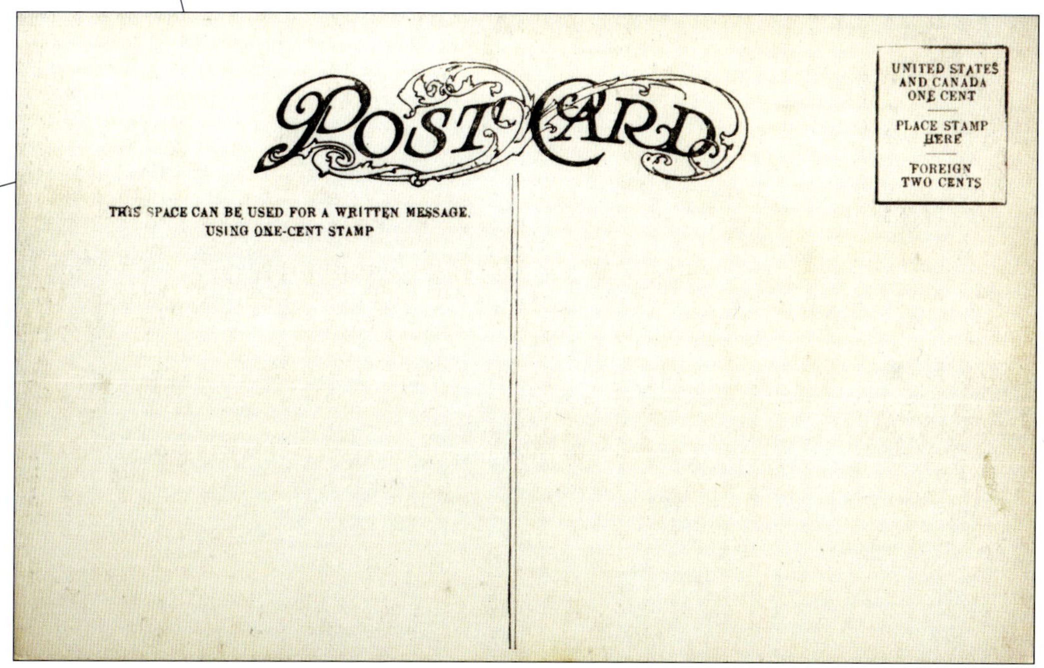

Sample of a postcard with a divided back. Senders were allowed to put an address on the right hand side of the postcard and a message on the left side.

About Colorado Springs

Introduction

When she first arrived in Colorado Springs, author Helen Hunt Jackson took an instant dislike to the city. "I shall never forget my sudden sense of hopeless disappointment at the moment when I first looked on the town [Colorado Springs]. It was a gray day in November. I had crossed the continent, ill, disheartened, to find a climate that would not kill. There stretched before me, to the east, a bleak, bare, unrelieved, desolate plain. There rose behind me, to the west, a dark range of mountains, snow-topped, rocky-walled, stern, cruel, relentless. Between lay the town – small, straight, new, treeless.

'One might die of such a place alone,' I said bitterly. 'Death by disease would be more natural'" (Jackson, 1878).

However, Jackson's opinion of Colorado Springs eventually changed and she came to love the city and the surrounding area. "To-day that plain and those mountains are to me well-nigh the fairest spot on earth. To-day I say, 'One might almost live on such a place alone.' I have learned it, [...] by heart; and there can be a heart and a significant record in the face of a plain and a mountain, as much as in the face of a man" (Jackson, 1878).

Helen Hunt Jackson continued to write the praises of Colorado and Colorado Springs in a number of her works, including a travel narrative called *Bits of Travel at Home*, written in 1878, and in numerous poems. Jackson, like many residents and visitors, appreciated the beauty of both Colorado Springs and the surrounding area, natural beauty that convinced many to come and many to stay.

From its founding, Colorado Springs was intended to be a tourist town. It was the founder's, General William Jackson Palmer, intention to create a high-class resort community. With the founding of the Denver & Rio Grande Railroad, travel to the town became as easy as buying a train ticket. Soon visitors arrived in droves, making Colorado Springs one of the most popular holiday destinations of the era.

Wherever they came from and whatever their reason for coming, every visitor found something worthwhile in Colorado Springs. Some visitors, like Jackson, came for their health – the warm, dry mountain air helping greatly in the treatment of tuberculosis, asthma, and other throat and lung diseases. Others came to see the sites they had read or heard about back East, to climb to the summit of Pikes Peak, wander among the strange and fantastic sandstone formations in the Garden of the Gods, and visit the many other natural attractions found in the region. Others still simply came to relax and to spend some time away from the noise and bustle of the big cities.

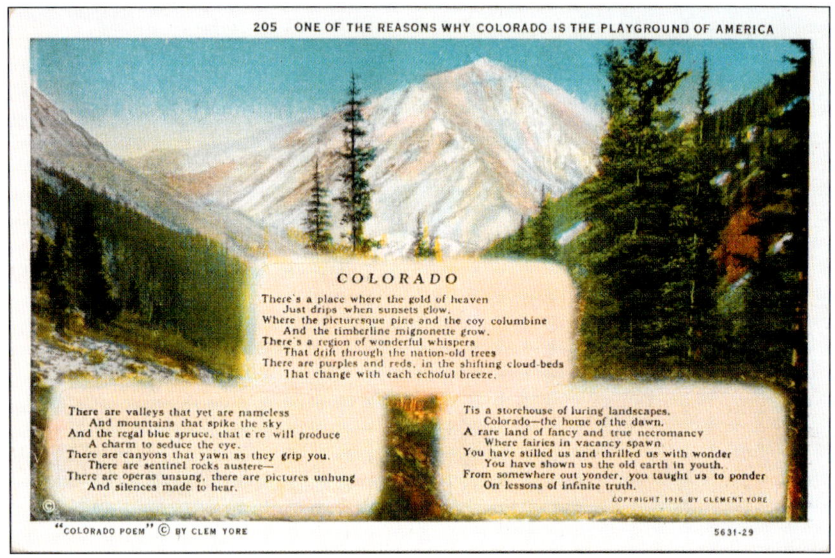

A poem by Clement Yore describes one of the reasons why Colorado was considered by many to be the playground of America.

Circa 1930s, $4-6

Of course, when visitors came to Colorado Springs, postcards left. Less expensive and far more convenient than the telephone, postcards were the traveler's best means of communication with the friends and family he had left at home. Taking time out from whatever activities occupied their days and nights, travelers would often sit and jot down a few lines to those back home, sending greetings, well wishes, and assurances of pleasant trips, speedy travels, and safe arrivals.

Vintage hand-tinted and black and white postcards from the 1900s to the 1950s will paint a picture of those times, showcasing some of Colorado Springs best features and well-known sites. Quoted material from the back of the cards, along with historical trivia included with the captions, will add some fun to the picture of this famous resort community.

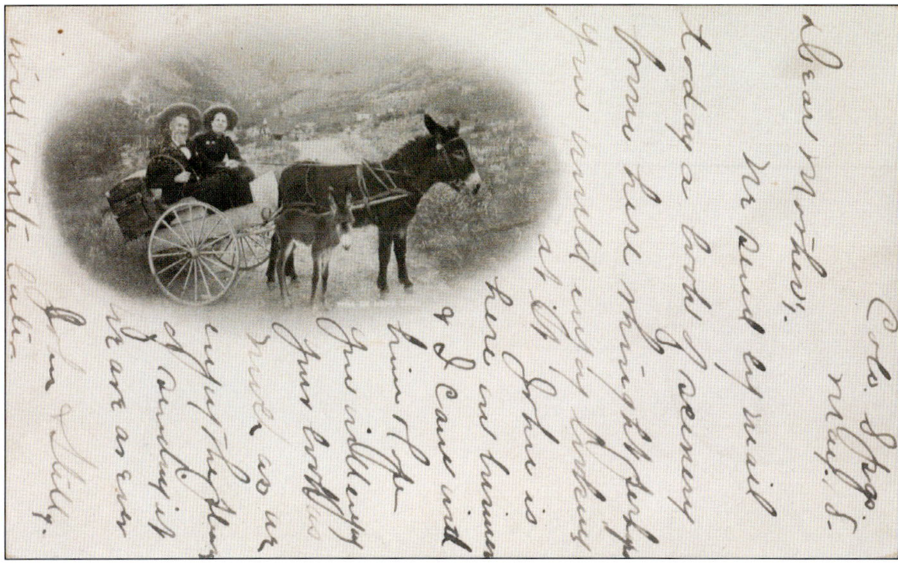

Greetings from Colorado Springs, will be home soon.

Cancelled 1903, $3-4

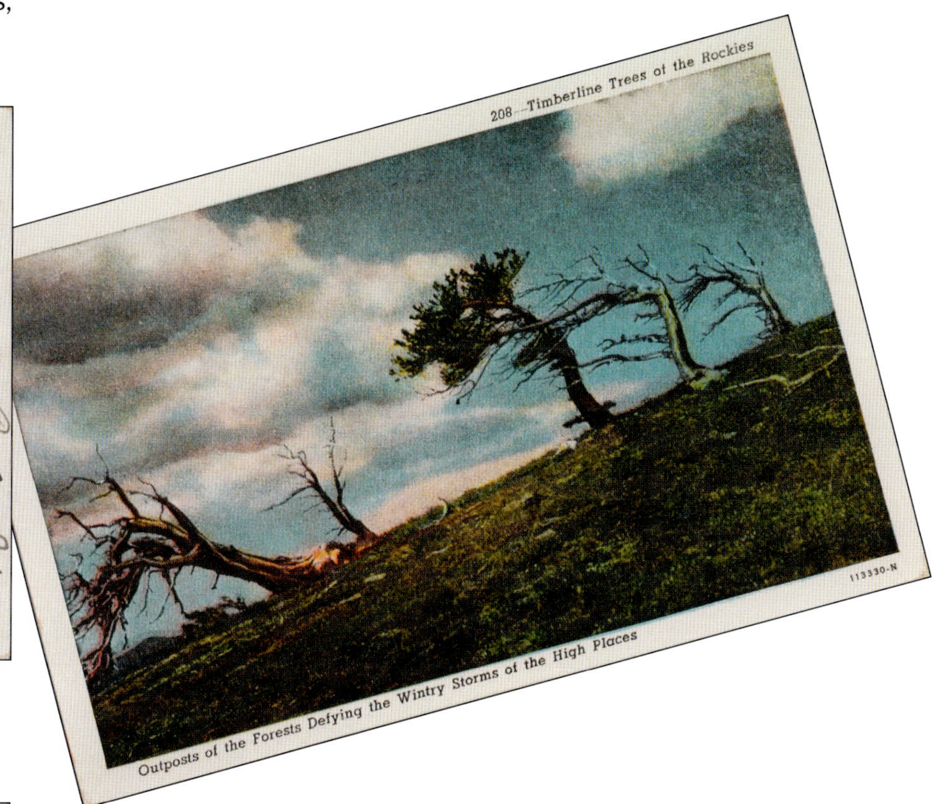

Trees along the timberline: Constantly battered by wind and rain, trees like these will often grow into twisted and unusual shapes.

Circa 1930s, $3-4

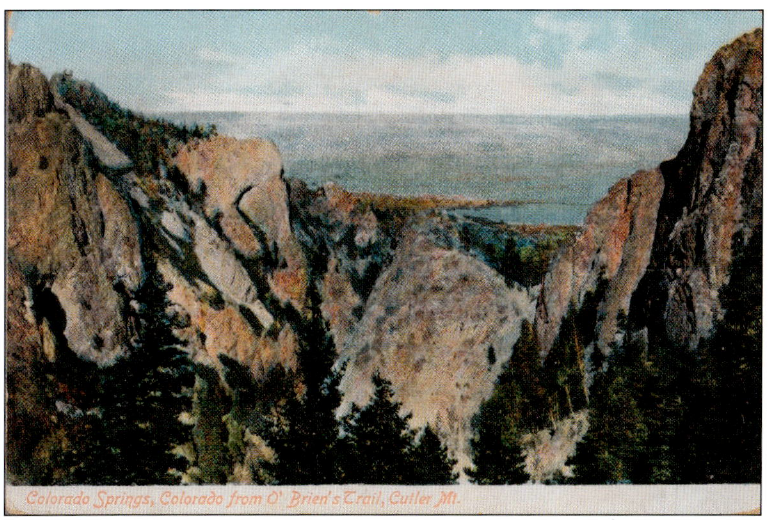

Colorado Springs as seen from the top of Cutler Mountain.

Cancelled 1907, $3-5

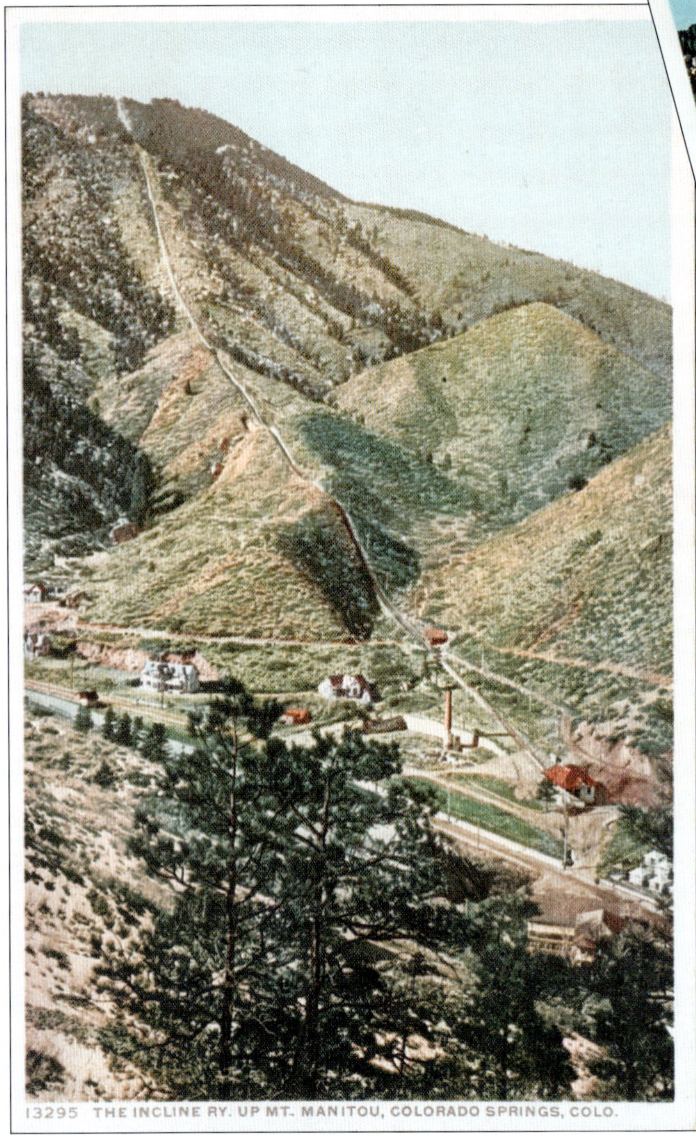

The Mount Manitou Incline Railway runs from Colorado Springs to the top of Mount Manitou.

Circa 1920s, $6-10

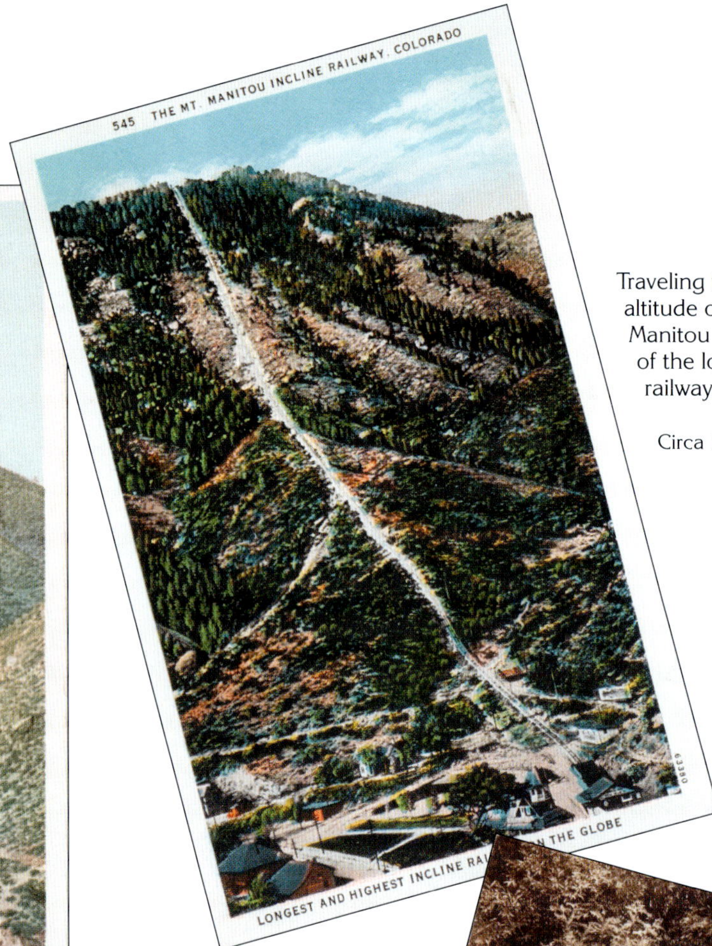

Traveling to the summit at an altitude of 9,000 feet, the Mount Manitou Incline Railway was one of the longest and highest incline railways in the world.

Circa 1920s, $4-6

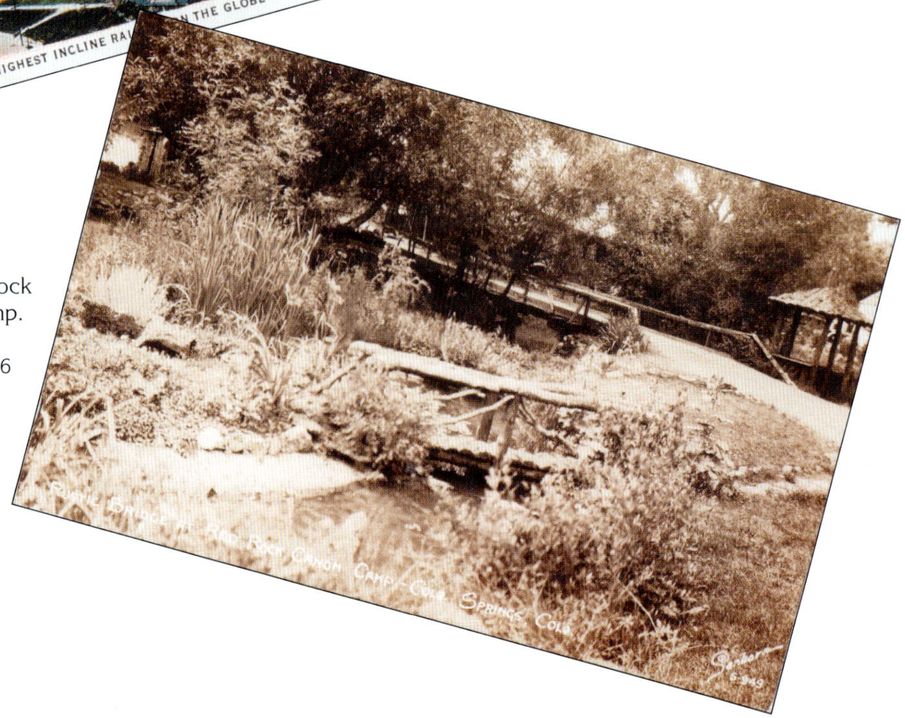

Bridge at Red Rock Canyon Camp.

Circa 1930s, $4-6

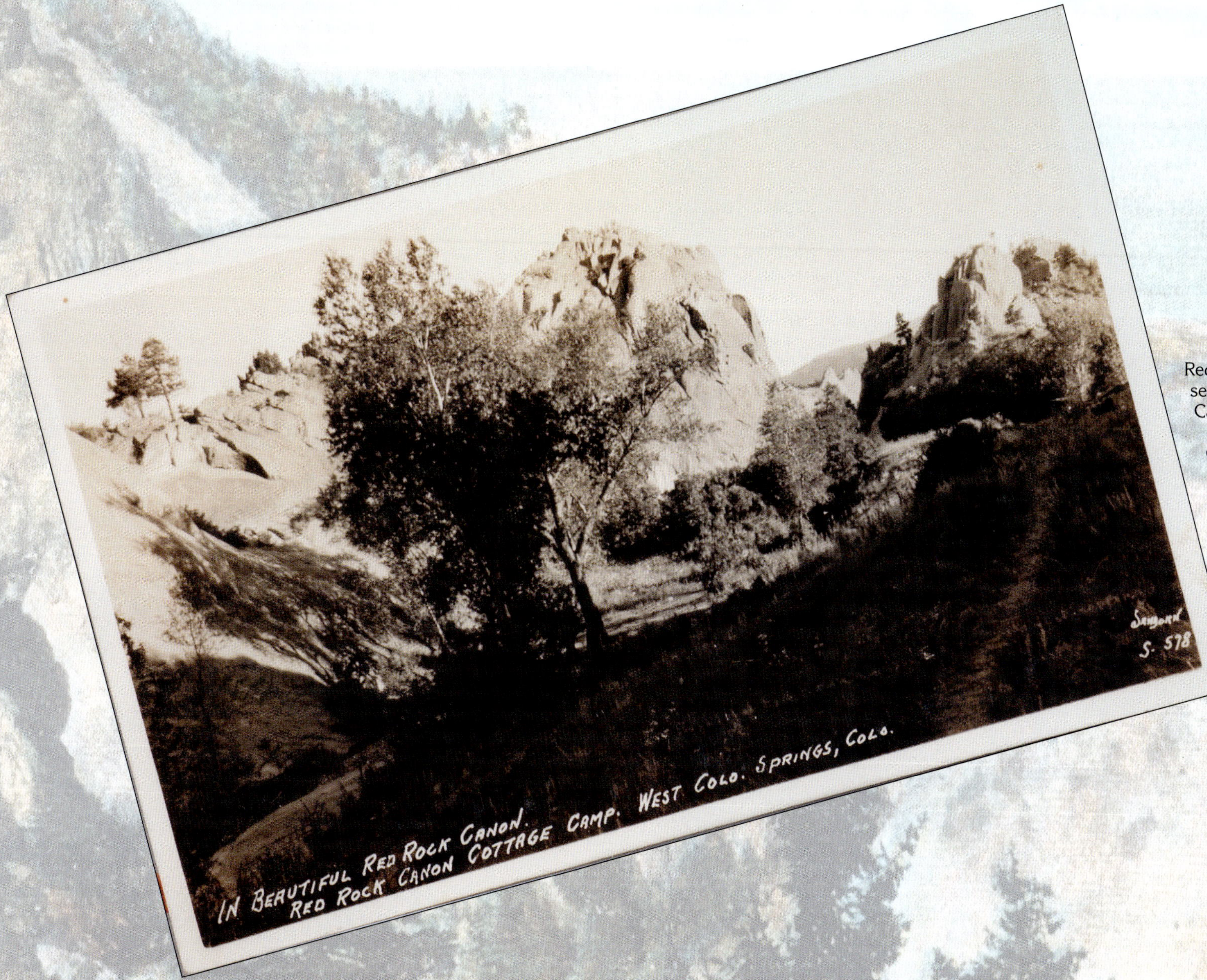

Red Rock Canyon as seen from the Red Rock Canyon Campground.

Circa 1930s, $6-10

History

Colorado Springs was founded in August 1871 by General William Jackson Palmer. While working for the Kansas Pacific Railroad in Colorado in 1867, General Palmer passed through the Pikes Peak Region, mapping out a proposed route from Kansas City to Denver. He was awed by the magnificent countryside around Pikes Peak and by the fascinating rock formations in a valley four miles from Colorado City.

After his marriage in 1870 to Mary Lincoln "Queen" Mellen, Palmer returned with his new wife to the area he had discovered in 1867. There he purchased 10,000 acres (with an additional 2,225 acres purchased near the Garden of the Gods for his personal home), at $1.25 an acre, and established the Fountain Colony, the town which would later be known as Colorado Springs. It was Palmer's intention to found a resort community and the land he had discovered seemed to be a natural location. That same year, in 1871, Palmer and William Bell founded the Denver & Rio Grande Railroad, opening up the Fountain Colony to the rest of the world.

Within two years, the Colony's population had risen to 15,000 people. With the opening of the Antlers Hotel a few years later, the Fountain Colony, a.k.a. Colorado Springs, was well on its way to becoming one of the most popular travel destinations in the country.

In 1891, major gold strikes in Victor and Cripple Creek on Pikes Peak led to the last major gold rush in the country, boosting the economy of nearby Colorado City. This strike made the fortunes of two of Colorado Springs early benefactors, Winfield Scott Stratton and Spencer Penrose. Both men contributed to a number of the city's civic institutions and charitable endeavors.

Colorado Springs continued to prosper, with tourism and the improvement of health being the city's main economic concerns through the 1900s until the 1940s. In 1942, the United States Army built Camp Carson near the southern edge of the city to train and house troops for World War II. During World War II, the army expanded Camp Carson, which revitalized the growth and economy of Colorado Springs and began the city's military boom. After the Korean War, Peterson Field (which was the Colorado Springs Municipal Airport before World War II) was re-christened Peterson Air Force Base, Camp Carson was made into Fort Carson, and Colorado Springs was chosen as the site of the United States Air Force Academy. The military boom continued in 1963 when the North American Aerospace Defense Command (NORAD) built its main facility in Cheyenne Mountain, contributing greatly to the city's economy and growth. The military boom attracted the high-tech industry that also became an integral part of the city's economy.

Today, Colorado Springs is still thriving, with an economy based on the military, high-tech industries, and tourism. Also, the city has recently become home to the headquarters of a number of Evangelical Christian organizations.

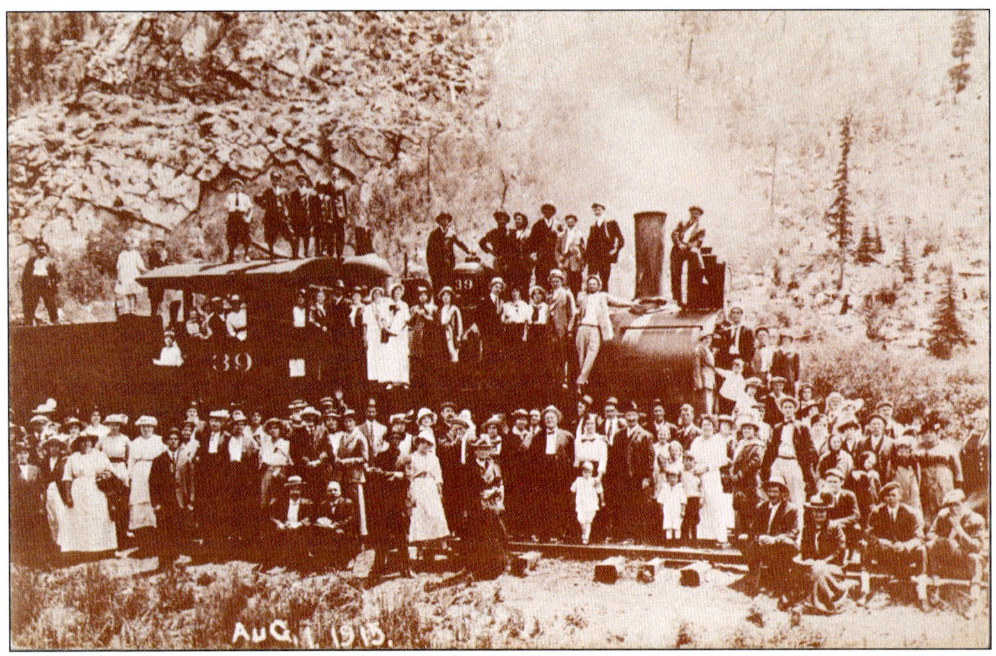

Taken on August 1, 1915, residents of Colorado Springs pose in front of the Wild Flower Train.

Circa 1950s, $6-10

Inside Colorado Springs

The City

Colorado Springs began with 10,000 acres of land, ten miles east of Pikes Peak. General William Jackson Palmer chose the site because of its location near Pikes Peak and the Garden of the Gods which, he believed, would make excellent tourist attractions. General Palmer also disliked the rough nature of nearby Colorado City, with its many bars and saloons. He wanted to build a high-quality resort community, without the negative influences of alcohol; in fact, Colorado Springs remained a dry community until Prohibition was repealed nationally in 1933.

Much of the land the city was built on came from General Palmer, who donated or sold a good portion of what he owned for parks, private development, and civic institutions. Other landowners, like Winfield Scott Stratton, also contributed land and funds towards the city's development.

Early Colorado Springs was quite a pleasant town, with broad avenues lined with cottonwood trees, churches, hotels, restaurants, mills, and plenty of parks and open spaces; all of which were reported frequently in the town's circulars, advertisements, and in pamphlets on Western immigration and the future of the state of Colorado. Colorado Springs remained a resort community and health center for much of its history, with most of the city's development and industry centered on tourism and the improvement of health. As of 2004, Colorado Springs was home to a population of 369,363 and occupies an area of 482 square kilometers in El Paso County, Colorado.

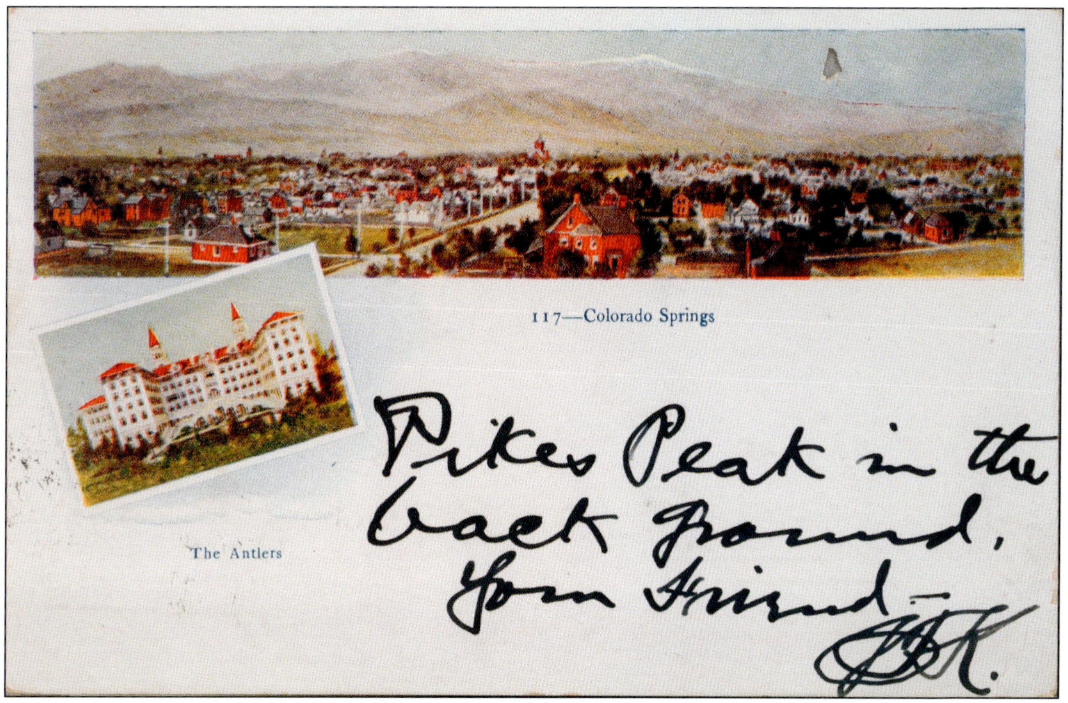

A panoramic view of Colorado Springs and the famous Antlers Hotel.

Cancelled 1906, $4-6

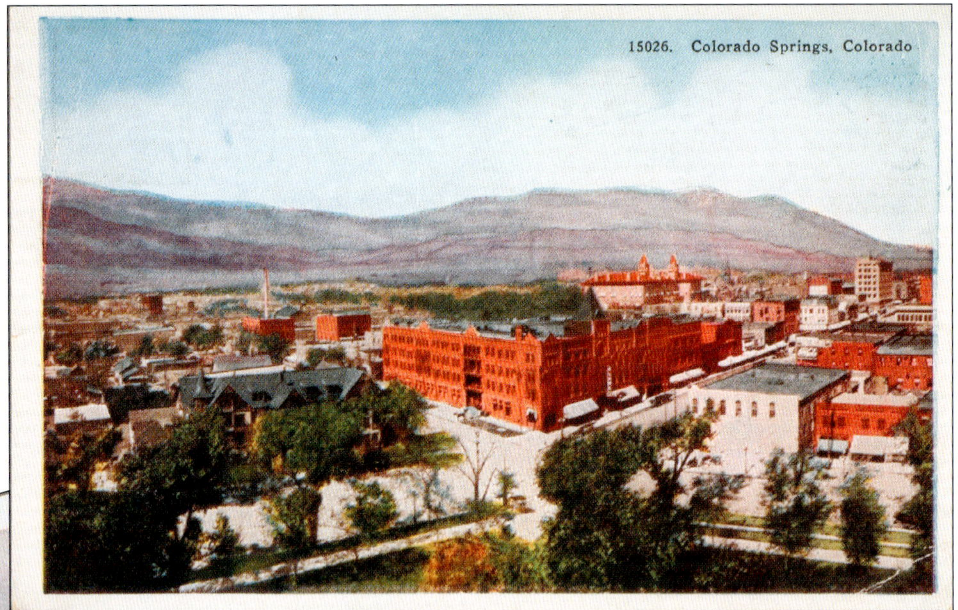

General William Jackson Palmer, a civil engineer, industrialist, and Civil War veteran, founded Colorado Springs as a high quality resort town in 1871.

Circa 1930s, $4-6

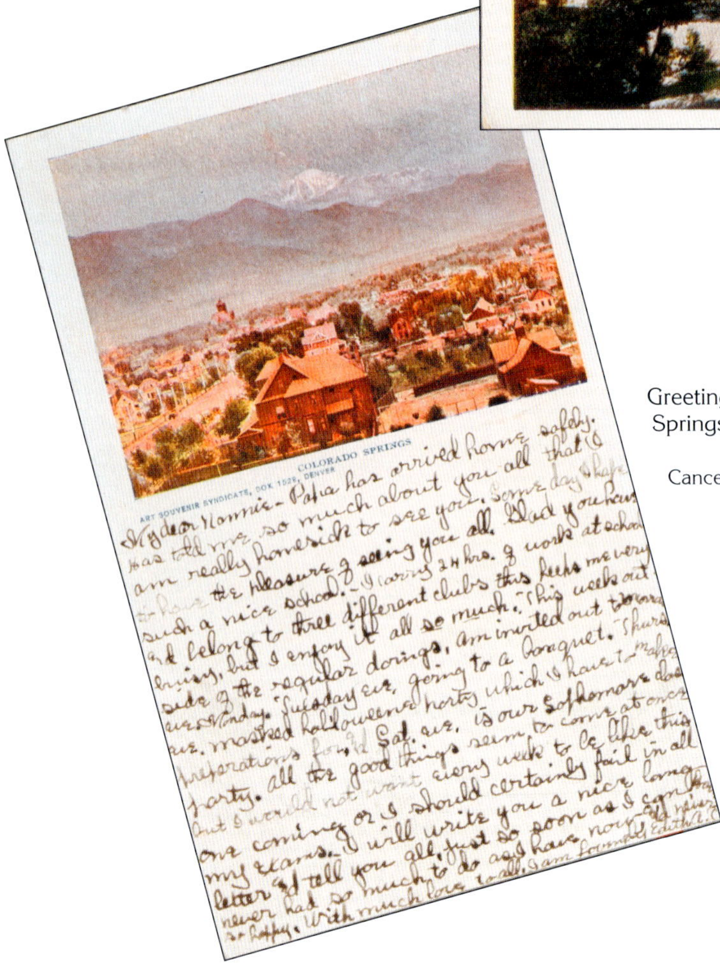

Greetings from Colorado Springs, Pikes Peak's City.

Cancelled 1907, $4-6

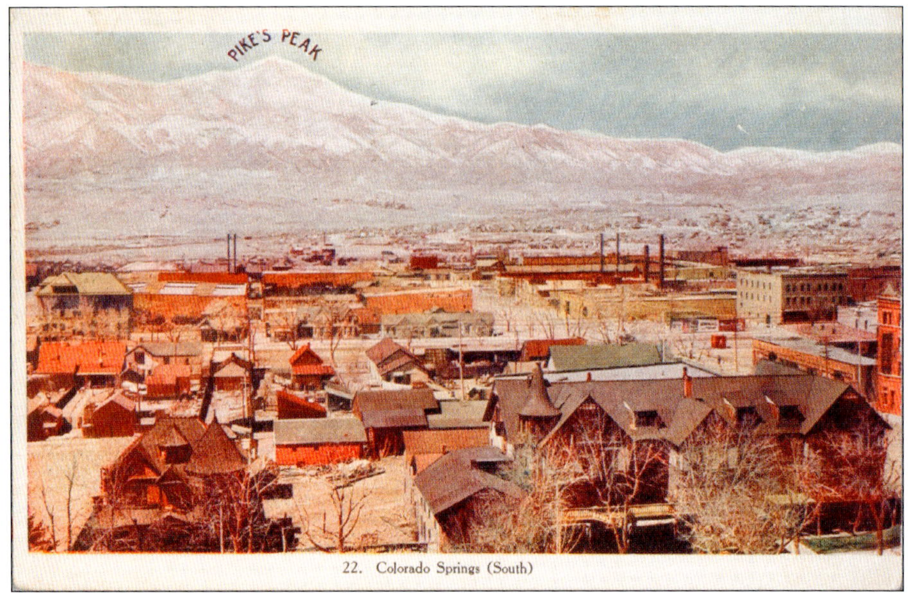

Colorado Springs was so popular with English tourists that it was known as "Little London."

Cancelled 1909, $4-6

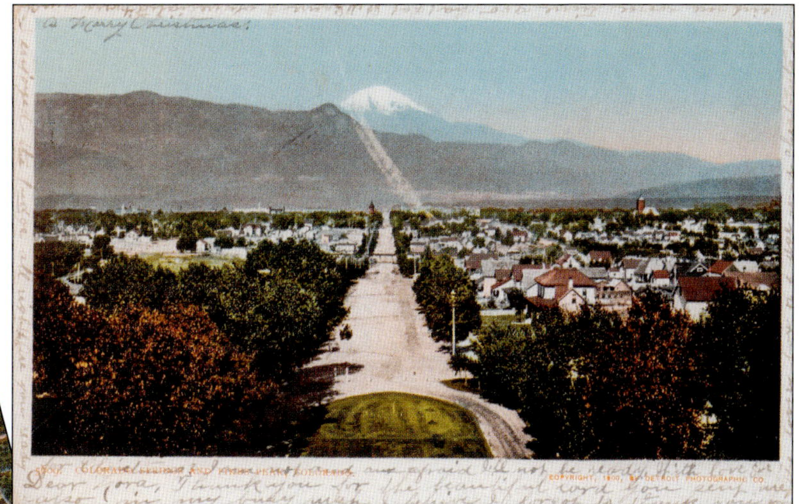

With a population of over 300,000 and an area of 482 square kilometers, Colorado Springs is the second largest city in Colorado and the forty-ninth largest city in the United States.

Cancelled 1906, $4-6

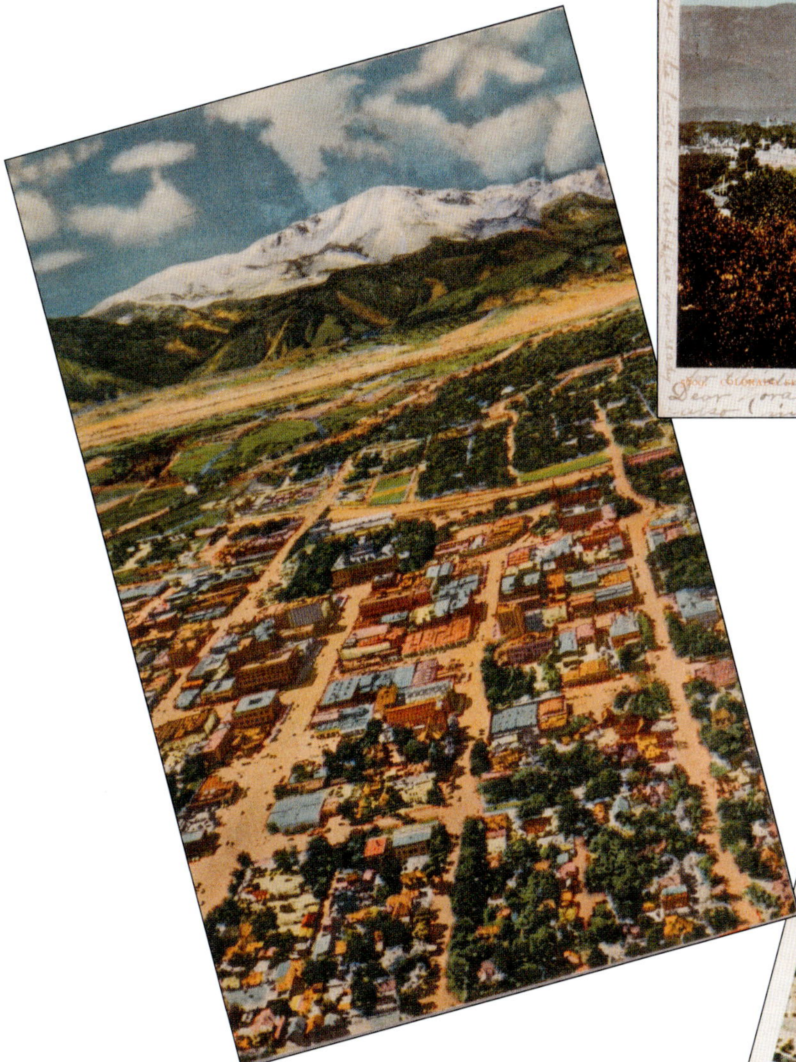

Aerial view of downtown Colorado Springs.

Circa 1940s, $4-6

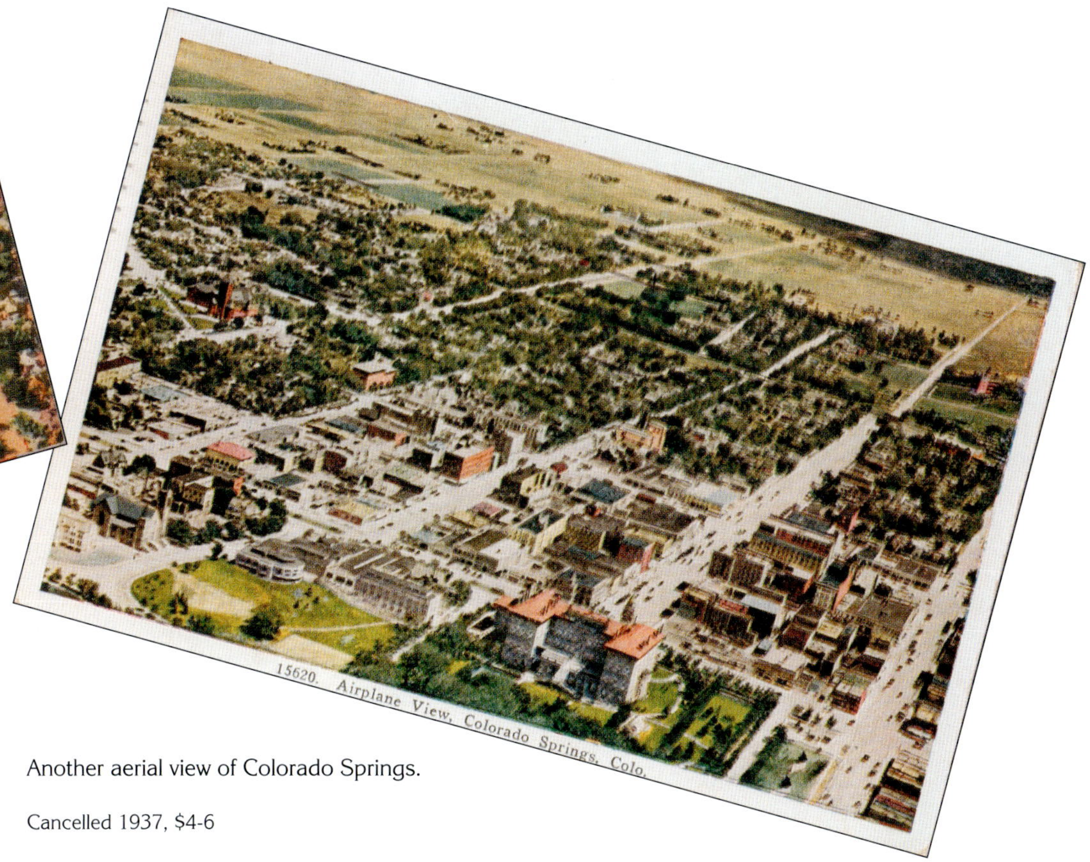

Another aerial view of Colorado Springs.

Cancelled 1937, $4-6

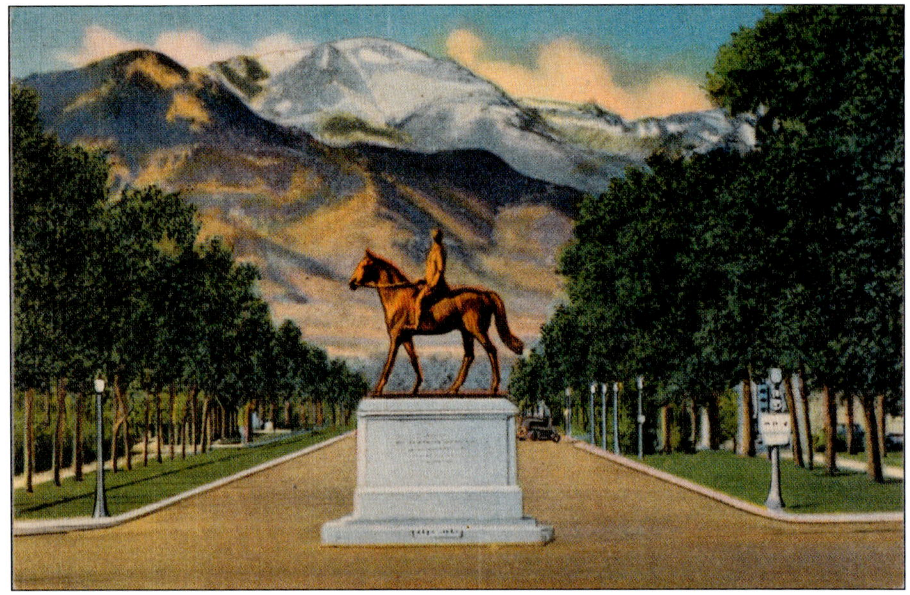

Monument dedicated to General William Jackson Palmer, the founder of Colorado Springs.

Circa 1940s, $4-6

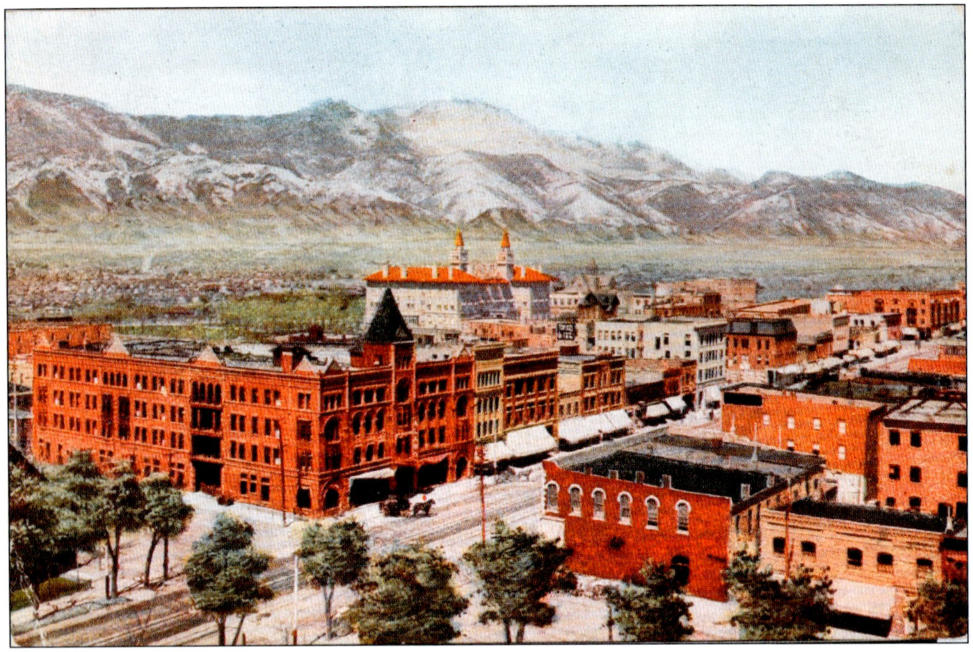

View of downtown Colorado Springs, with the Antlers Hotel and Pikes Peak in the distance.

Circa 1920s, $5-7

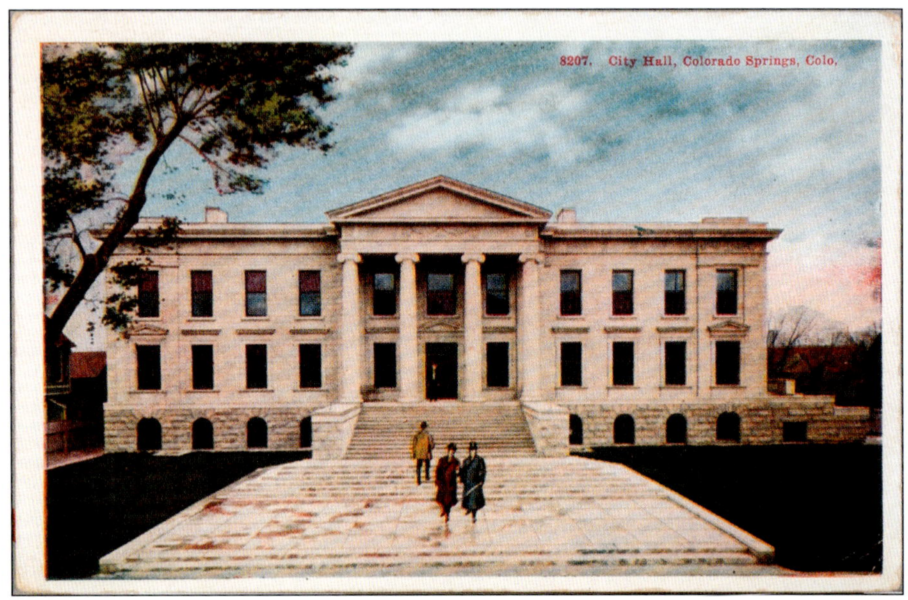

The land for City Hall was donated by Winfield Scott Stratton, one of the early benefactors of Colorado Springs.

Circa 1930s, $4-6

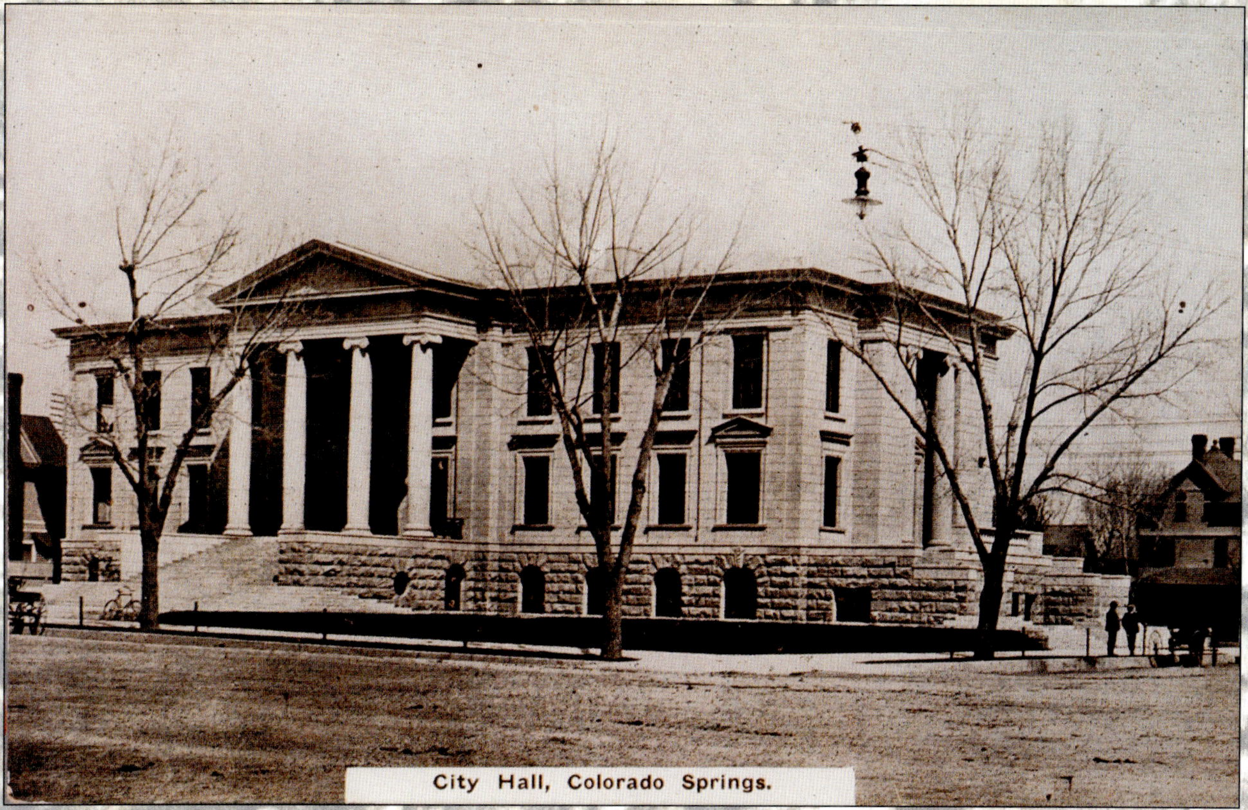

Colorado Springs City Hall was dedicated and opened in 1904. Today it is the subject of a restoration and revitalization project.

Circa 1910s, $6-10

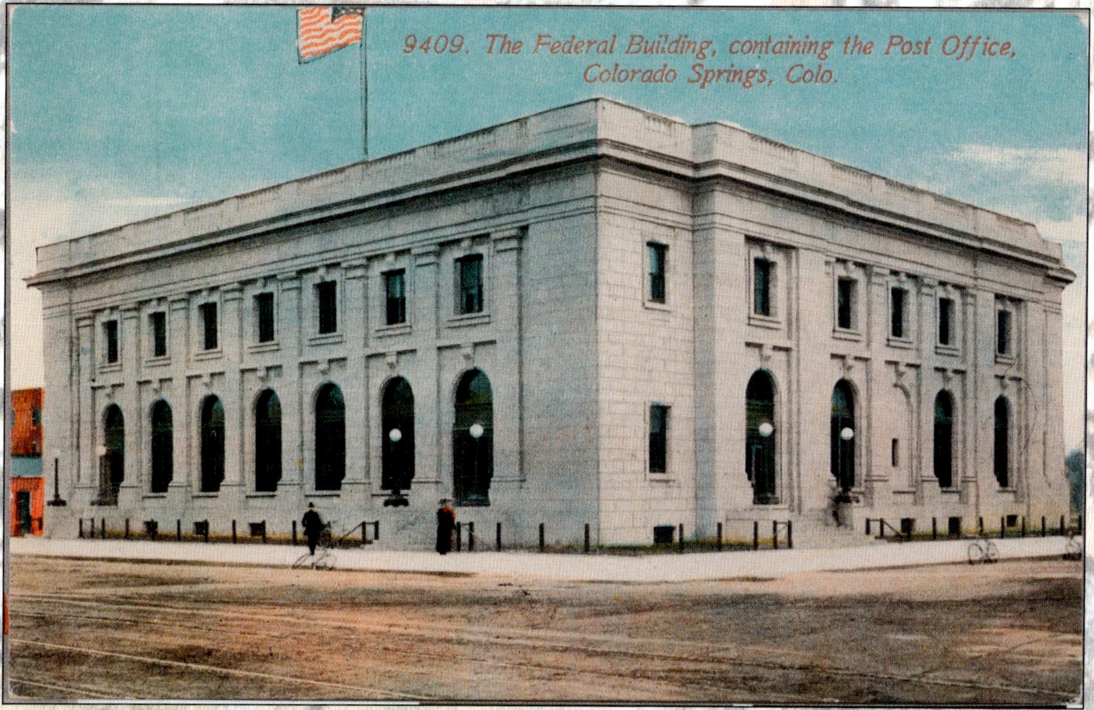

In addition to housing the city's federal offices, the Federal Building was also home to Colorado Springs' post office.

Circa 1910s, $4-6

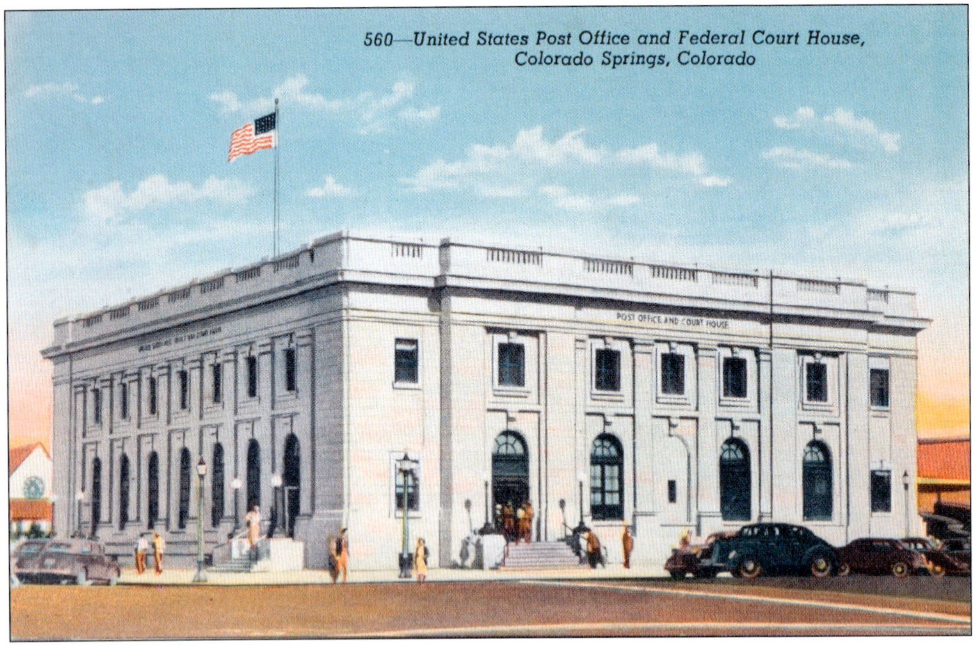

The Post Office and Federal Building located at the intersection of Pikes Peak and Nevada Avenues.

Circa 1940s, $4-6

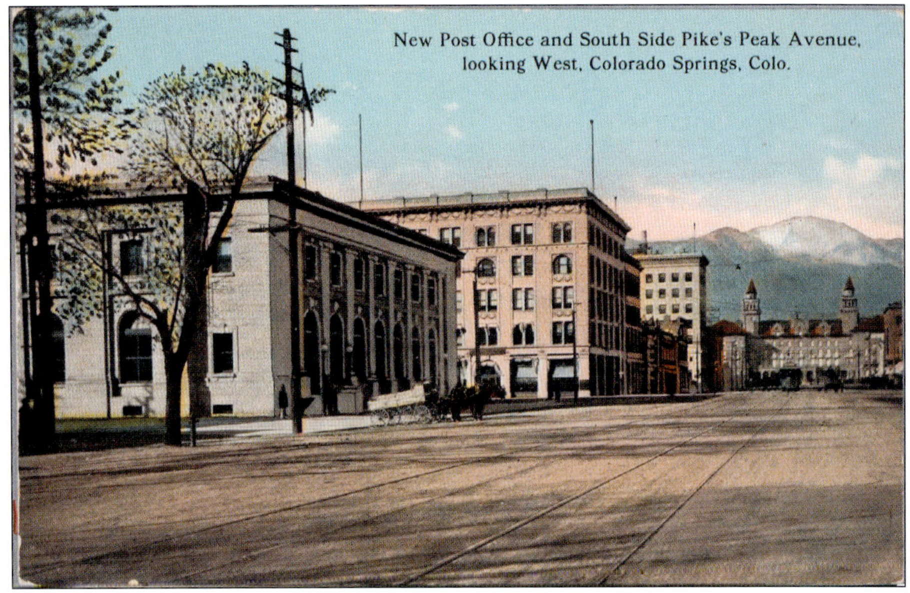

The Post Office, as seen from Pikes Peak Avenue.

Circa 1910s, $4-6

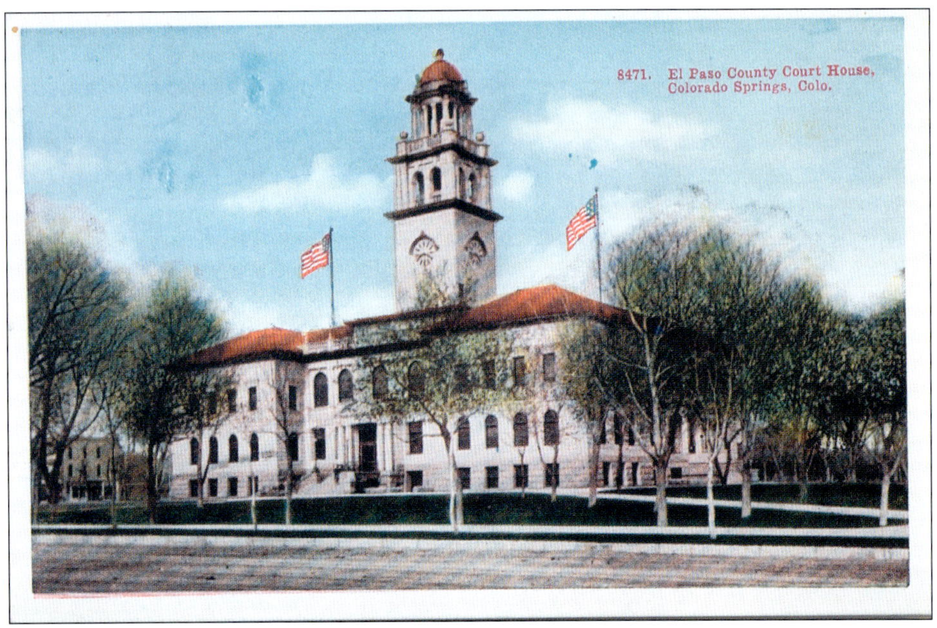

Since Colorado Springs was the county seat of El Paso County, it was also the home of the county courthouse.

Circa 1930s, $4-6

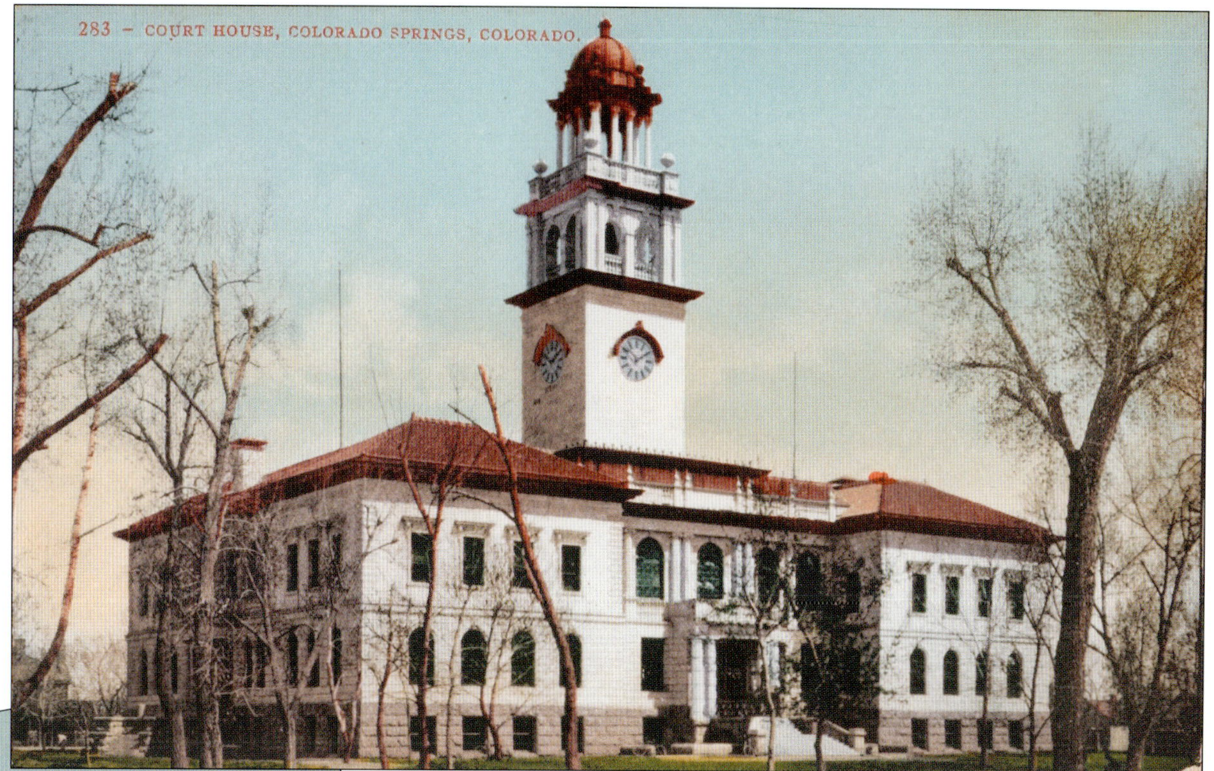

The Courthouse itself was dedicated in 1903, and is located on South Tejon Street.

Circa 1910s, $5-7

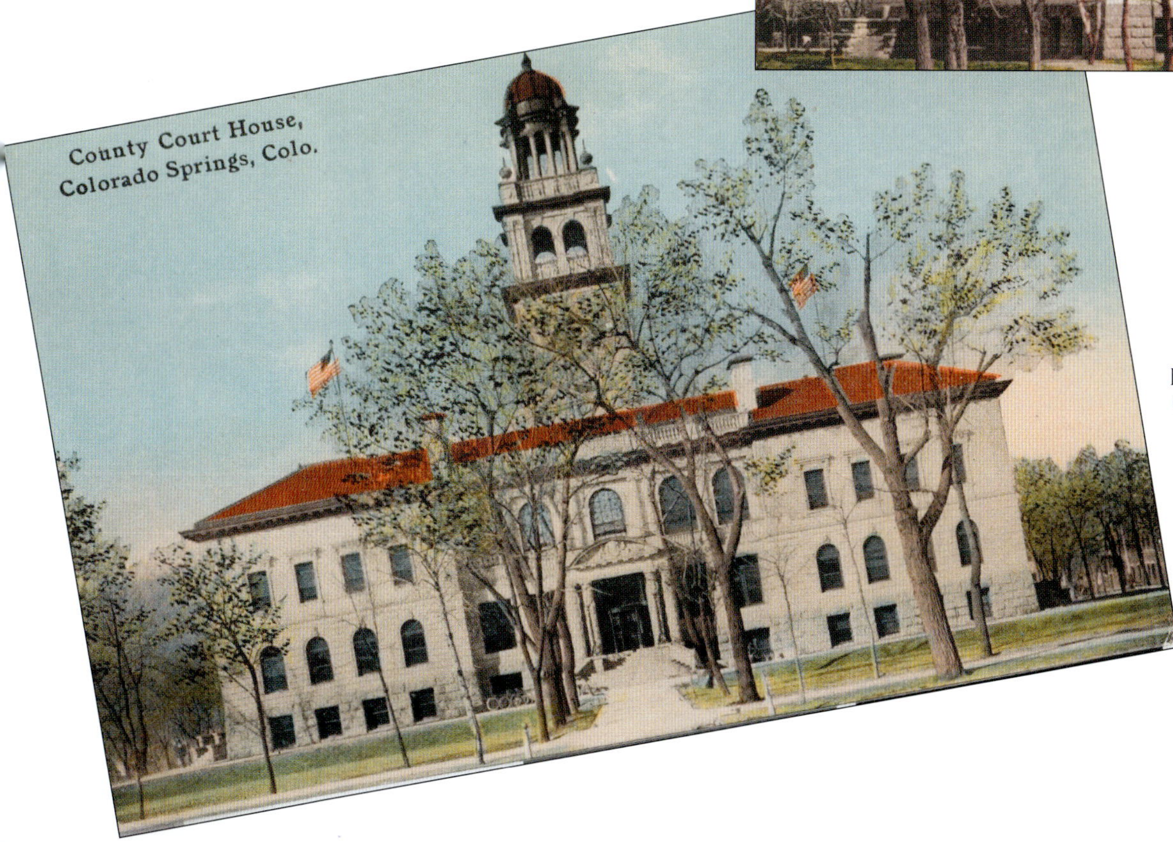

Like the City Hall, the El Paso County Courthouse was built on land donated to the city by Winfield Scott Stratton.

Circa 1910s, $4-6

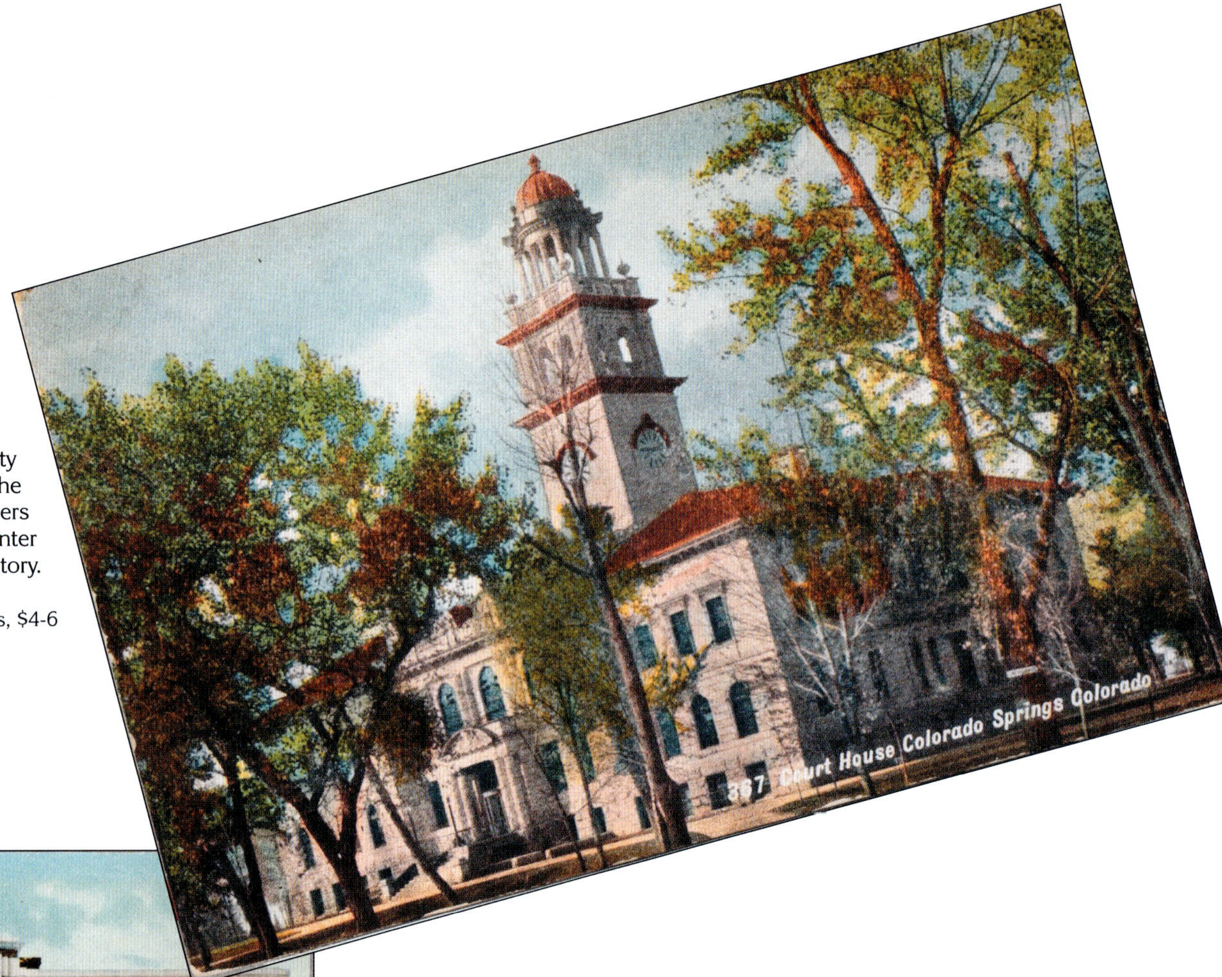

Today, the El Paso County Courthouse is home to the Colorado Springs Pioneers Museum and Starsmore Center for Local History.

Circa 1910s, $4-6

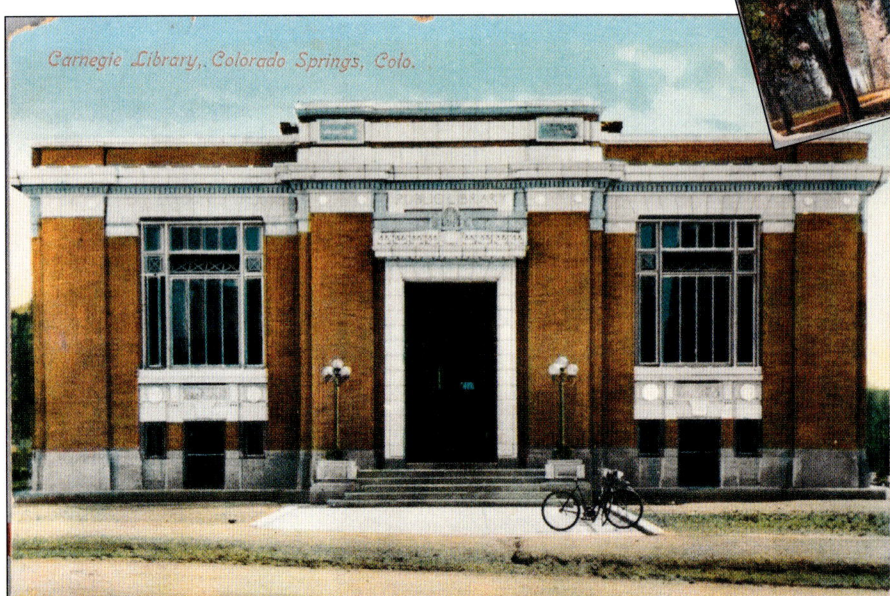

The funds for building the Public Library were donated to the city of Colorado Springs by Andrew Carnegie.

Circa 1910s, $5-7

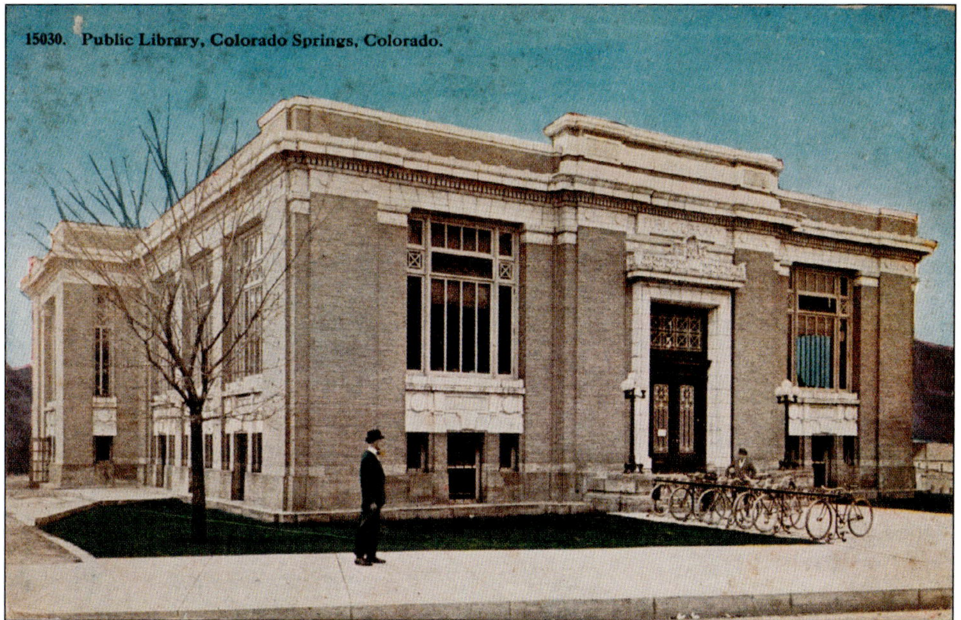

Andrew Carnegie funded 2,509 libraries between 1883 and 1929. He would provide funding for the construction of a library on the condition that the city find the site and provide the maintenance for the finished building.

Circa 1920s, $4-6

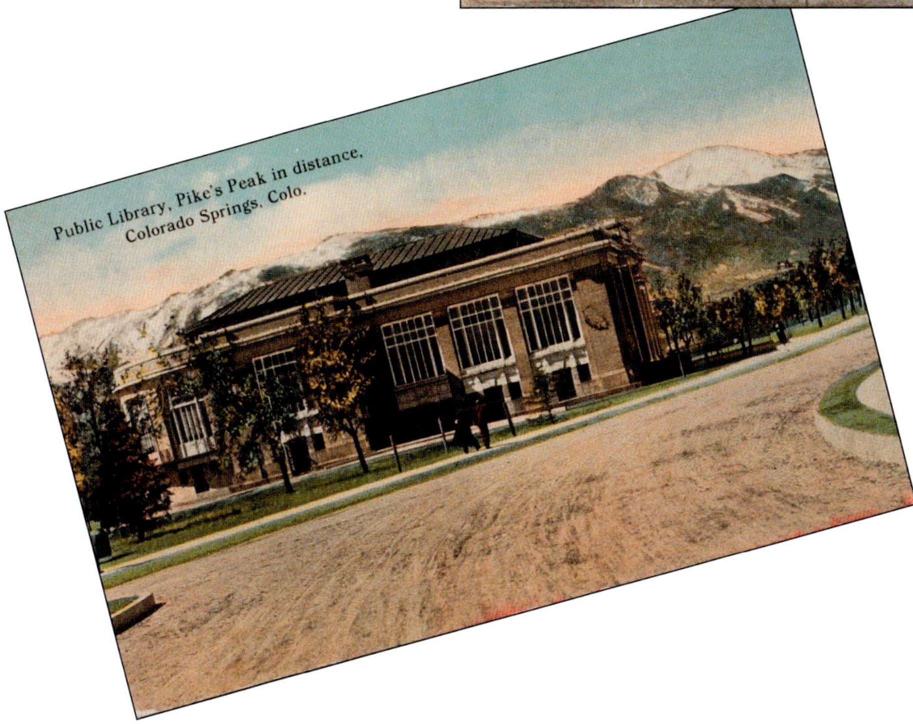

A view of the Colorado Springs Public Library with Pikes Peak in the distance.

Circa 1910s, $4-6

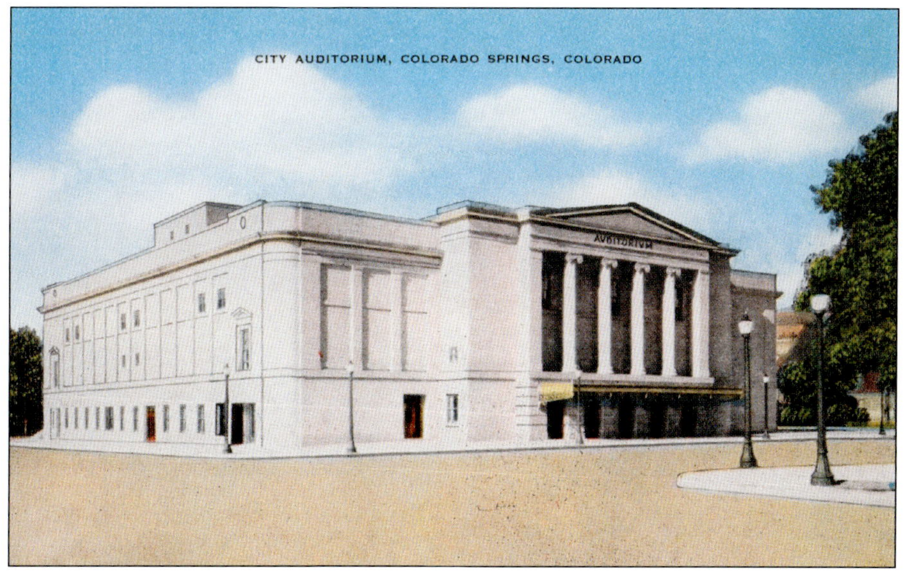

The Colorado Springs City Auditorium.

Circa 1940s, $4-6

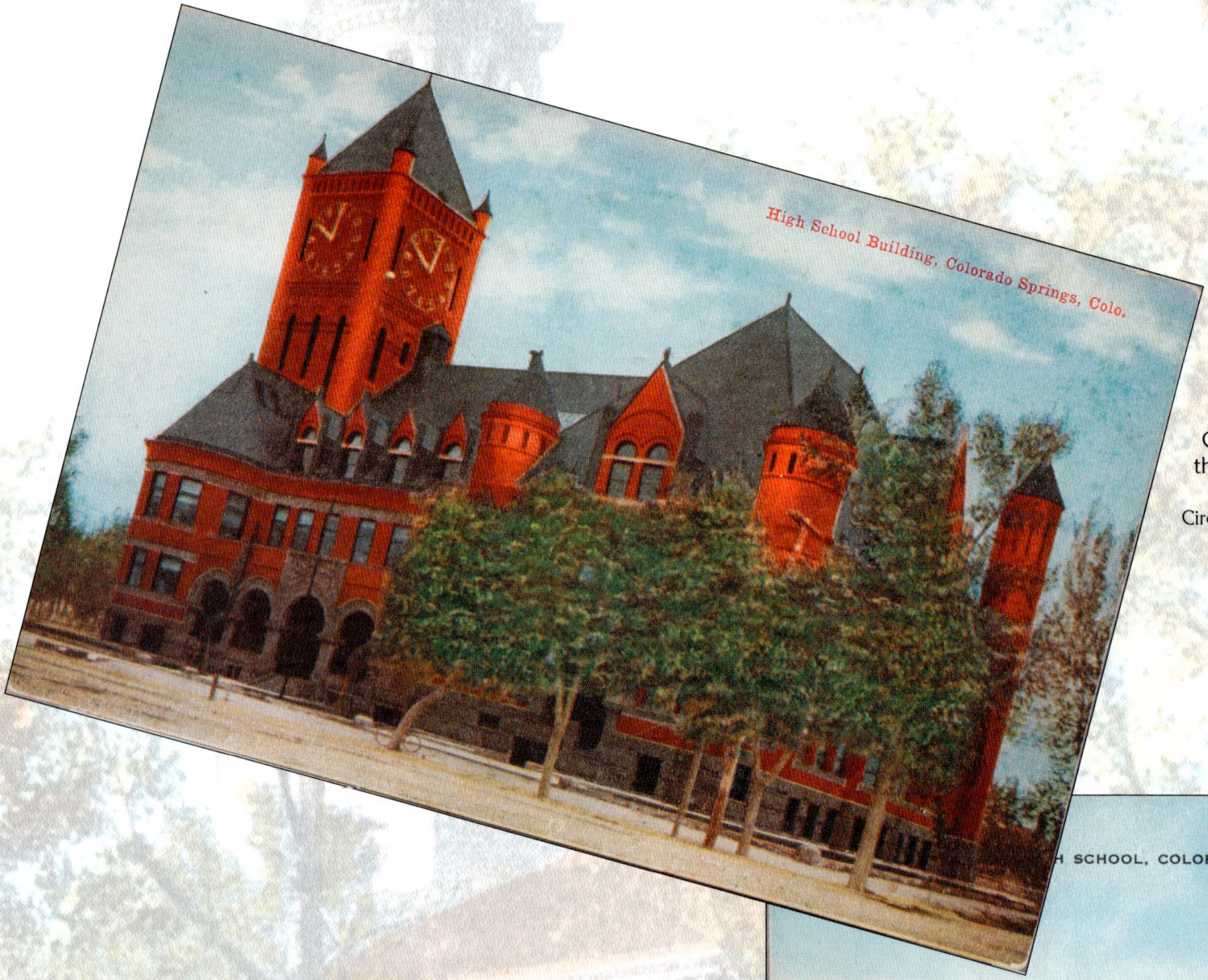

Colorado Springs High School dates back to the 1870s when the city was founded.

Circa 1910s, $4-6

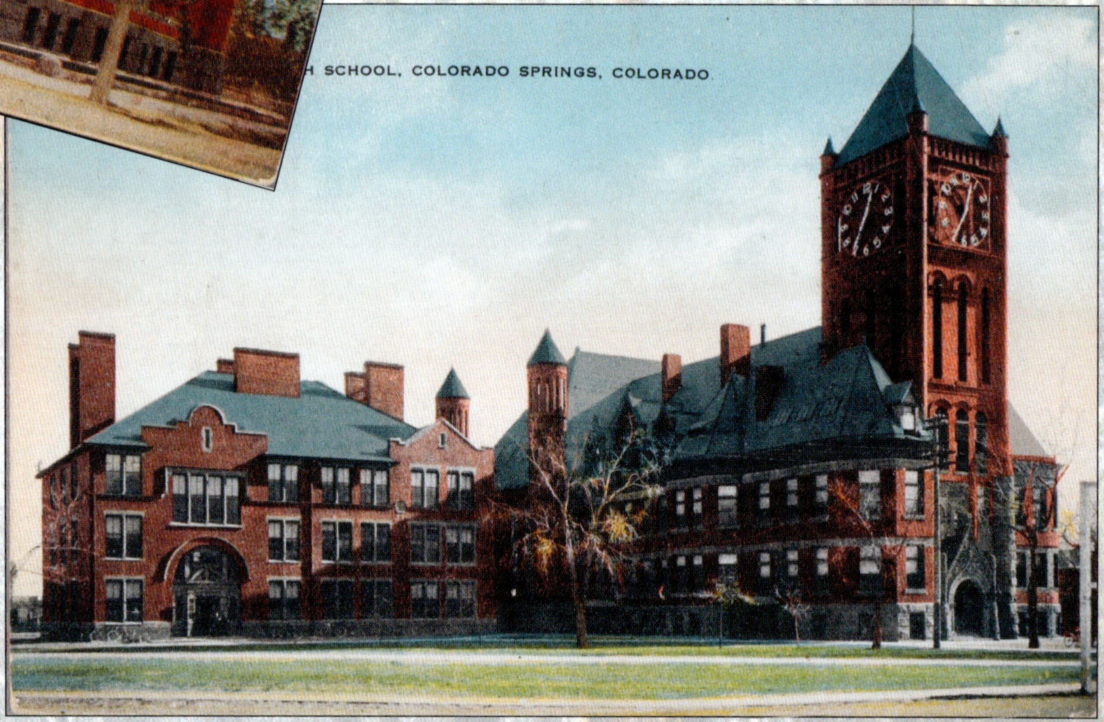

Colorado Springs High School was renamed Palmer High School in 1959 after the city's founder, General William Jackson Palmer.

Circa 1920s, $4-6

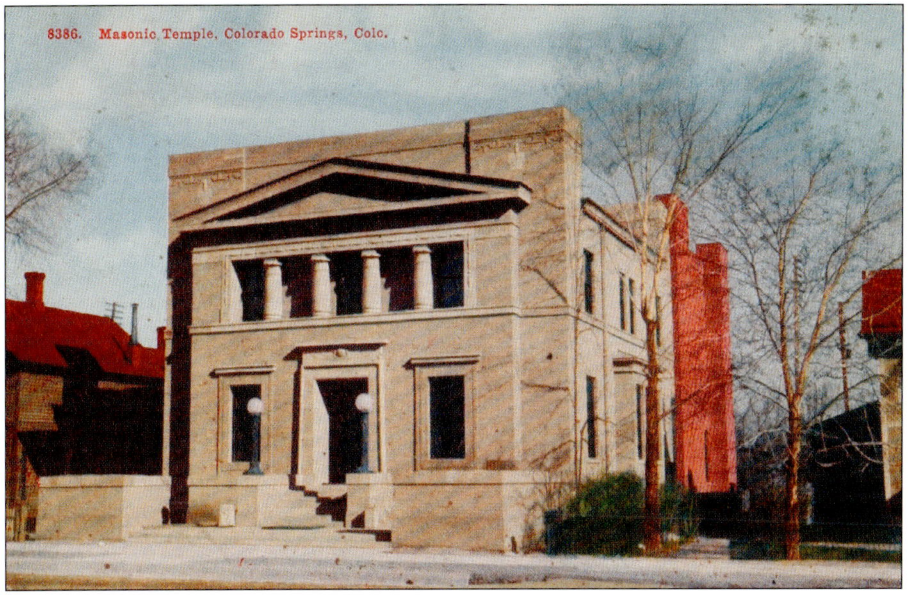

Colorado Springs Masonic Temple.

Circa 1910s, $7-9

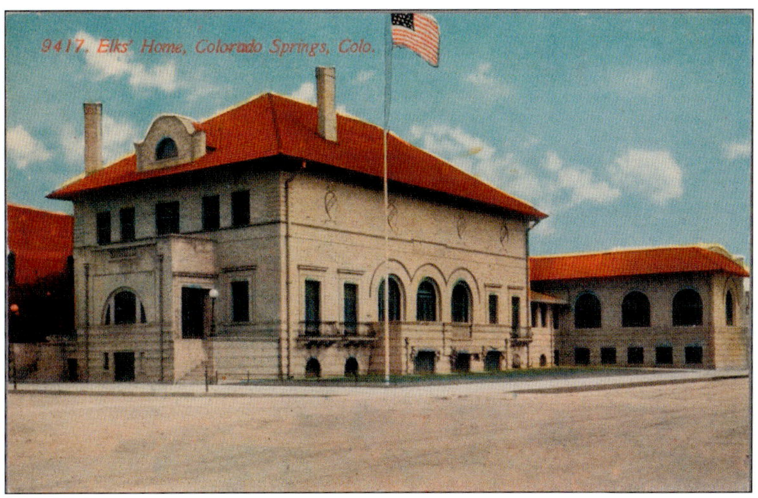

The home of Colorado Springs Lodge Number 309 of the Benevolent Party of the Elks.

Circa 1910s, $5-7

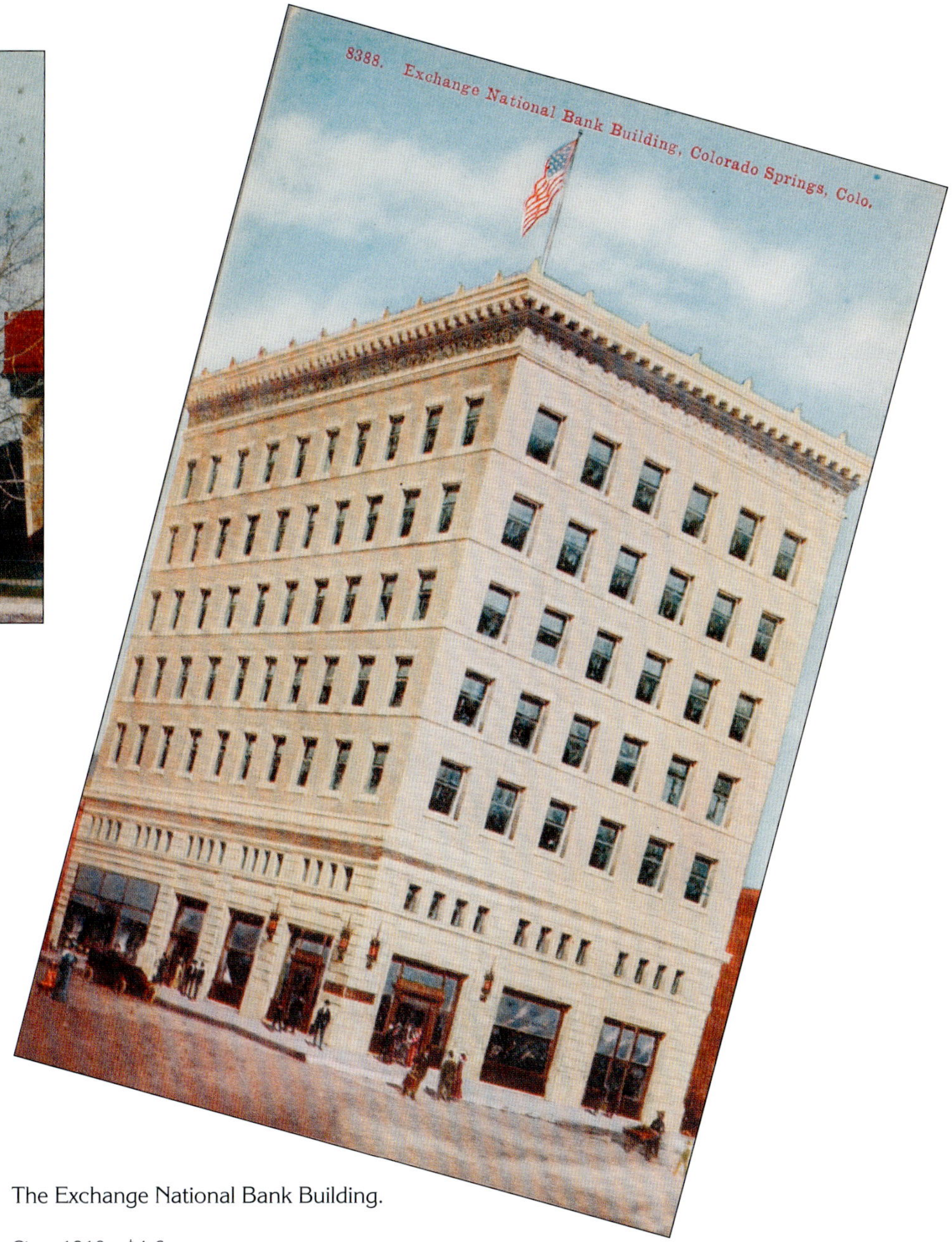

The Exchange National Bank Building.

Circa 1910s, $4-6

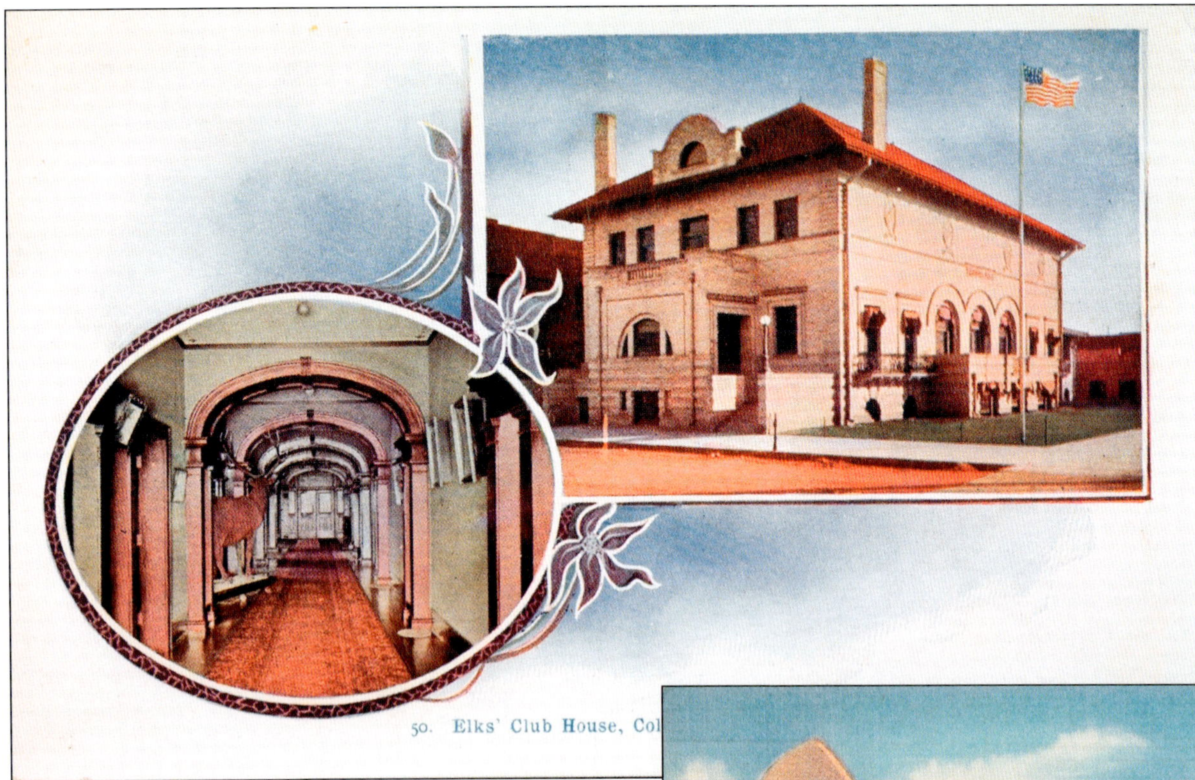

The interior and exterior of the Elk's Club House.

Circa 1900s, $4-6

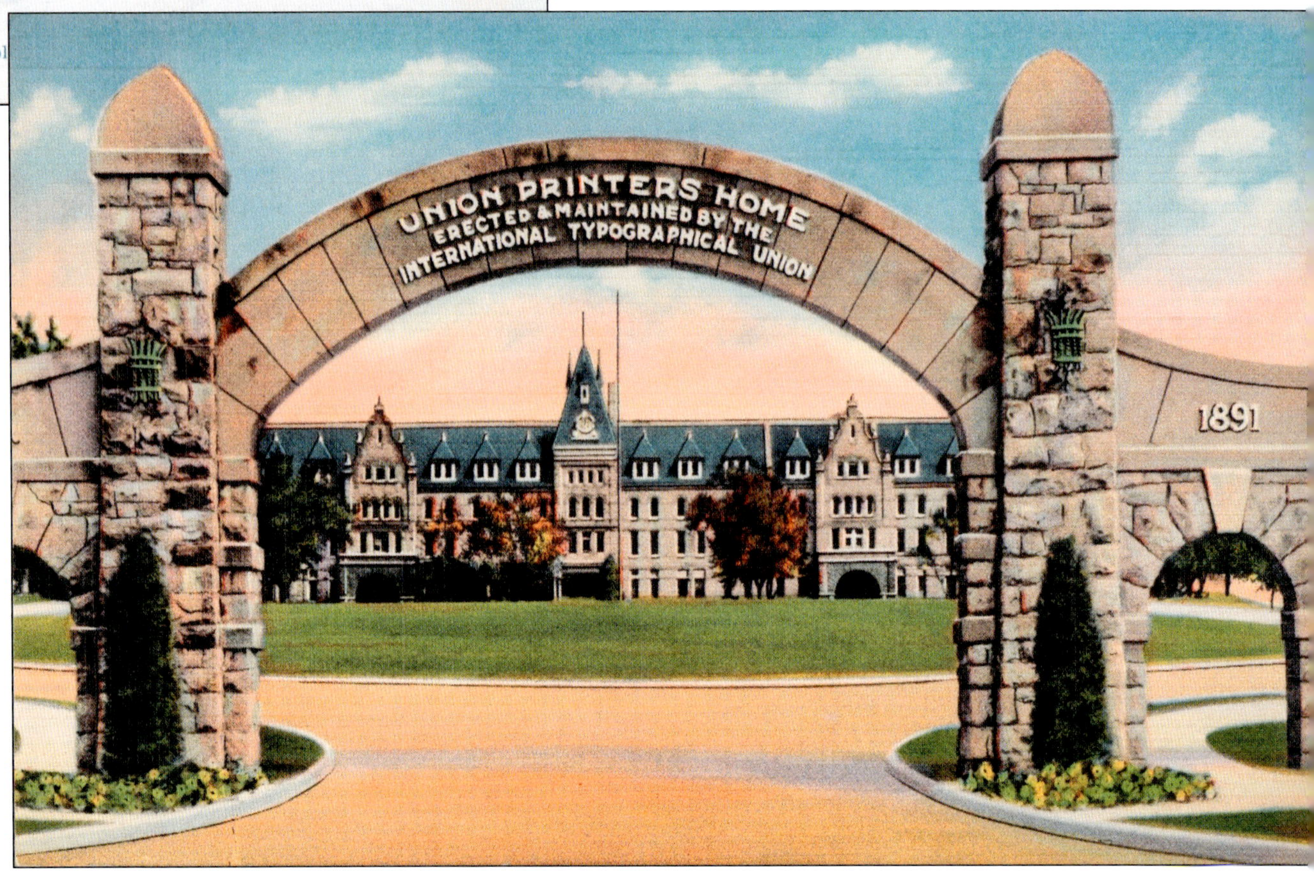

The gateway of the Union Printers Home.

Circa 1940s, $4-6

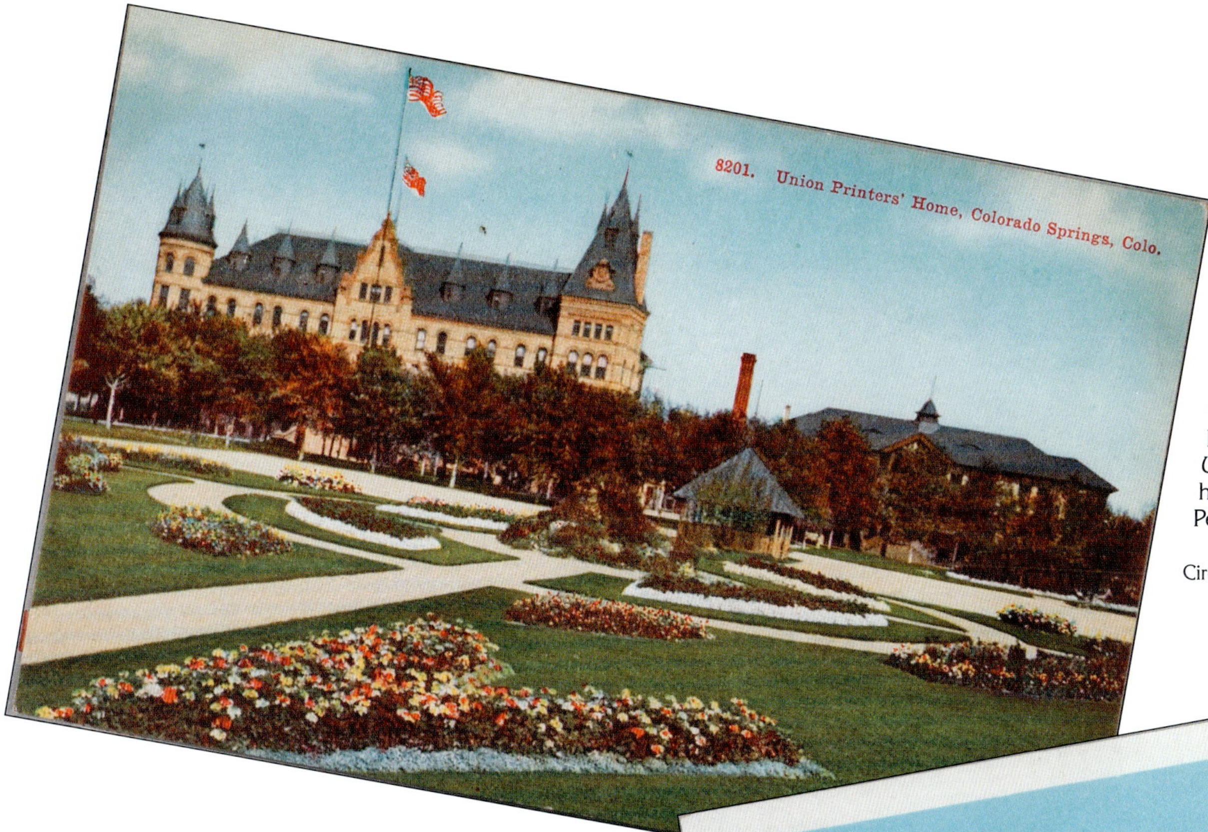

Established in 1891 and run by the International Typographical Union, the Union Printers Home was the first national health institution to be built in the Pikes Peak Region.

Circa 1910s, $4-6

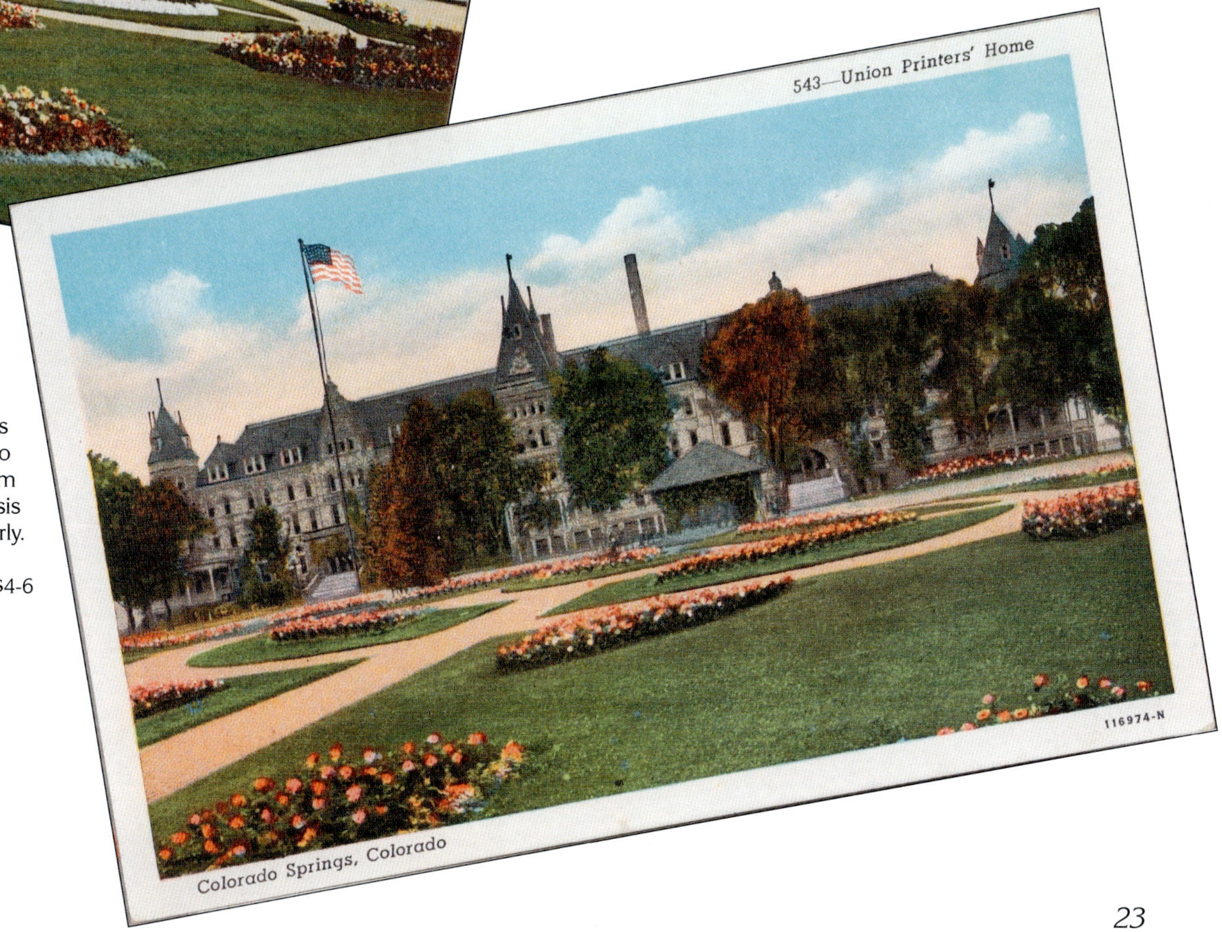

The Union Printers Home was situated just outside of Colorado Springs and included a sanatorium for the treatment of tuberculosis and a home for the elderly.

Circa 1930s, $4-6

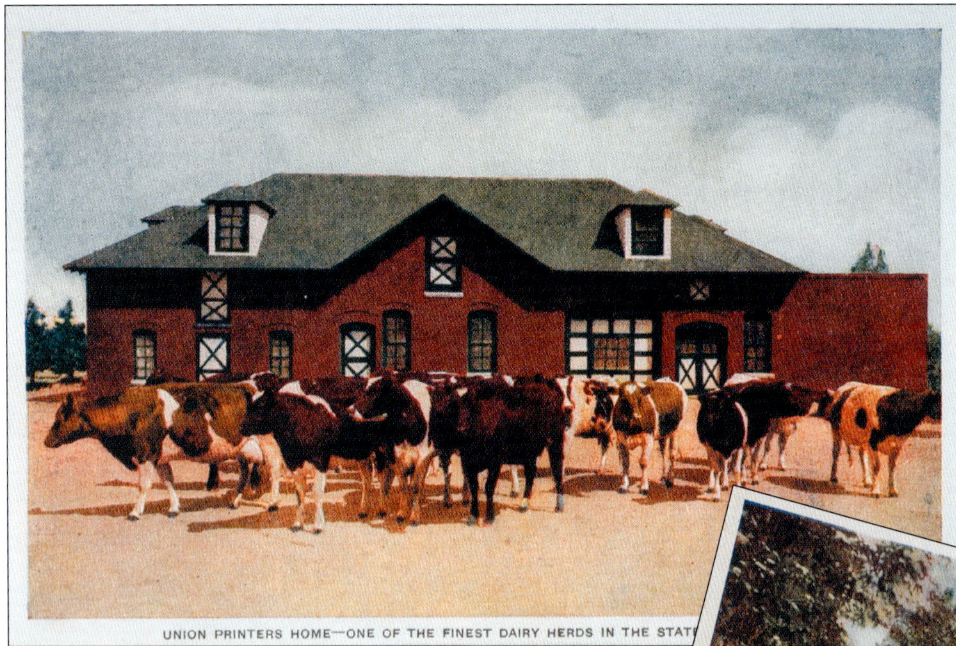

Dairy herd housed on the grounds of the Union Printers Home.

Circa 1930s, $4-6

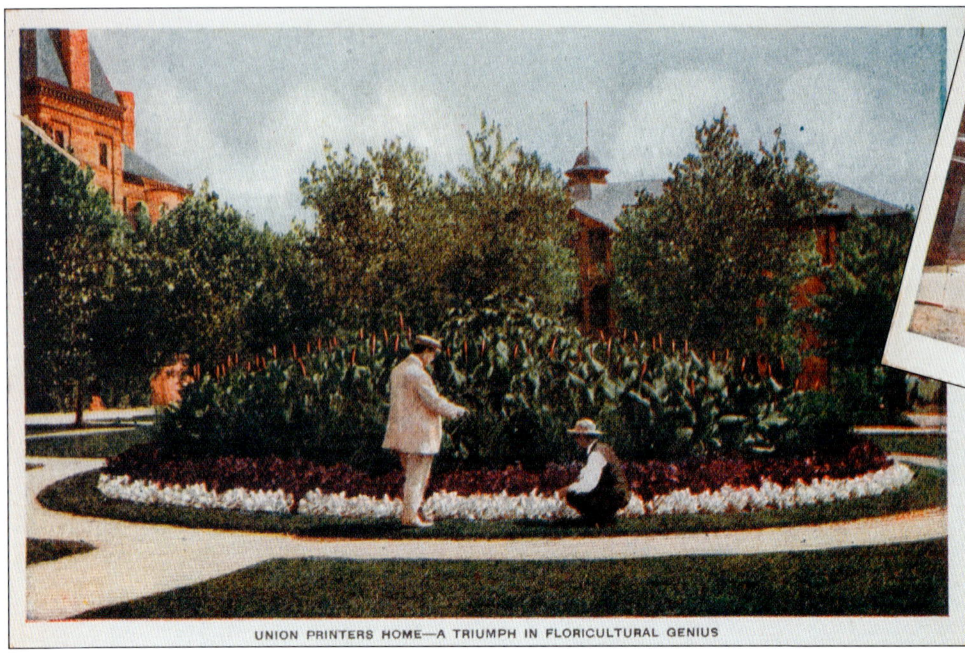

A section of the grounds of the Union Printers Home.

Circa 1920s, $4-6

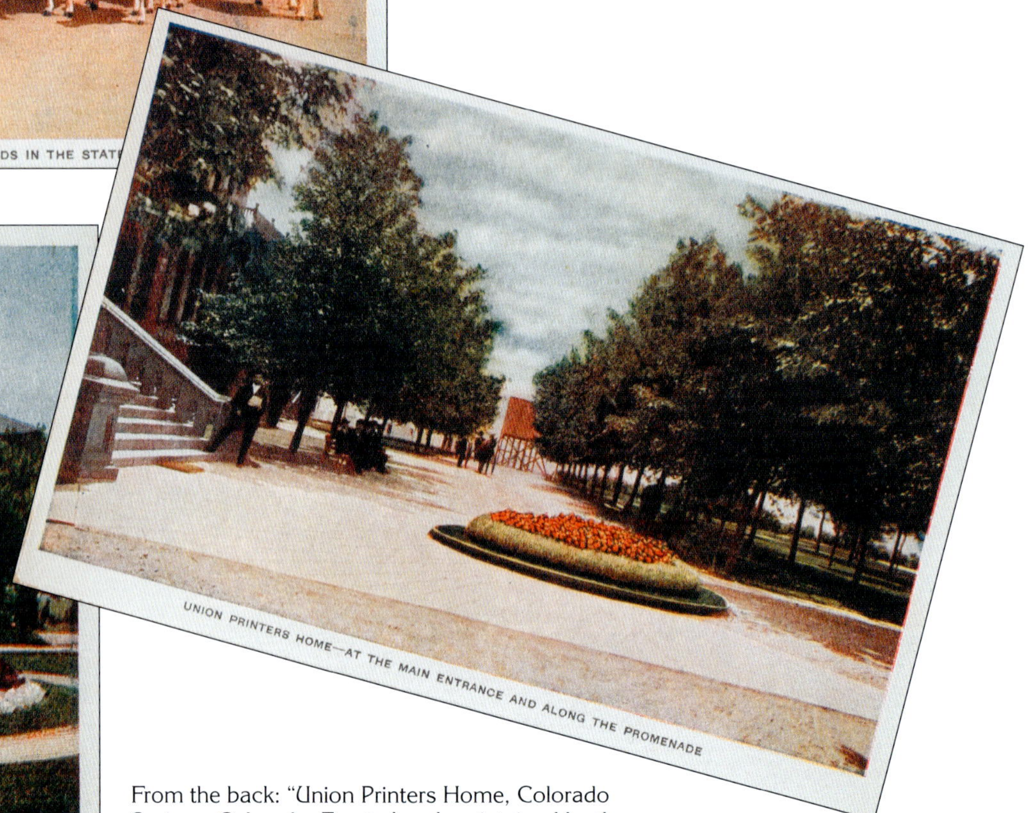

From the back: "Union Printers Home, Colorado Springs, Colorado. Erected and maintained by the International Typographical Union. Its bounty unpurchasable; its charity without price. Estimated physical value of the home and grounds, $1,000,000."

Circa 1920s, $4-6

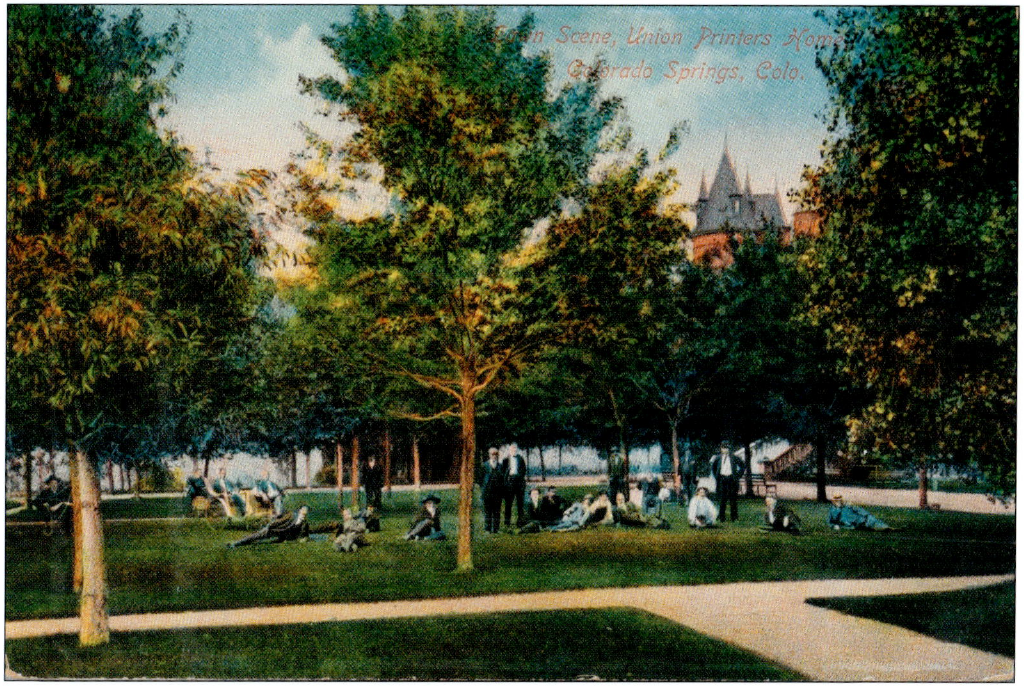

As part of their treatments, patients at the Union Printers Home were encouraged to get plenty of fresh air and sunlight each day.

Cancelled 1911, $4-6

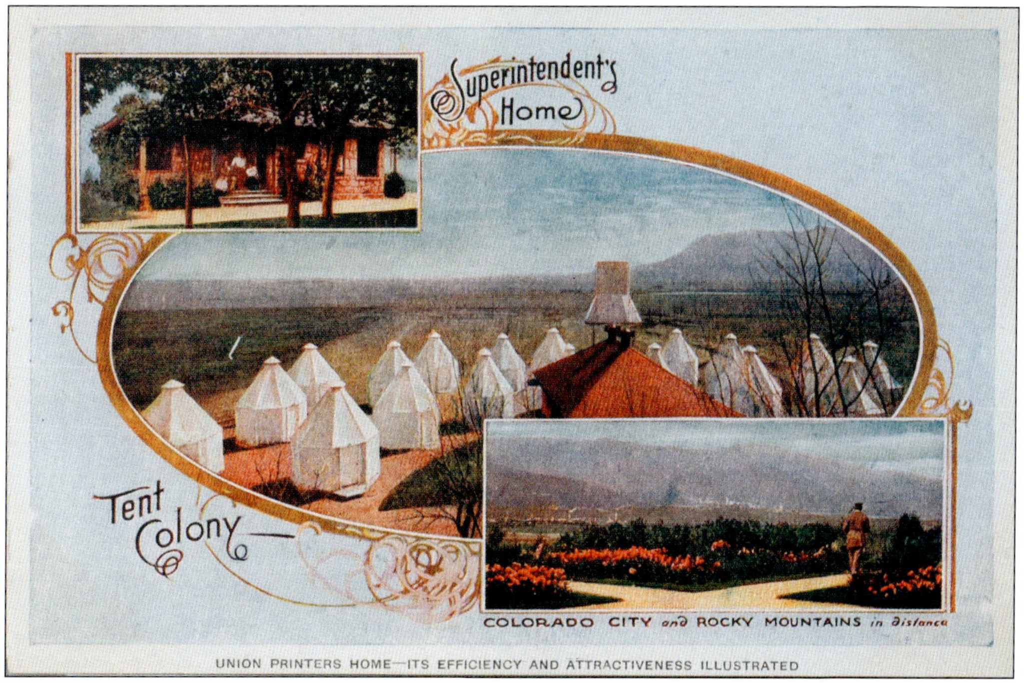

Multiple views of the Union Printers Home including the Superintendents home, the Tent Colony, and a view of Colorado City and the Rocky Mountains as seen from the Home's grounds.

Circa 1920s, $4-6

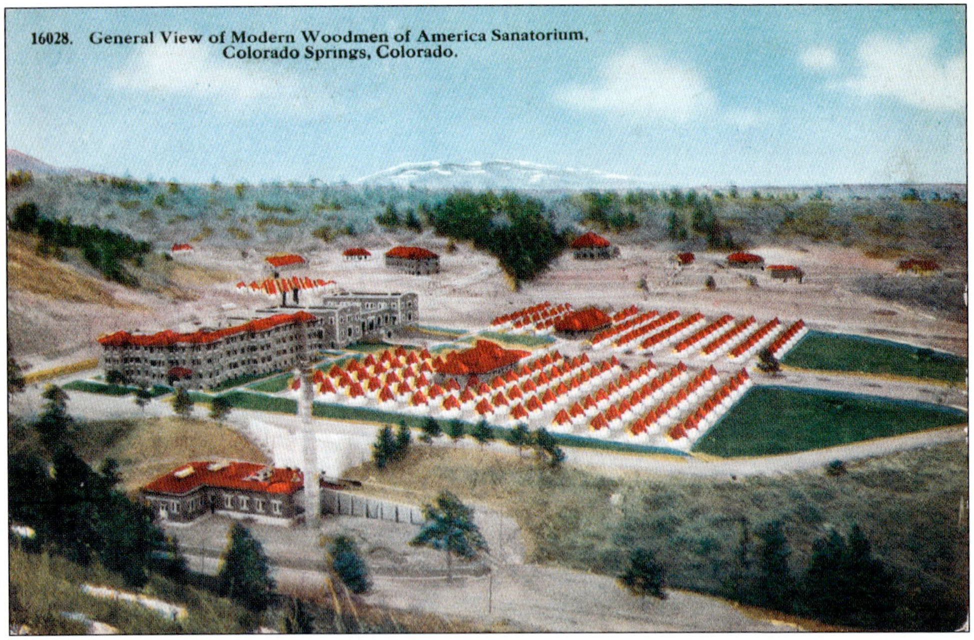

The Modern Woodmen of America Sanatorium, like the Union Printers Home, was also built for the purpose of treating people with tuberculosis and other pulmonary ailments.

Circa 1920s, $4-6

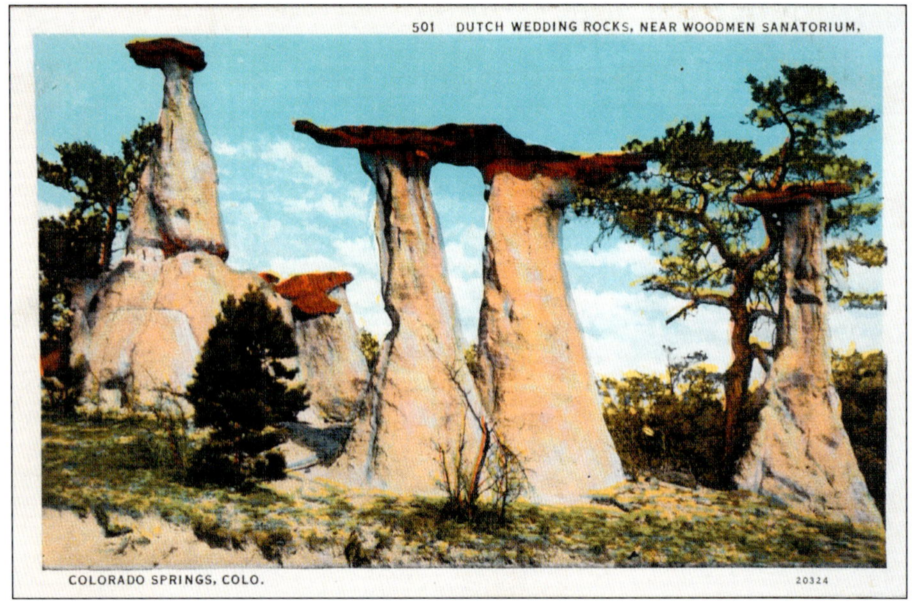

The Dutch Wedding Rocks, a formation in the valley east of the Modern Woodmen of America Sanatorium.

Circa 1930s, $4-6

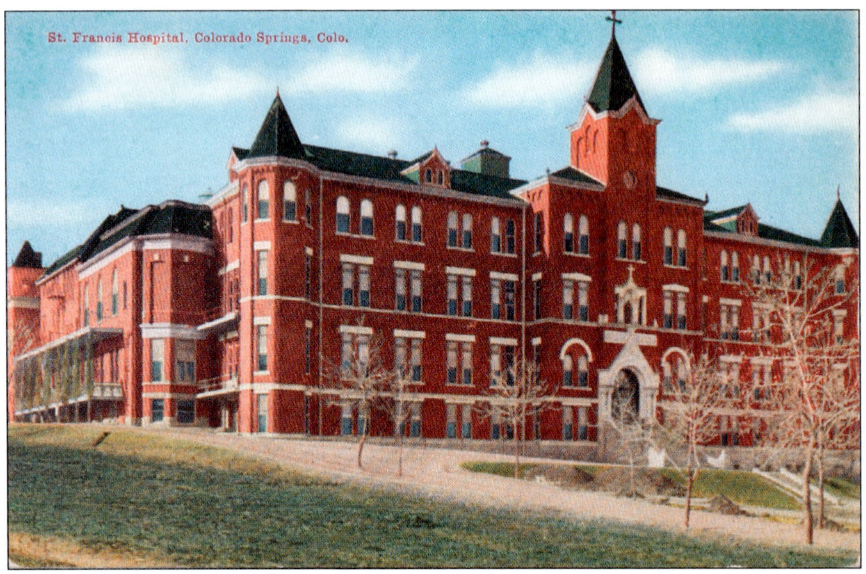

The St. Francis Hospital.

Circa 1910s, $4-6

In many Protestant denominations, deaconesses (women called or commissioned to serve in a church or church-related agency) often fulfilled the role of spiritual and physical caregiver and ran and staffed a number of hospitals in the United States and abroad, like the Deaconess Hospital in Colorado Springs.

Circa 1910s, $4-6

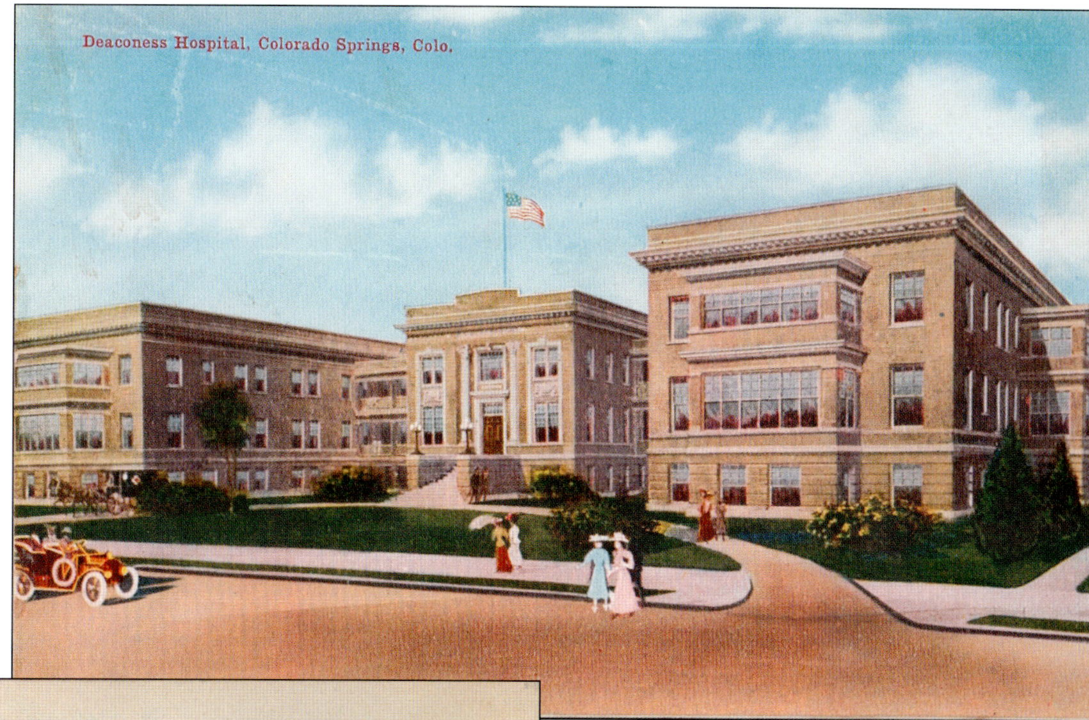

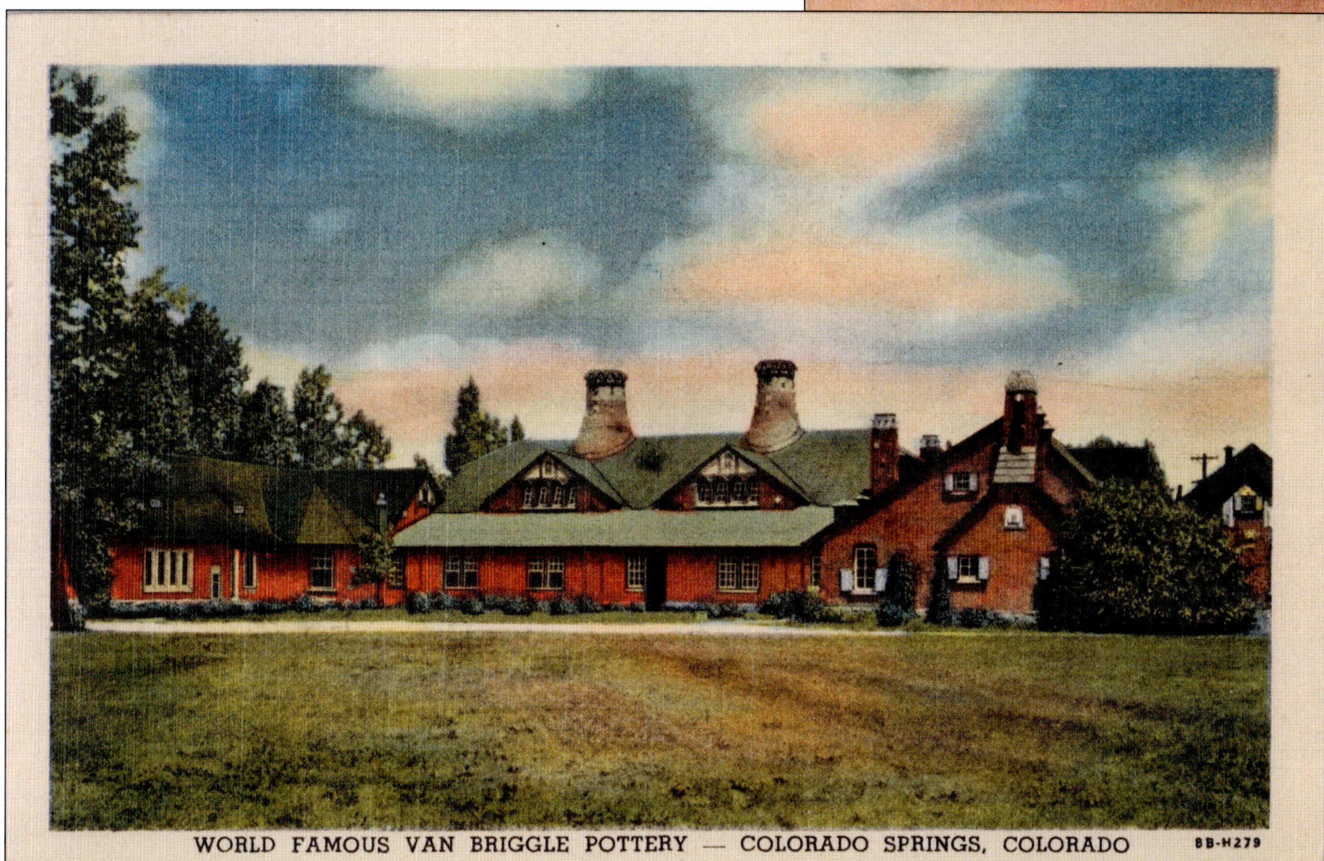

The world famous Van Briggle Pottery, situated at the foot of Pikes Peak. Here potters worked throughout the day, drawing inspiration for the work from the beautiful scenery around them.

Cancelled 1954, $4-6

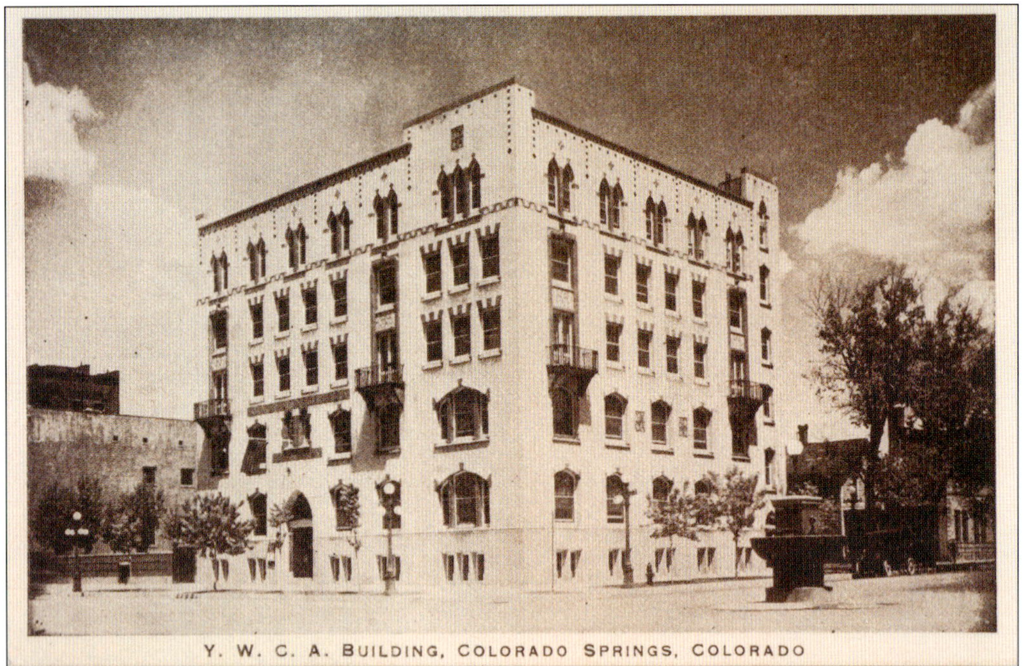

The YWCA (Young Women's Christian Association) functions along the same lines as the YMCA, except its programs are geared towards women.

Circa 1920s, $4-6

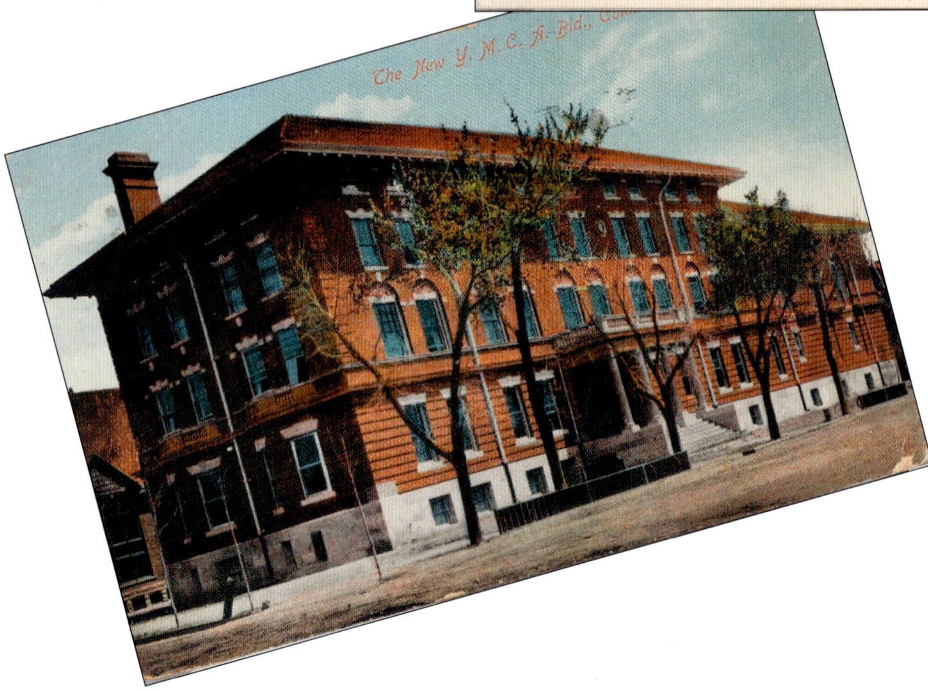

The new Colorado Springs YMCA Building, circa 1910s.

Cancelled 1922, $4-6

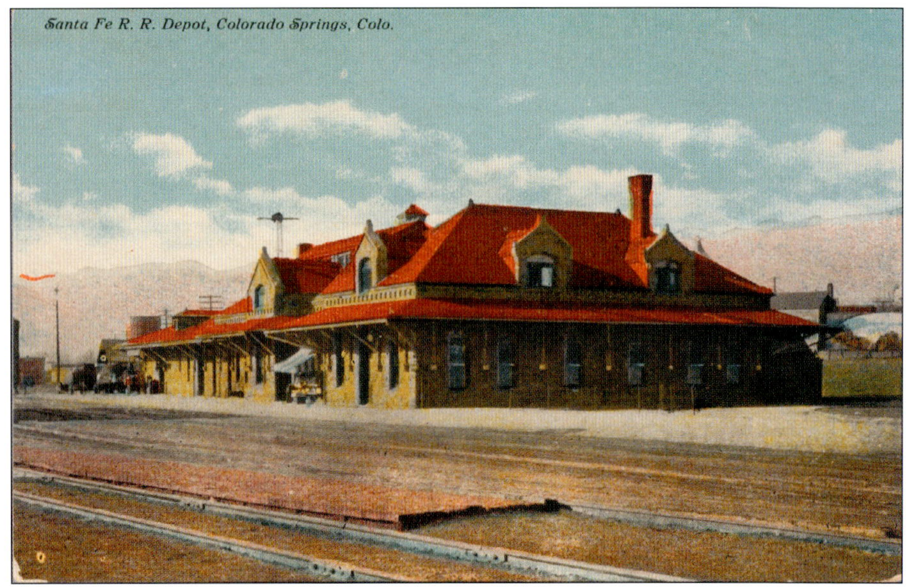

Atchison, Topeka, and Santa Fe Railway depot in Colorado Springs.

Circa 1910s, $10-12

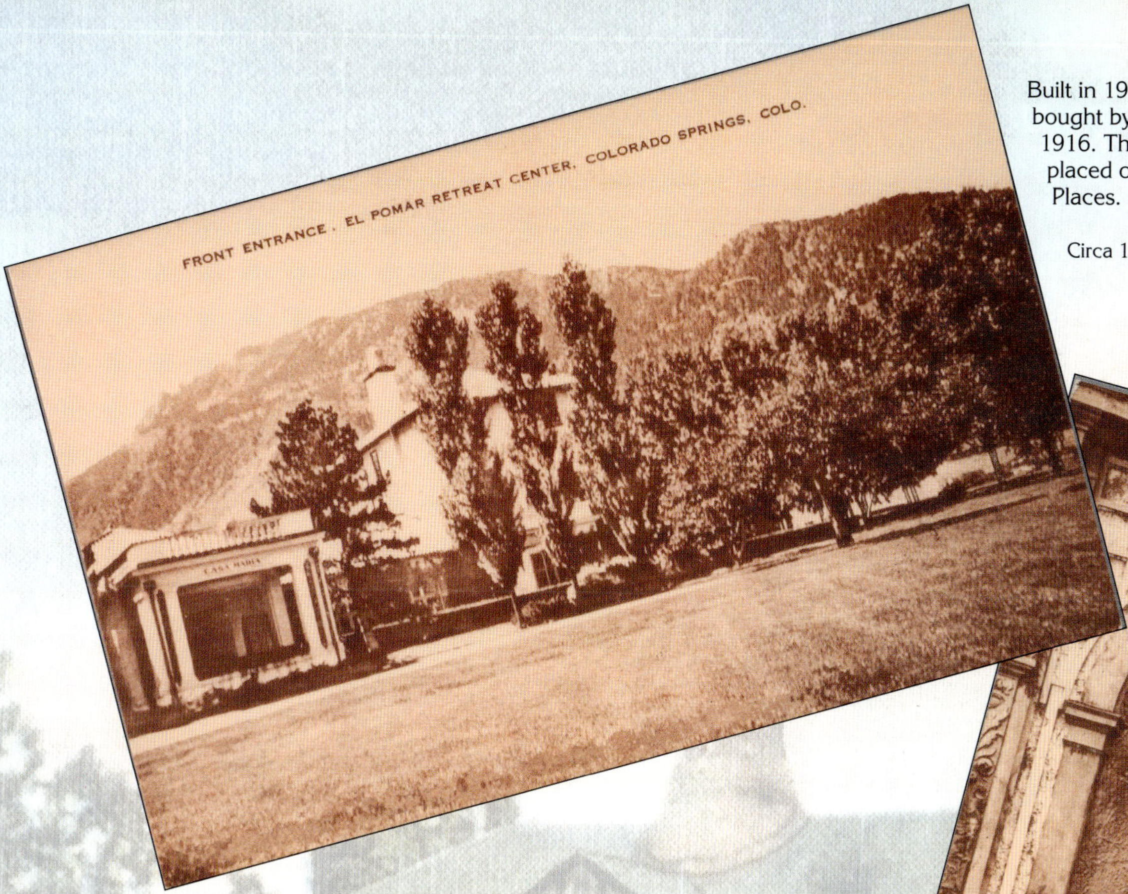

Built in 1910, the Penrose House was bought by Spencer and Julie Penrose in 1916. The house itself has since been placed on the National Register of Historic Places.

Circa 1920s, $4-6

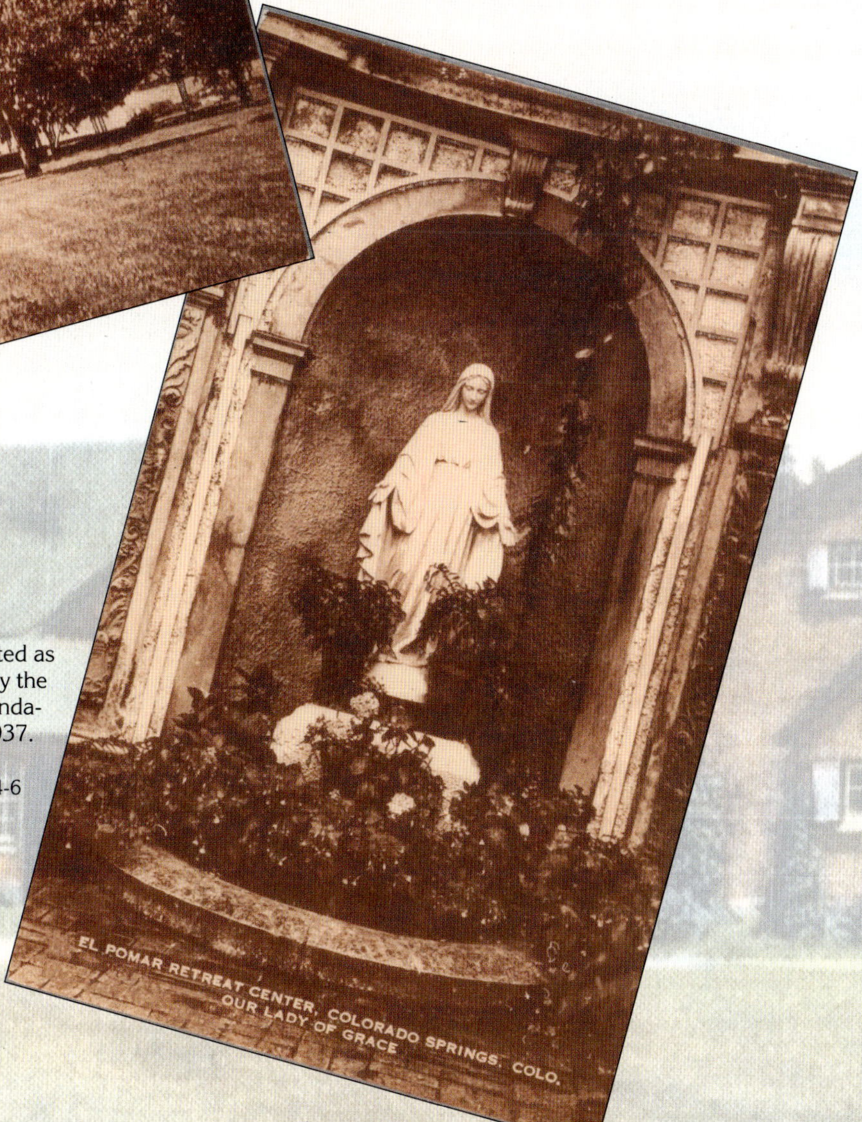

Today the Penrose House is operated as a retreat and conference center by the El Pomar Foundation, a private foundation started by the Penroses in 1937.

Circa 1920s, $4-6

Streets

In accordance with General Palmer's early plan, the streets in Colorado Springs were one hundred feet wide and avenues were 140 feet wide. The idea for the width was attributed to General Palmer who wanted to avoid the traffic congestions that was so common in Eastern cities. To keep the streets free of congestions, he designed them to be wide enough that a multiple horse carriage could turn around without needing to back up. The streets ran on a north-south axis and alternated with avenues. Streets that ran on an east-west axis were placed two between two avenues. At first these early thoroughfares were dirt, but they were eventually covered with gravel and later paved over when residents complained of dust and rainwater puddles. In 1872, the city planted cottonwoods along the irrigation ditches on each side of the streets and along some of the medians as well.

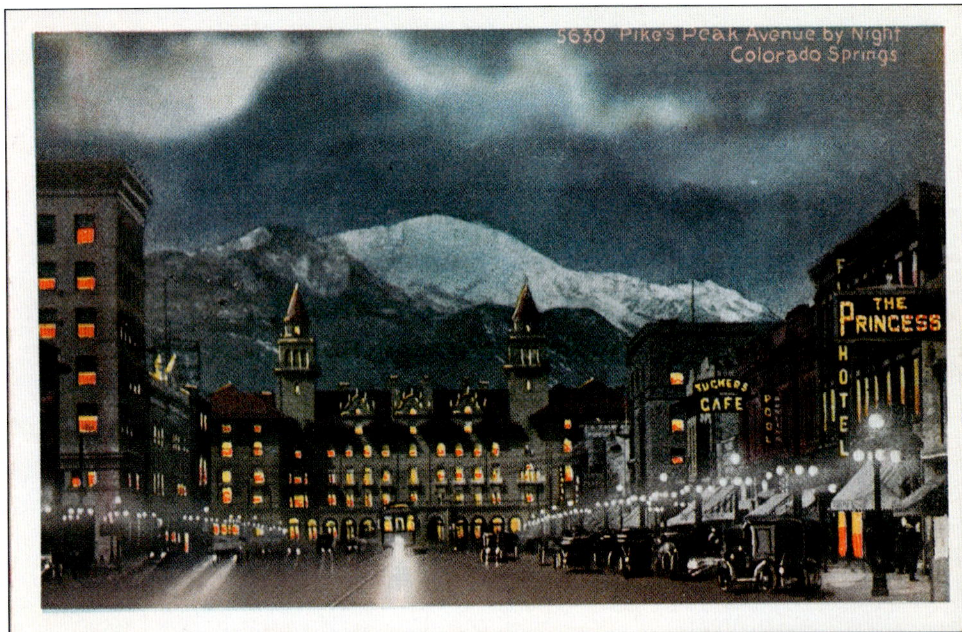

Pikes Peak Avenue, as seen at night.

Circa 1930s, $5-7

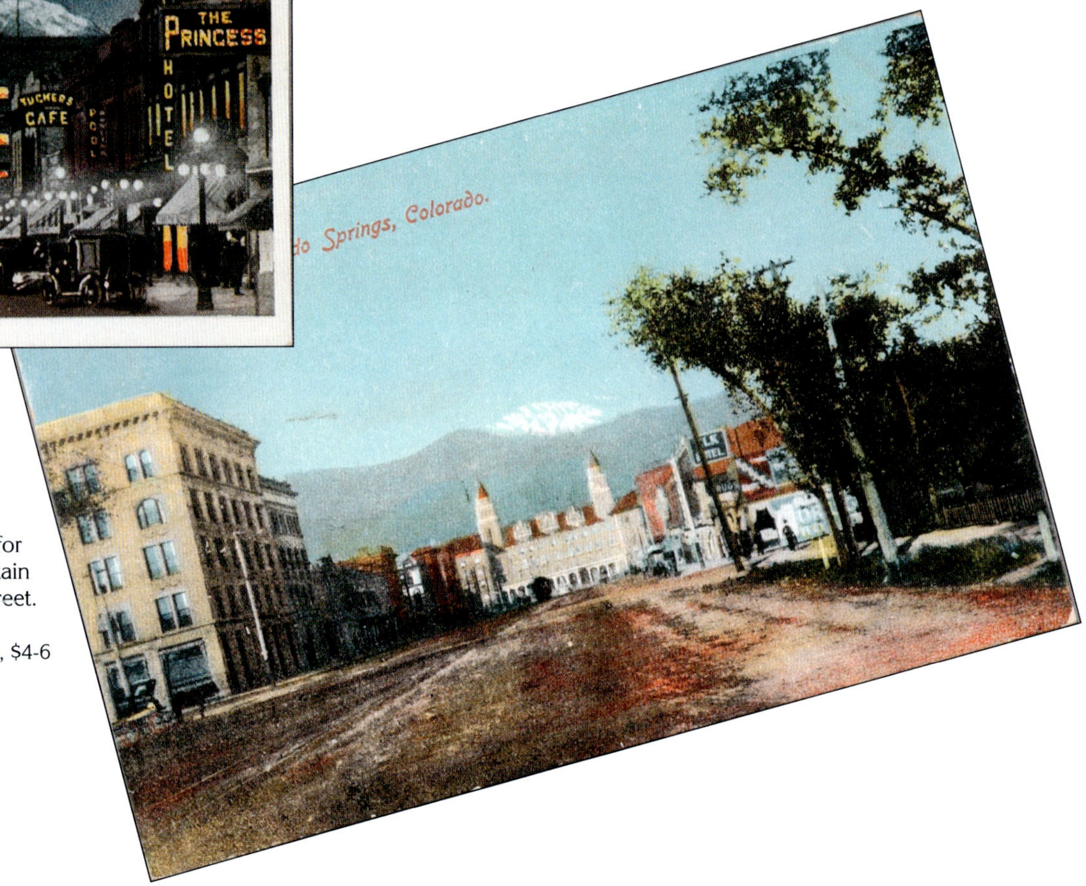

Pikes Peak Avenue is named for Pikes Peak, the famous mountain that looms above the street.

Circa 1910s, $4-6

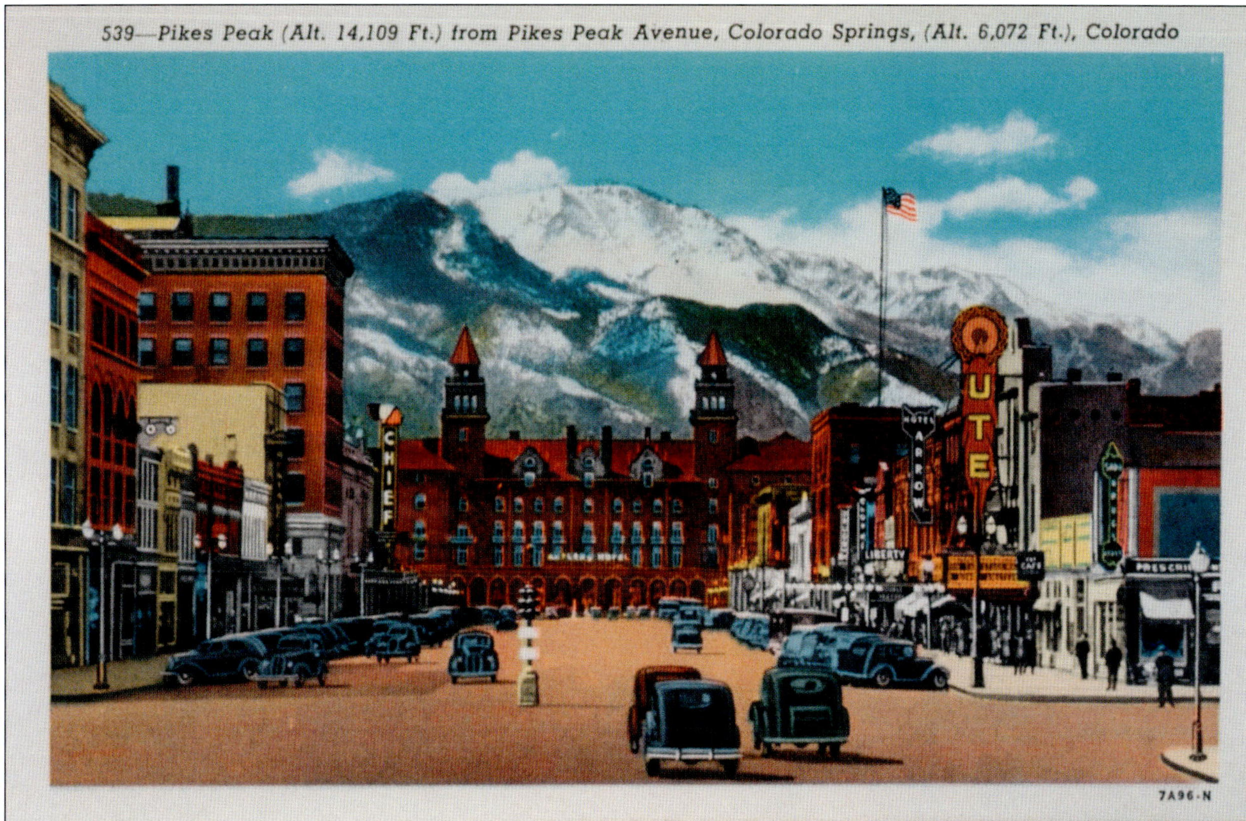

From the back: "Few who have traversed its [Pikes Peak Avenue] broad pavements will forget it as it is one of the most impressive street spectacles of the world."

Circa 1940s, $5-7

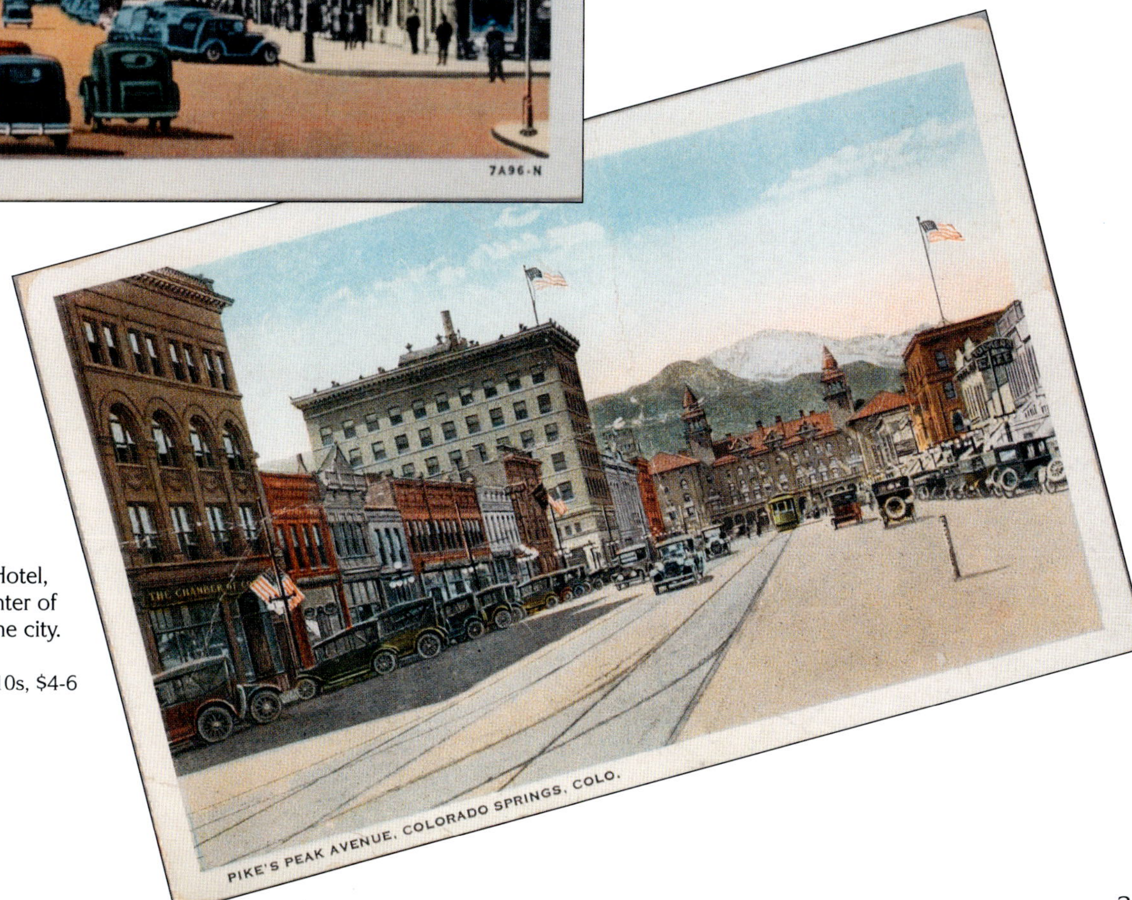

The location of the Antlers Hotel, Pikes Peak Avenue was the center of tourist activity for the city.

Circa 1910s, $4-6

Pikes Peak as seen from the Midland Railway Bridge.

Cancelled 1912, $4-6

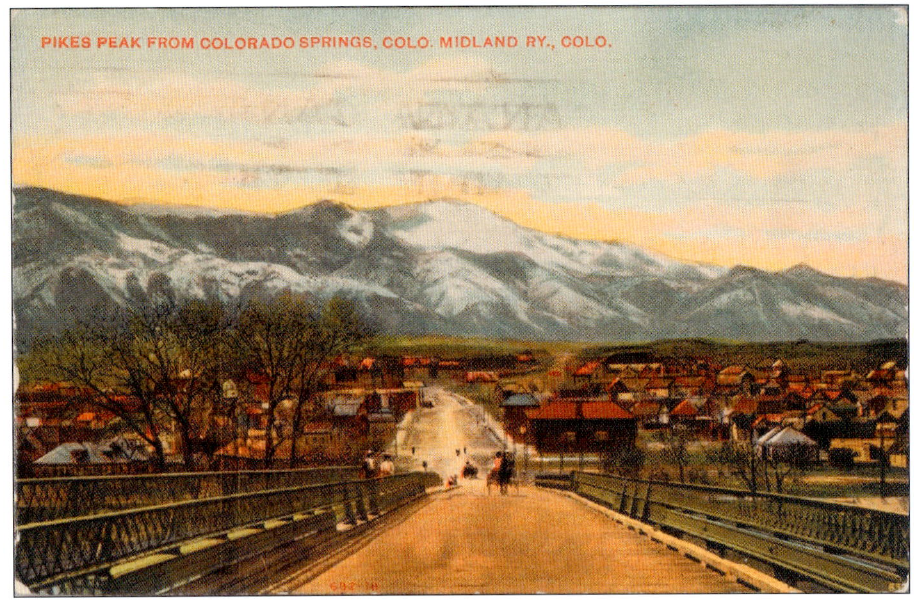

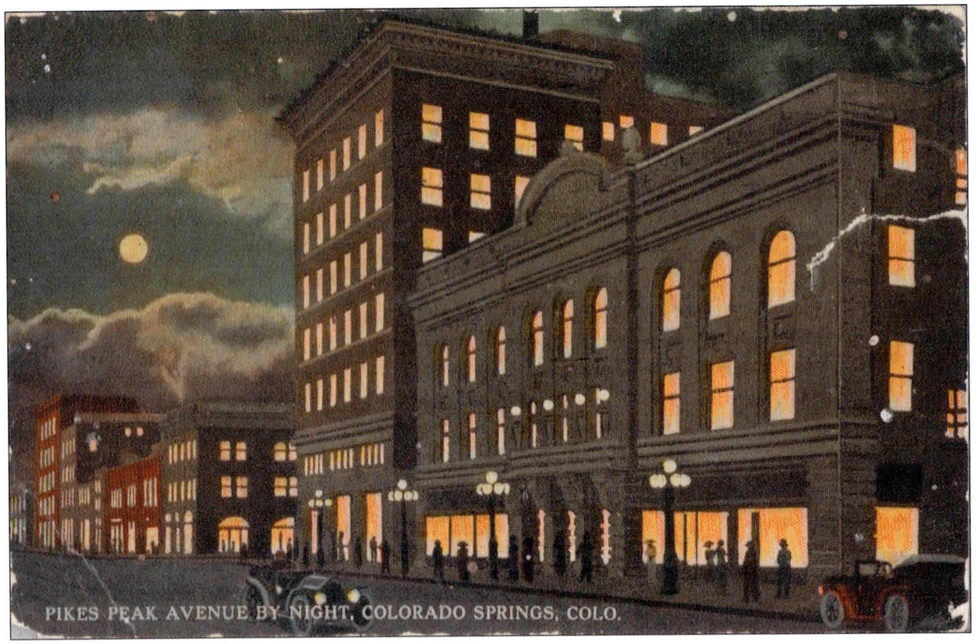

Another nighttime view of Pikes Peak Avenue.

Circa 1910s, $4-6

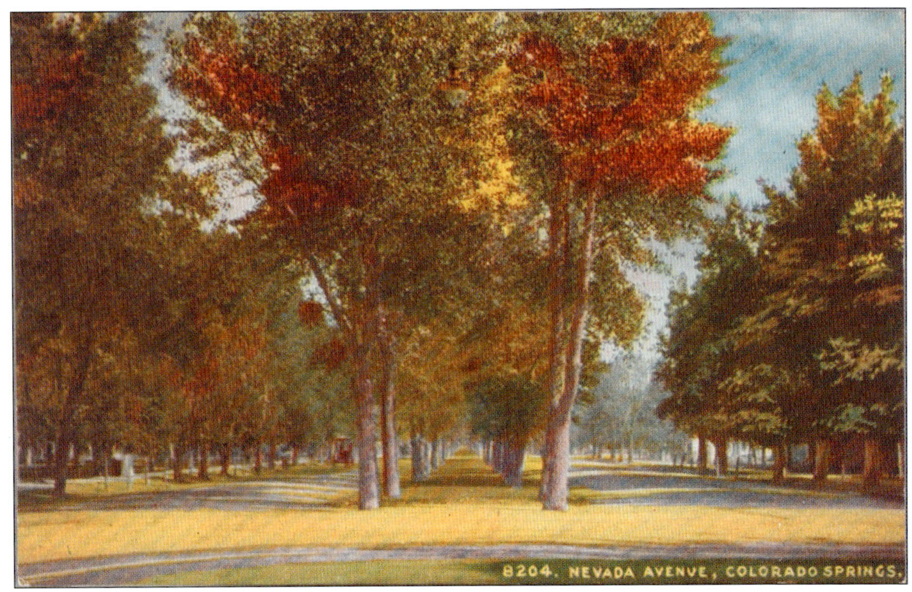

Nevada Avenue.

Circa 1910s, $4-6

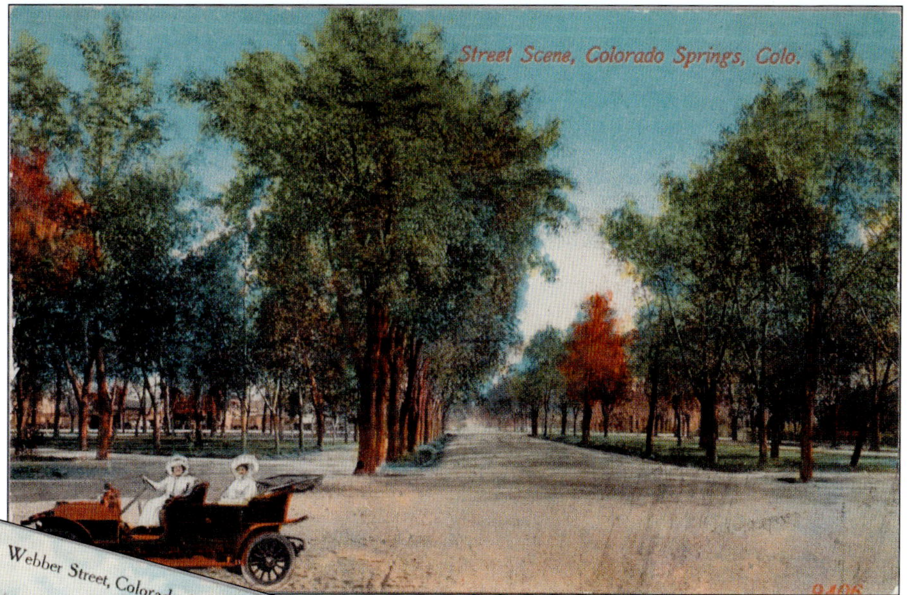

A street scene: The original plan for Colorado Springs called for streets that were 100 feet wide and avenues that were 140.

Circa 1910s, $4-6

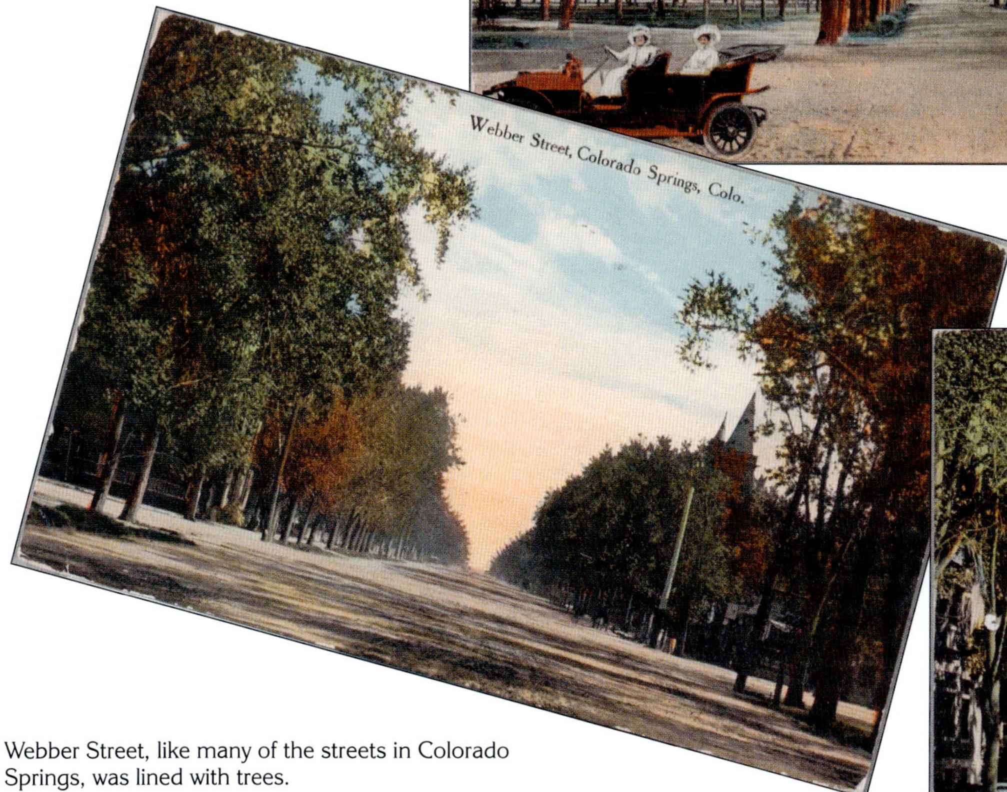

Webber Street, like many of the streets in Colorado Springs, was lined with trees.

Cancelled 1911, $4-6

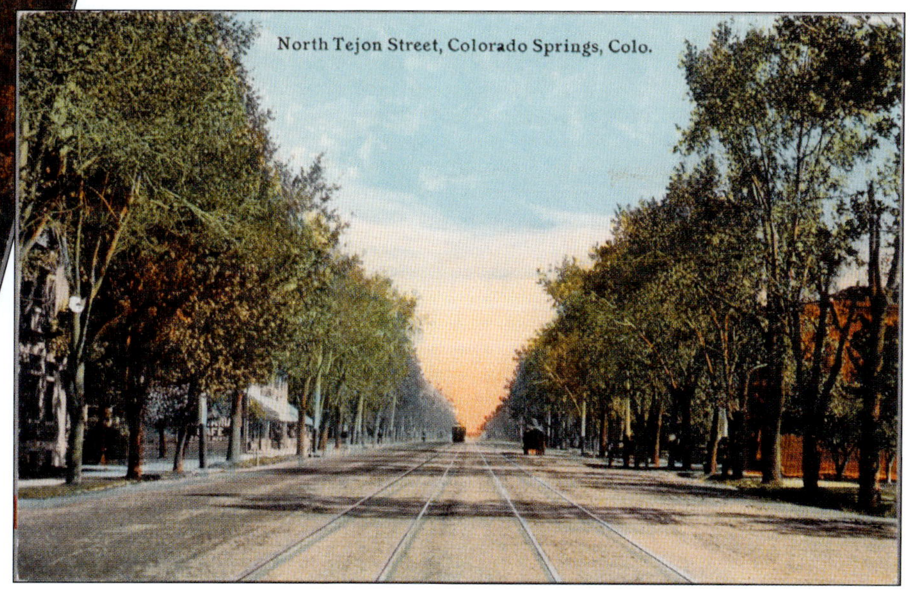

Looking down North Tejon Street.

Circa 1910s, $4-6

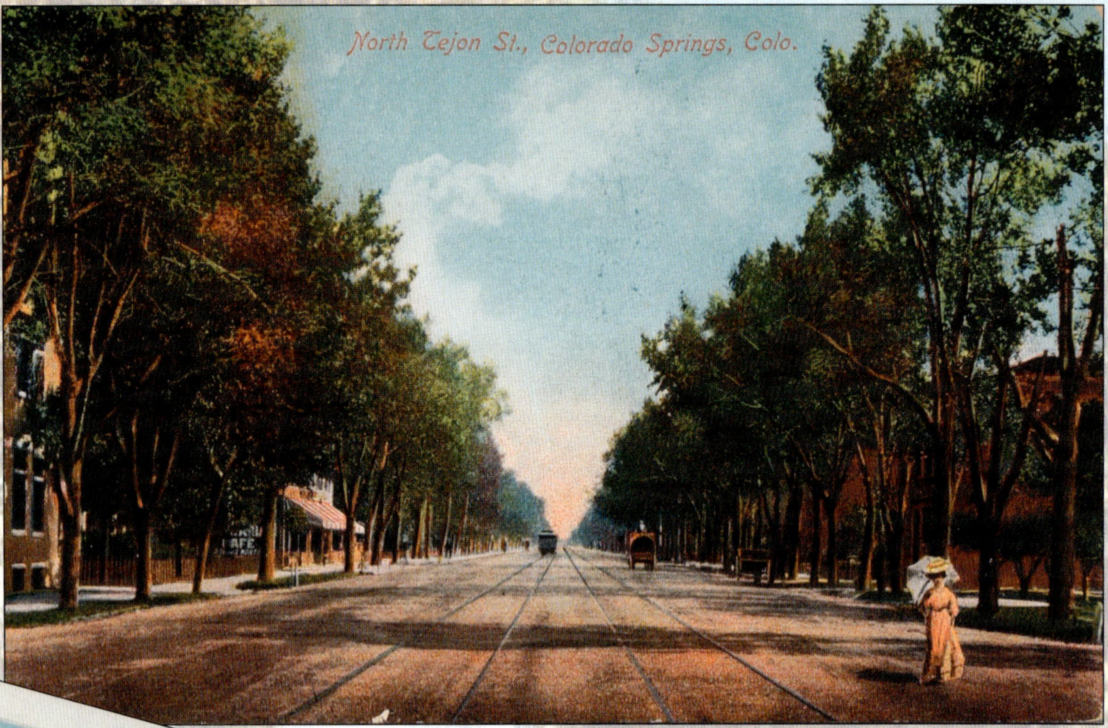

Another view of Tejon Street.

Circa 1910s, $4-6

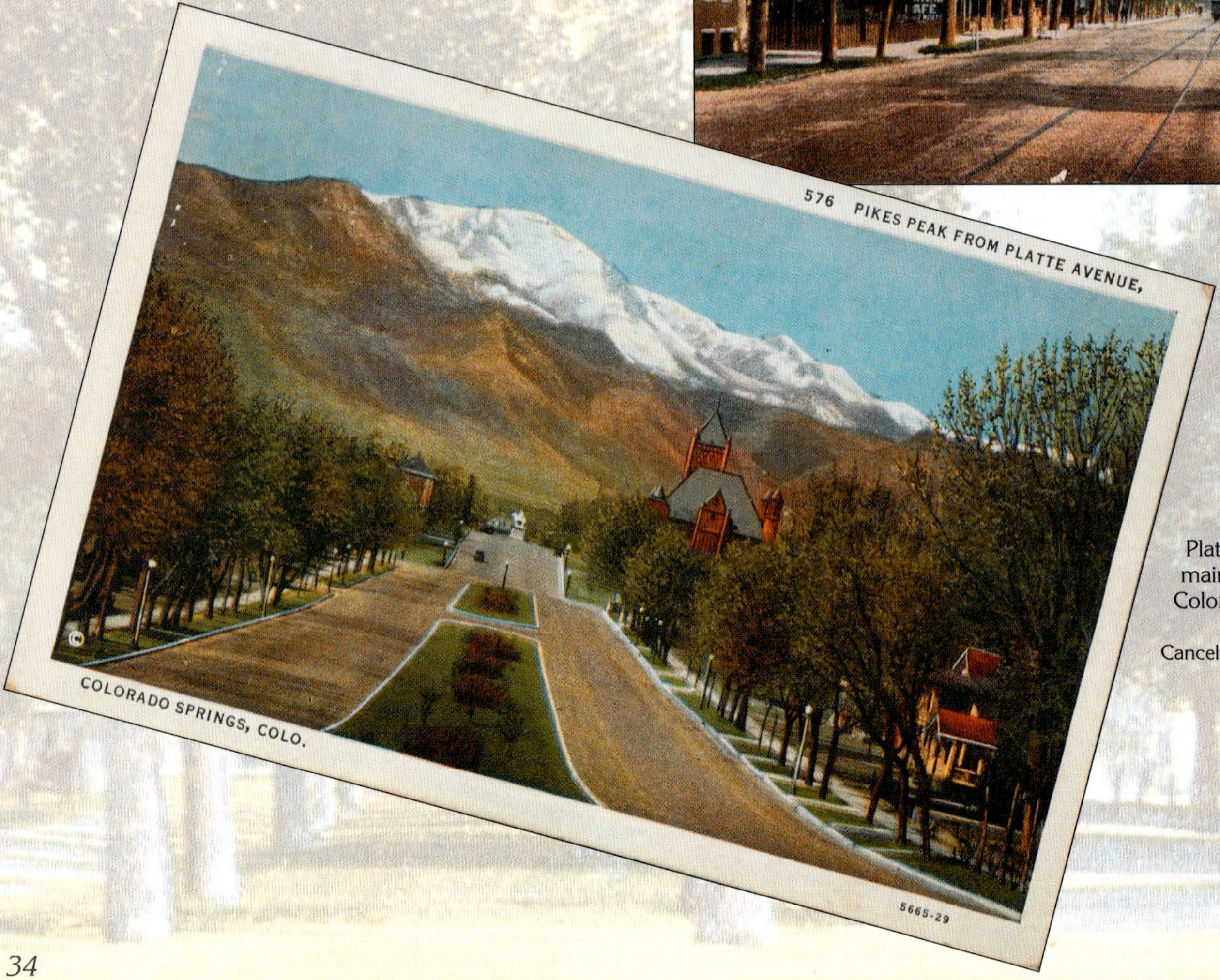

Platte Avenue, one of the main thoroughfares into Colorado Springs.

Cancelled 1937, $5-7

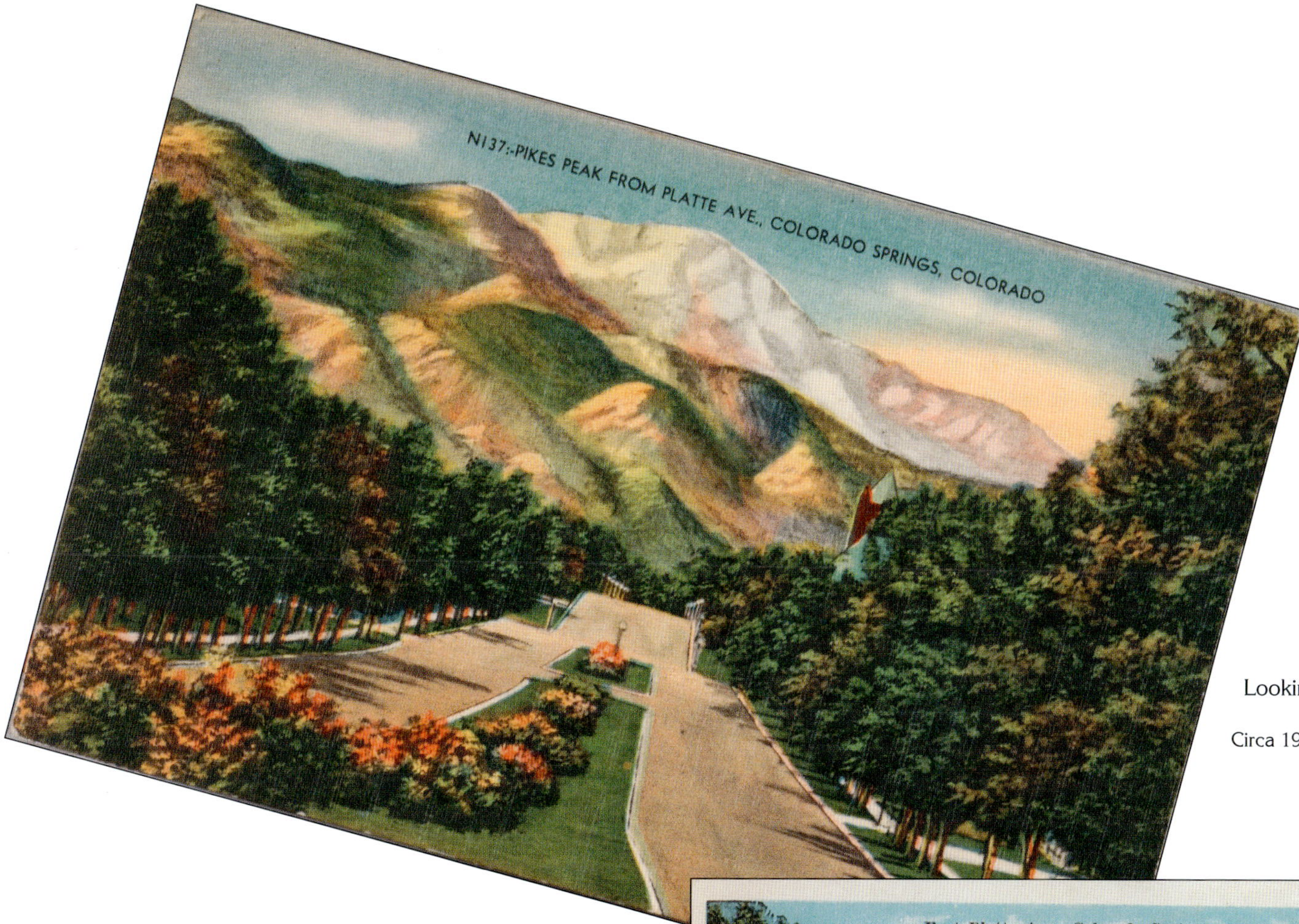

Looking west down Platte Avenue.

Circa 1940s, $4-6

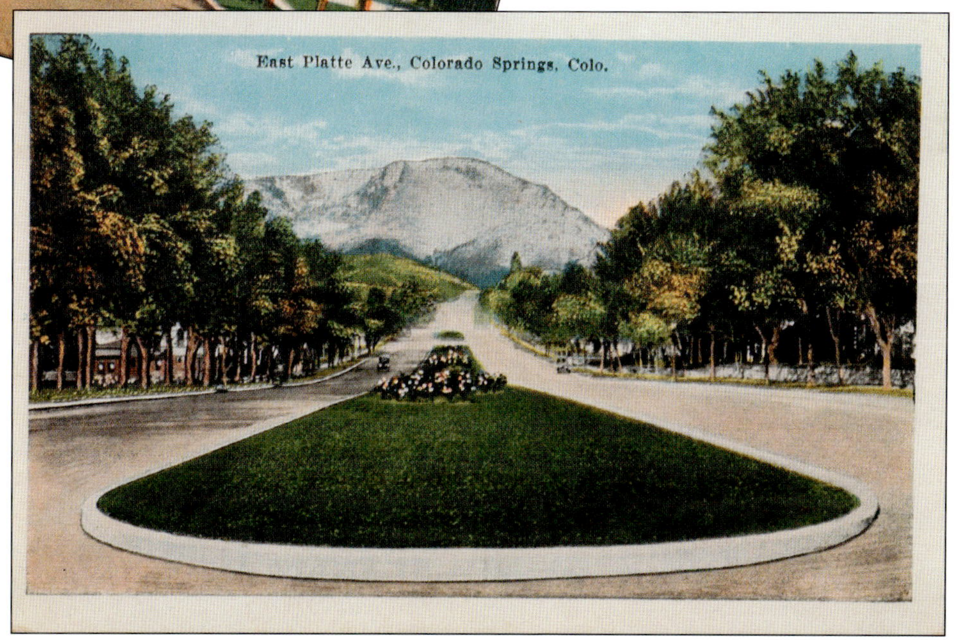

Platte Avenue was also the main eastern entrance to Colorado Springs.

Circa 1920s, $4-6

Churches

As a dry, high-class resort town, there was little to impede the process of "civilization" and ministers had little or no trouble setting up churches and organizing congregations. As largely Anglo-Americans settled the town, the early churches were all Protestant. By 1878, there were eight churches in Colorado Springs, two Presbyterians, two Methodists, a Baptist, an Episcopalian, a Unitarian, and a Congregationalist.

In recent years, Colorado Springs has attracted a large number of Evangelical Christians and Evangelical organizations. It was estimated that the city was home to at least eighty-one different religious organizations, which has earned it the nickname "the Protestant Vatican."

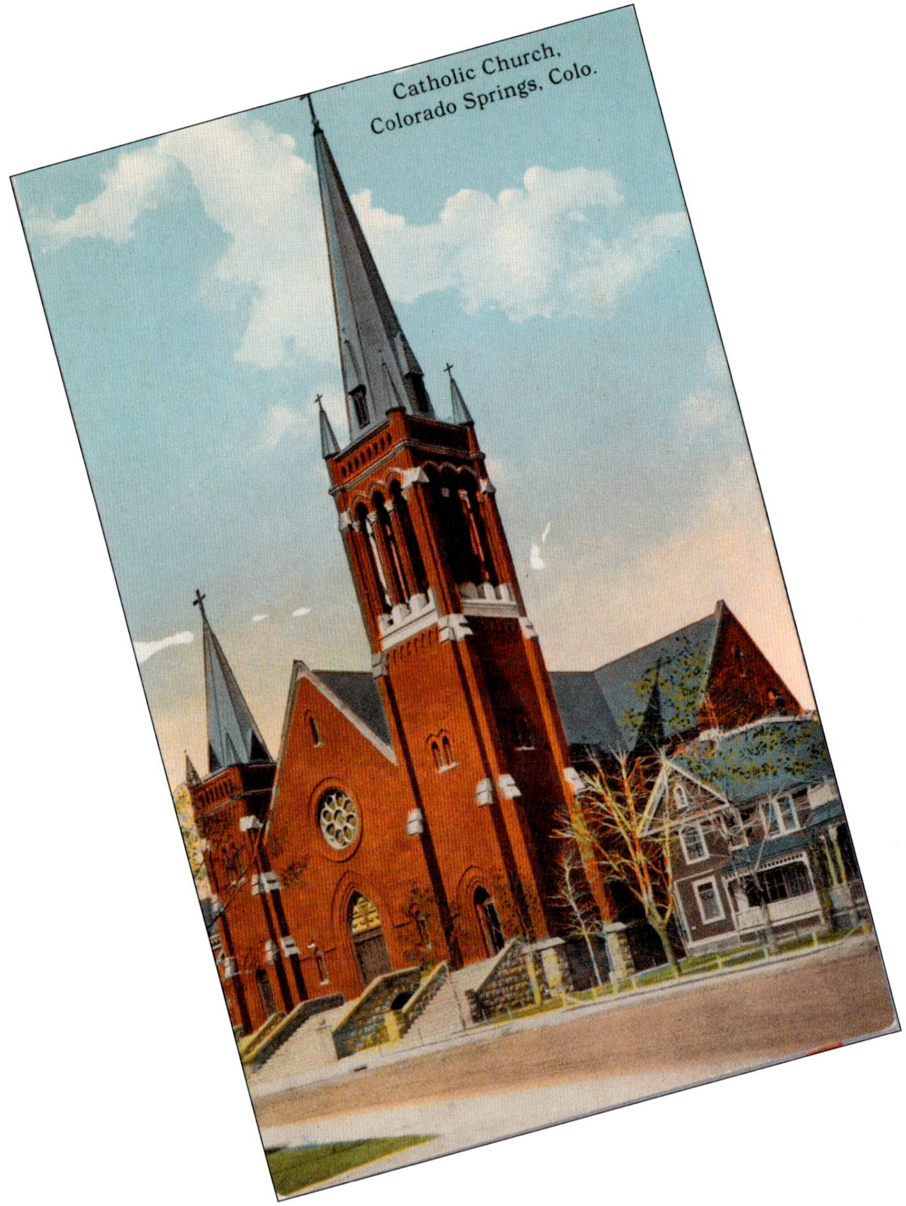

Catholic church in Colorado Springs.

Circa 1910s, $4-6

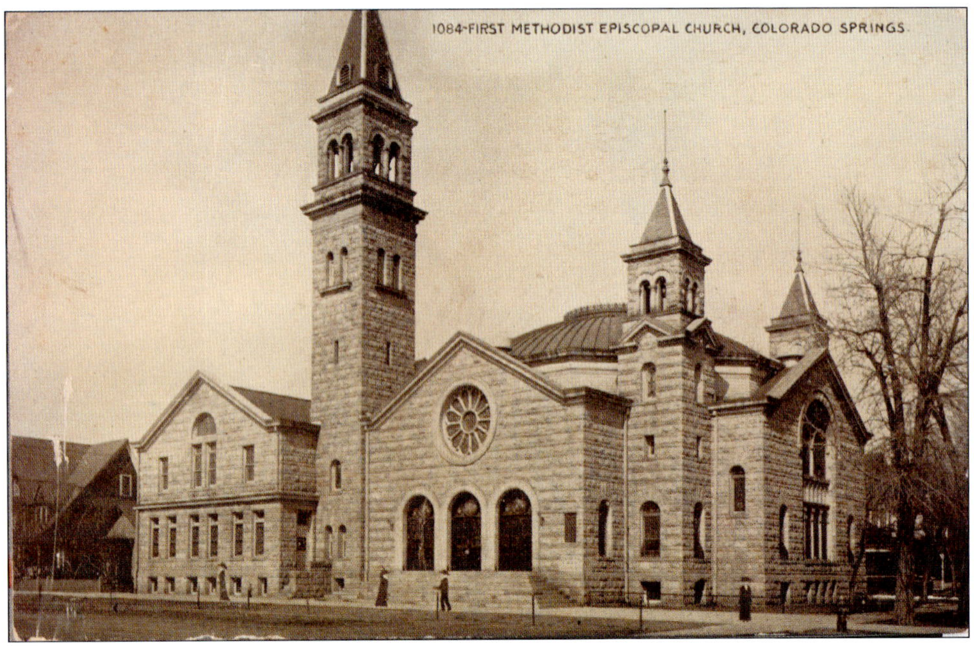

The First Methodist Episcopal Church of Colorado Springs.

Circa 1920s, $4-6

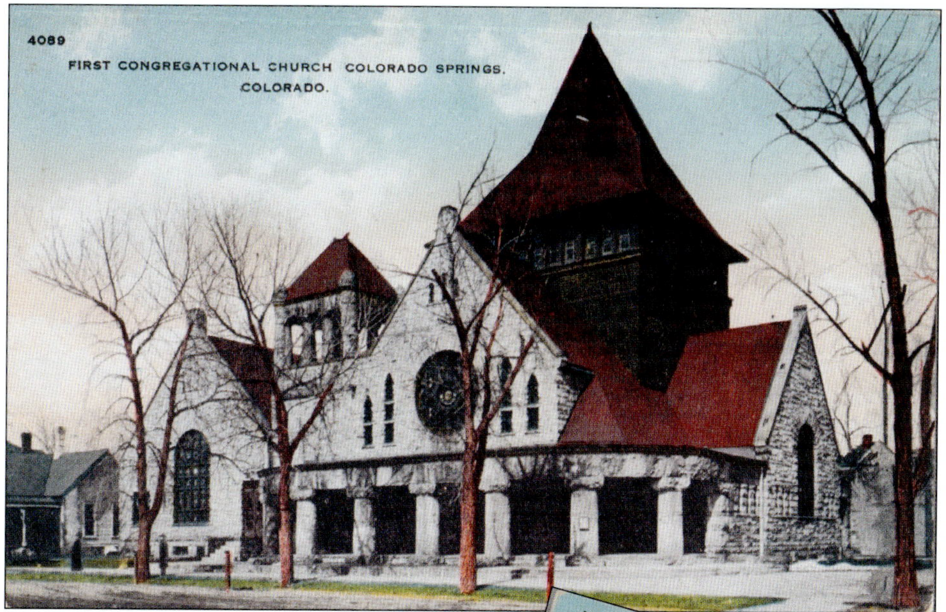

Finished in 1889, the design and building of the First Congregational Church was a collaborative effort between an architect from New York, Henry Rutgers Marshall; a contractor, Joseph Dozier; and Robert Roeschlaub, a local doctor.

Circa 1920s, $4-6

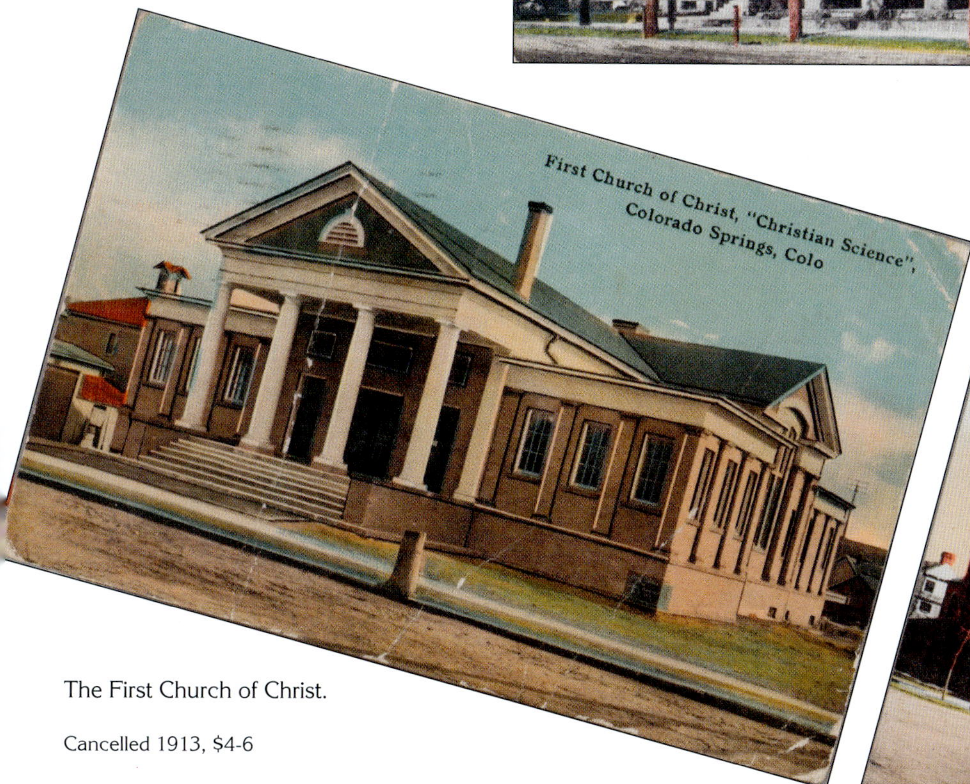

The First Church of Christ.

Cancelled 1913, $4-6

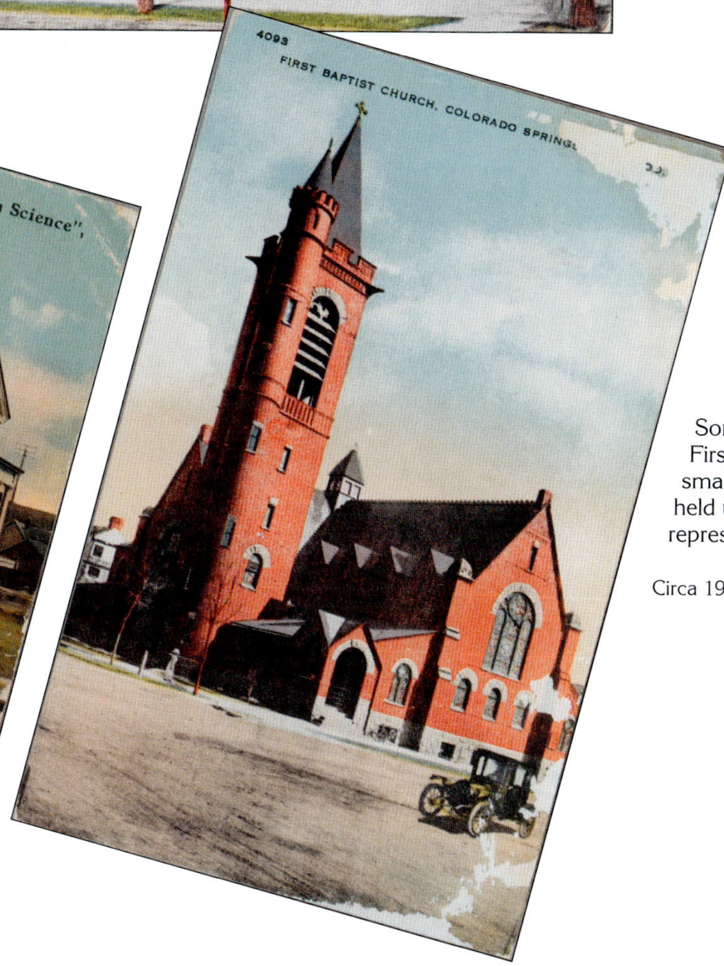

Some who see the towers of the First Baptist Church believe that smaller tower represents man, being held up by the larger tower, which represents God.

Circa 1920s, $4-6

The first Grace Episcopal Church building was built on the corner of Webber Street and Pikes Peak Avenue in 1874. The present building was completed in 1926 and is located on North Tejon Street.

Circa 1920s, $4-6

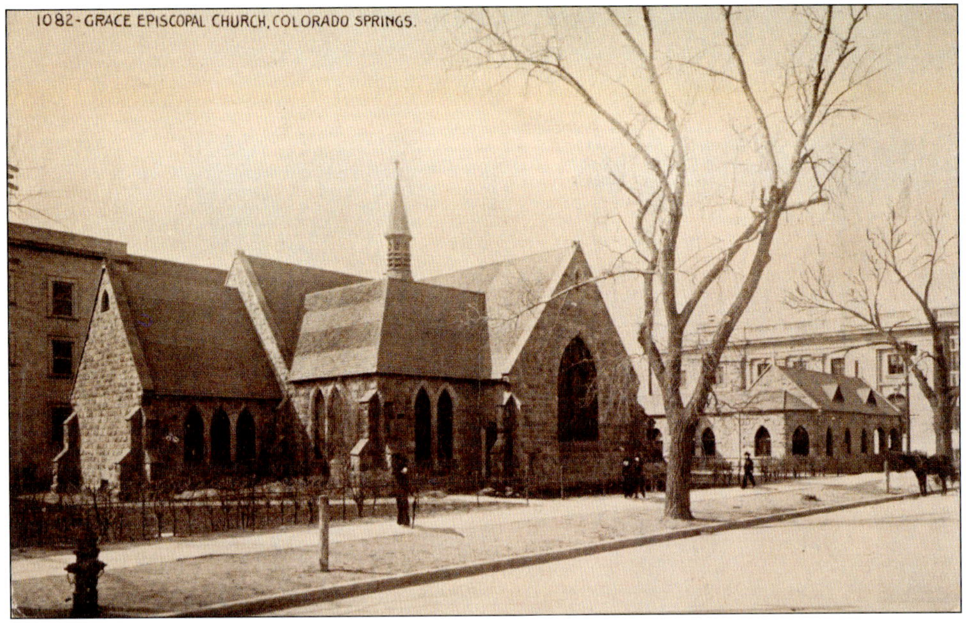

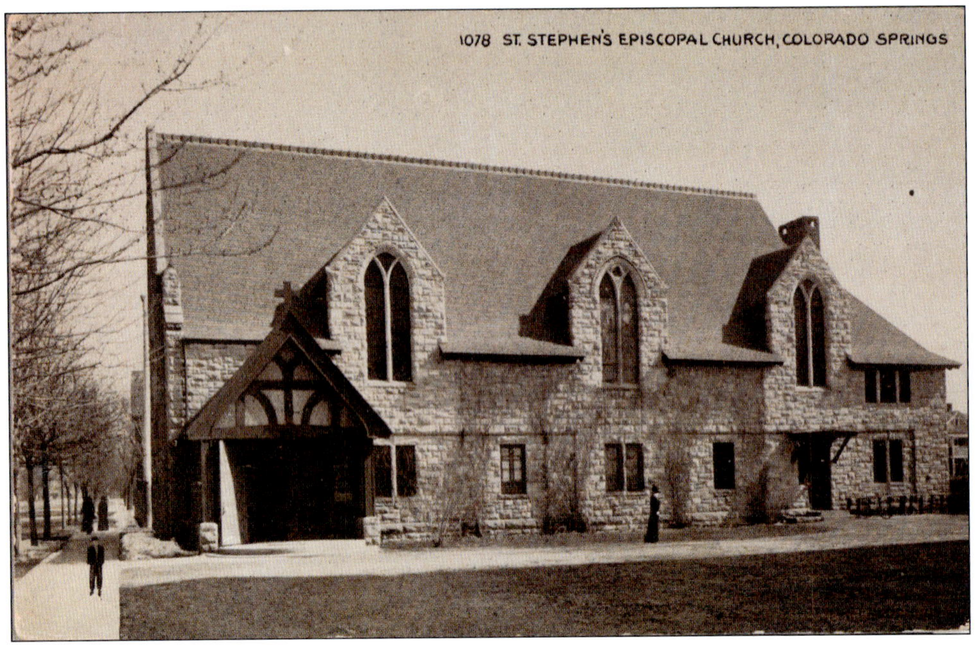

In 1893 a group split off from Grace Episcopal Church, forming St. Stephen's Episcopal Church, building a house of worship on the corner of Monument Avenue and Tejon Street.

Circa 1920s, $4-6

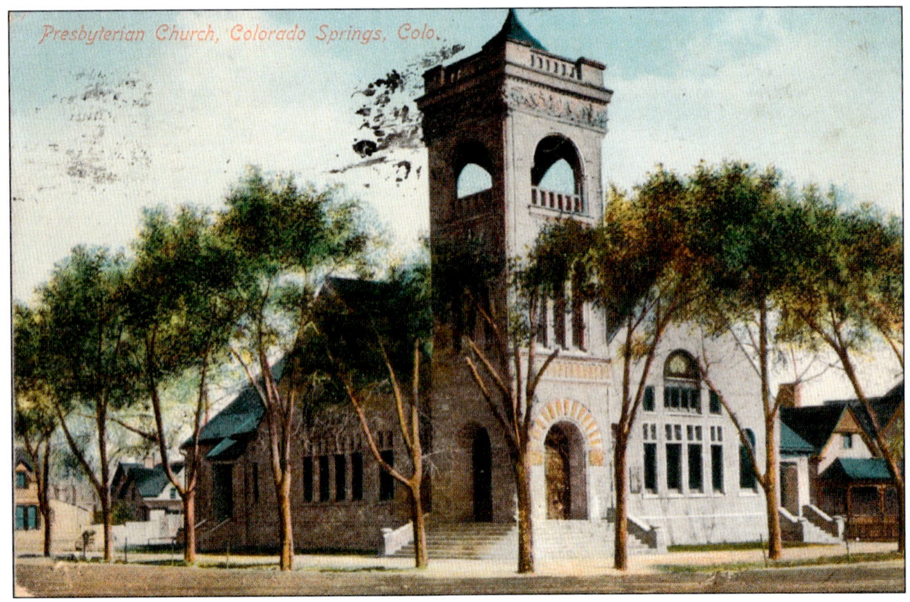

First Presbyterian Church: After Catholics and Methodists, Presbyterians are the third largest Christian denomination in the state of Colorado.

Cancelled 1910, $4-6

Colorado College

Instituted as a liberal arts school, Colorado College was also founded by General Palmer and opened its doors to students on May 6, 1874. The principals of the school were based on the tradition of New England schools, which fostered Christian outreach through their faculty and graduates.

Academically, Colorado College follows a block plan in which a student studies only one subject for three and a half weeks, a system which allows time for more "hands on" learning, i.e. labs, field trips, etc. The college offers over eighty different academic majors and minors as well as a number of specialty programs.

Though it had opened in 1874, Colorado College's first permanent building was not opened until 1880. During the 1950s, the face of the College changed again. The campus was almost completely renovated as new, more modern residence halls and academic buildings were constructed.

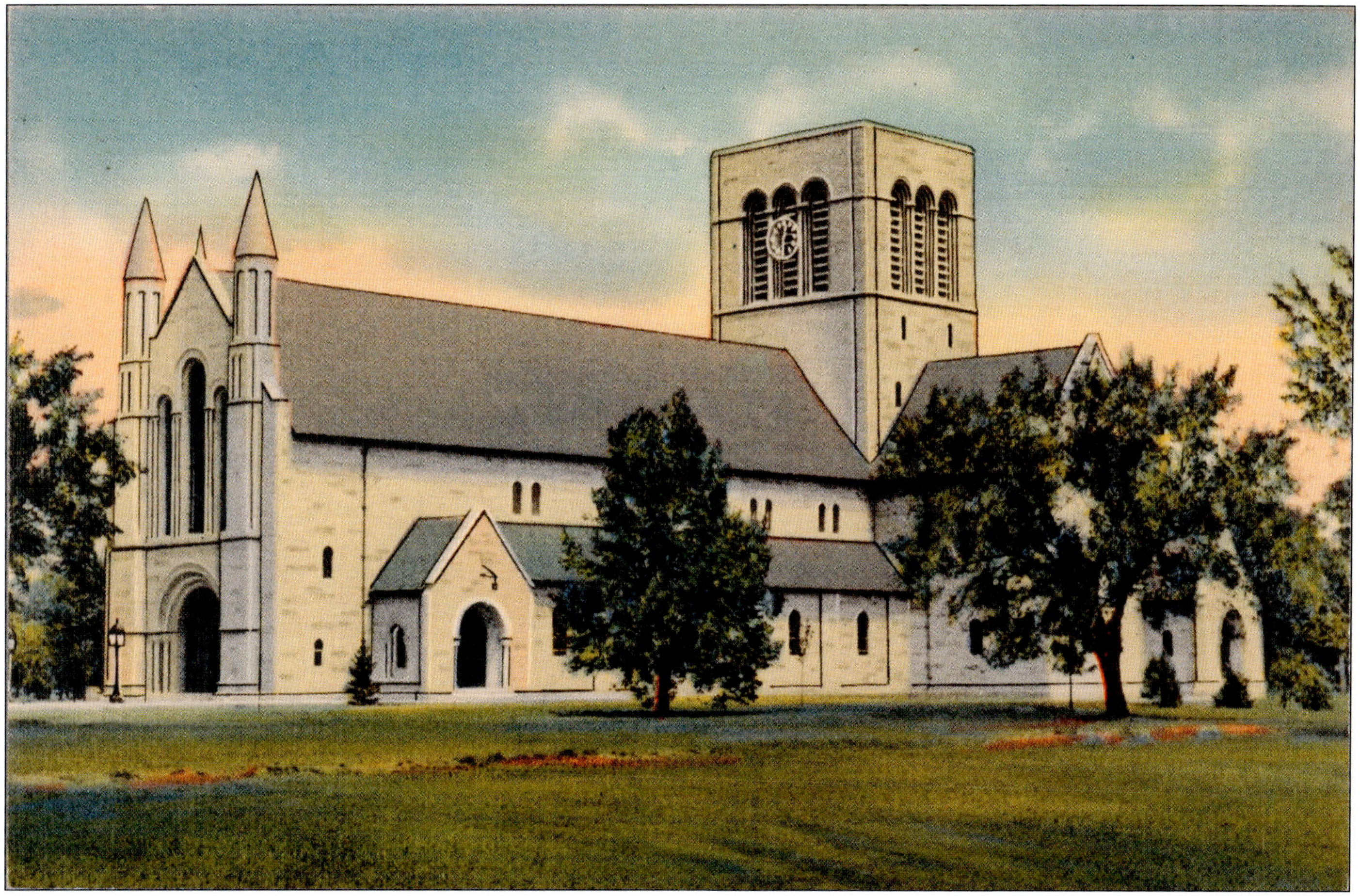

A gift from Eugene Percy Shove in 1930, the design for Shove Chapel was inspired by the Winchester Cathedral in England.

Circa 1940s, $4-6

Colorado College's oldest dormitory, Hagerman Hall, was demolished in 1956.

Cancelled 1911, $4-6

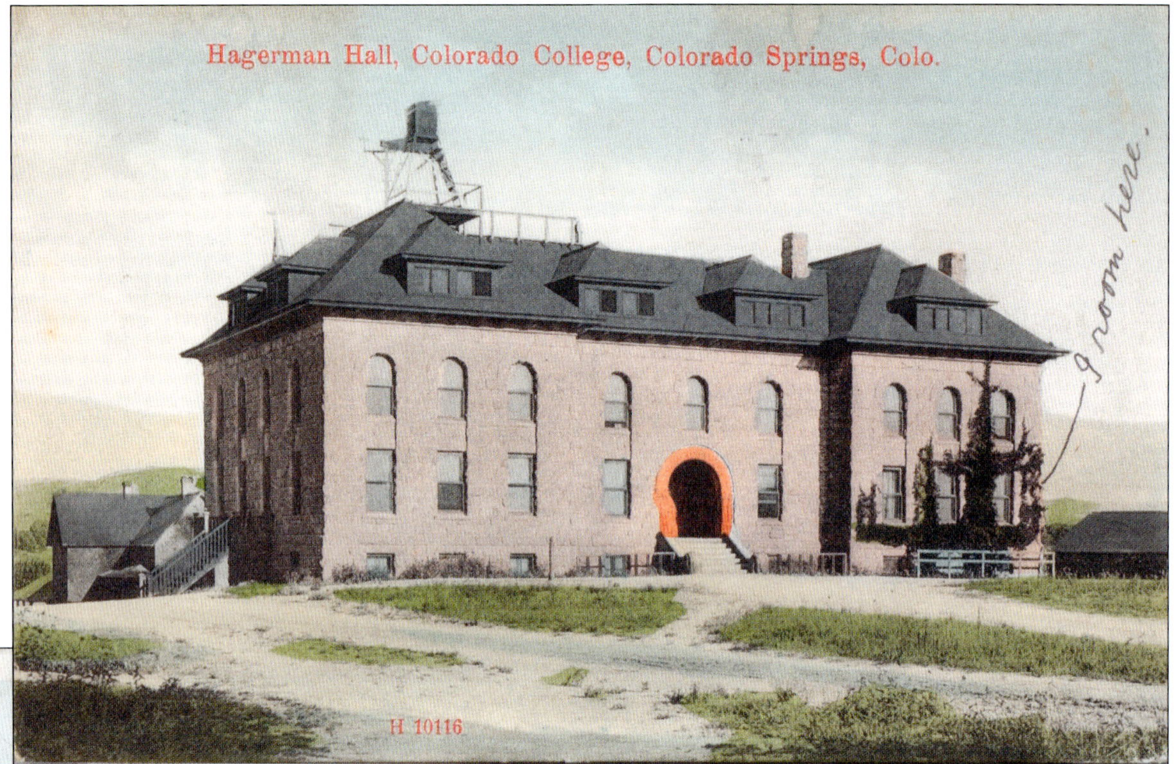

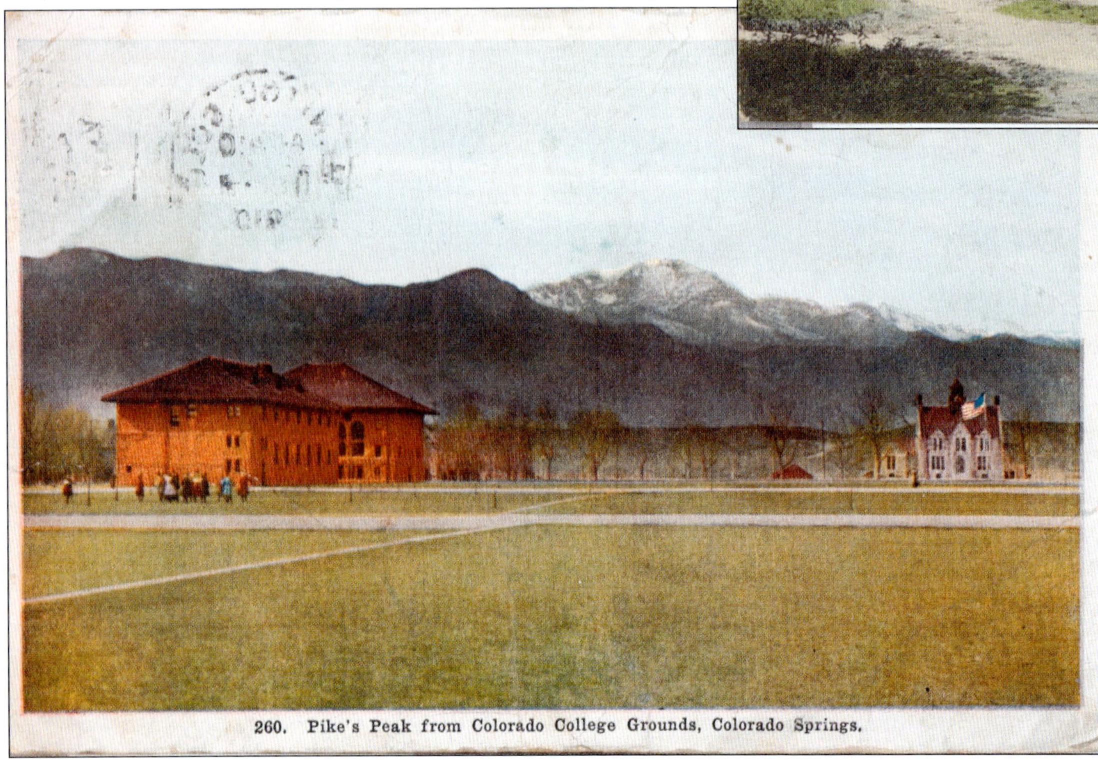

Colorado College was founded in 1874 by General William Jackson Palmer as a liberal arts college that would also promote Christian evangelism and outreach through its students and its faculty.

Cancelled 1910, $4-6

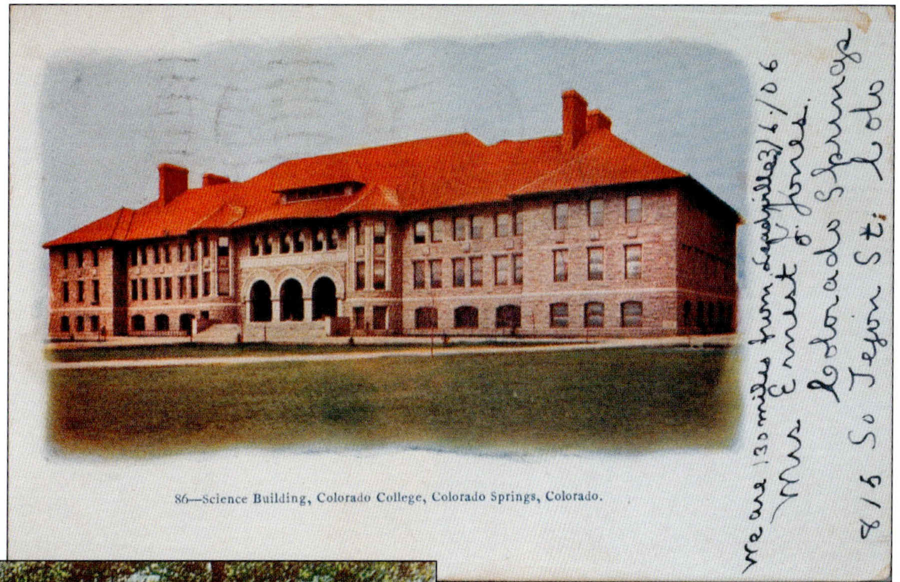

Named after the College's founder, William Jackson Palmer, Palmer Hall was built in 1904.

Cancelled 1906, $4-6

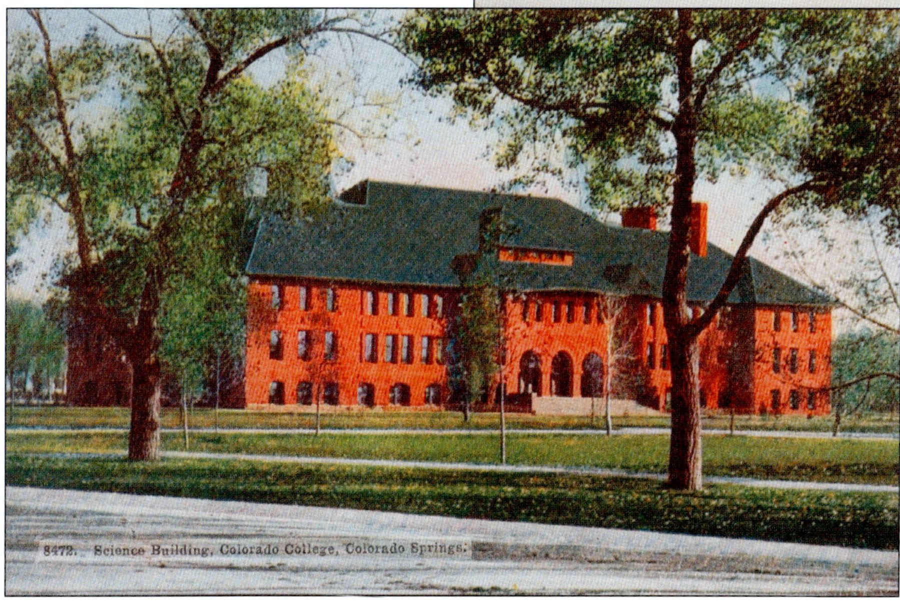

Originally Palmer Hall was the College's science and administrative building. Today it houses the Political Science, History, Sociology, Economics, Psychology, Mathematics, and Geology Departments.

Circa 1910s, $4-6

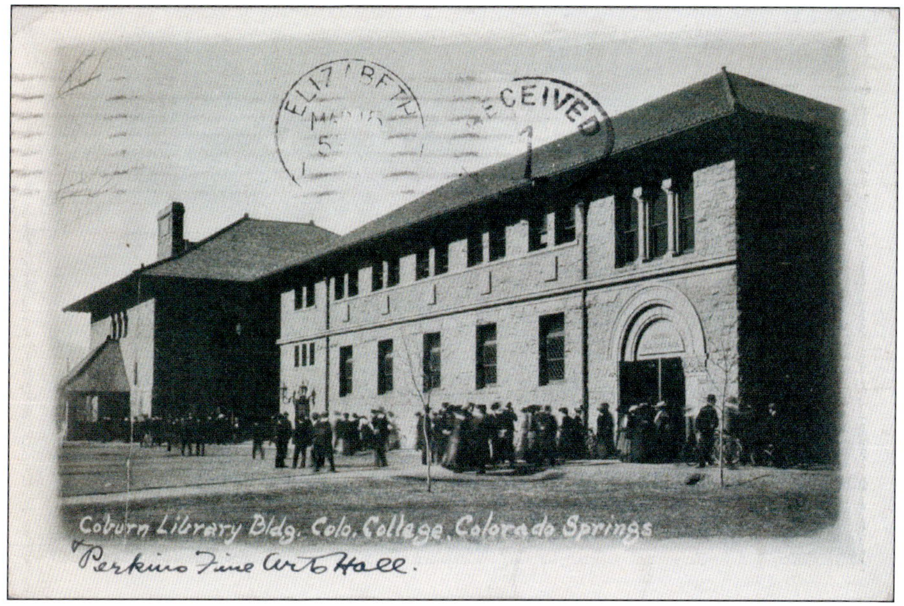

Students congregate outside of the Coburn Library Building.

Cancelled 1907, $4-6

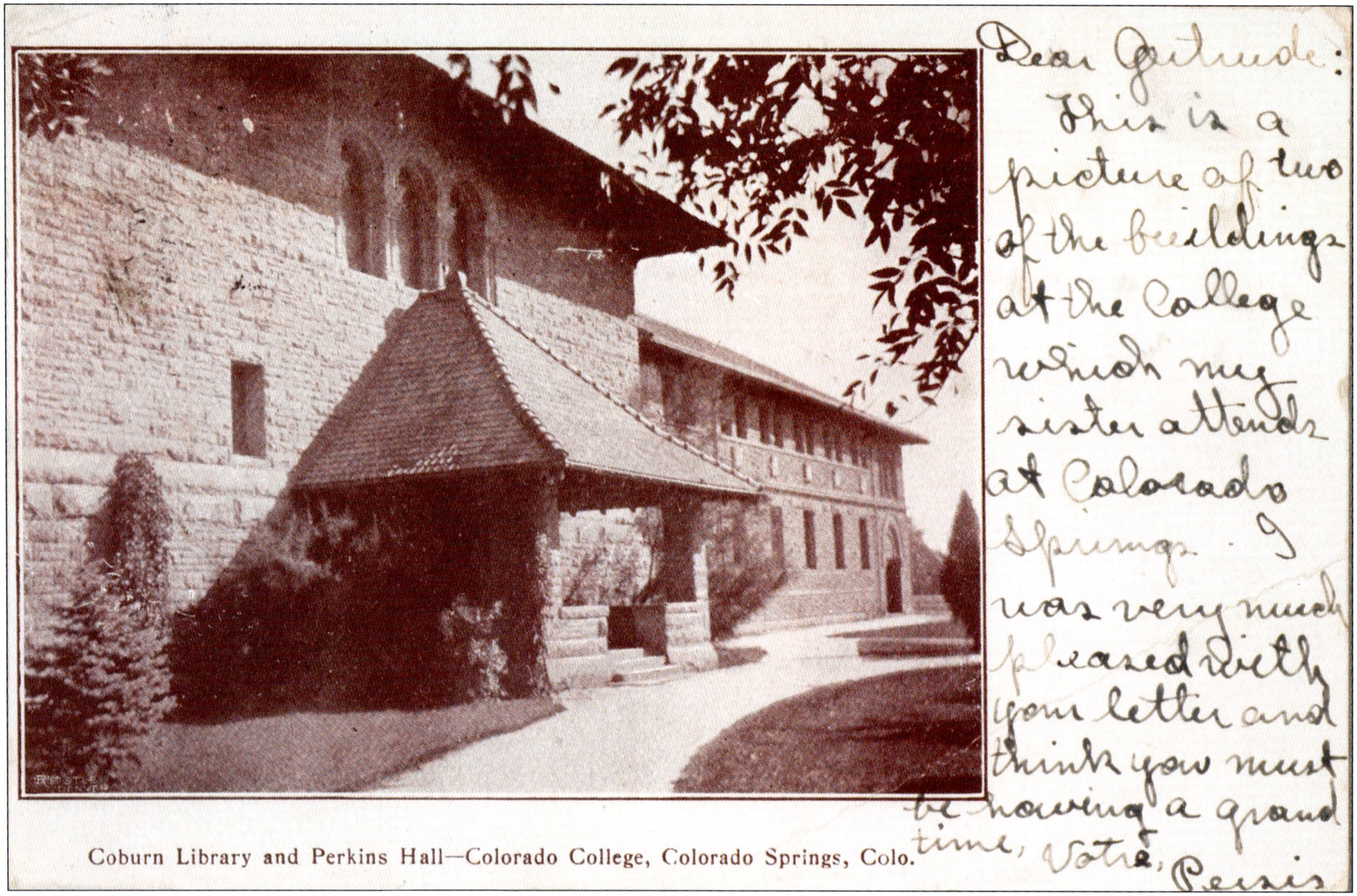

Coburn Library and Perkins Hall. The Coburn Library was replaced in 1962 by the Tutt Library.

Cancelled 1905, $4-6

Hotels

As a resort community, Colorado Springs was known for the quality of its hotels. Catering to well-to-do travelers from both the United States and Europe, these hotels were known for the beauty of their design, the comfort of their rooms and facilities, the quality of their food, and the skill and politeness of their staff.

One of Colorado Spring's first, the Antlers Hotel opened on June 1, 1883. It was built by General Palmer, who intended the Antlers to be his flagship hotel. It was in this hotel that Katherine Lee Bates wrote the words to the poem that would become the patriotic song, "America the Beautiful."

Another influential Colorado Springs hotel, the Broadmoor Hotel was built sometime later in 1918, the enterprise of gold rush millionaire Spencer Penrose. Modeled after some of the finest hotels of Europe, the Broadmoor, like the Antlers Hotel, attracted wealthy clientele drawn to Colorado Springs for the beauty of the natural scenery or to recover from illness. Unlike the Antlers, the Broadmoor was a resort hotel located just outside the city, with plenty of room for additional facilities like golf courses, tennis courts, and a stadium, as well as extensive grounds.

For those unable to stay at the Antlers or the Broadmoor, places like the Alamo, the Plaza, and the Alta Vista were also highly recommended by both residents and frequent visitors.

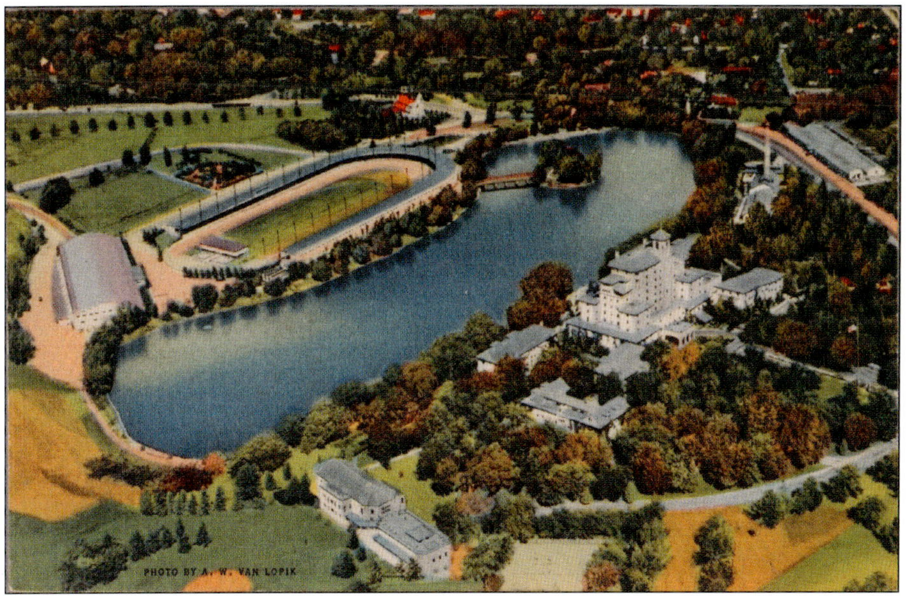

A panoramic view of the Broadmoor Hotel and the surrounding grounds.

Circa 1940s, $4-6

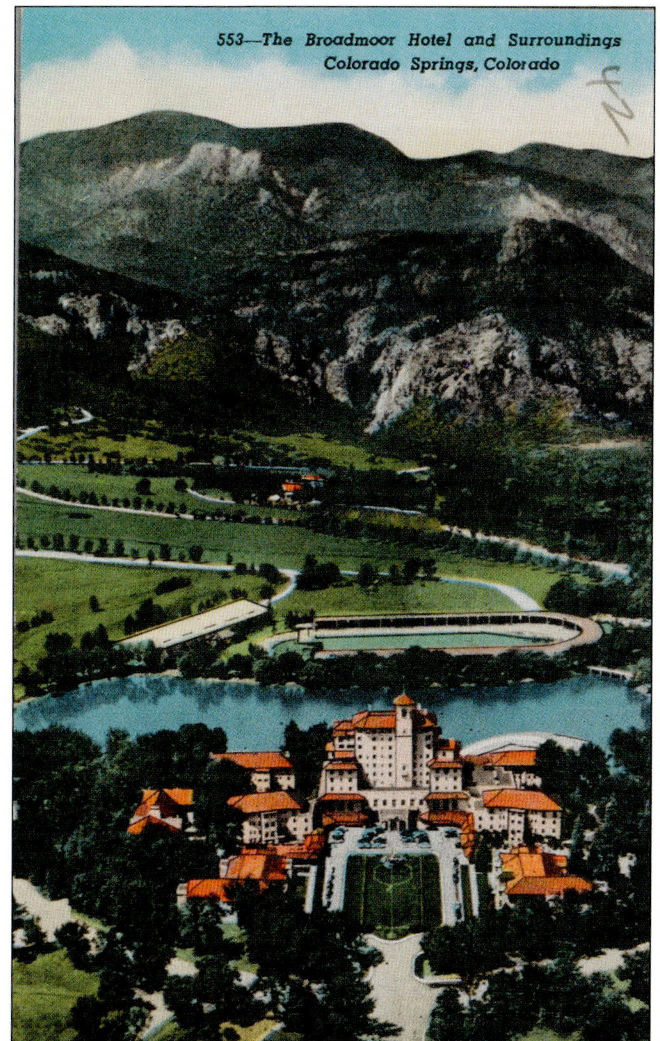

The Broadmoor Hotel dates back to 1891 when it was just a small hotel and casino. The resort as it is known today was built by Spencer Penrose in 1918.

Circa 1940s, $4-6

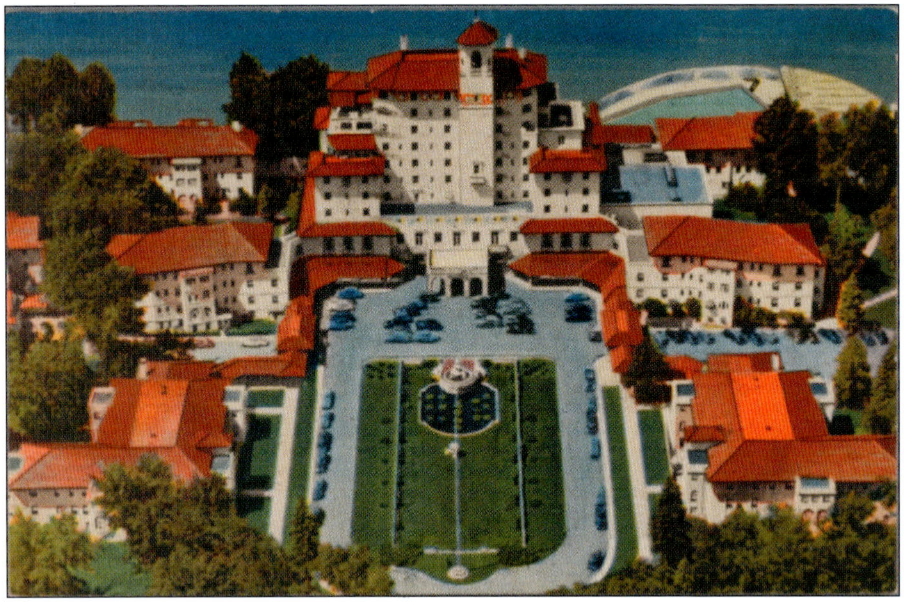

Known as "Grande Dame of the Rockies," the Broadmoor Hotel was, and still is, considered one of the finest hotel/resorts in Rocky Mountains.

Circa 1940s, $4-6

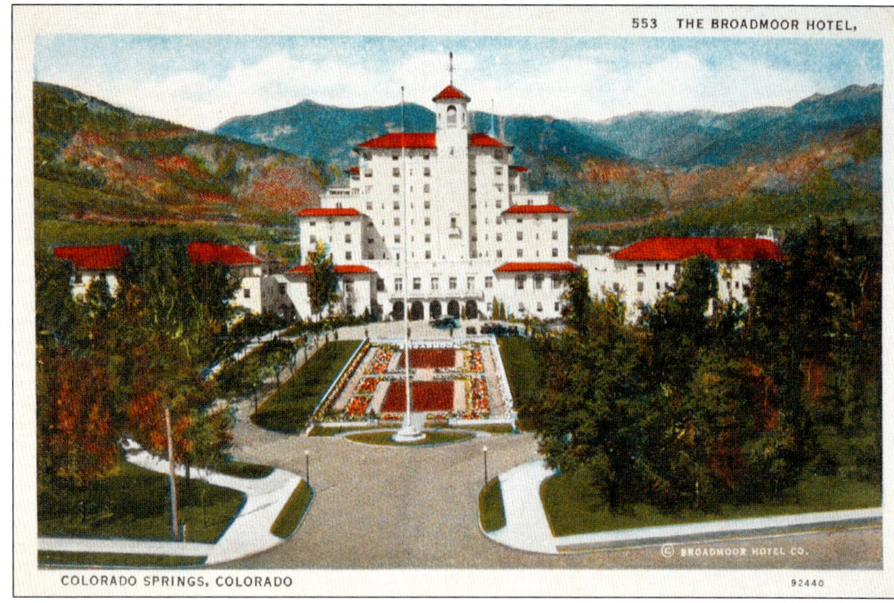

Spencer Penrose bought the land for the Broadmoor Hotel from the estate of W. S. Stratton in 1916.

Circa 1930s, $4-6

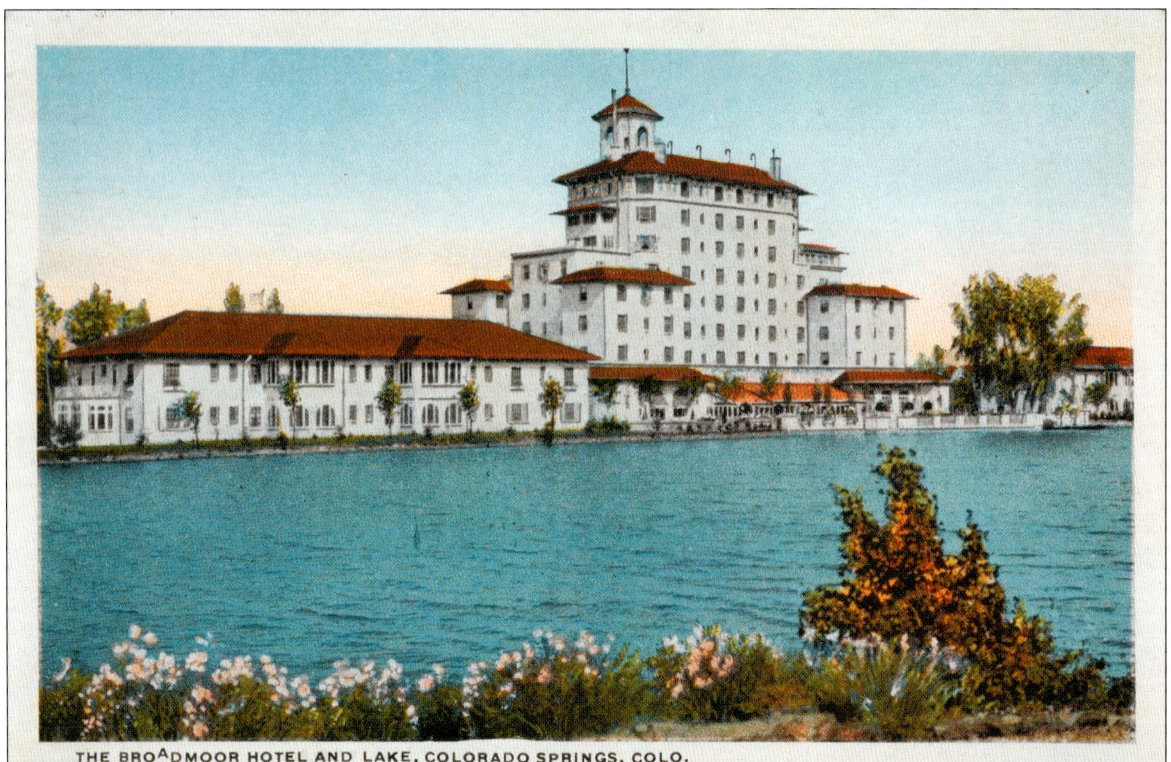

Determined to build the most beautiful resort in the world, Spencer Penrose imported artists and craftsmen from around the world to create elaborate architectural and decorative details inspired by the finest hotels of Europe and the Orient.

Circa 1920s, $4-6

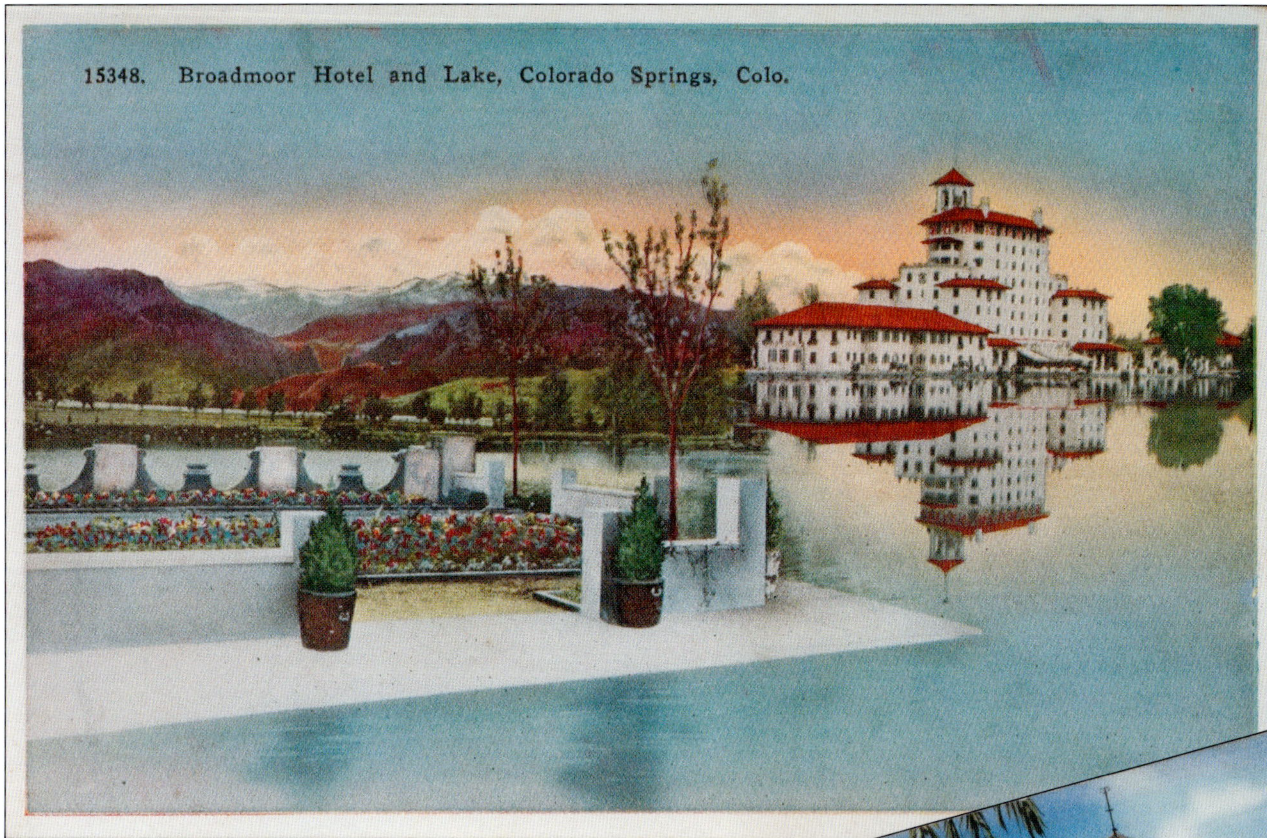

The Broadmoor Hotel opened to the public on June 29, 1918, and has remained open to this day.

Circa 1930s, $4-6

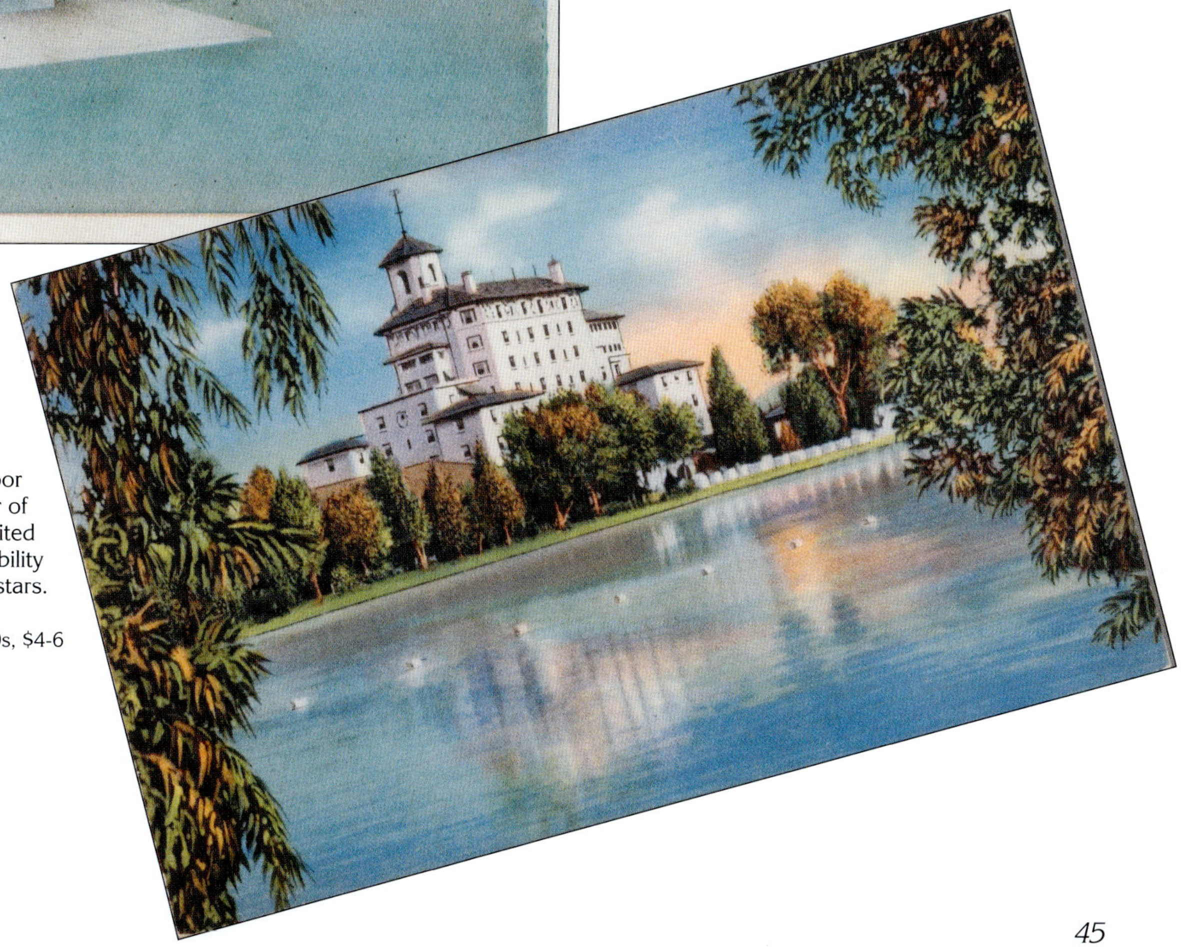

Since its opening, the Broadmoor Hotel has played host to a number of notable guests ranging from United States presidents and foreign nobility to sports and movie stars.

Circa 1940s, $4-6

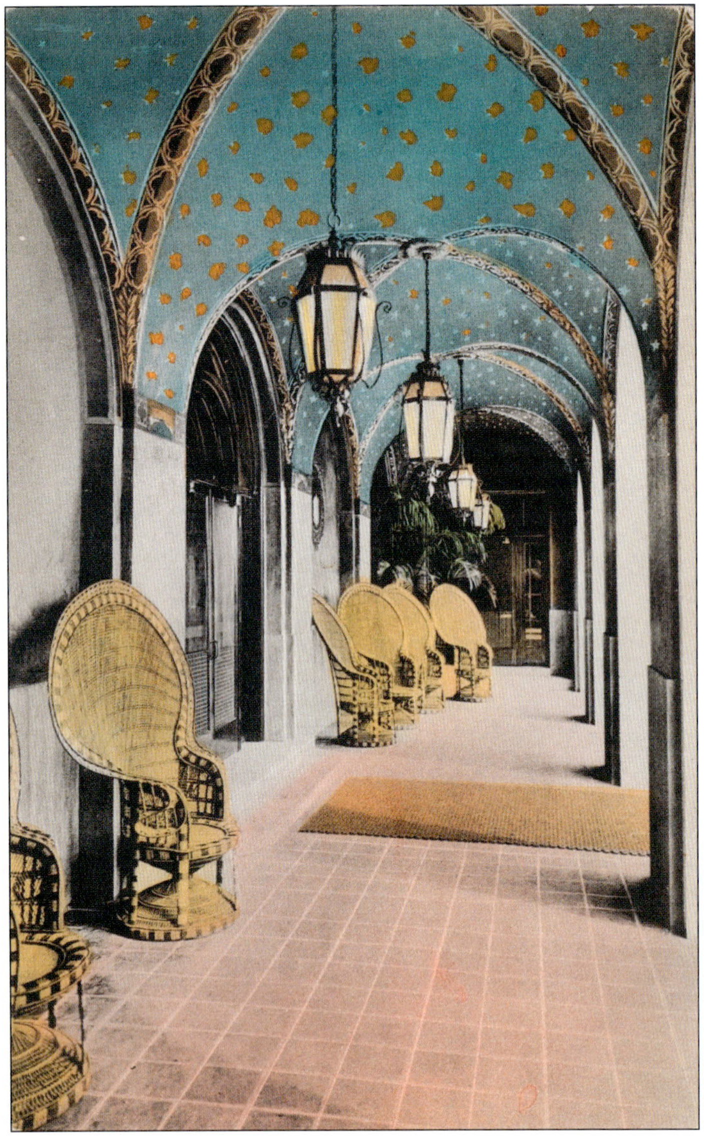

An outside corridor at the Broadmoor Hotel.

Circa 1930s, $4-6

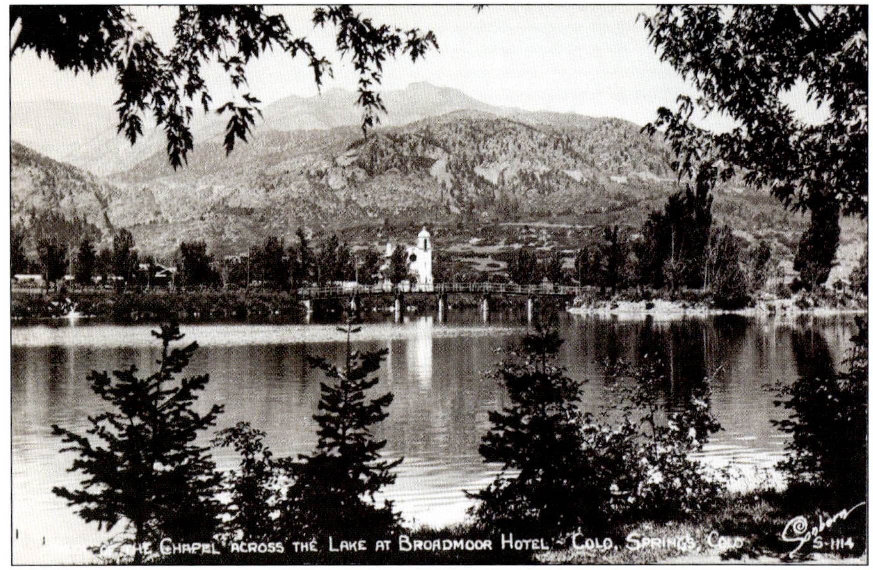

View of the Chapel from across Cheyenne Lake.

Circa 1930s, $4-6

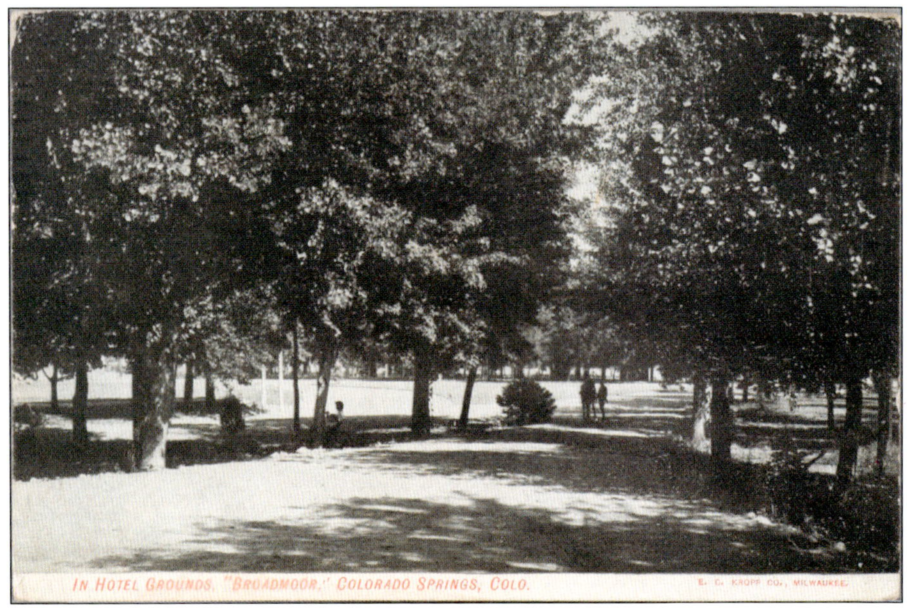

At present, the grounds of the Broadmoor consist of 3,000 acres in southwestern Colorado Springs.

Cancelled 1907, $4-6

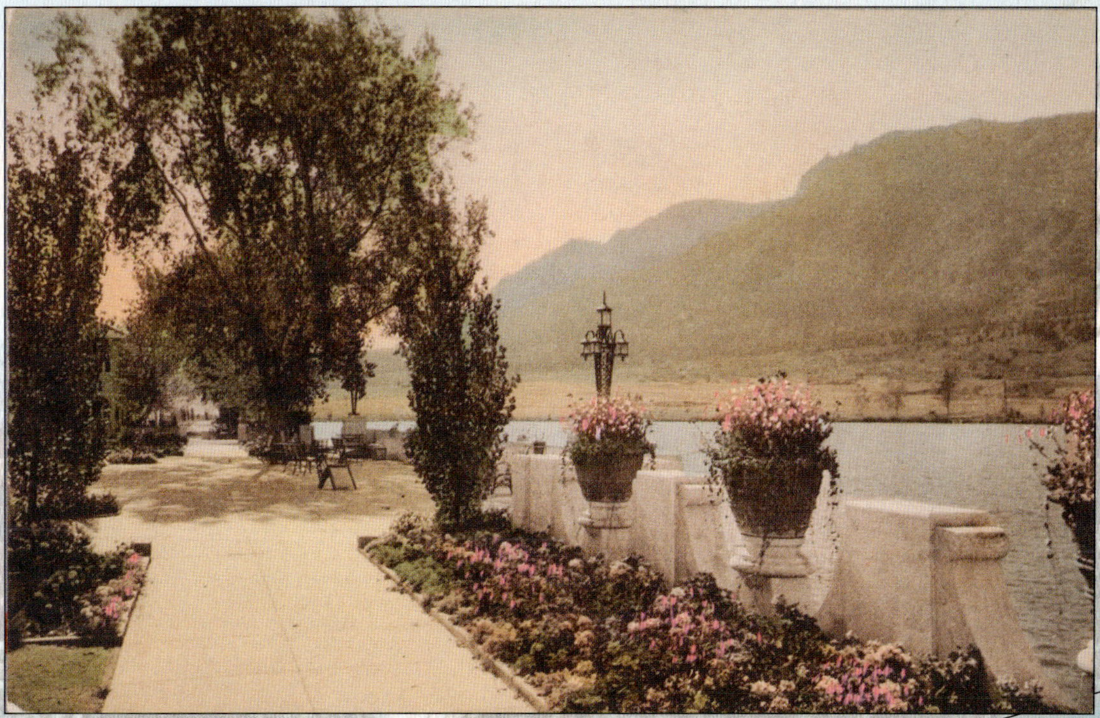

The gardens along the shore of Cheyenne Lake.

Circa 1930s, $4-6

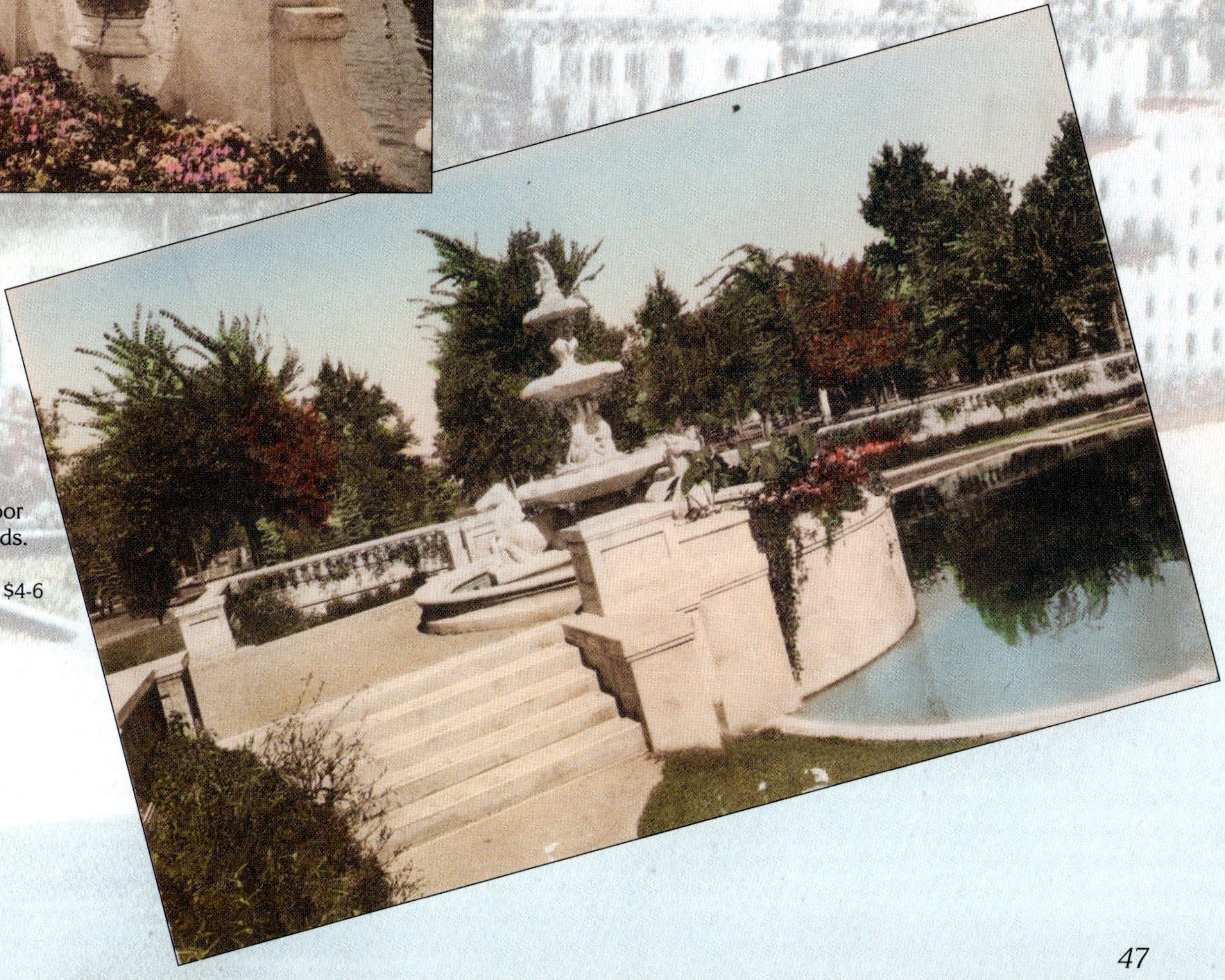

Another view of the Broadmoor Hotel grounds.

Circa 1930s, $4-6

Before the Broadmoor Hotel was built, the land was home to the Broadmoor Casino, operated by James Pourtales, a Prussian nobleman who had come to Colorado Springs in 1884. A small hotel was also constructed on that spot a few years later.

Cancelled 1911, $4-6

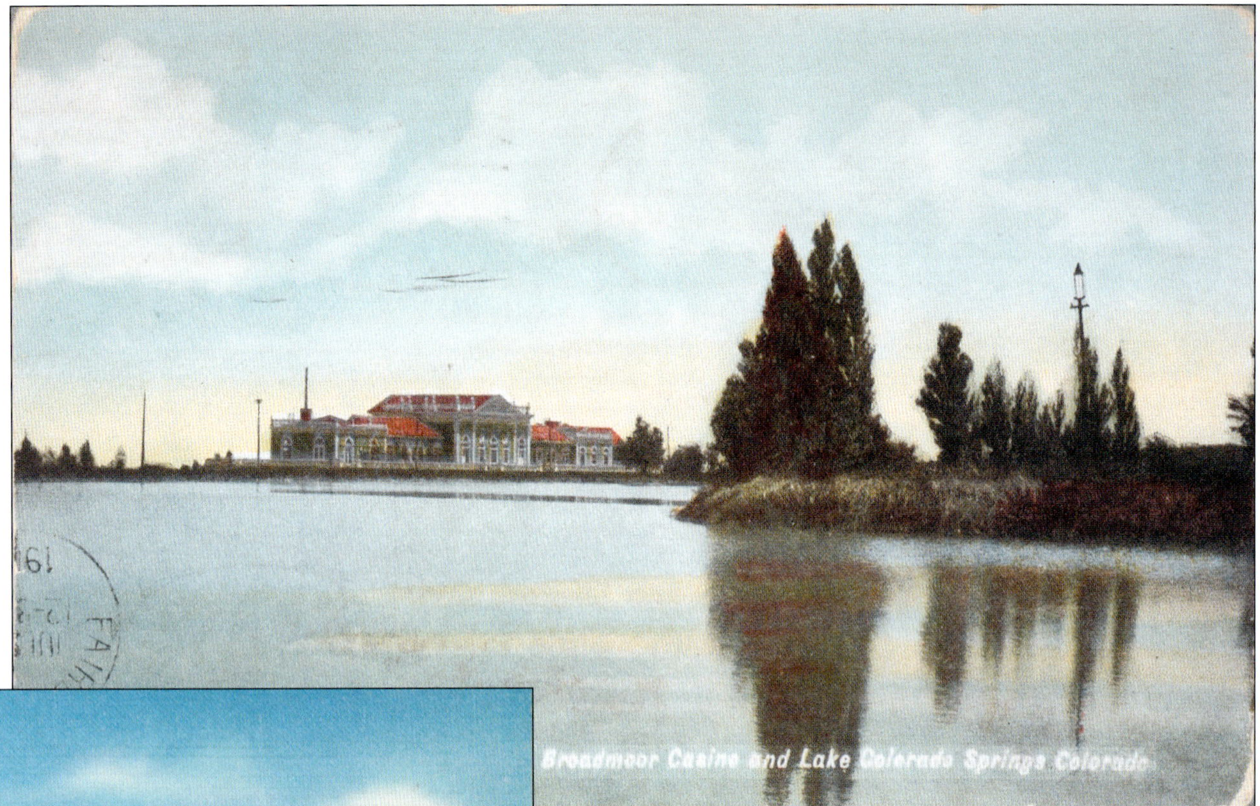

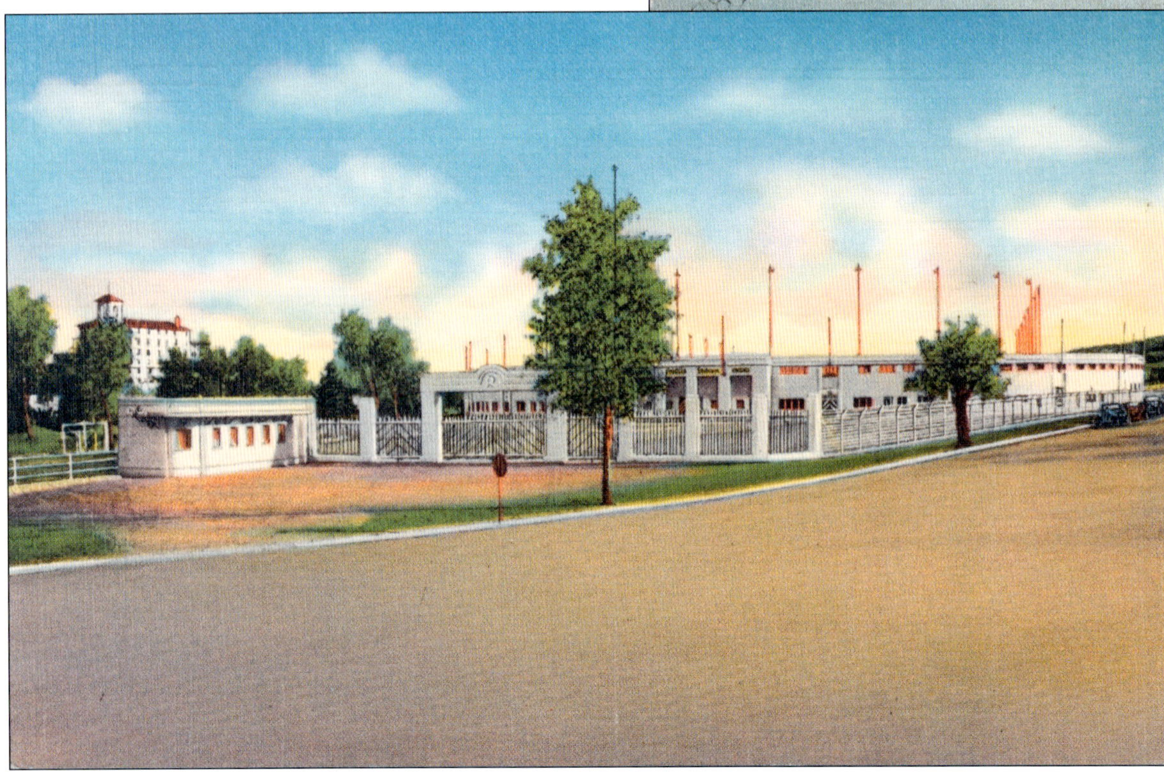

The Will Rogers Stadium was named after the famous American humorist and entertainer, who was also a friend of Spence Penrose.

Circa 1940s, $4-6

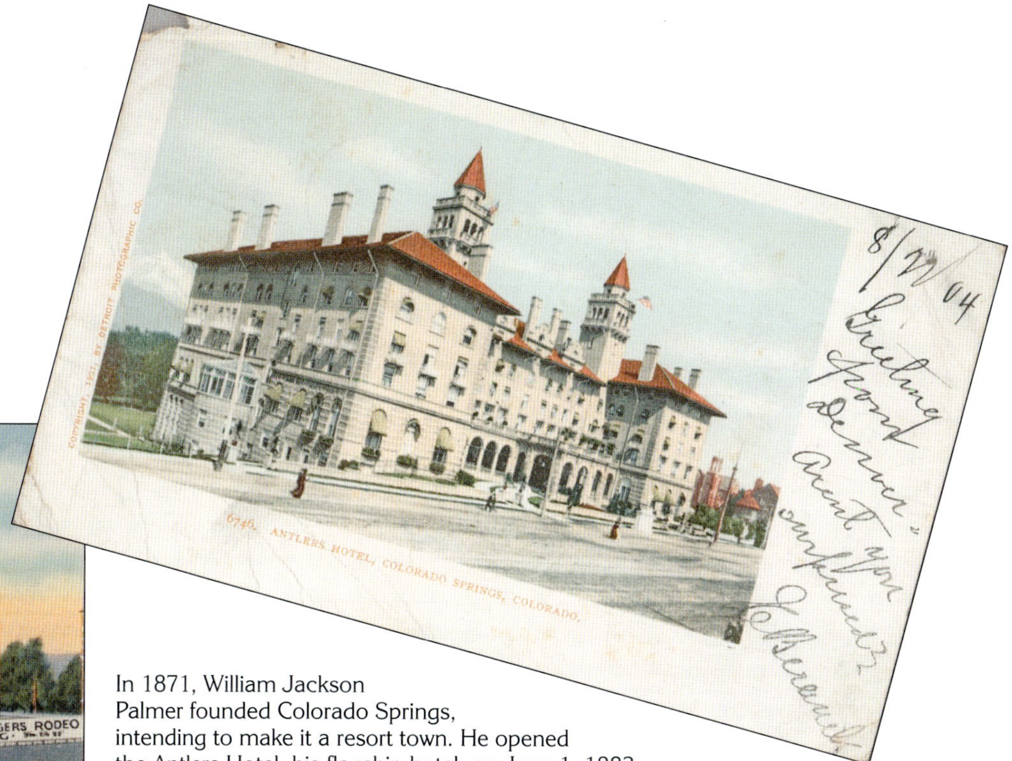

In 1871, William Jackson Palmer founded Colorado Springs, intending to make it a resort town. He opened the Antlers Hotel, his flagship hotel, on June 1, 1883.

Cancelled 1904, $4-6

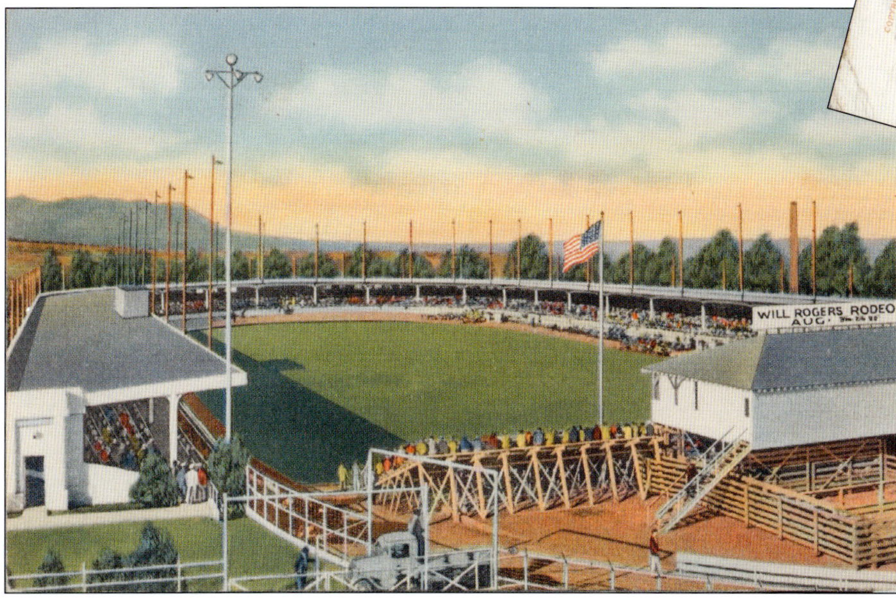

The Will Rogers Stadium was host to a number of special sporting events, including the Will Rogers Rodeo held in late August.

Circa 1940s, $4-6

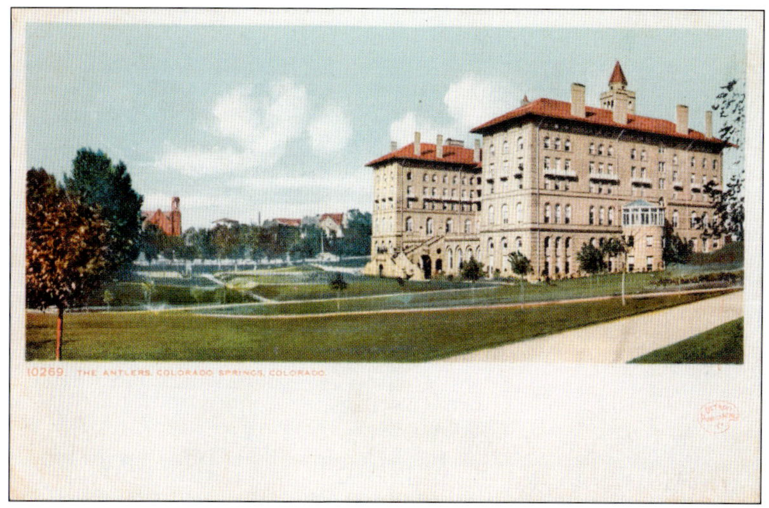

The Antlers Hotel was named for General Palmer's large collection of elk and deer trophies, which he kept in the hotel.

Circa 1900s, $4-6

While staying at the Antlers in the summer of 1893, Katherine Bates, a visiting English professor from Massachusetts, wrote the words to the poem that would become "America the Beautiful."

Circa 1910s, $5-7

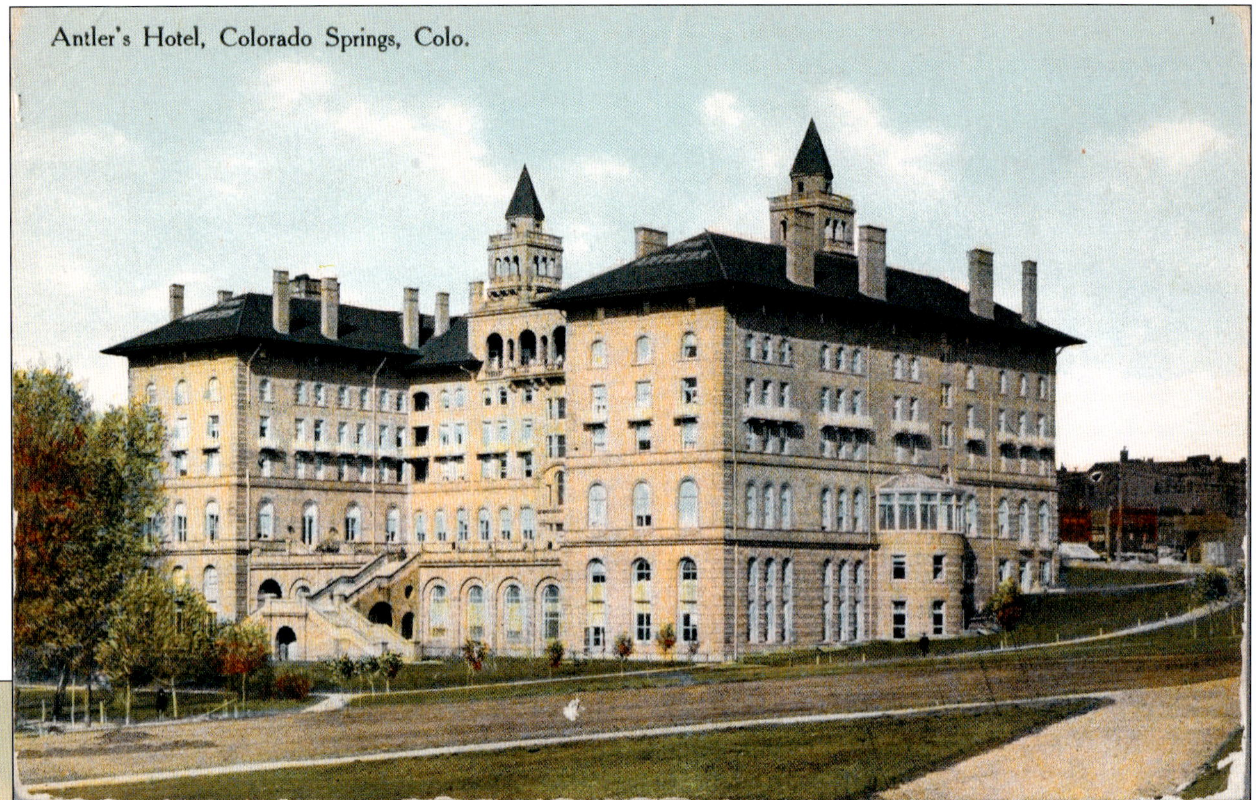

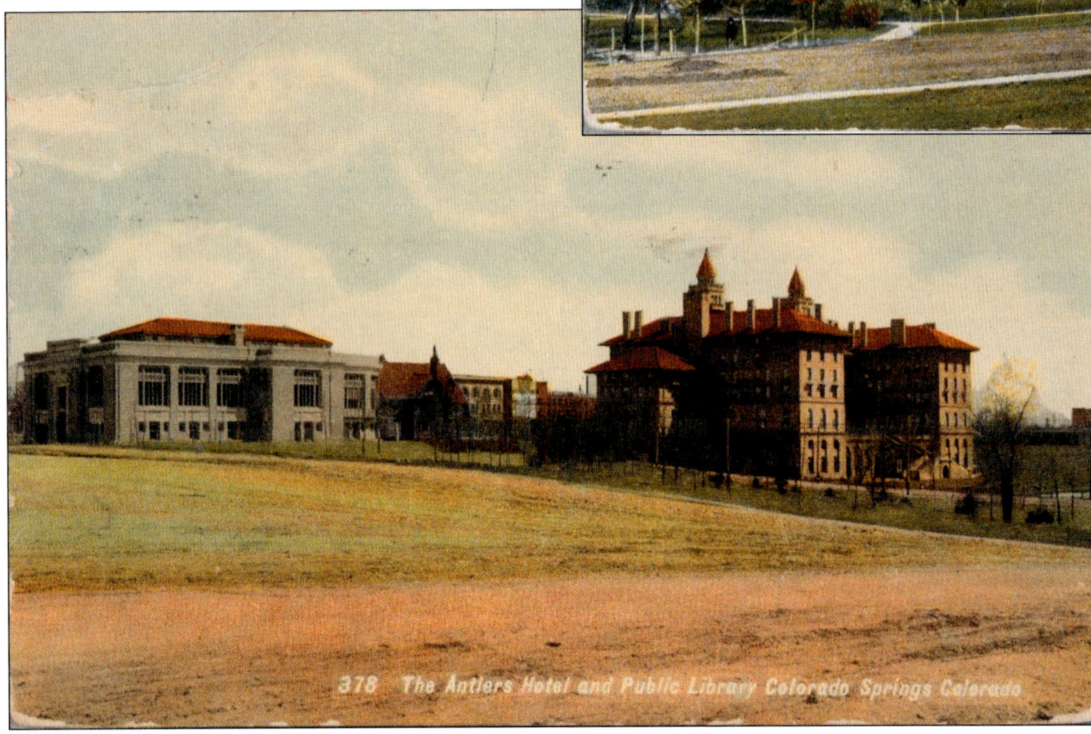

The hotel itself featured seventy-five guestrooms and two bathrooms on each floor, a unique and attractive feature at the time.

Cancelled 1912, $4-6

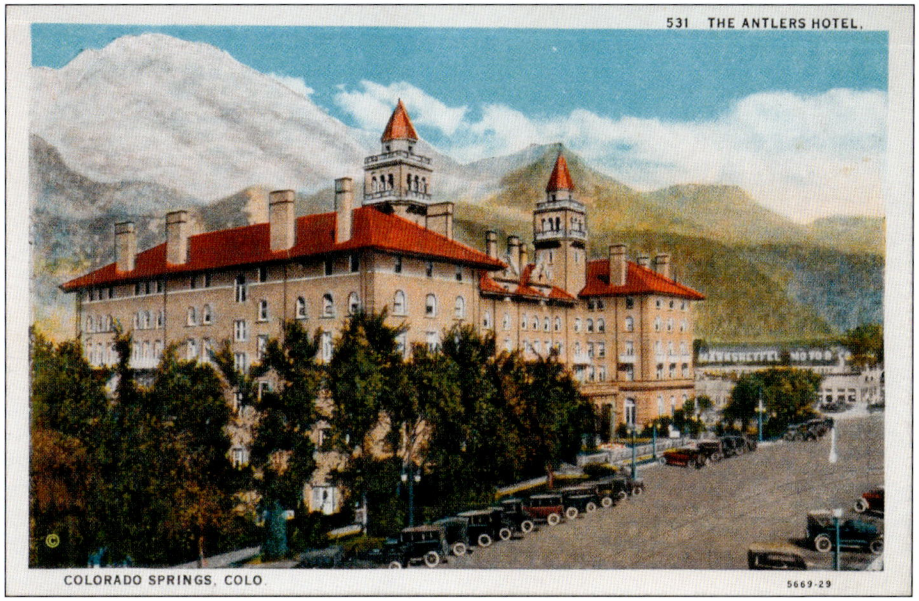

From the back: "The view of Pikes Peak from the Antlers Hotel is absolutely unobstructed at any point, and is pronounced to be one of the finest views of a great mountain to be seen from any hotel in the world."

Circa 1920s, $4-6

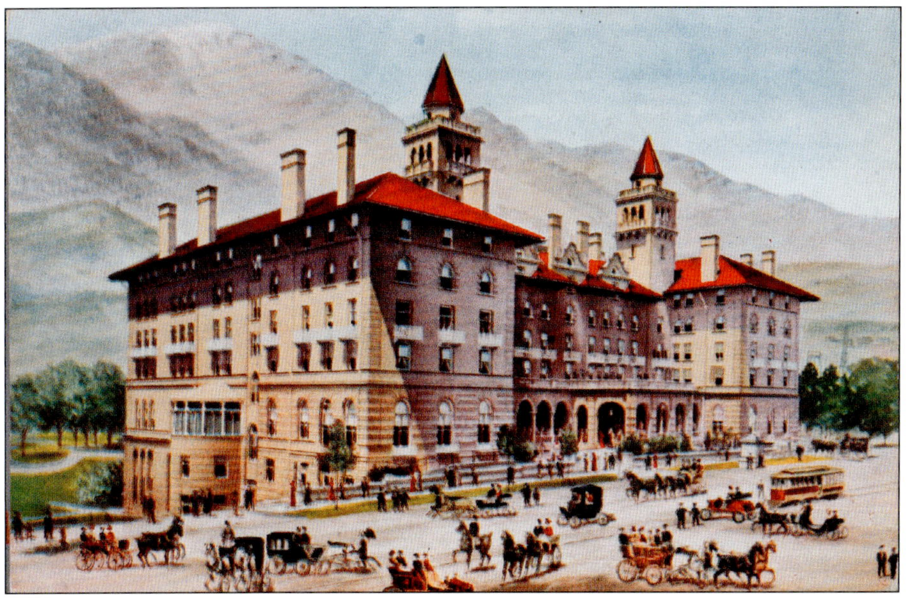

Since it opened in 1883, the Antlers Hotel has been rebuilt twice. The first time it was rebuilt was in 1901, after the building was destroyed in a fire in 1898. In 1964, the years of wear and tear on the building had taken its toll and Antlers was demolished again, rebuilt, and reopened in 1967. The Antlers Hotel is currently owned by the Hilton Hotel Chain.

Circa 1910s, $4-6

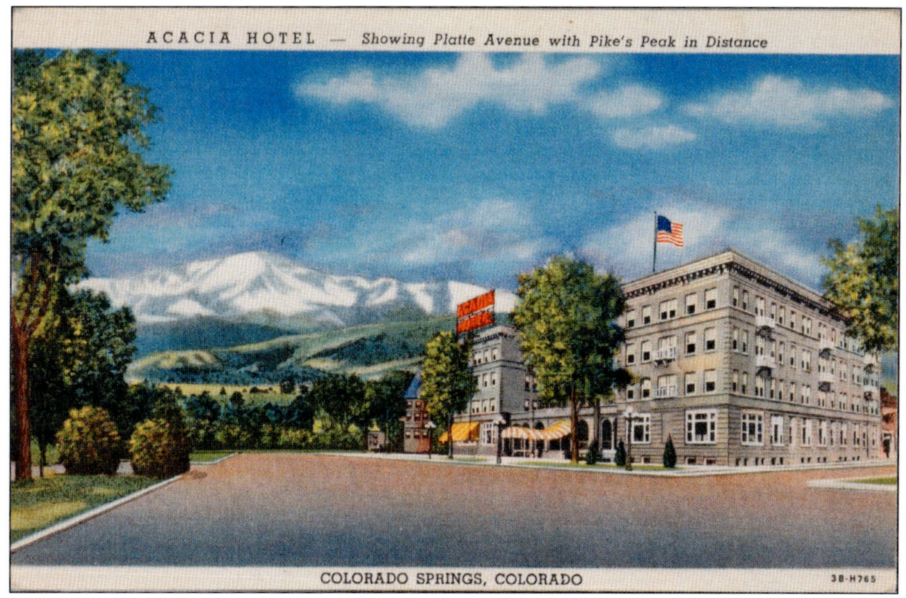

The Acacia Hotel on Platte Avenue. Pikes Peak is visible in the distance.

Circa 1940s, $4-6

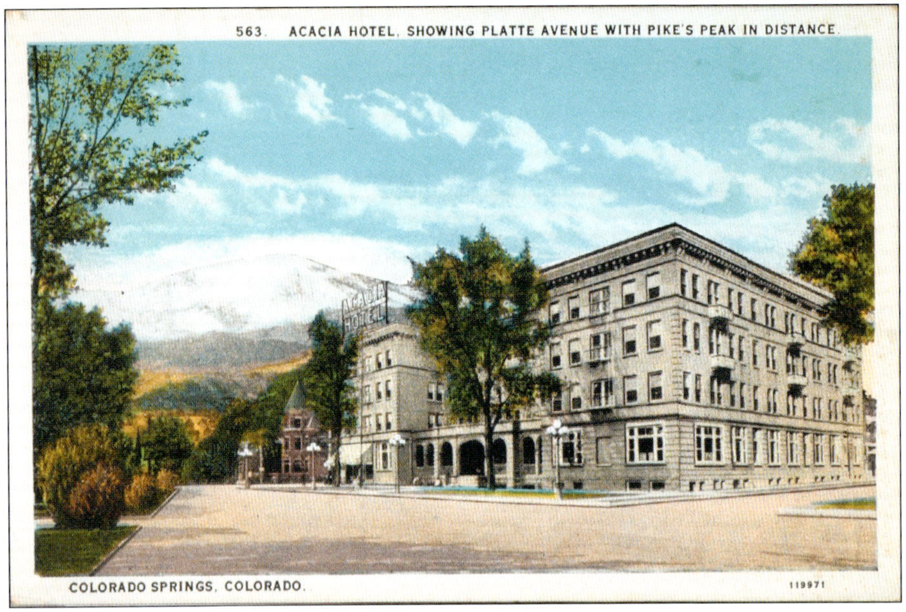

From the back: "The Acacia Hotel is one of the best of the many fine hotels in Colorado Springs. Situated just north of the business district, opposite Acacia Park, it fronts on beautiful Pikes Peak Avenue from the end of which Pike's Peak seems to rise majestically."

Circa 1920s, $4-6

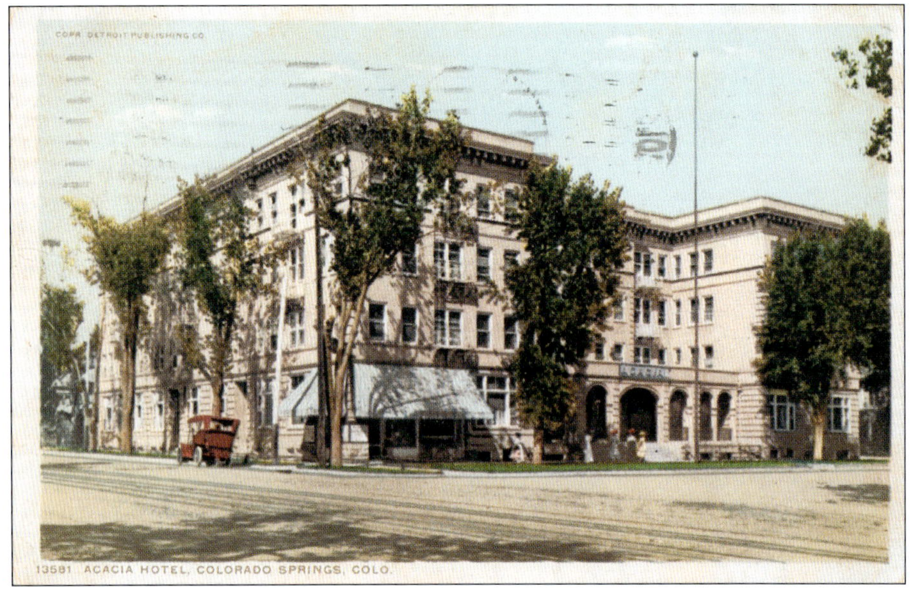

Another view of the Acacia Hotel.

Cancelled 1915, $4-6

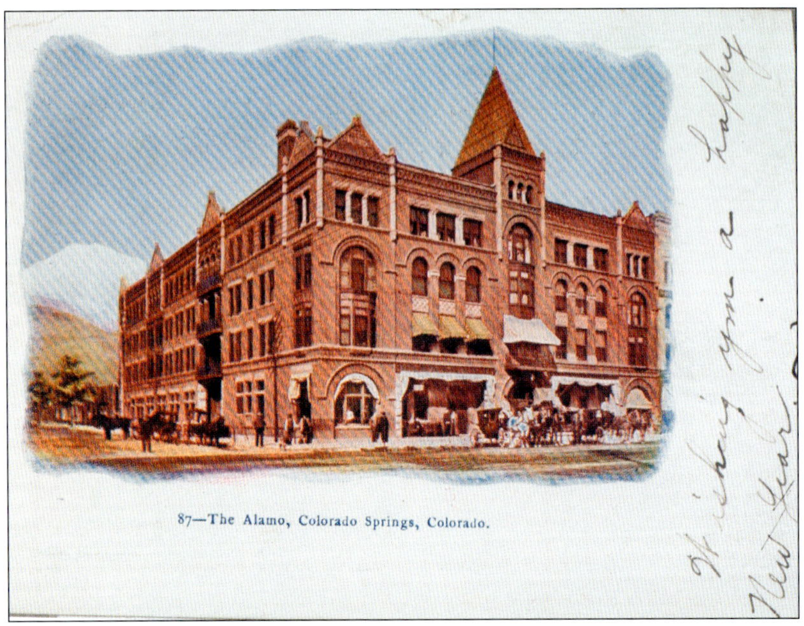

The Alamo Hotel, named for the Alamo in San Antonio, Texas.

Cancelled 1905, $4-6

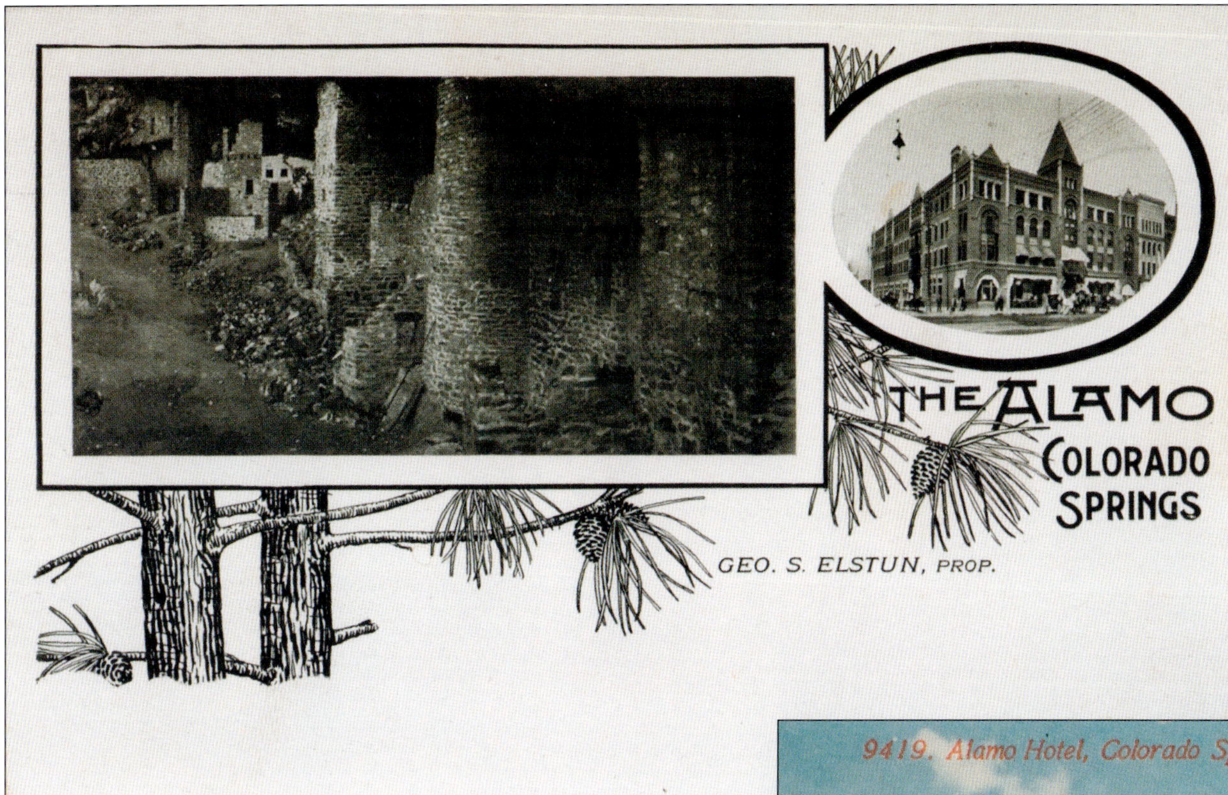

Postcard featuring the Alamo Hotel and the nearby Manitou Cliff Dwellings. It was not uncommon for hotels to publish postcards with pictures of nearby attractions.

Circa 1900s, $4-6

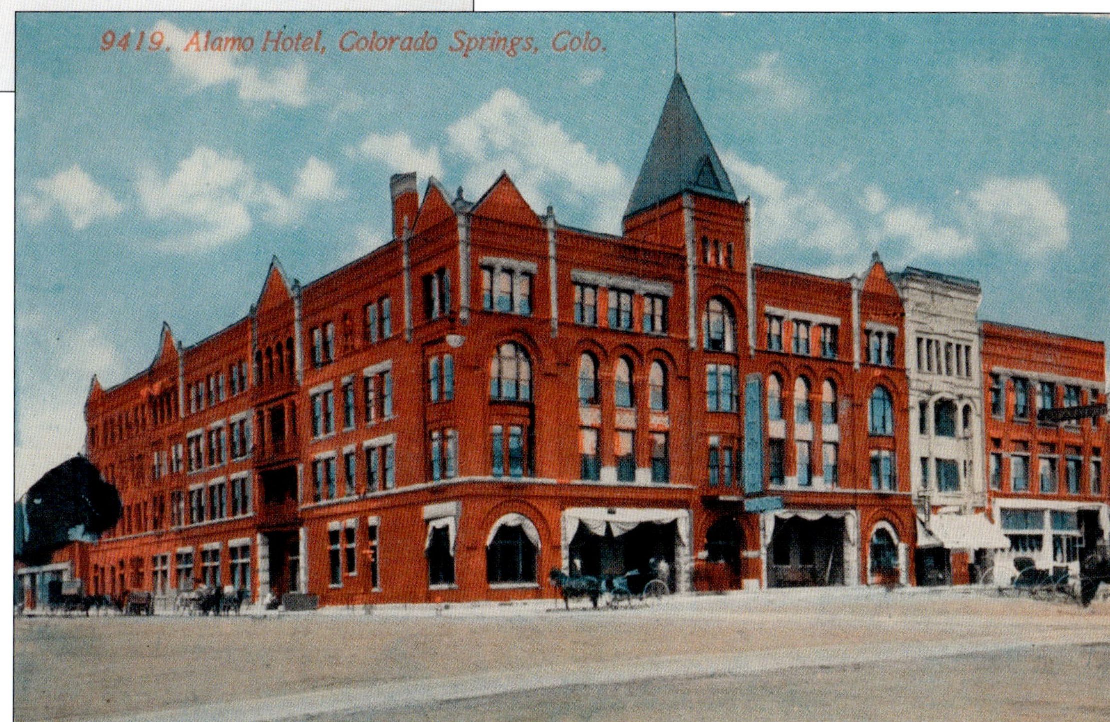

Another view of the Alamo Hotel.

Circa 1910s, $4-6

Even in its early days, Colorado Springs was visited by thousands of tourists each year. Numerous hotels, like the Plaza Hotel pictured here, were built to accommodate the large number of arriving visitors.

Circa 1910s, $4-6

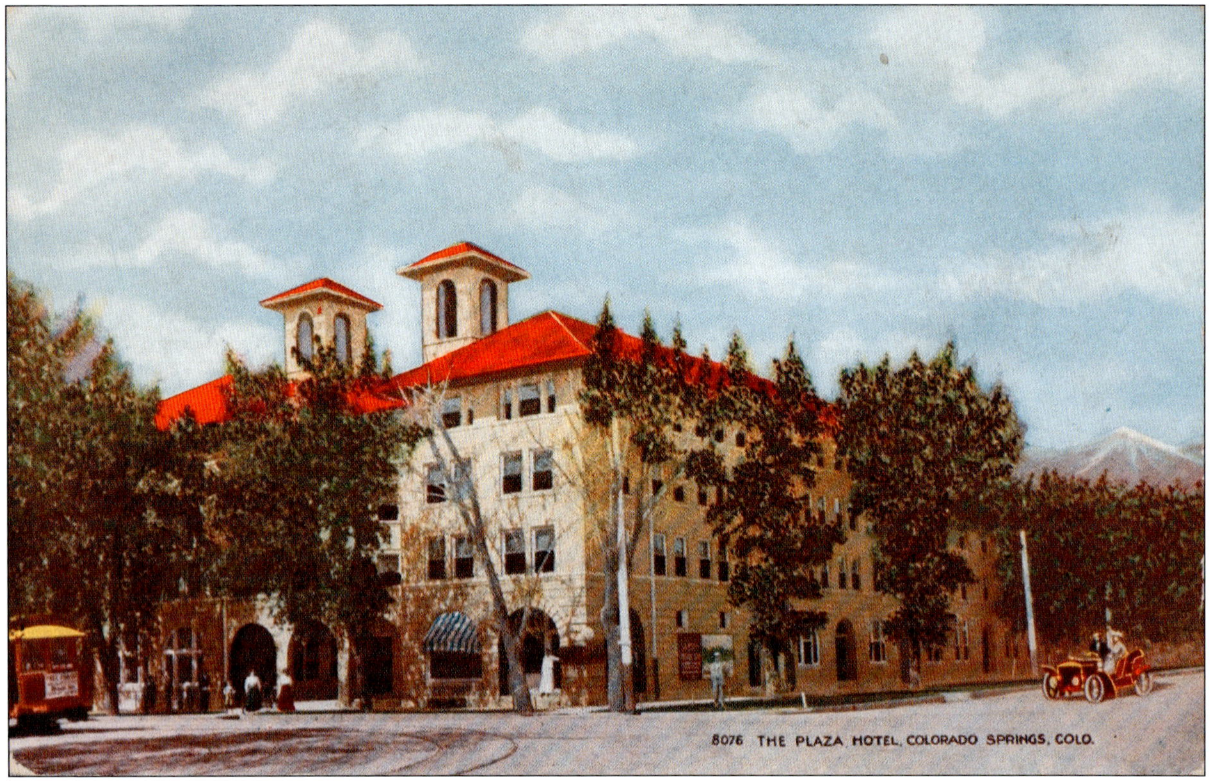

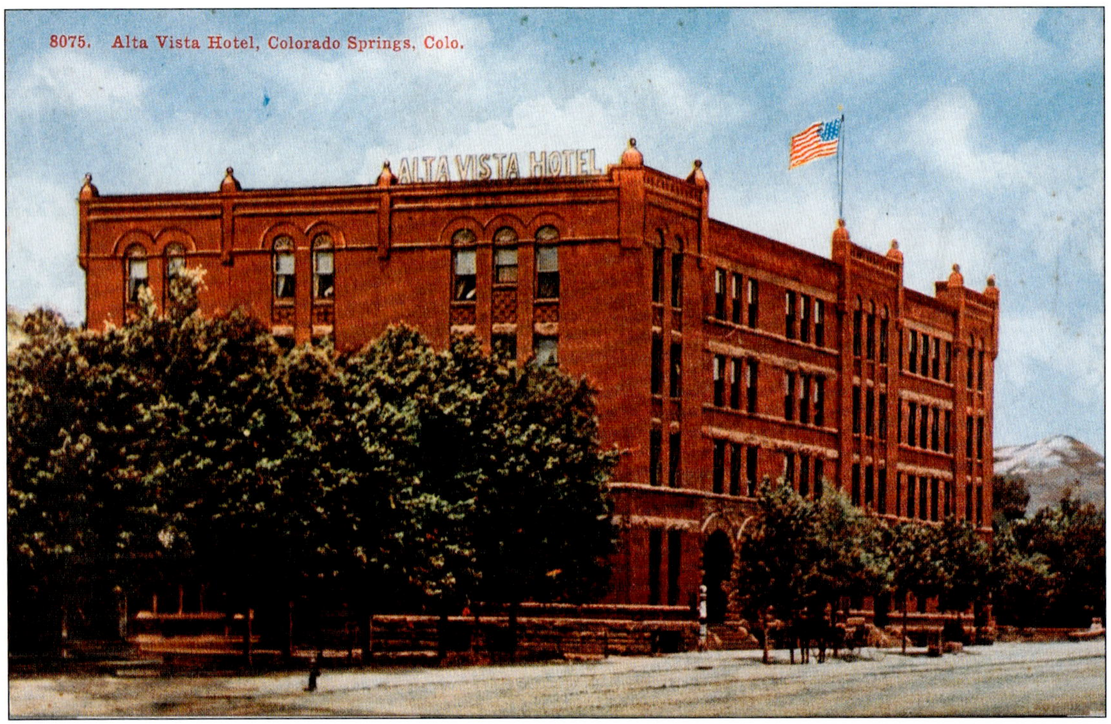

Famed inventor, physicist, and electrical engineer Nikola Tesla lived in the Alta Vista Hotel for eight months in 1899 while waiting for his new lab to be built.

Circa 1910s, $4-6

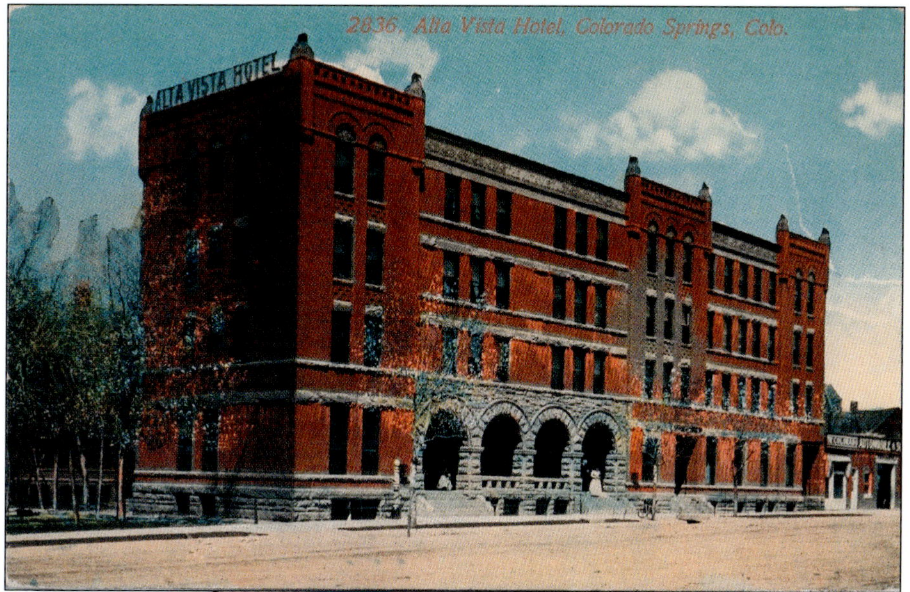

The Alta Vista Hotel, located on Cascade Avenue, was not too far from the city's business section or Monument Valley Park.

Circa 1910s, $4-6

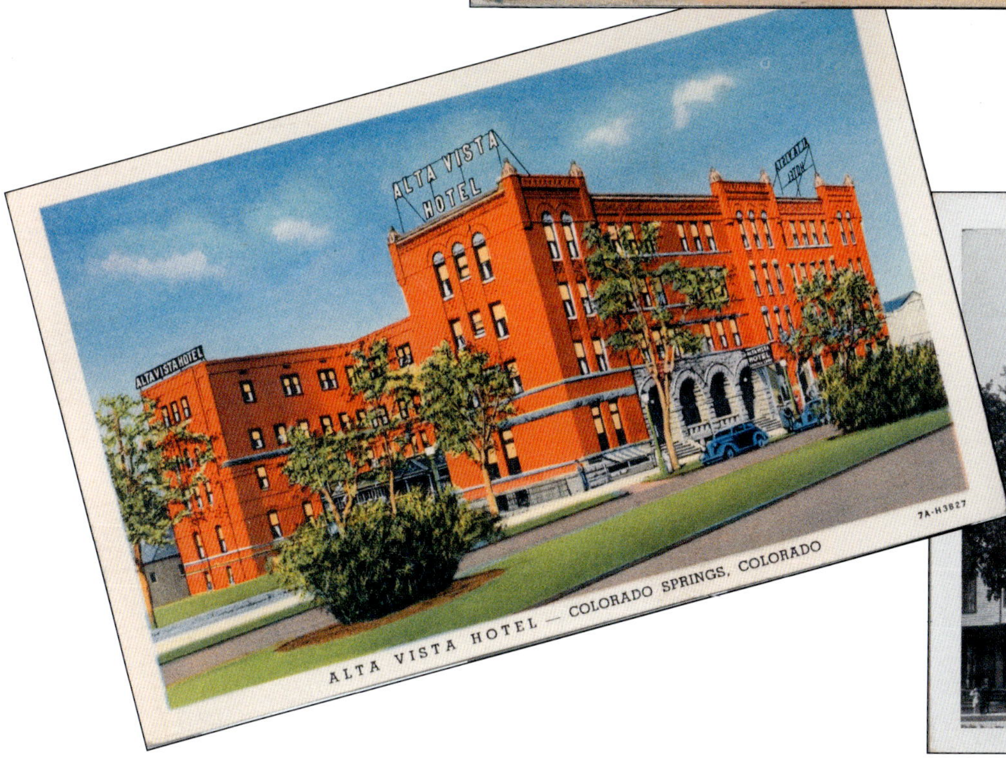

Another view of the Alta Vista Hotel.

Circa 1940s, $4-6

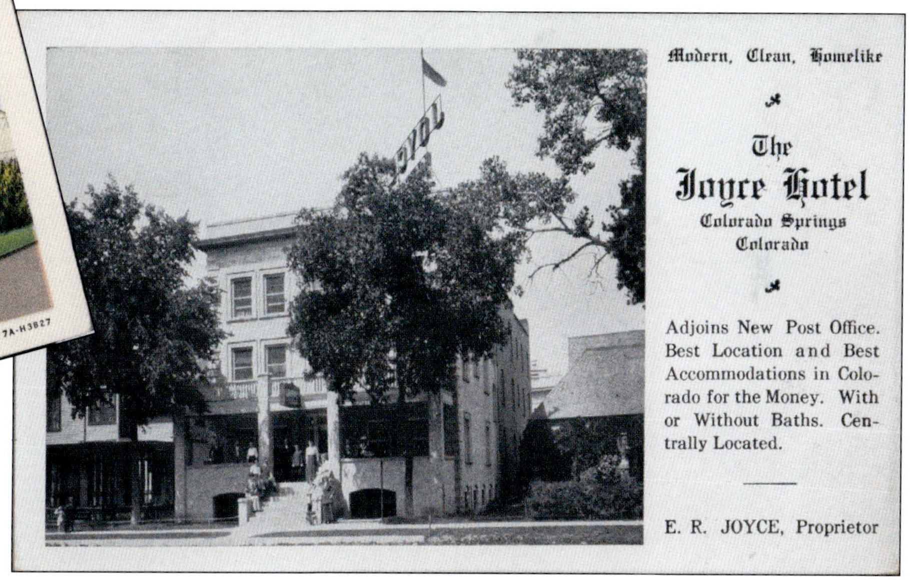

The Joyce Hotel, "Best Location and Best Accommodations in Colorado for the Money."

Circa 1910s, $4-6

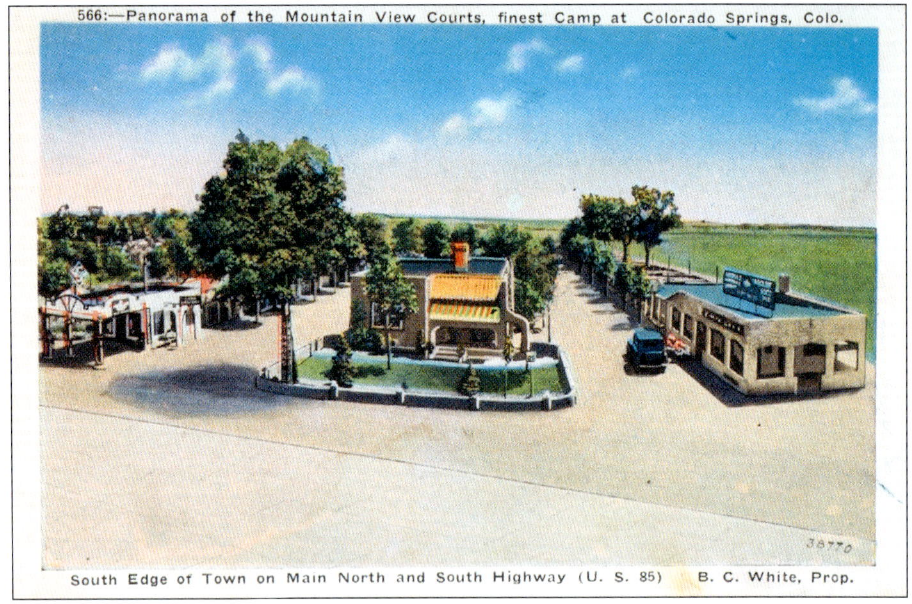

The Mountain View Courts were ideally located, a five-minute drive from Colorado Springs and a ten-minute drive to the mountains.

Circa 1920s, $4-6

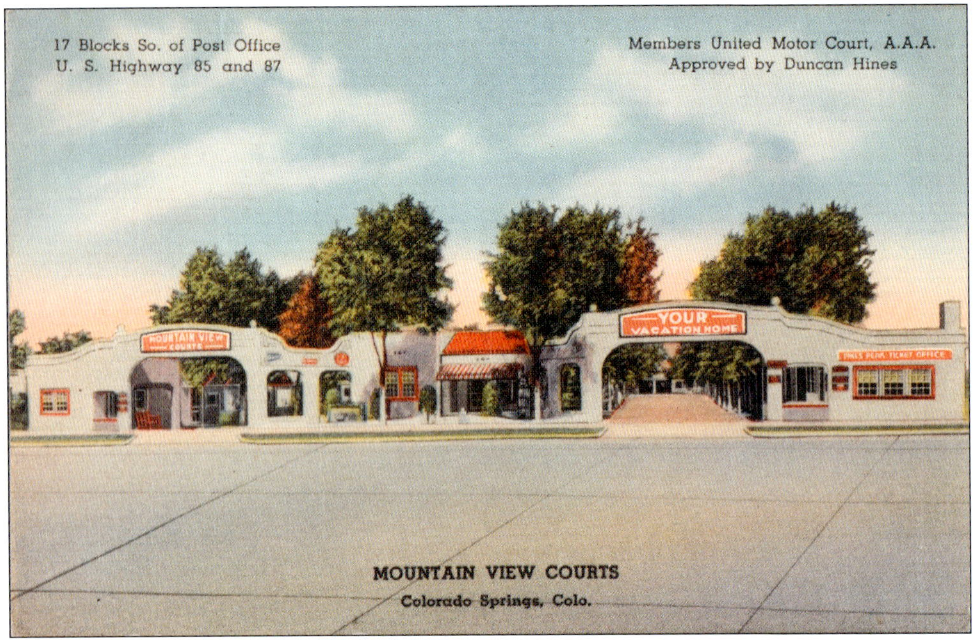

When the use of the automobile became widespread and the national highway system was put in place, more and more tourists began traveling the country via automobile staying at motor courts like the Mountain View Courts pictured here.

Circa 1940s, $4-6

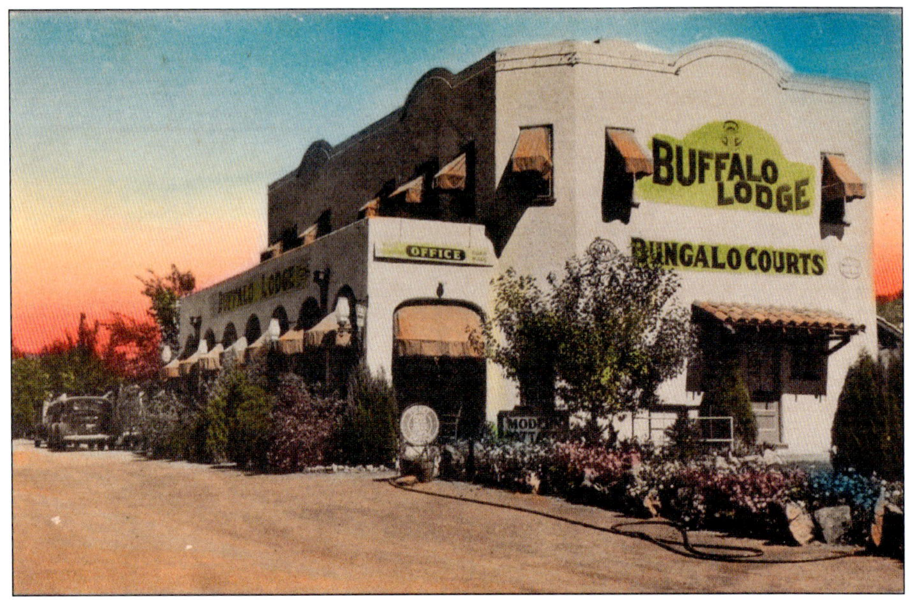

The Buffalo Lodge, located at the foot of Pikes Peak on 37th Street.

Circa 1940s, $4-6

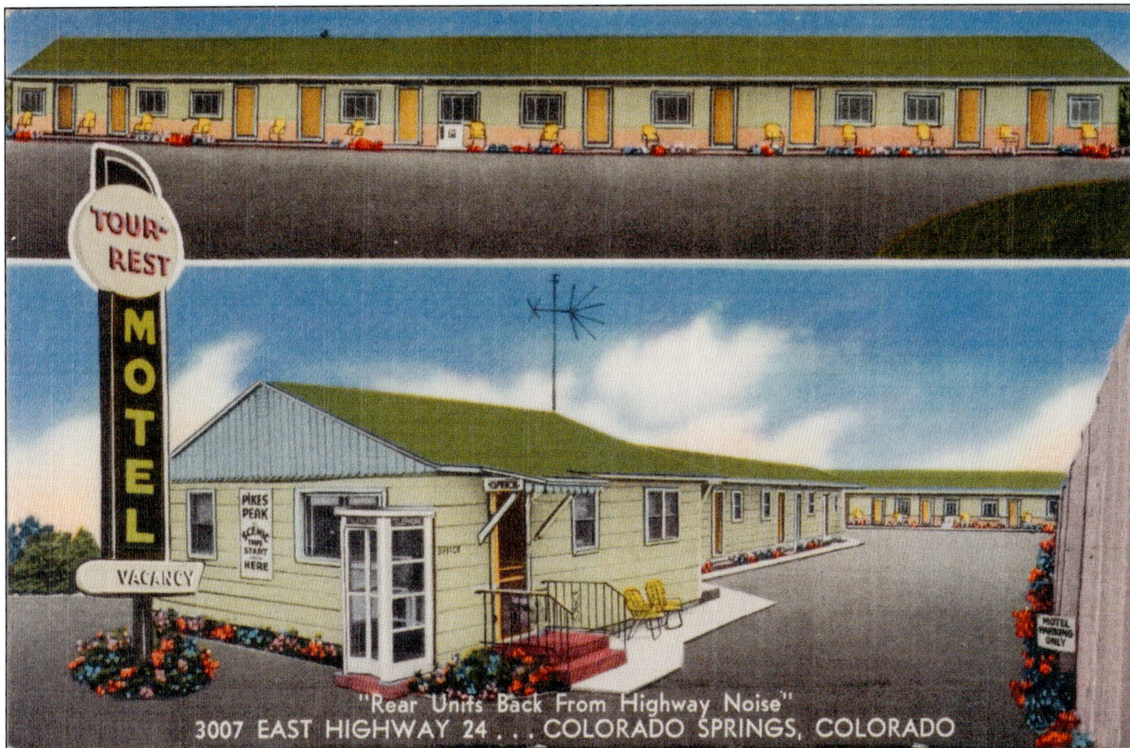

The rear units of the Tour Rest Motel were intentionally set back from the highway so as to be far from any noise.

Circa 1940s, $4-6

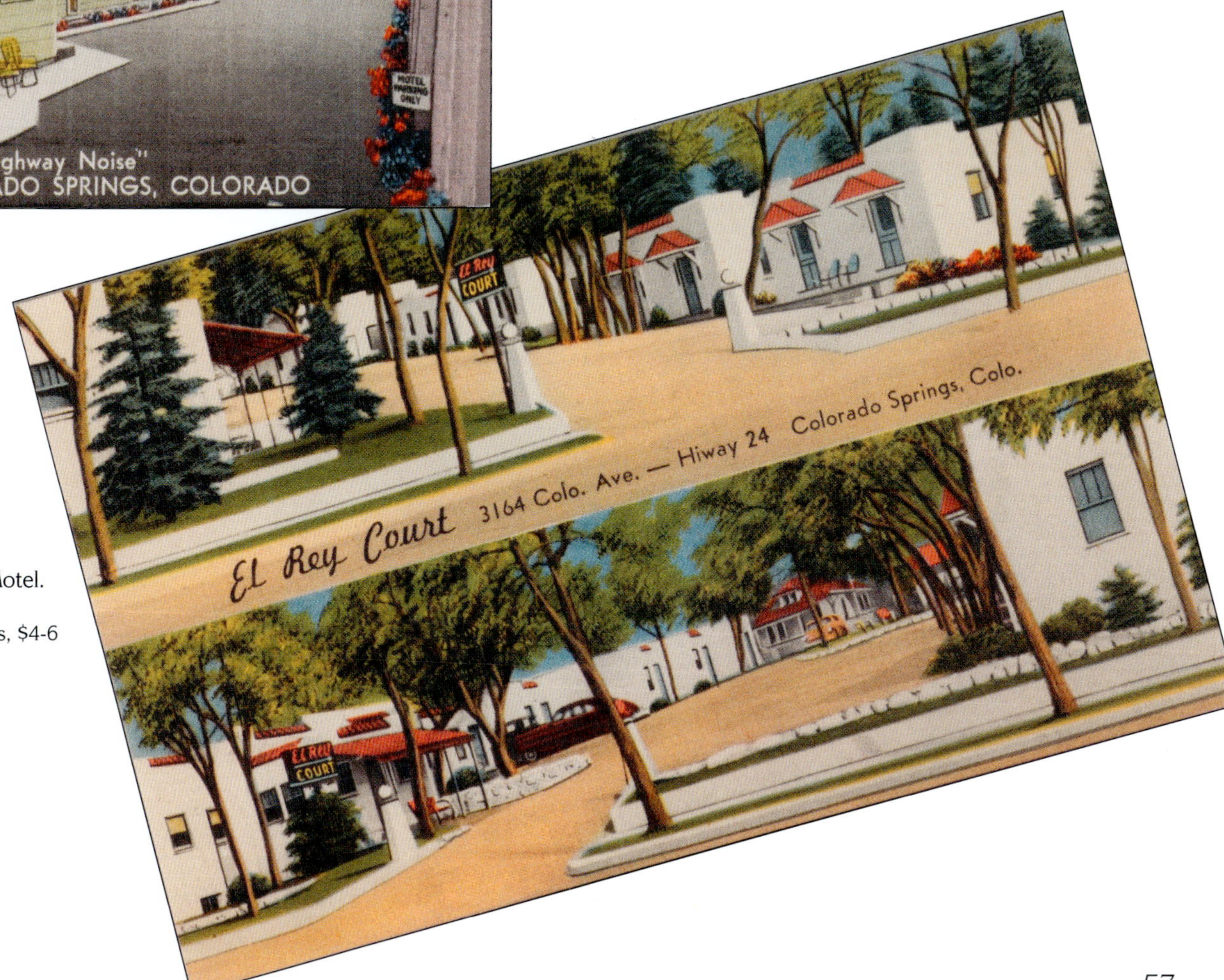

The El Rey Court Motel.

Circa 1940s, $4-6

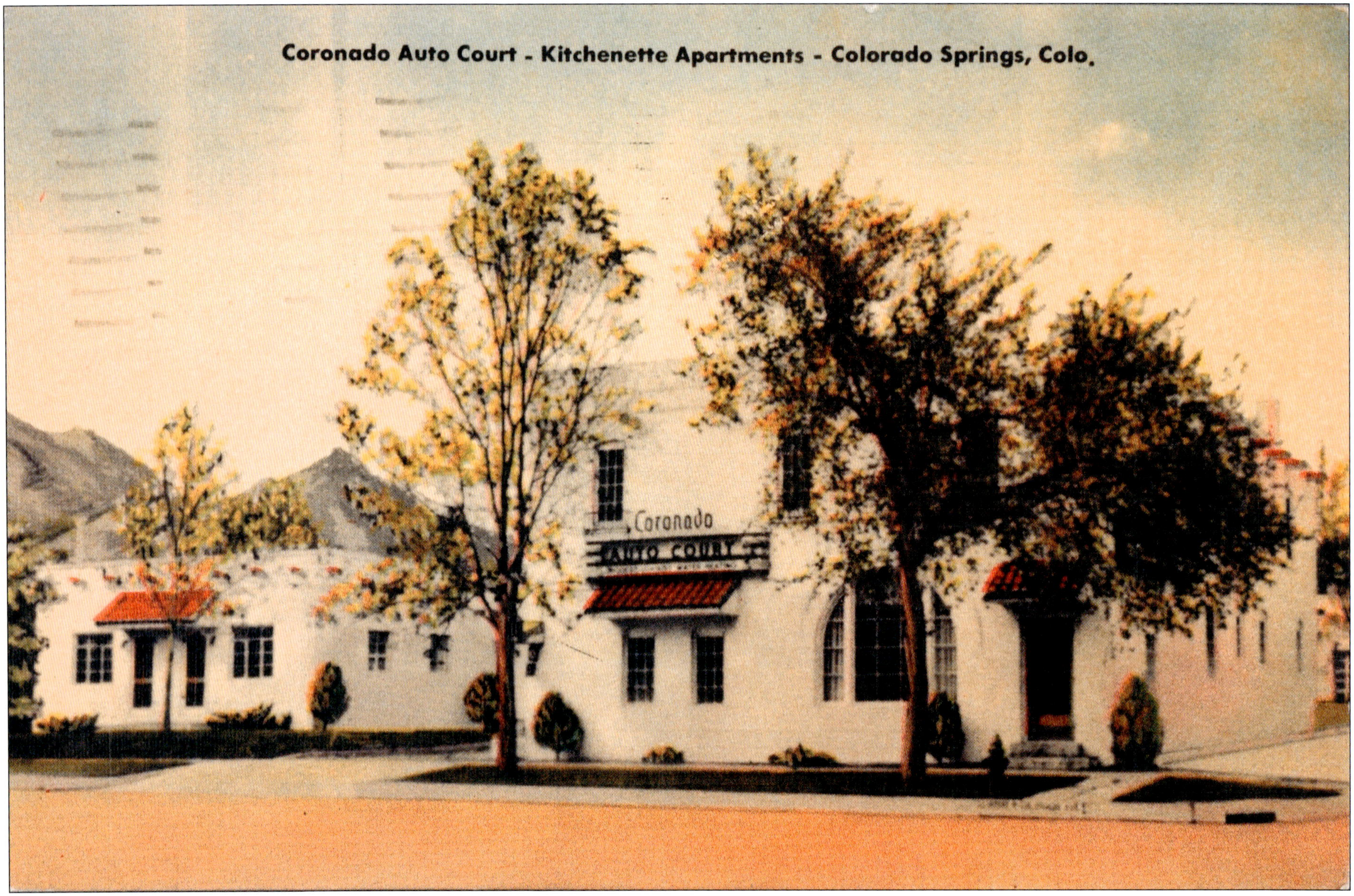

Coronado Auto Court, two miles west of downtown Colorado Springs.

Cancelled 1952, $4-6

Parks

Of the 10,000 acres purchased by General Palmer in 1870 for the future site of Colorado Springs, 1,270 acres were used to create parks, scenic drives, open spaces, and foot and bridle paths. The first was Acacia Park, which was included in the original plans for the layout of the city. Over the years, the general continued to contribute land for parks, including Monument Valley Park, North Cheyenne Cañon Park, and Antlers Park, all of which remain treasured parts of Colorado Springs.

Since then, the city has expanded well beyond its original boundaries and the creation and maintenance of parks and open spaces has remained an ongoing concern with the city and its private citizens. The Colorado Springs Parks, Recreation & Cultural Services oversees seven regional parks, nine community parks, 123 neighborhood parks, forty-five open spaces, and five sports complexes; a total 12,000 acres worth of parks, trails, and open spaces.

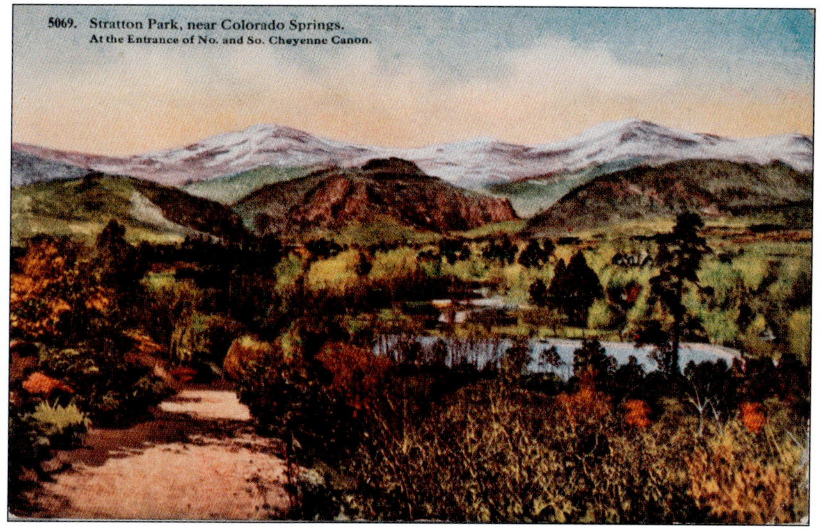

Stratton Park was built on land donated to Colorado Springs by Winfield Scott Stratton.

Circa 1910s, $4-6

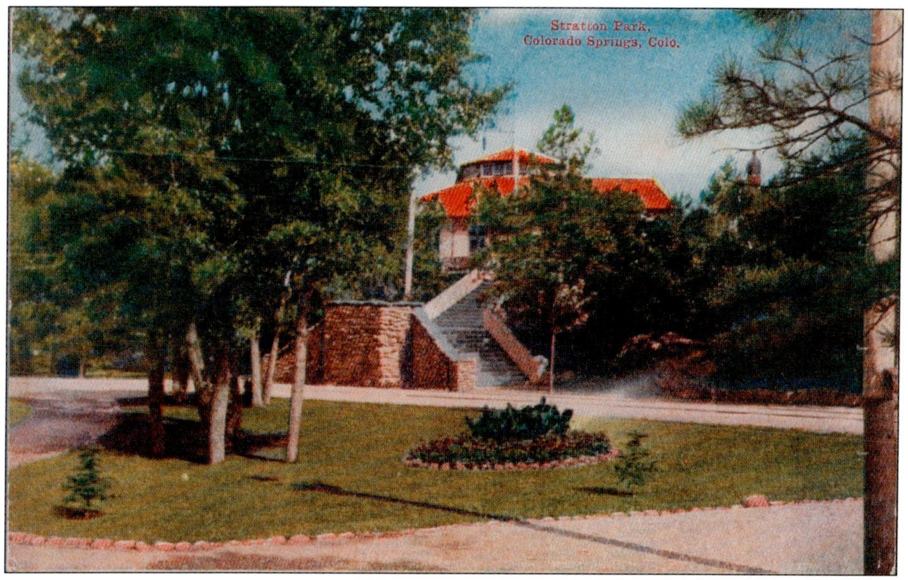

Stratton Park was located a half-hour's drive outside of Colorado at the entrance to North Cheyenne Cañon.

Circa 1910s, $4-6

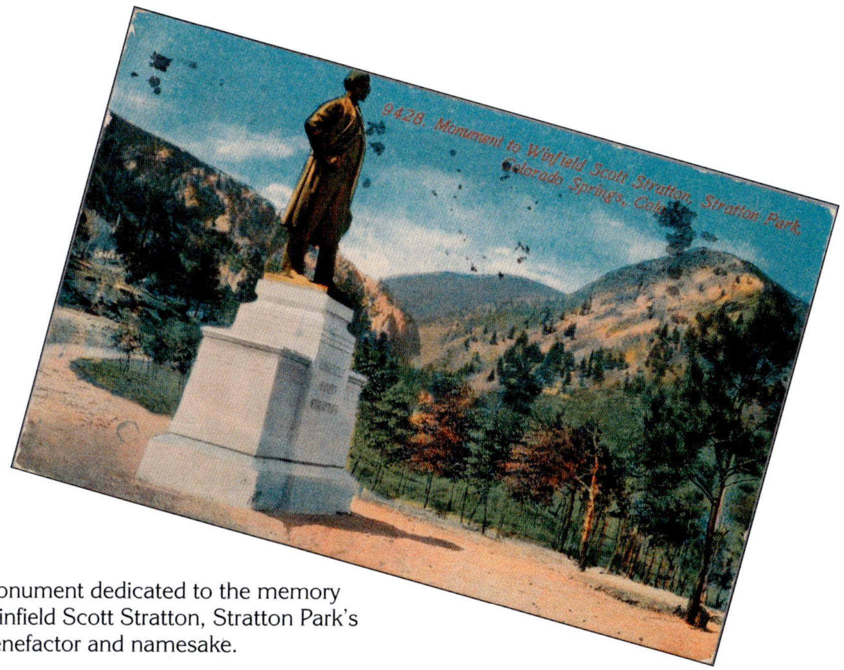

Monument dedicated to the memory Winfield Scott Stratton, Stratton Park's benefactor and namesake.

Cancelled 1916, $4-6

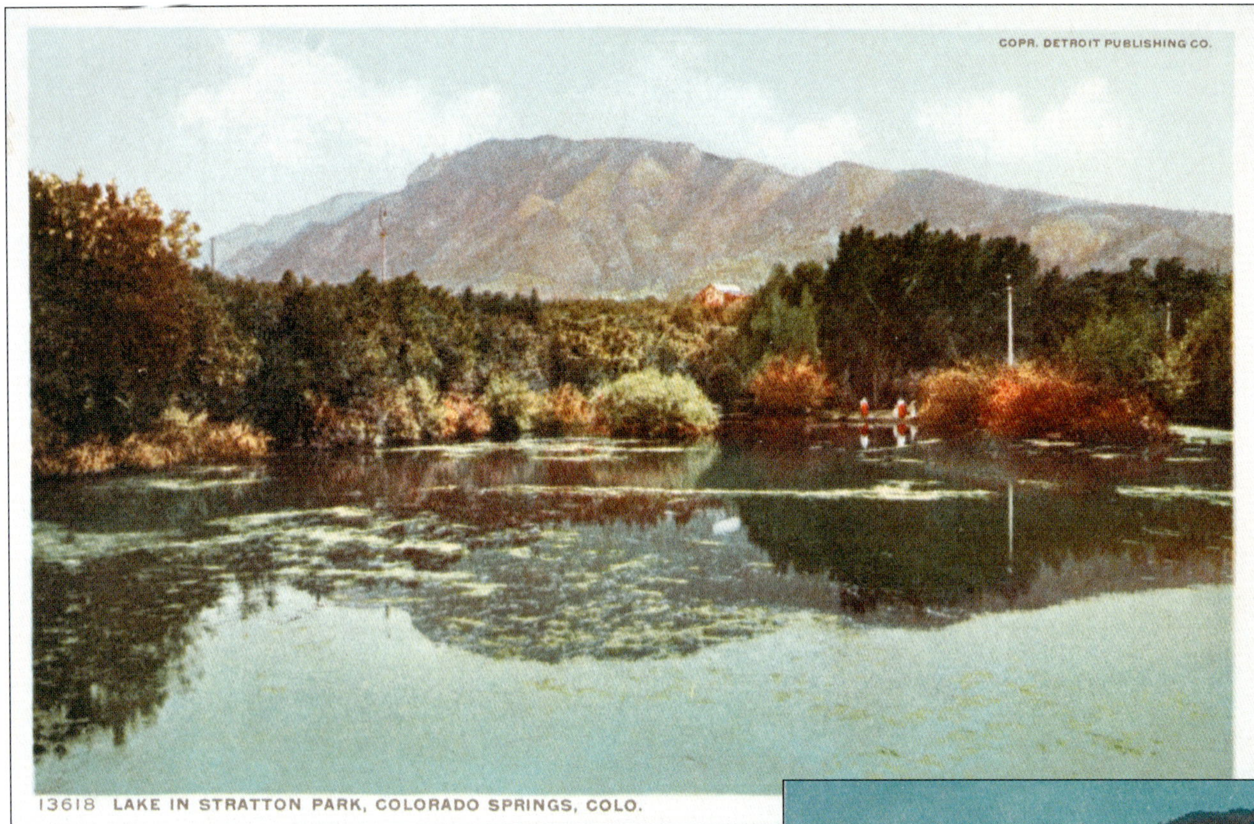

In addition to donating the land, Winfield Scott Stratton was also responsible for the design and layout of Stratton Park.

Circa 1920s, $4-6

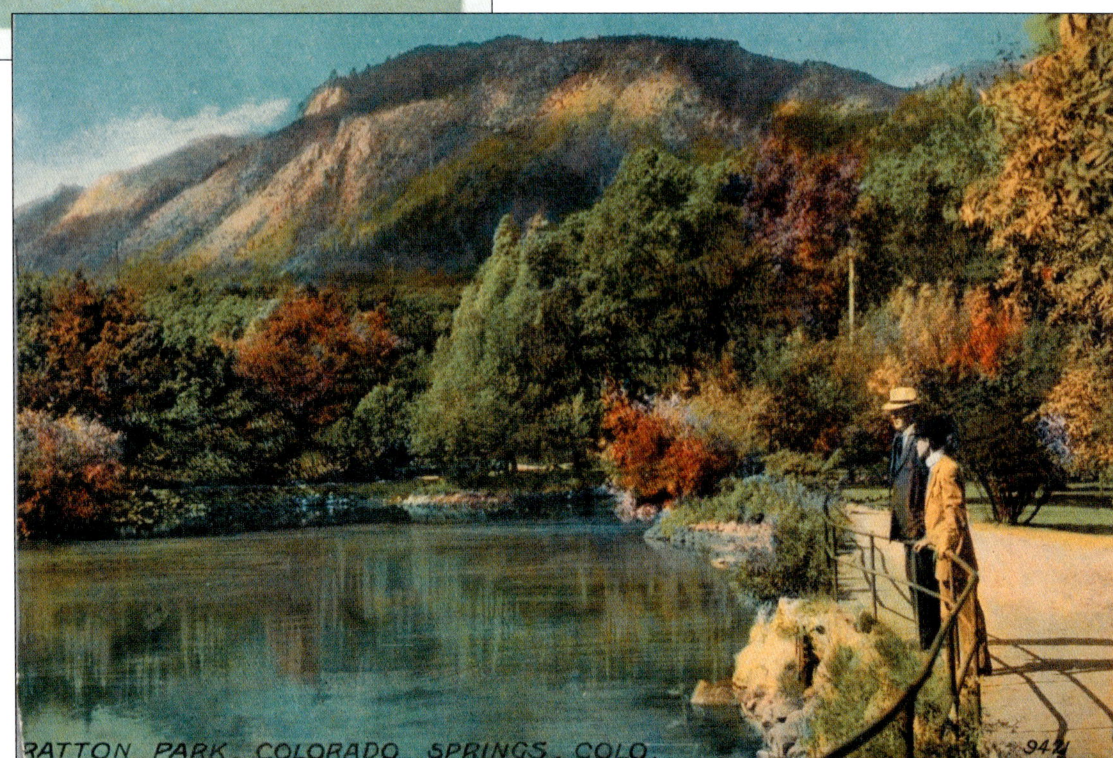

Park goers pause by a lake in Stratton Park.

Cancelled 1914, $4-6

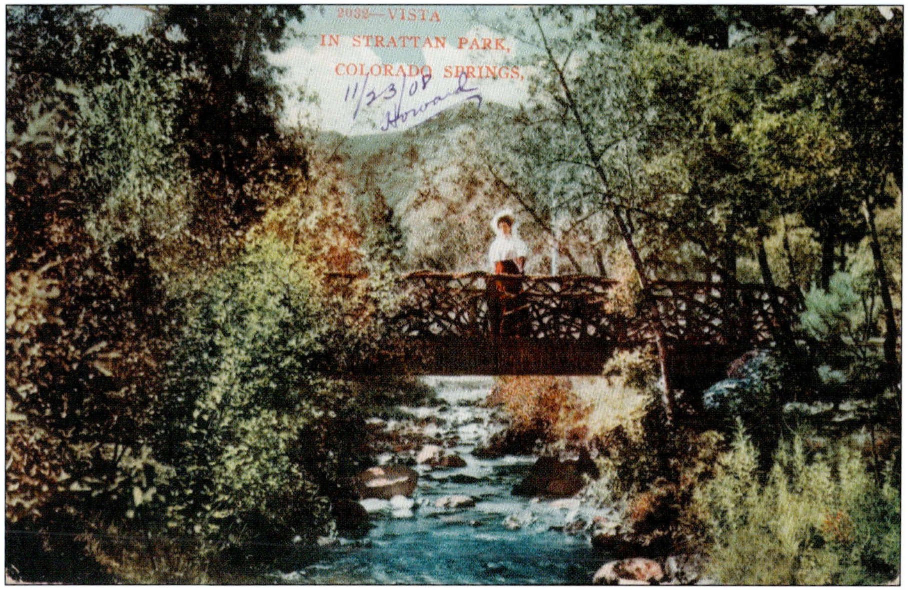

Another vista in Stratton Park.

Cancelled 1908, $4-6

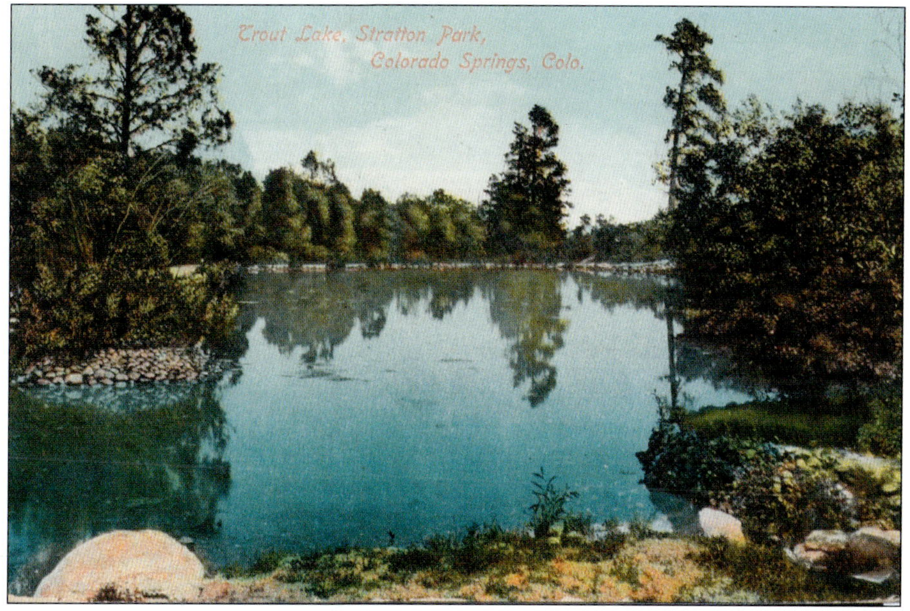

Because Stratton Park has remained largely within its natural state, meaning it has not been overly developed and the vegetation growing there is naturally occurring, it has been designated an "open space" by the city's Parks and Recreation Department.

Cancelled 1910, $4-6

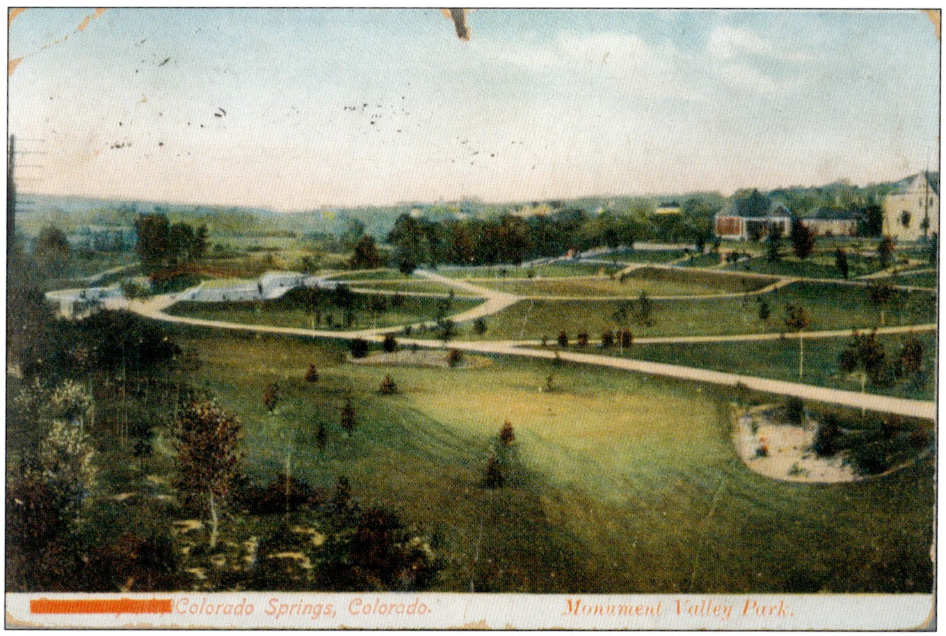

Monument Valley Park was a gift to the city of Colorado Springs from its founder, General William Jackson Palmer. Today it is one of the city's most popular parks.

Cancelled 1910, $4-6

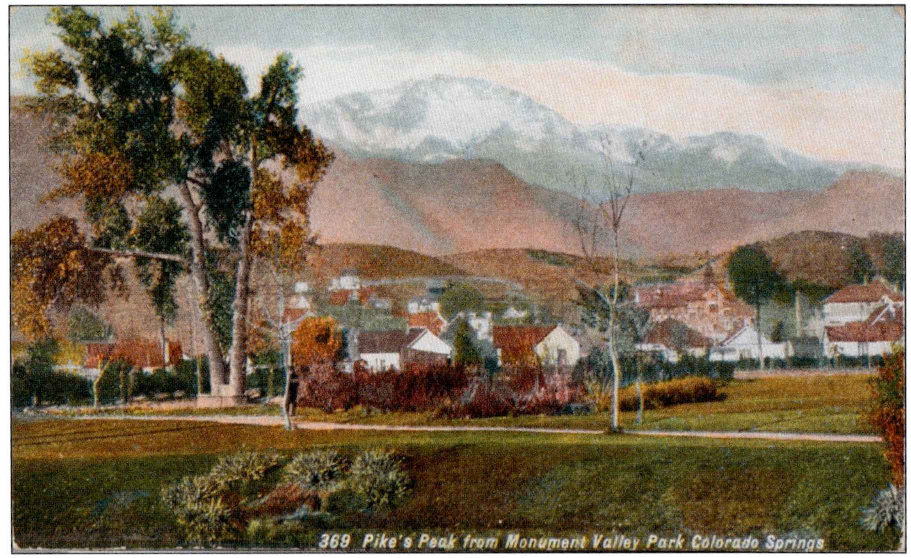

A view of Pikes Peak from Monument Valley Park.

Circa 1910s, $4-6

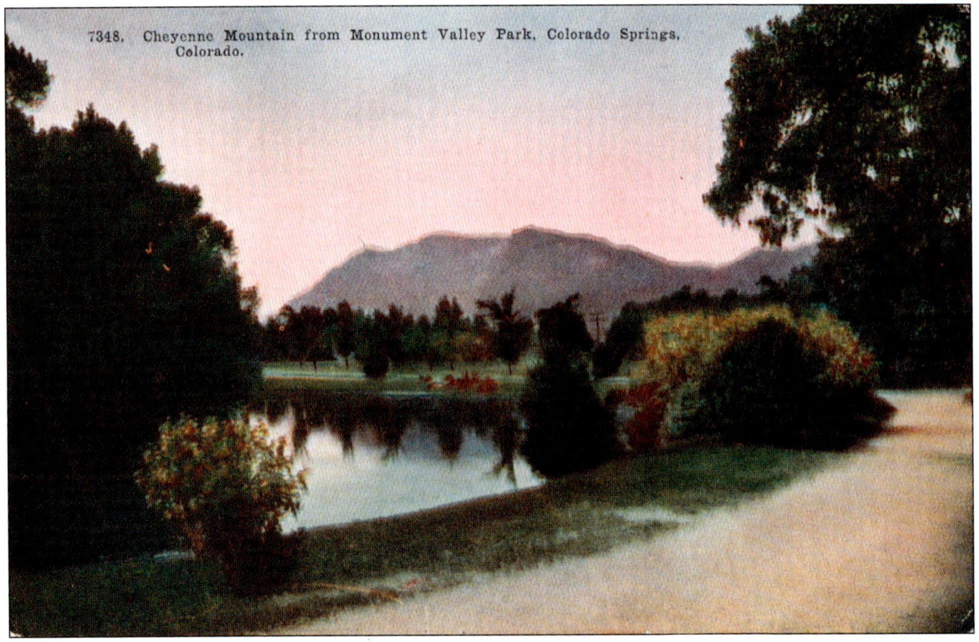

Cheyenne Mountain, as seen from Monument Valley Park.

Circa 1910s, $4-6

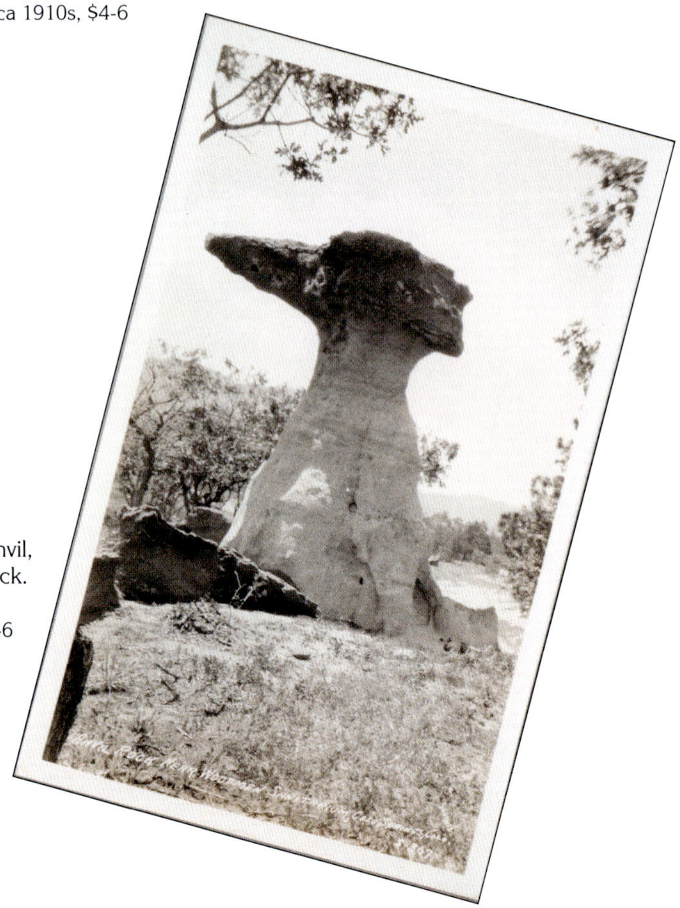

Another view of Volcano Anvil, also known as Anvil Rock.

Circa 1930s, $4-6

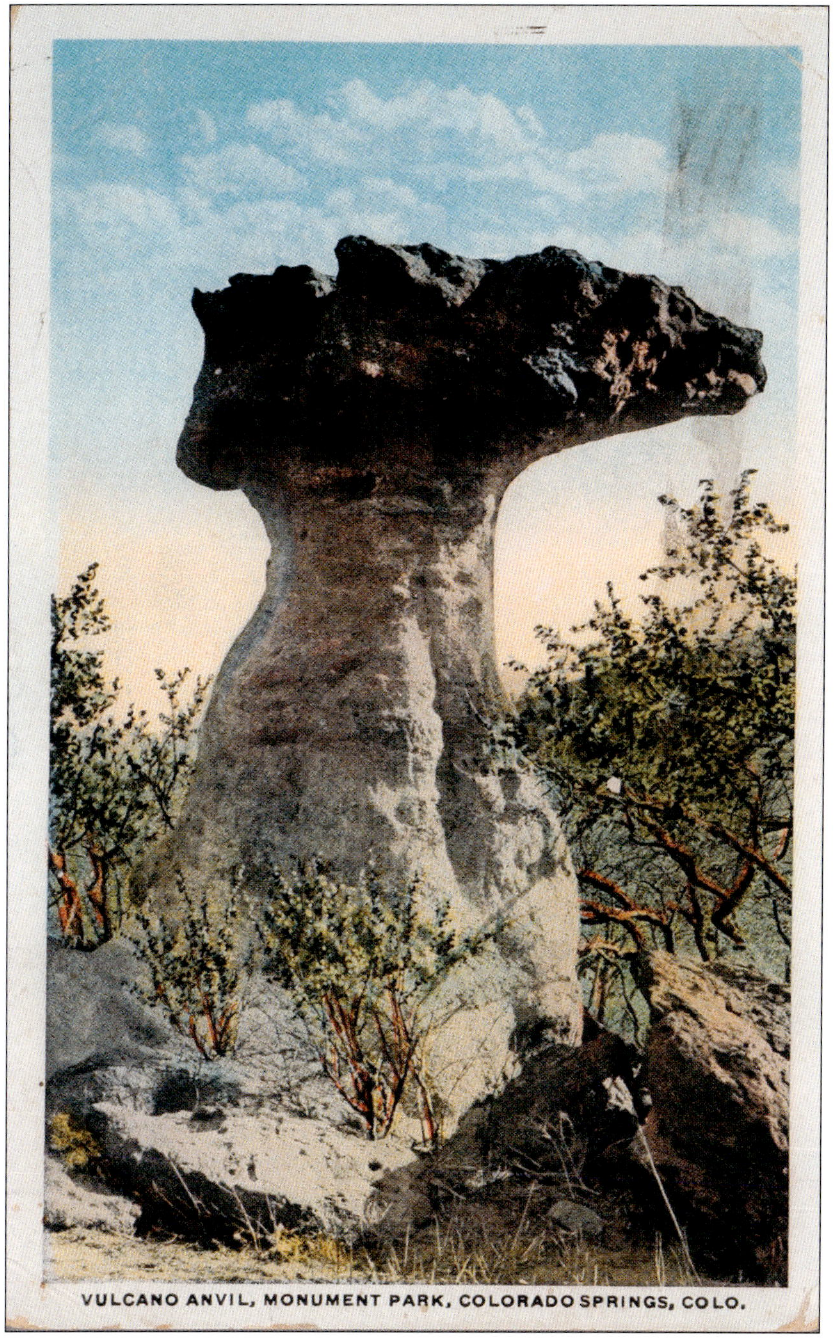

Volcano Anvil, a rock formation in Monument Valley Park.

Circa 1920s, $4-6

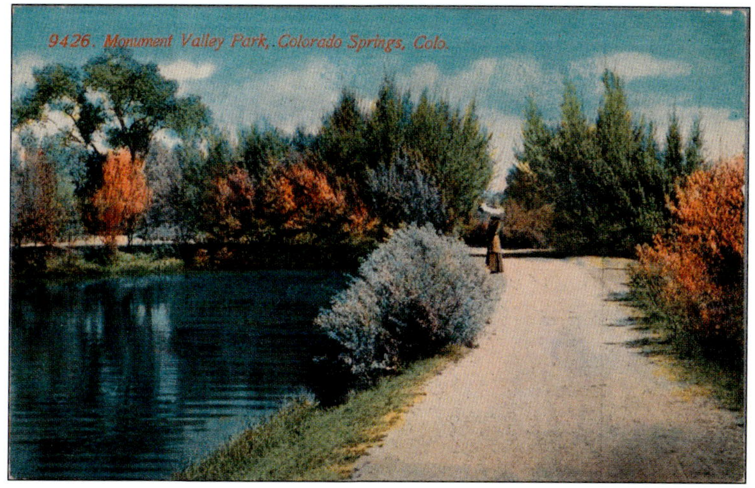

General Palmer built Monument Valley Park in 1904 at a cost of $75,000. Early features of the park included a tennis court, playgrounds, and numerous gardens including a wildflower garden made up of native Colorado flowers and an arboretum featuring specimens of every species of tree and shrub found in Colorado.

Circa 1910s, $4-6

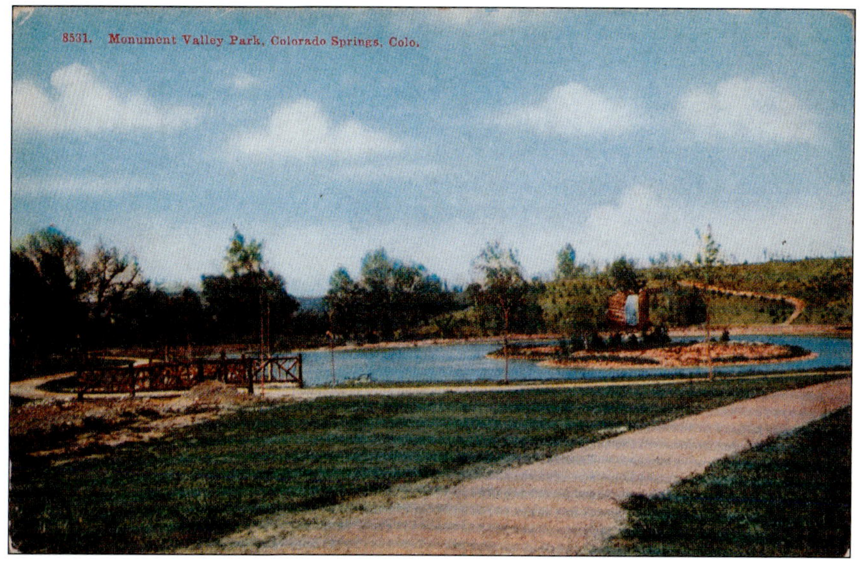

In 1935, the park suffered a massive flood that caused a large amount of damage to many of the park's features. It was eventually rebuilt, though some features were never replaced.

Circa 1910s, $4-6

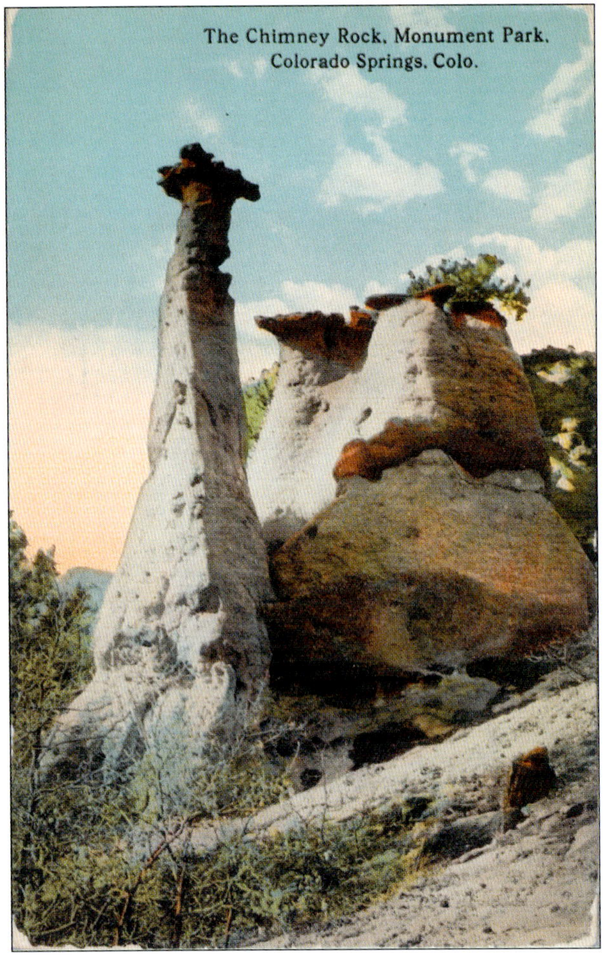

Chimney Rock, another of Monument Valley Park's unusual rock formations.

Circa 1910s, $4-6

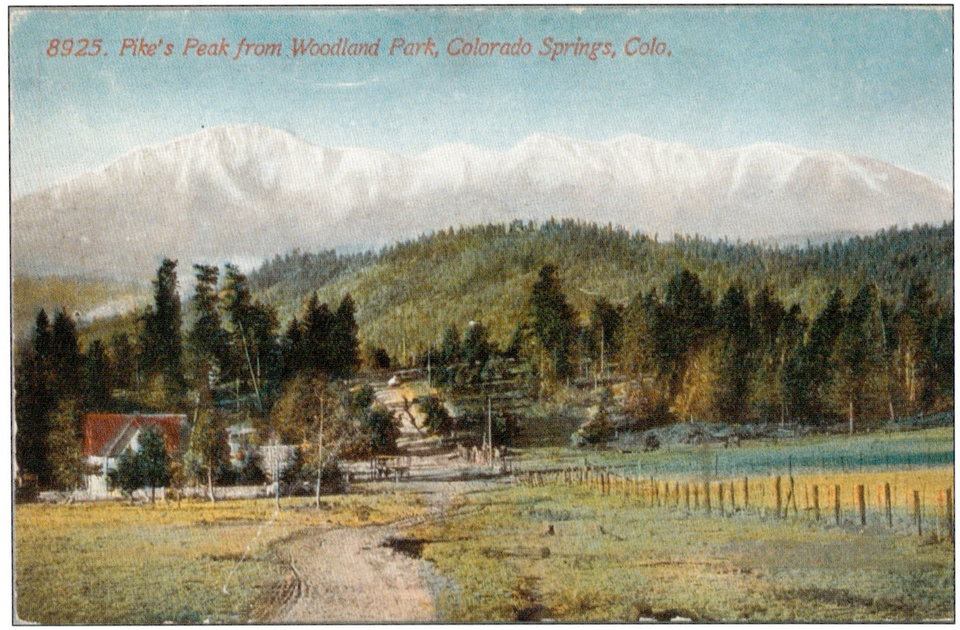

Woodland Park.

Circa 1910s, $4-6

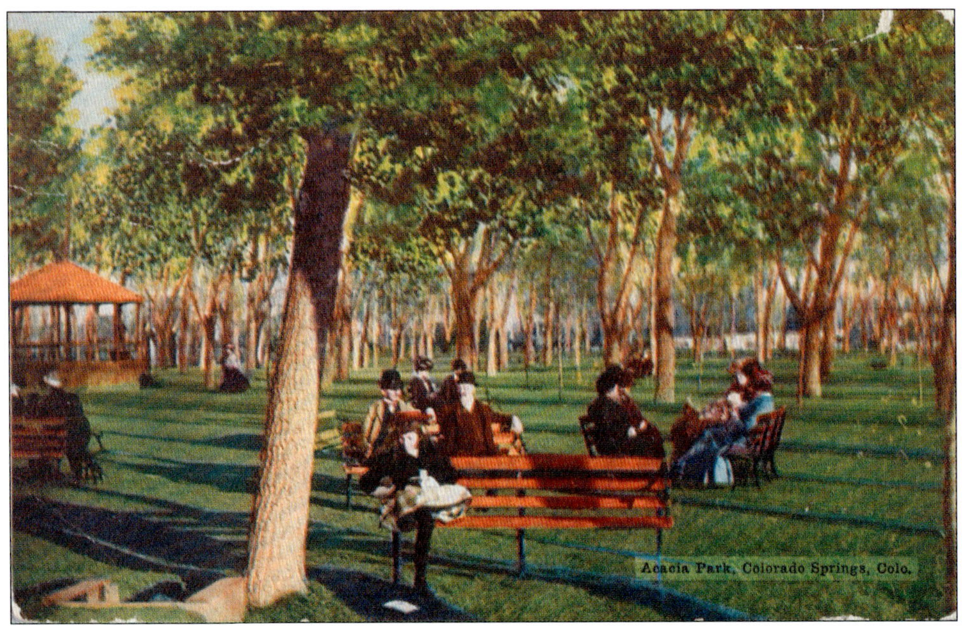

Part of the original city plan of 1871, Acacia Park was the first park built in Colorado Springs.

Cancelled 1910, $4-6

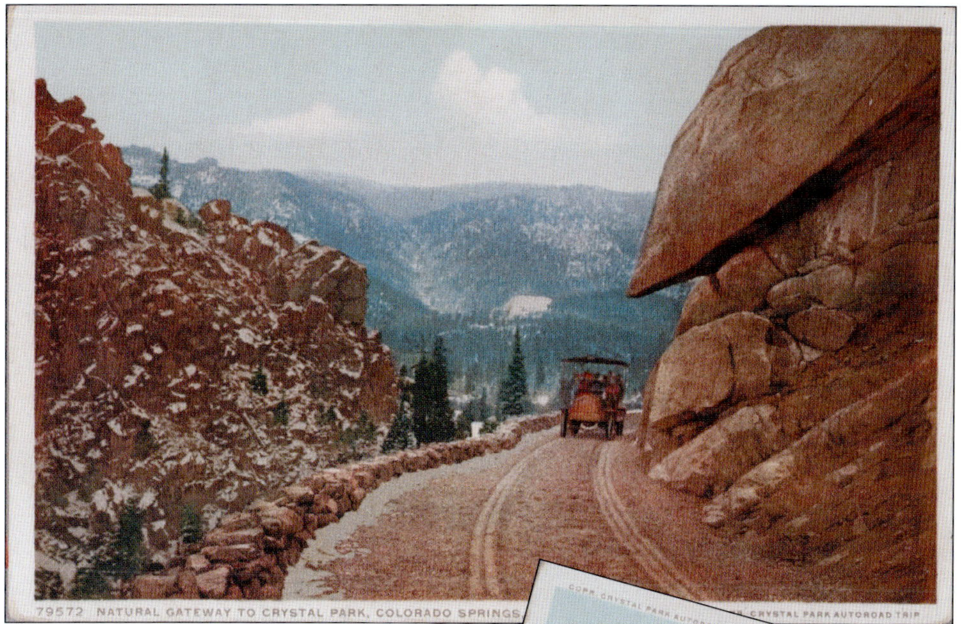

The entrance to Crystal Park.

Circa 1920s, $4-6

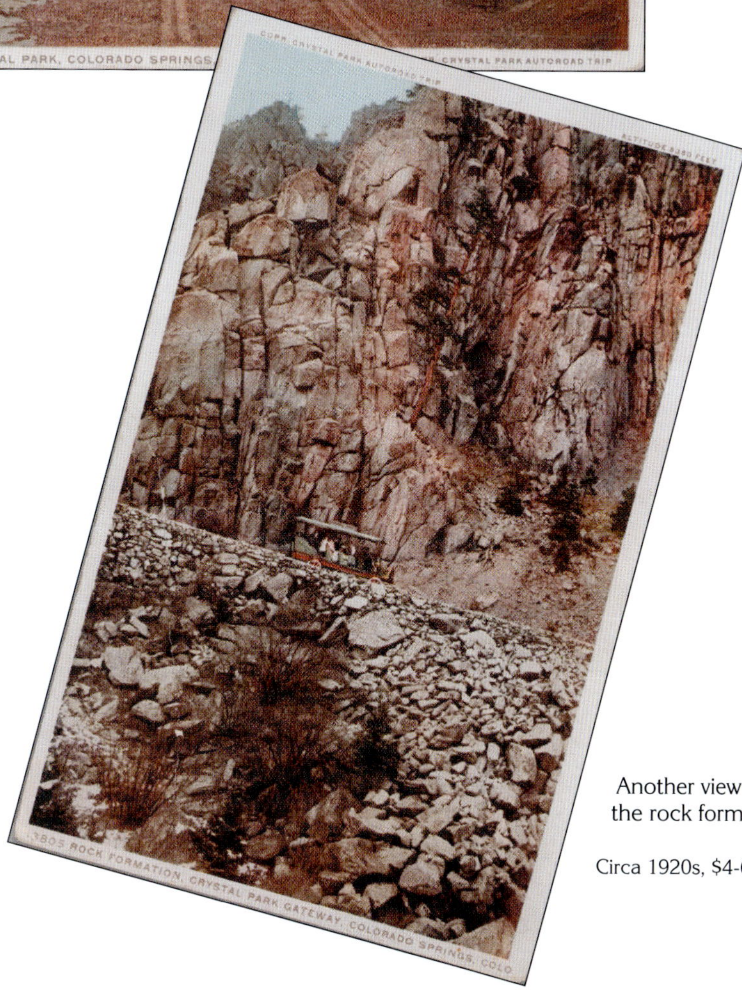

Another view of the entrance to Crystal Park showing the rock formations making up the gateway.

Circa 1920s, $4-6

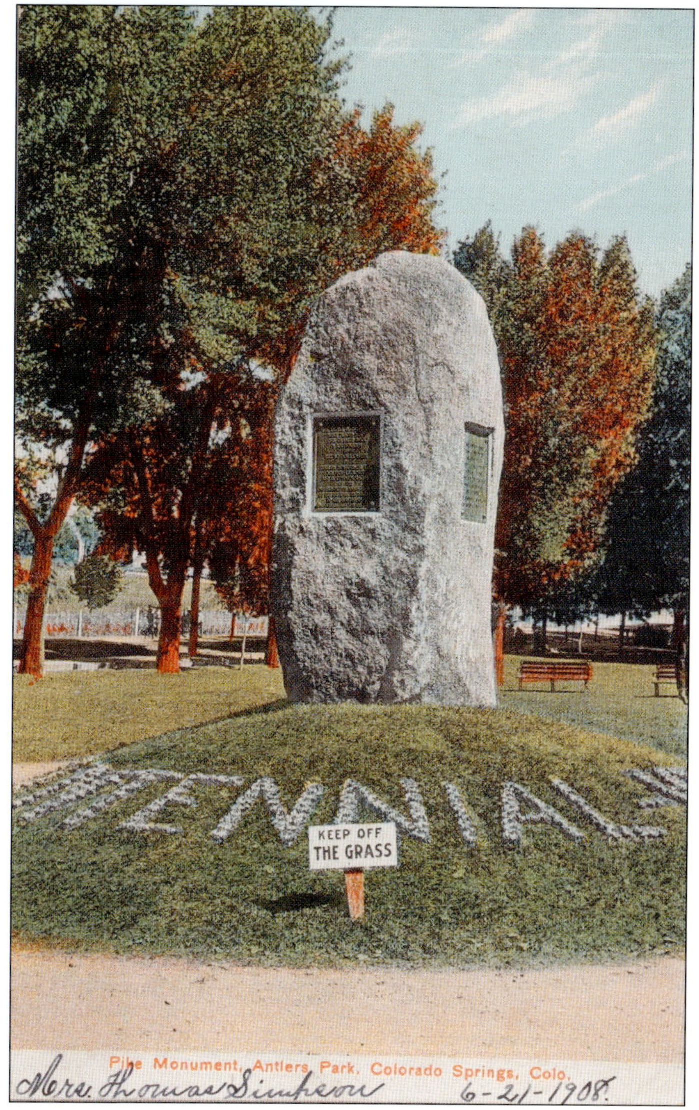

Monument in Antlers Park commemorating the discovery of Pikes Peak by Zebulon Pike in 1806.

Circa 1900s, $4-6

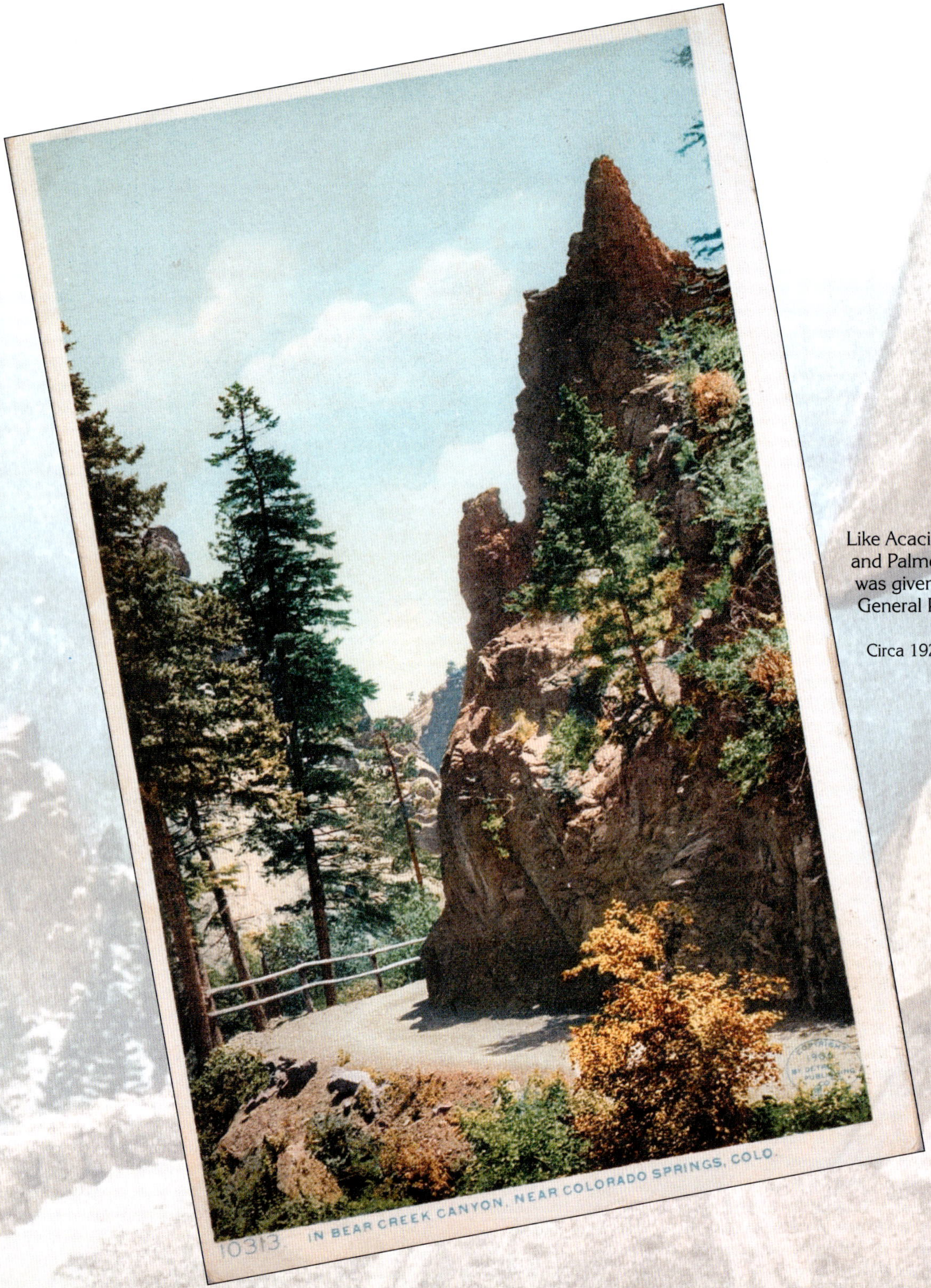

Like Acacia, Monument Valley, Antlers, and Palmer Parks, Bear Creek Canyon was given to Colorado Springs by General Palmer.

Circa 1920s, $4-6

Visiting Colorado Springs

Garden of the Gods

In August 1859, two surveyors, M.S. Beach and Rufus Cable, traveled from Denver City to survey a location for the future town of Colorado City. Exploring possible locations around Pikes Peak they came upon an area filled with sandstone formations that had been weathered into a variety of fantastic shapes. Beach believed that the area would be an excellent place for a beer garden. Cable, who was described as young and more poetic, exclaimed, "Beer Garden? Why this is a fit place for the Gods to assemble. We will call it the Garden of the Gods." The name stuck, and has remained ever since.

After the founding of Colorado Springs, General Palmer urged his friend Charles Elliot Perkins, head of the Burlington Railroad, to settle in Colorado Springs and to build a home. In 1879, Perkins purchased 240 acres in the Garden of the Gods and built a summer home there. Though he had left his land open to the public for many years, Perkins had planned to eventually present the land to the city of Colorado Springs or propose the site as a National Park; however, he passed away in 1907 before he could put any plans into motion. A year later his children turned the land (480 acres) over to three trustees who in turn gave the land to the city for use as a public park. There were three conditions to be met – or the land would revert back to the children or their heirs. The conditions were: the park was to remain free to the public; no intoxicating beverages were to be manufactured, bought, or sold anywhere on the property; and no building was to be built there unless it was for the maintenance and care of the land as a public park. Since then, the Garden of the Gods has become one of Colorado Spring's most popular attractions, frequently visited by residents and tourists alike.

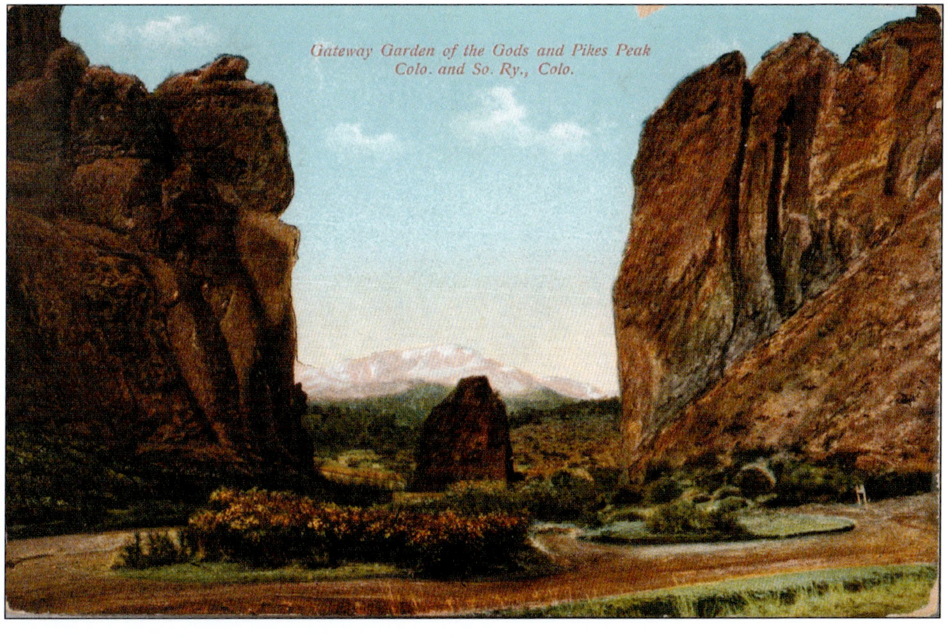

While helping explore the area for a suitable location for the future town of Colorado City, surveyors M.S. Beach and Rufus Cable came across a place filled with magnificent sandstone formations. Beach suggested that it would be an excellent place for a beer garden. Cable exclaimed, "Beer Garden? Why this is a fit place for the Gods to assemble. We will call it the Garden of the Gods."

Cancelled 1909, $4-6

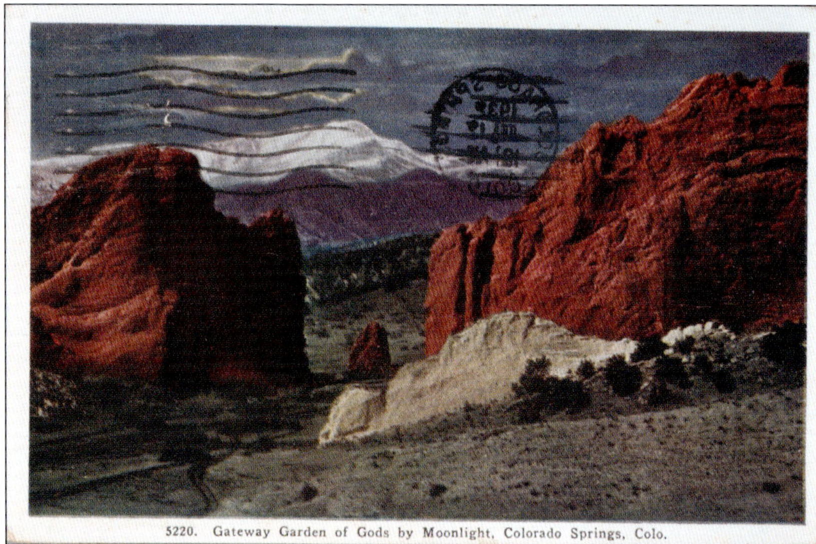

The Gateway to the Garden of the Gods.

Cancelled 1932, $4-6

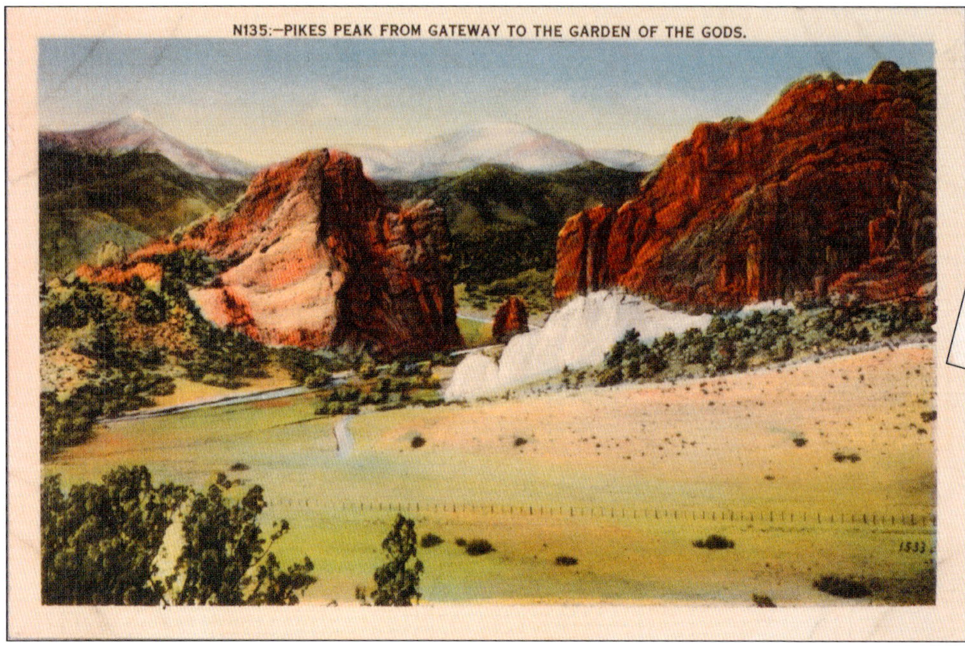

In 1879, Charles Elliot Perkins, the head of the Burlington Railroad and a friend of General Palmer, bought 240 acres in the Garden of the Gods and built a summer home there.

Circa 1940s, $4-6

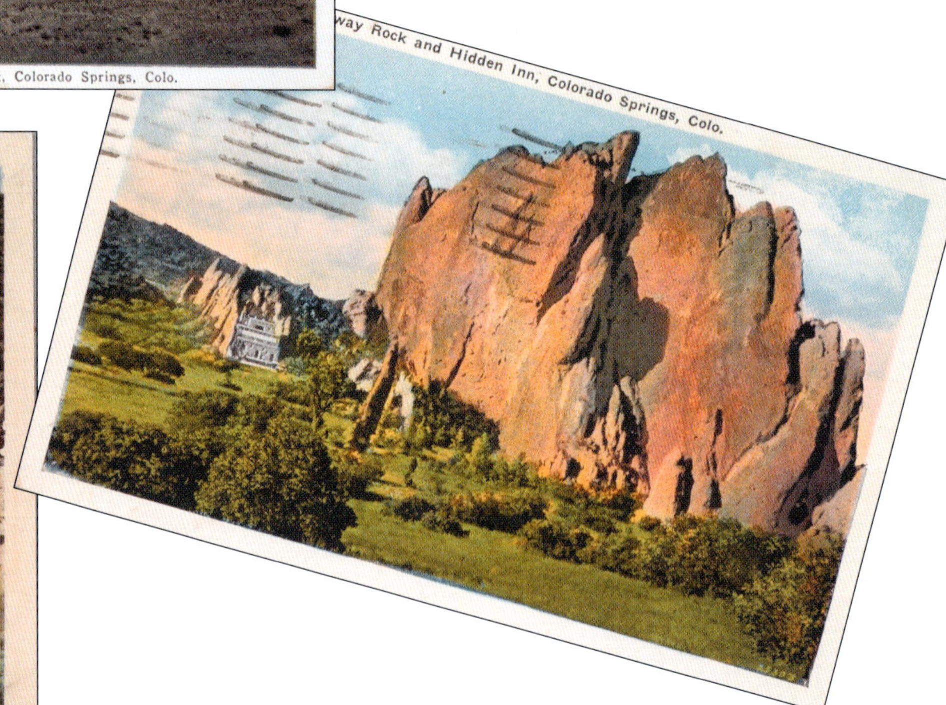

Perkins had intended to give his land in the Garden of the Gods to the city of Colorado Springs for use as a public park. Unfortunately he died before he could amend his will to convey his wish. His children gave the land to the city in 1909 on the condition that it would be kept free to the public; that no intoxicating beverages were sold, made, or dispensed in the park; and that no building would be built in the park unless it was for the purpose of maintaining, protecting, or caring for the area as a public park. If these conditions were not met, the ownership of the land would revert back to Perkins' heirs.

Cancelled 1928, $4-6

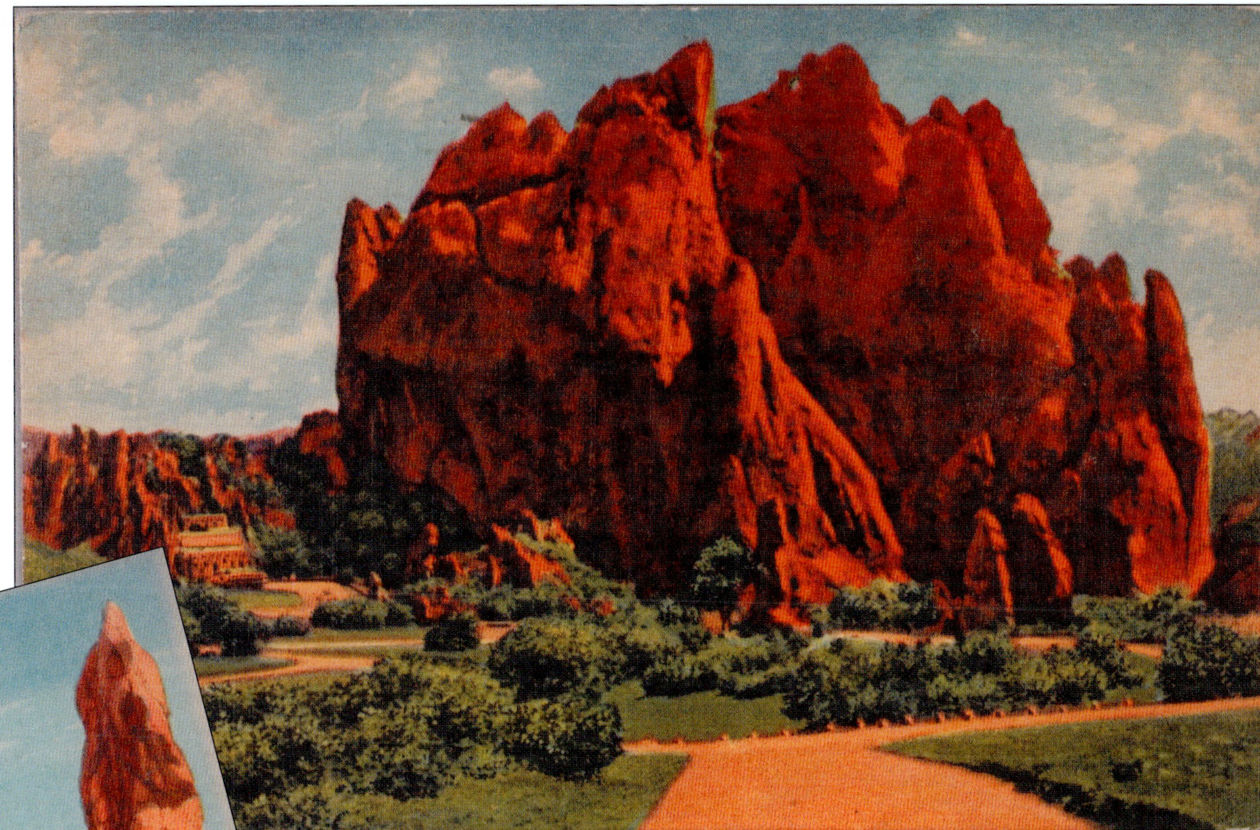

At dawn on Easter Sunday a church service is held in the Garden of the Gods just as the sun rises over Gateway Rock. One of several ongoing activities held in the Garden annually, it has served to draw thousands of visitors to the park since the first service was held in 1921.

Cancelled 1958, $4-6

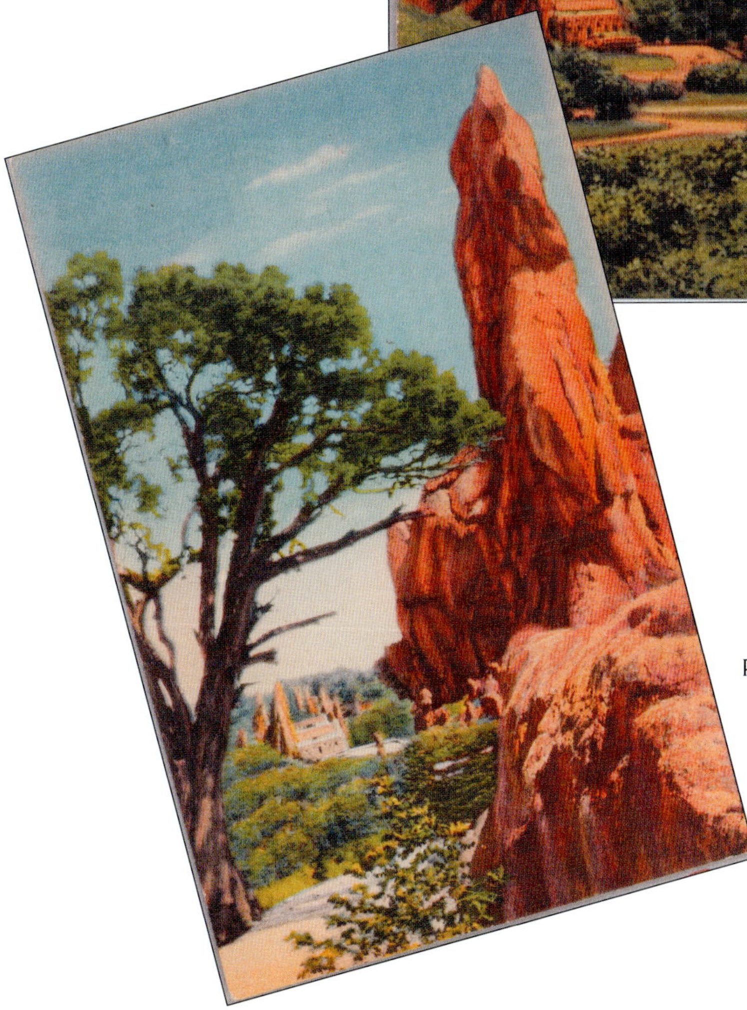

Pulpit Rock and the Hidden Inn.

Circa 1940s, $4-6

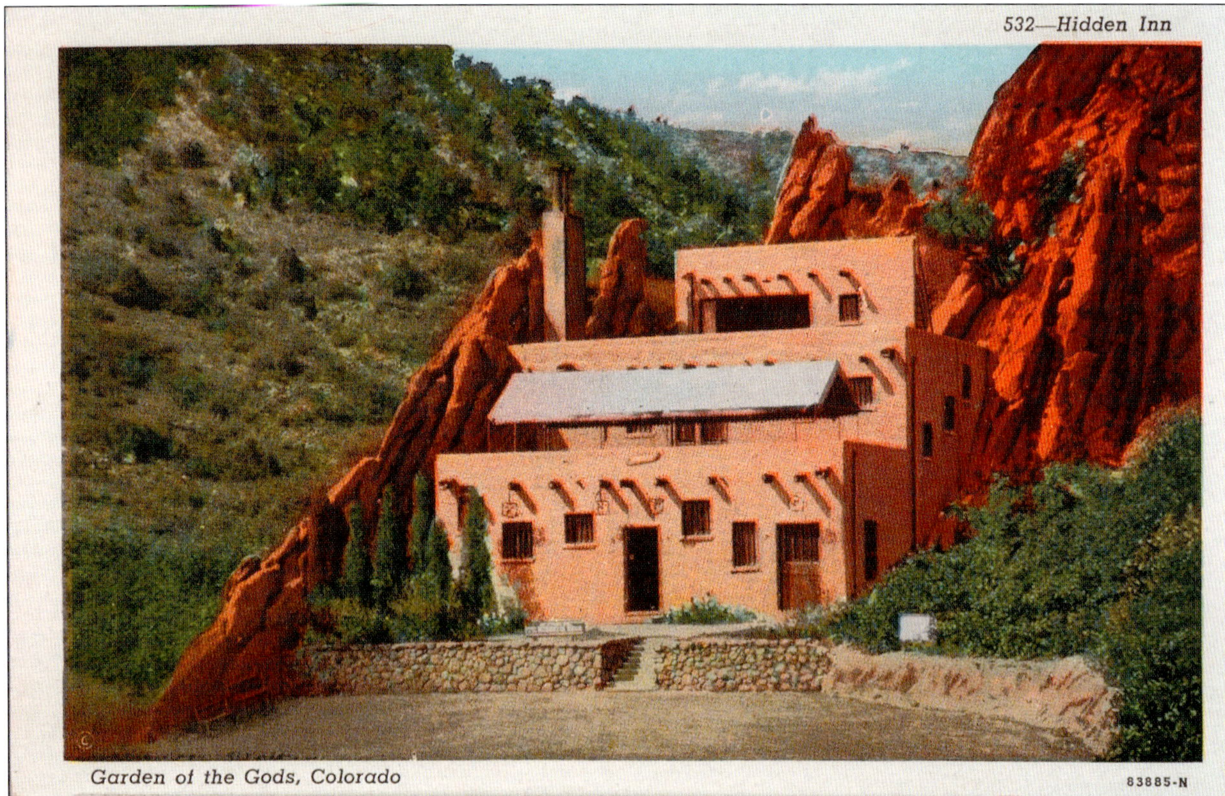

The Hidden Inn was built by the Park Commission of Colorado Springs in 1914 so that visitors to the Garden of the Gods would have a place to rest and partake of some refreshments.

Circa 1920s, $4-6

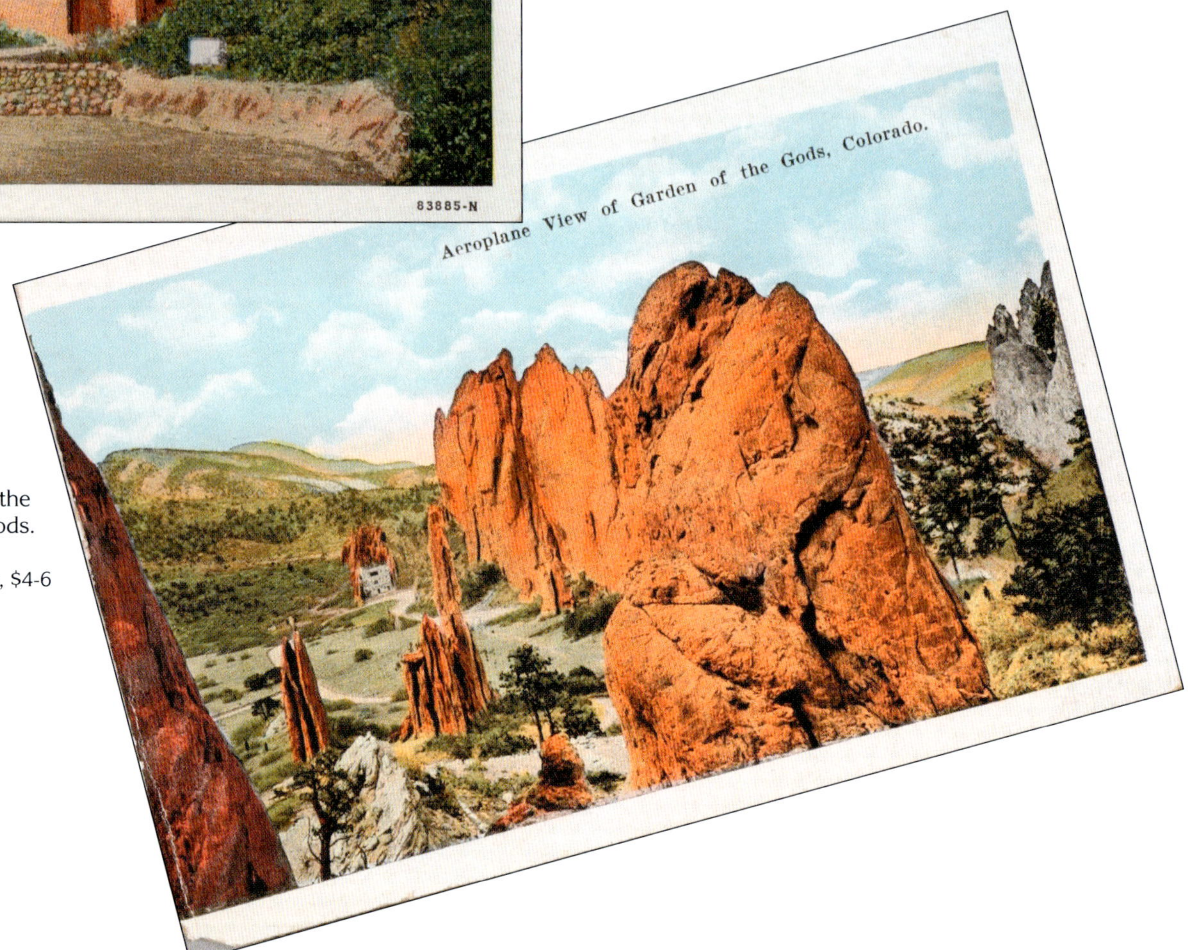

An aerial view of the Garden of the Gods.

Circa 1920s, $4-6

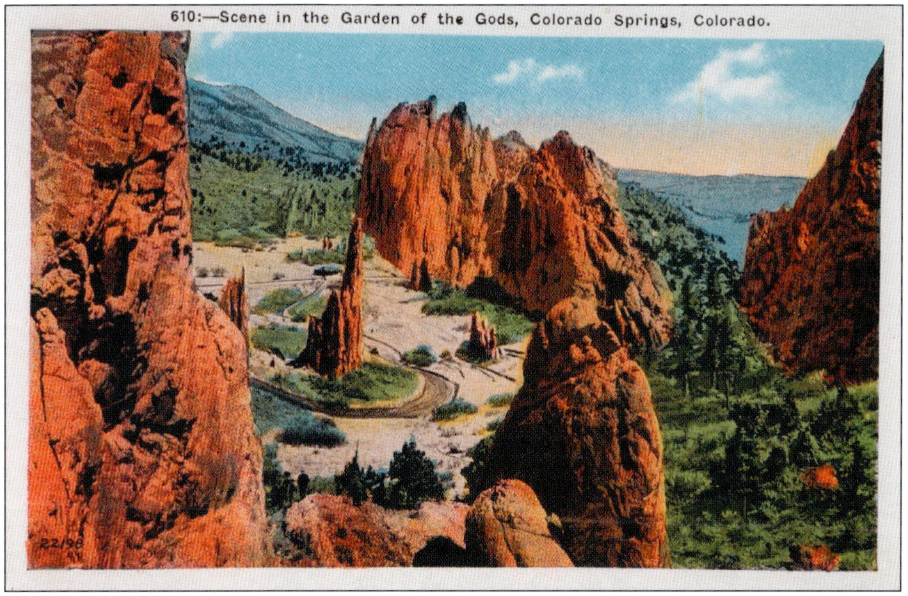

The formations in the Garden of the Gods are made from red sandstone. They are called hogback formations because the layers in the sandstone ridges are vertical or tilted instead of horizontal, resembling the back of a pig.

Circa 1920s, $4-6

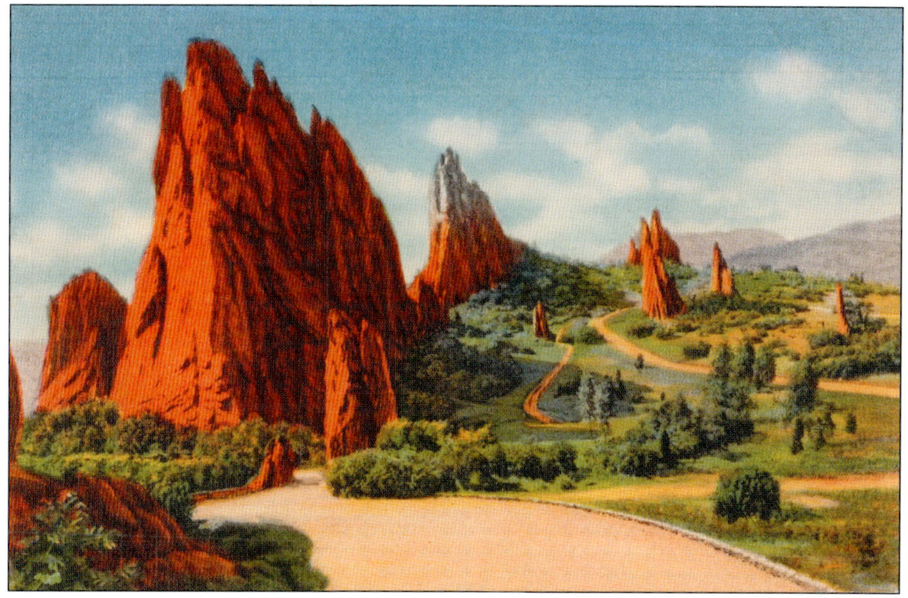

The first people to visit the Garden of the Gods were prehistoric hunters who camped, foraged, and hunted in the Garden. Recently, discoveries have revealed campsites, bones, and stone tools 3,300 years old.

Circa 1940s, $4-6

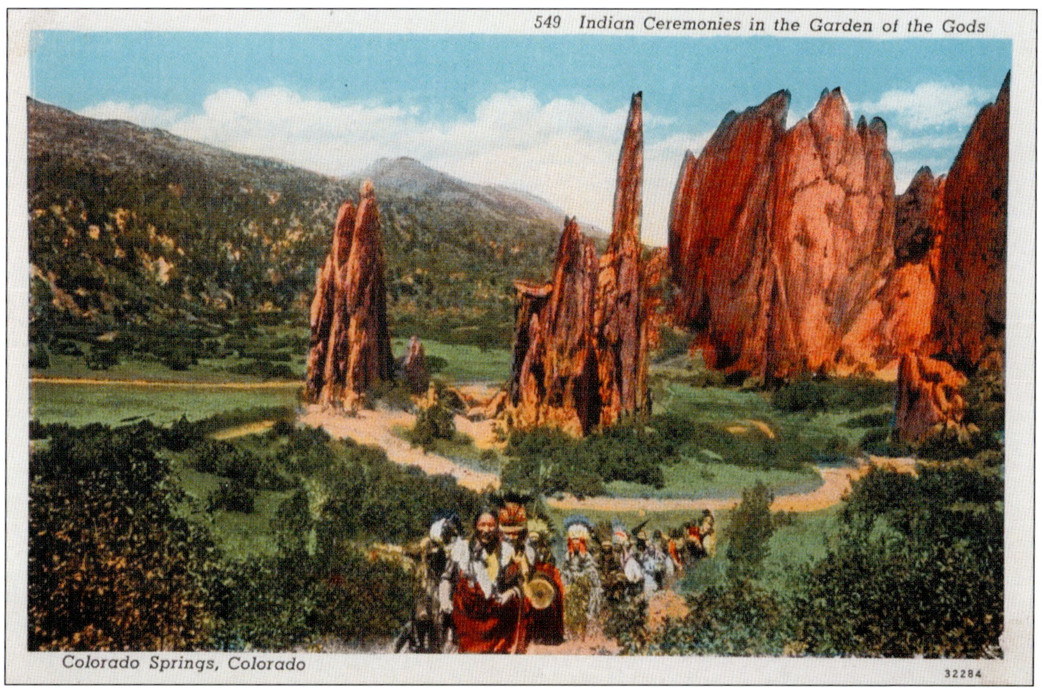

Before the arrival of Anglo settlers, the Ute Indians used the Garden of the Gods as a winter camp before traveling through Ute Pass to their hunting grounds in South Park.

Circa 1920s, $4-6

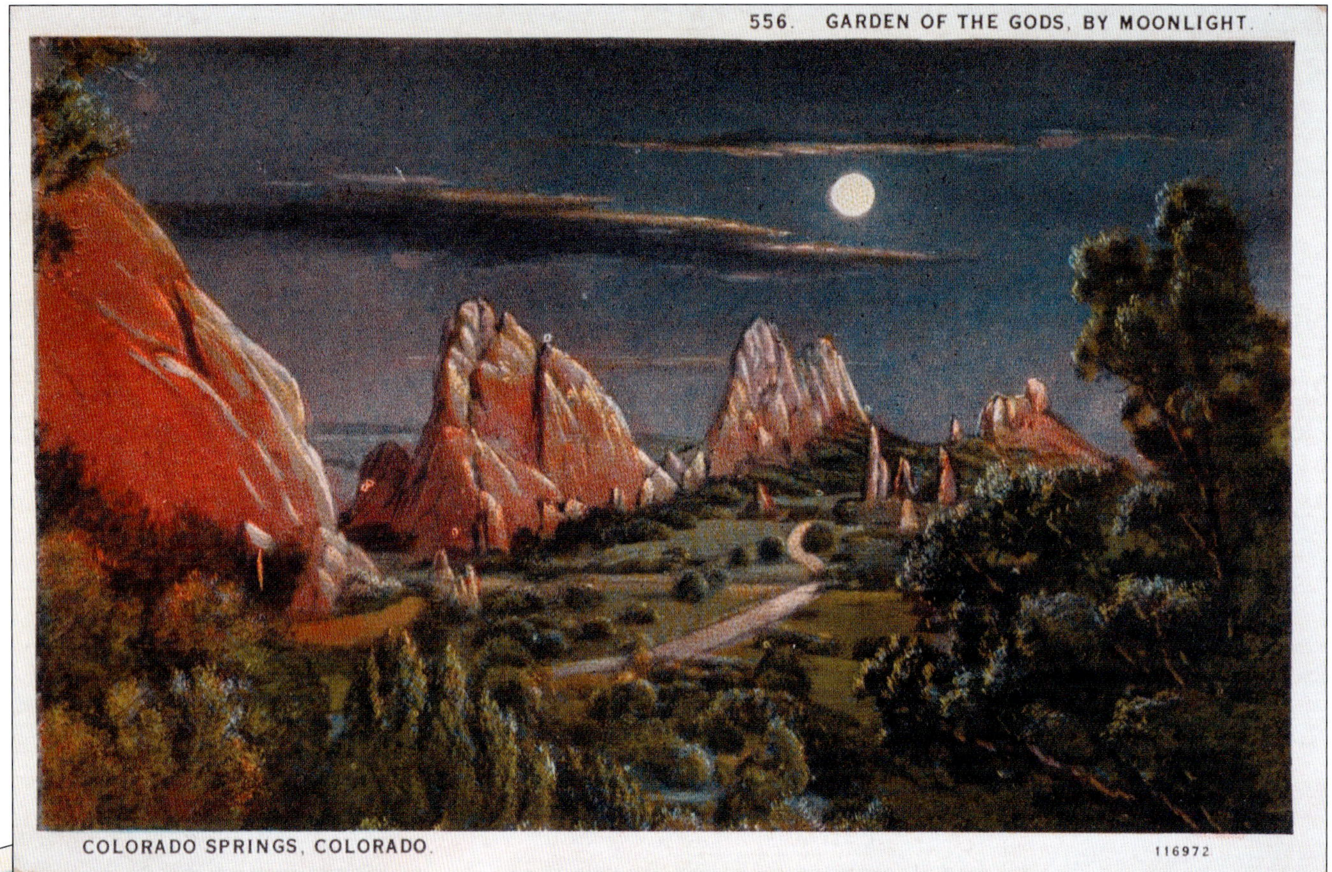

From the back: "By moonlight the Garden is more wonderful than ever, with the great masses of rock dimly outlined and the moonlight gleaming over its bright surfaces."

Circa 1920s, $4-6

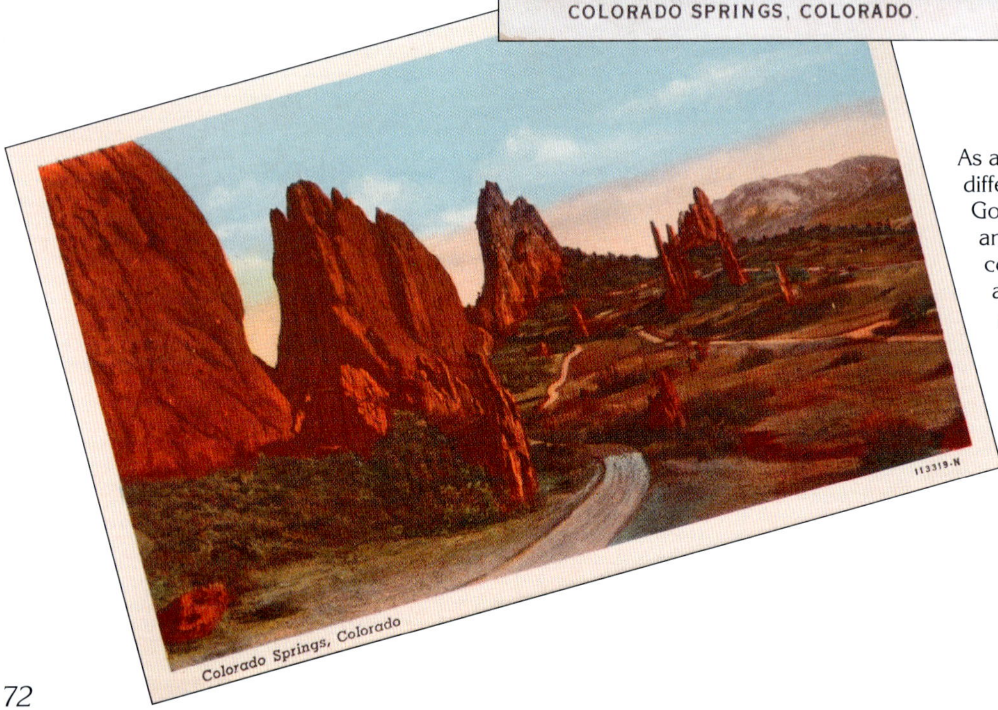

As an ecotone, a transition area where several different ecosystems meet, the Garden of the Gods is well known for the diversity of flora and fauna within its boundaries. It is often compared to the United States of America as the United States are a convergence of many different peoples and cultures and the Garden of the Gods is a convergence of many different plants and animals.

Circa 1920s, $4-6

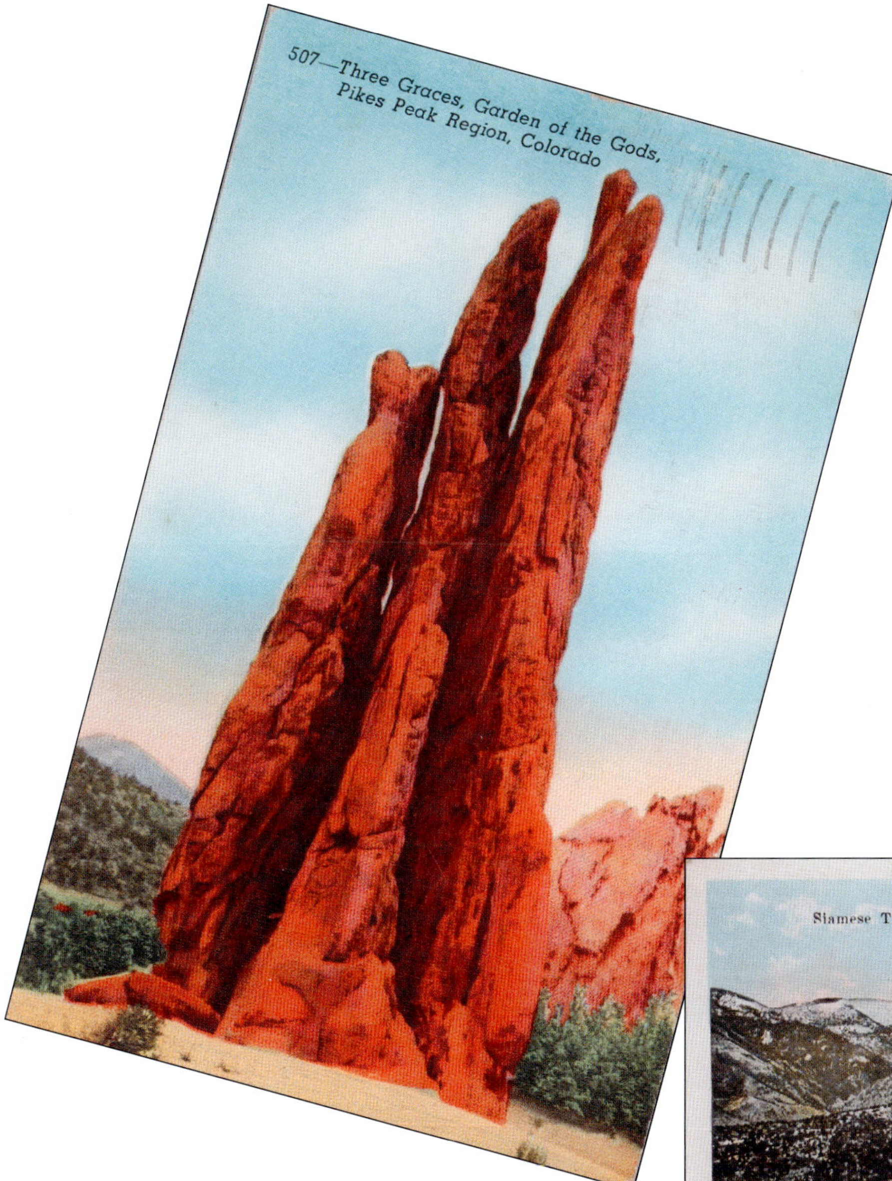

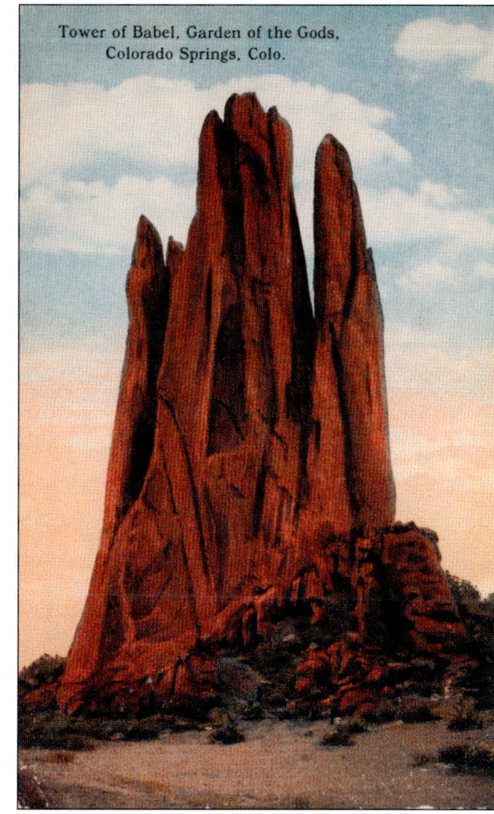

Many of the formations in the Garden of the Gods were given classical or biblical names, like the Tower of Babel pictured here, named after the tower mentioned in the Book of Genesis in the Bible.

Circa 1920s, $4-6

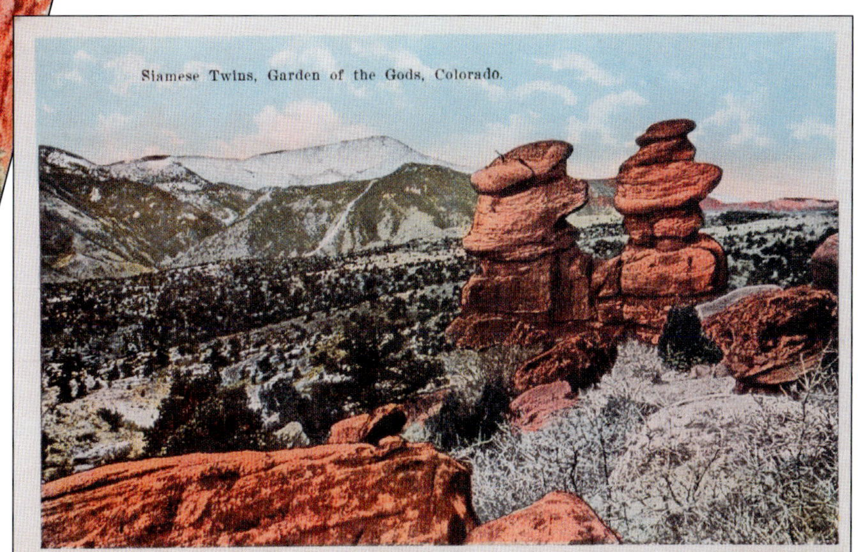

The Three Graces, one of many formations in the Garden of the Gods. In Greek Mythology, the Three Graces (or Charities) were the personification of charm and beauty in both the human and natural worlds. They are often depicted in art and many classical works make reference to them.

Cancelled 1950, $4-6

The Siamese Twins, from the back: "Two grotesque figures about 50 feet in height. It was because of such fantastic formations that the Garden of the Gods was named."

Circa 1920s, $4-6

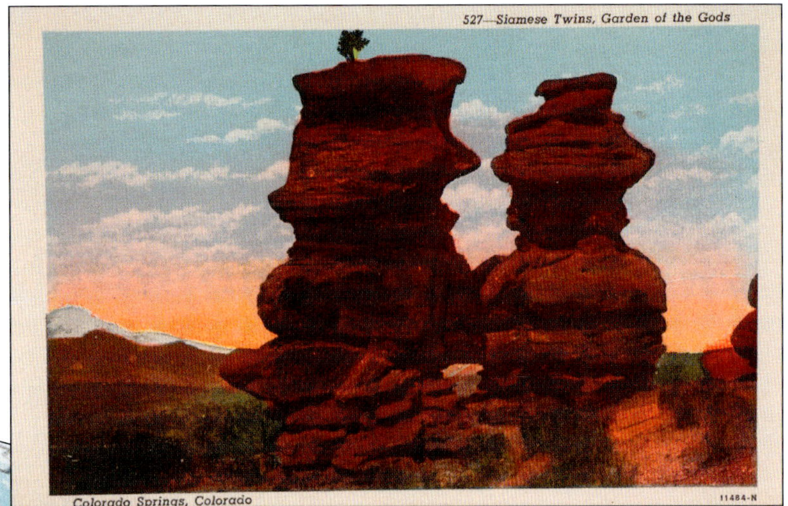

The Siamese Twins are among the first formations a visitor to the Garden will see after traveling through Mushroom Park.

Circa 1920s, $4-6

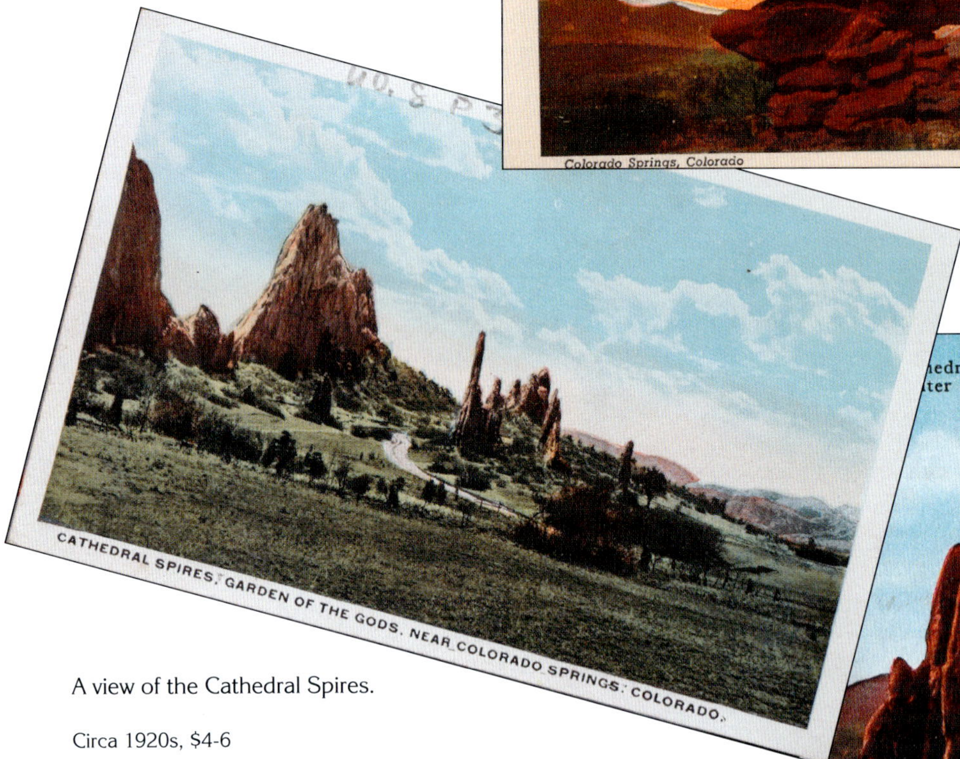

A view of the Cathedral Spires.

Circa 1920s, $4-6

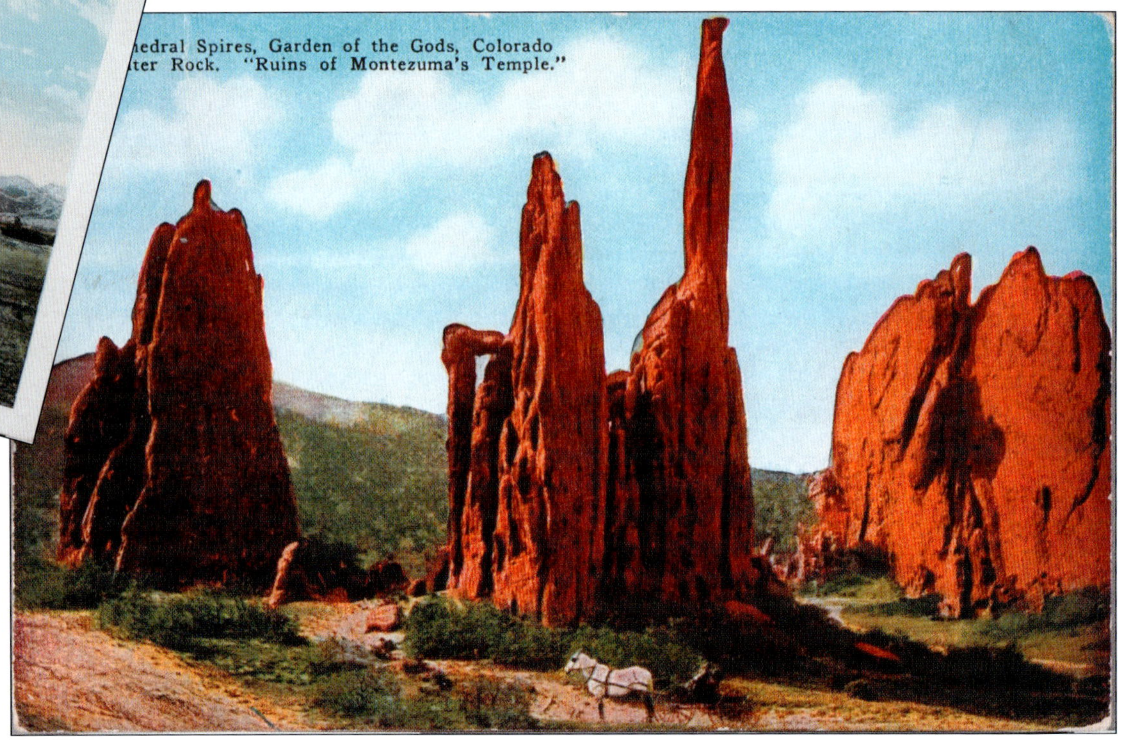

The Cathedral Spires, also known as the Ruins of Montezuma's Temple.

Cancelled 1920, $4-6

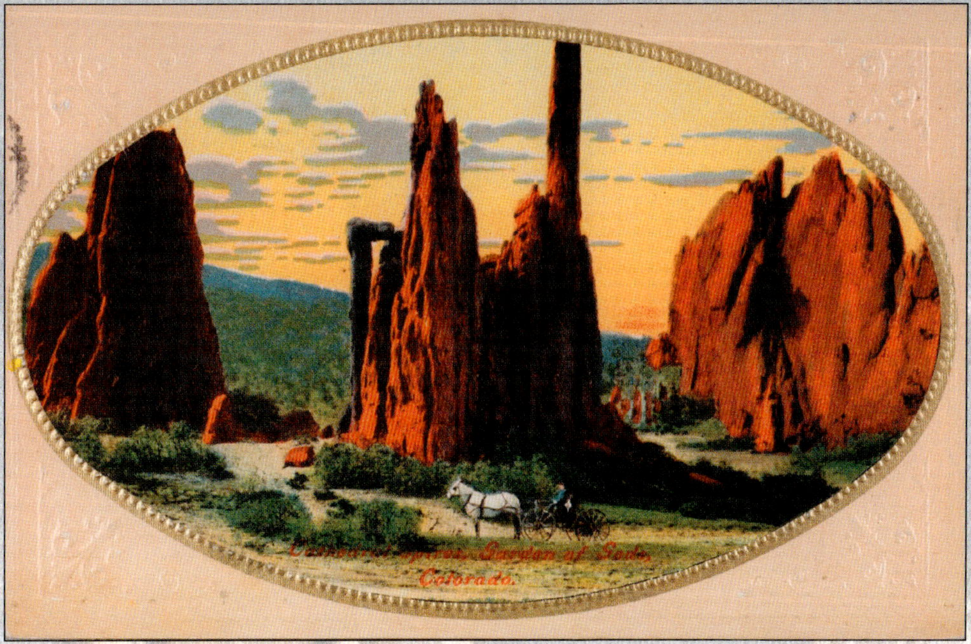

Tourists in a horse-drawn carriage pose in front of the Cathedral Spires.

Cancelled 1911, $4-6

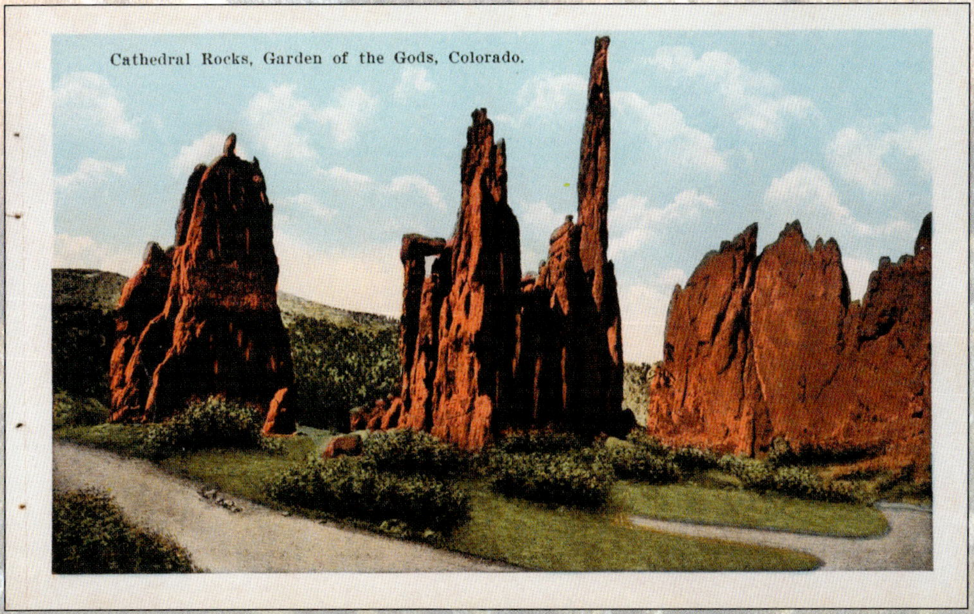

Standing 250 feet tall, the Cathedral Spires are among the first formations seen after passing through the Gateway to the Garden of the Gods.

Circa 1920s, $4-6

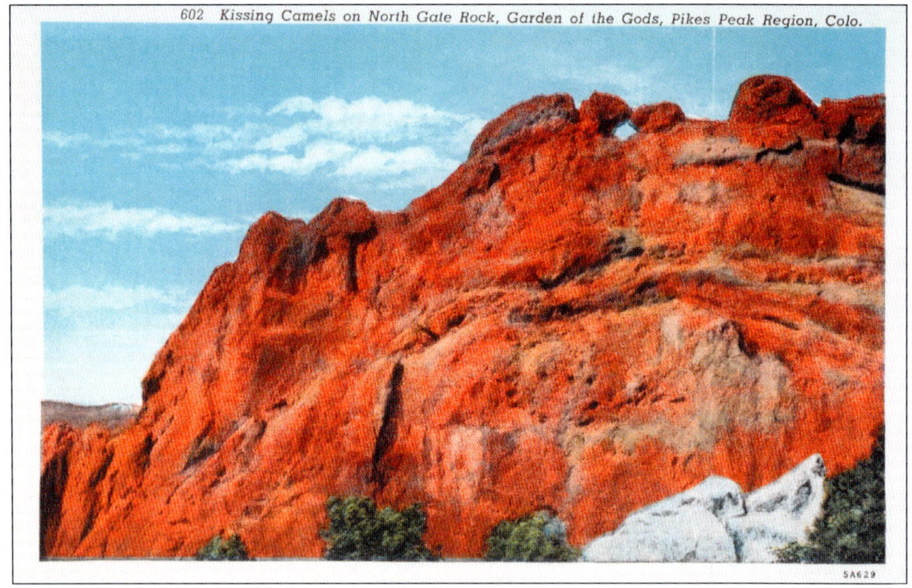

Located on the top of Gateway Rock, the Kissing Camels are among the most visible formations in the park.

Circa 1920s, $4-6

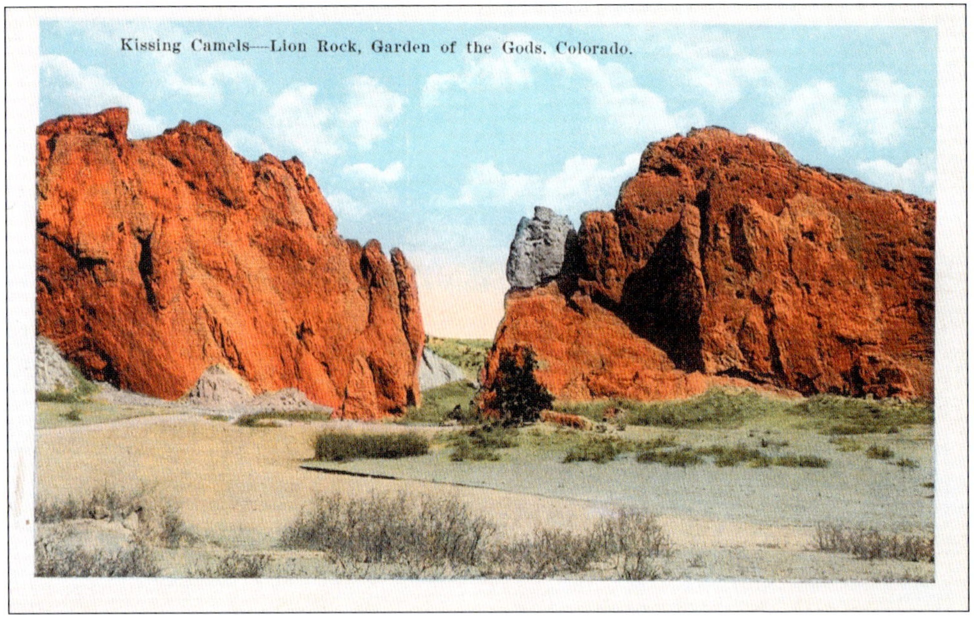

Lion Rock and the Kissing Camels.

Circa 1920s, $4-6

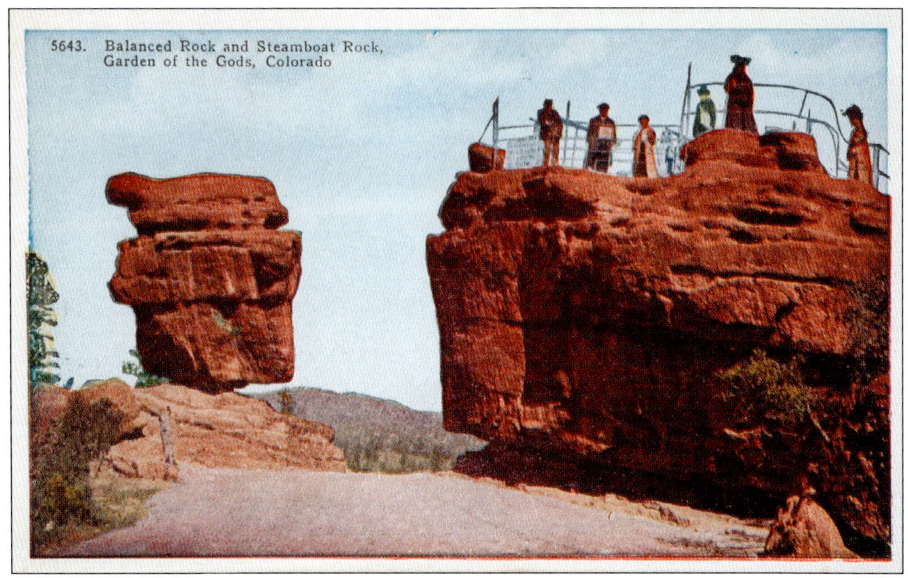

Balanced and Steamboat Rocks, two formations located in the southern end of the Garden.

Circa 1930s, $4-6

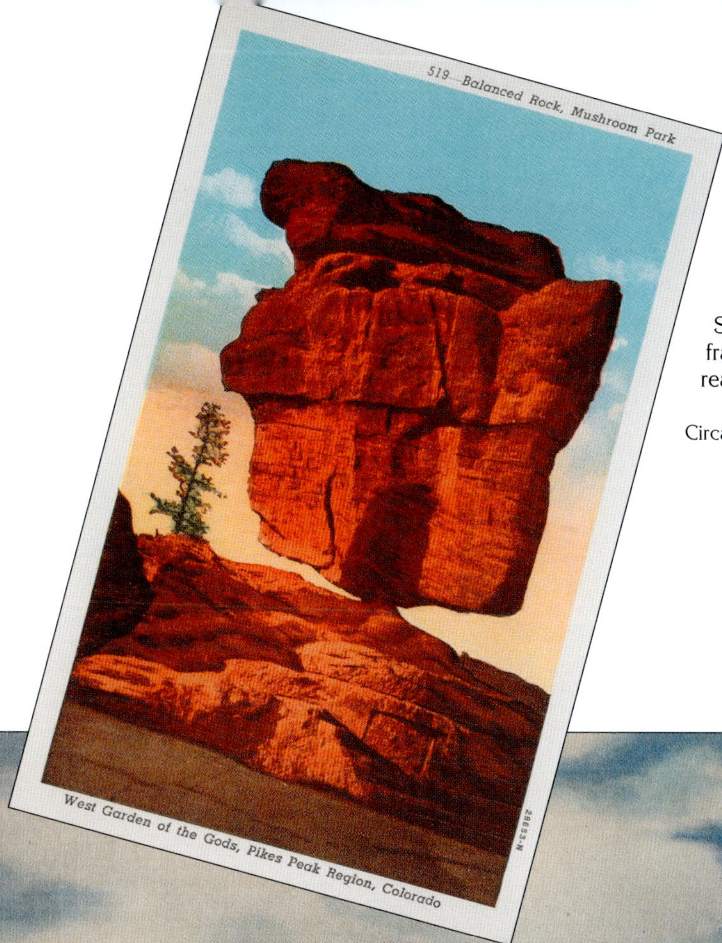

Sitting precariously atop a seemingly frail base, Balanced Rock appears ready to topple at any moment.

Circa 1940s, $4-6

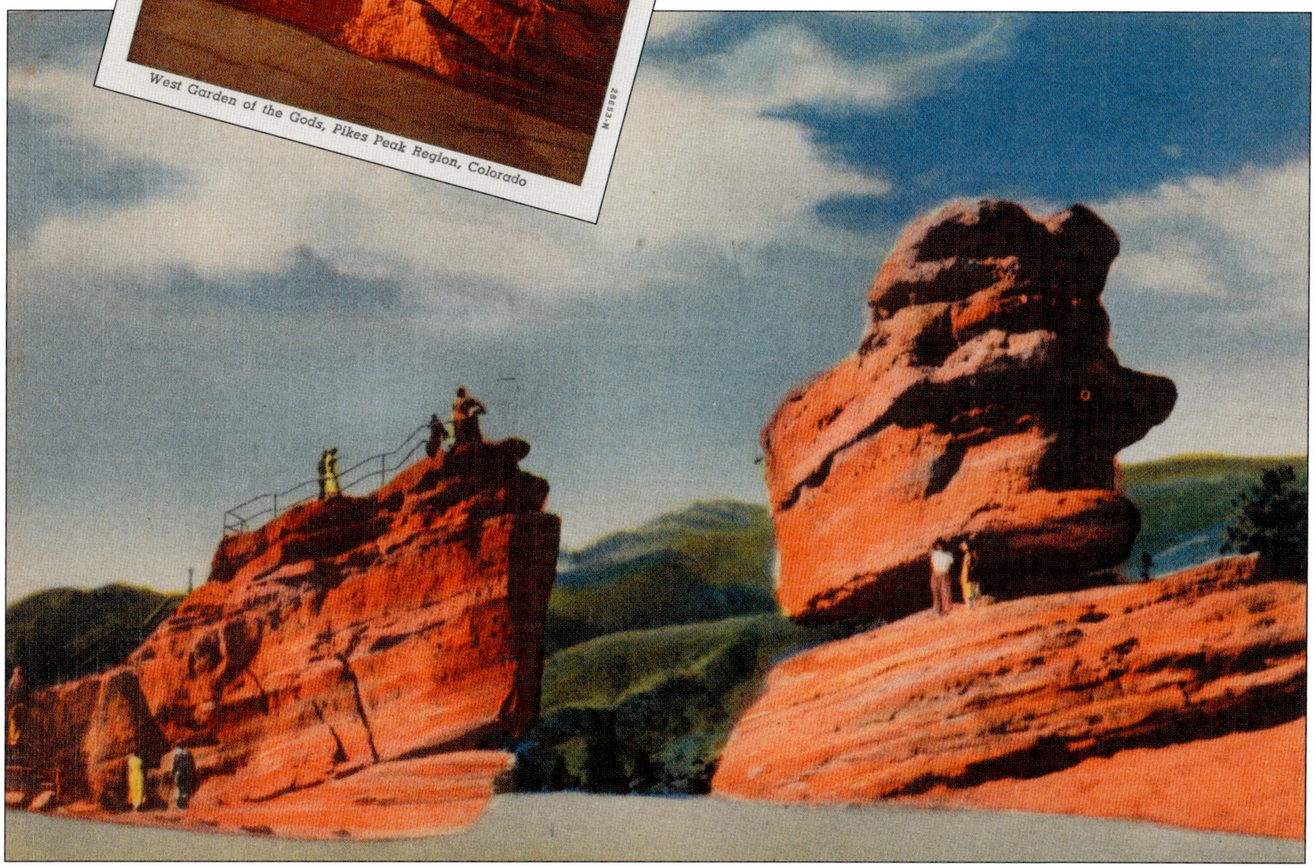

Steamboat Rock, named for its resemblance to the prow of a steamboat.

Circa 1940s, $4-6

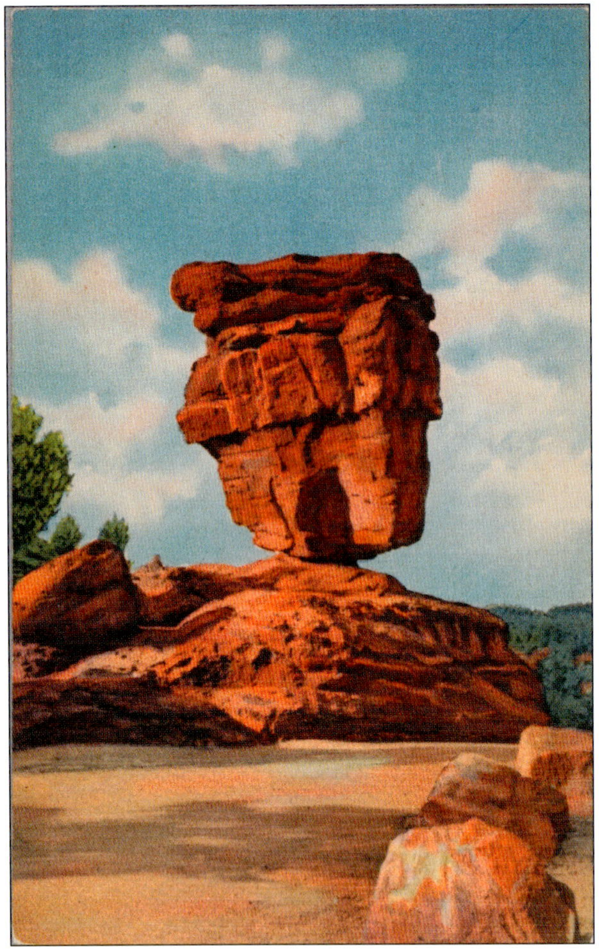

Before it became part of the Garden of the Gods, Balanced Rock was part of the privately owned Mushroom Park. The owners of the park did not charge visitors admission, but reserved the right to photograph Balanced Rock.

Circa 1940s, $4-6

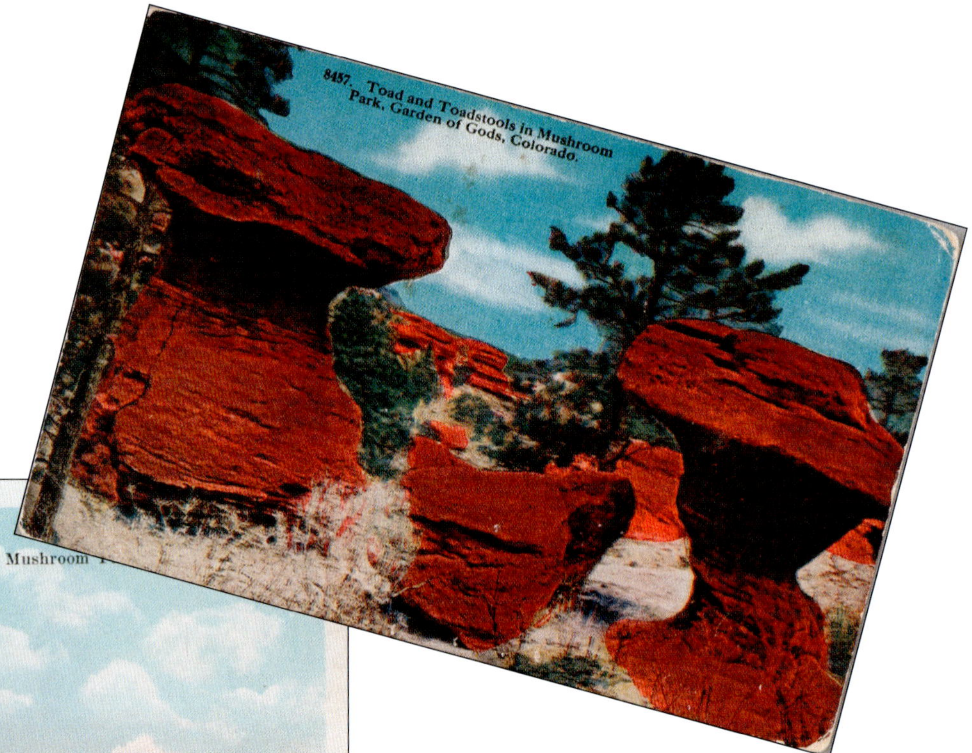

Toad and Toadstools, some of the many mushroom-shaped formations that gave Mushroom Park its name.

Circa 1930s, $4-6

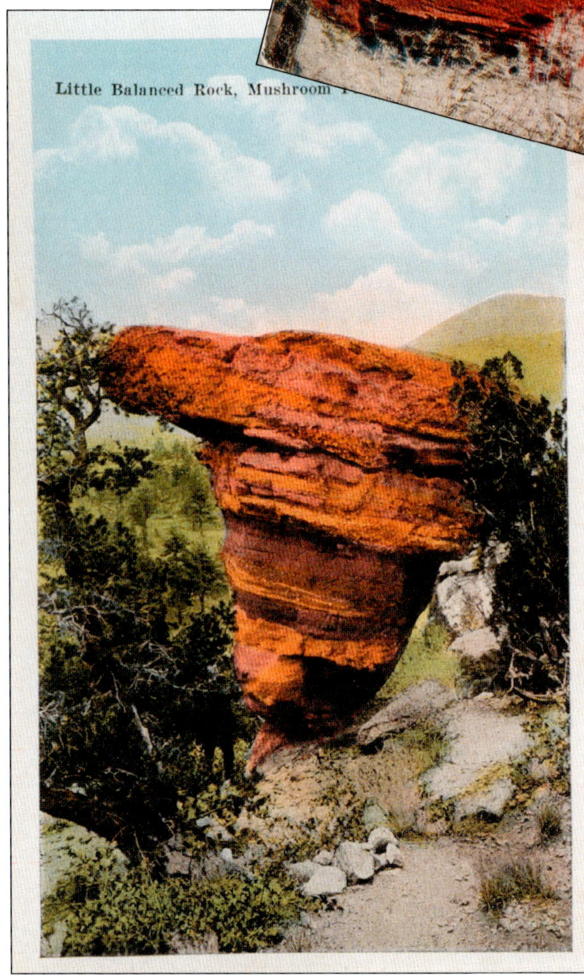

Little Balanced Rock, so named to distinguish it from its larger cousin, Balanced Rock.

Circa 1920s, $4-6

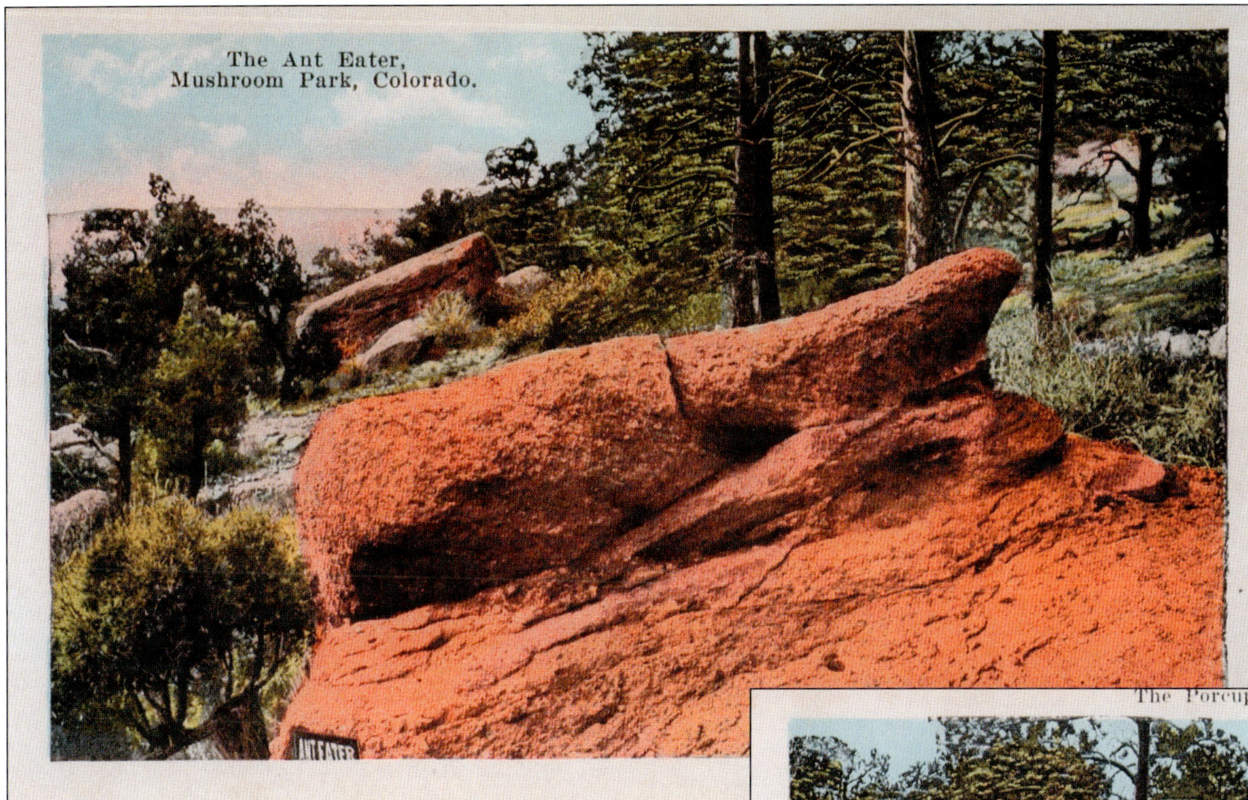

Ten feet long and sitting on a base of red sandstone, the Anteater is situated near Balanced Rock.

Circa 1920s, $4-6

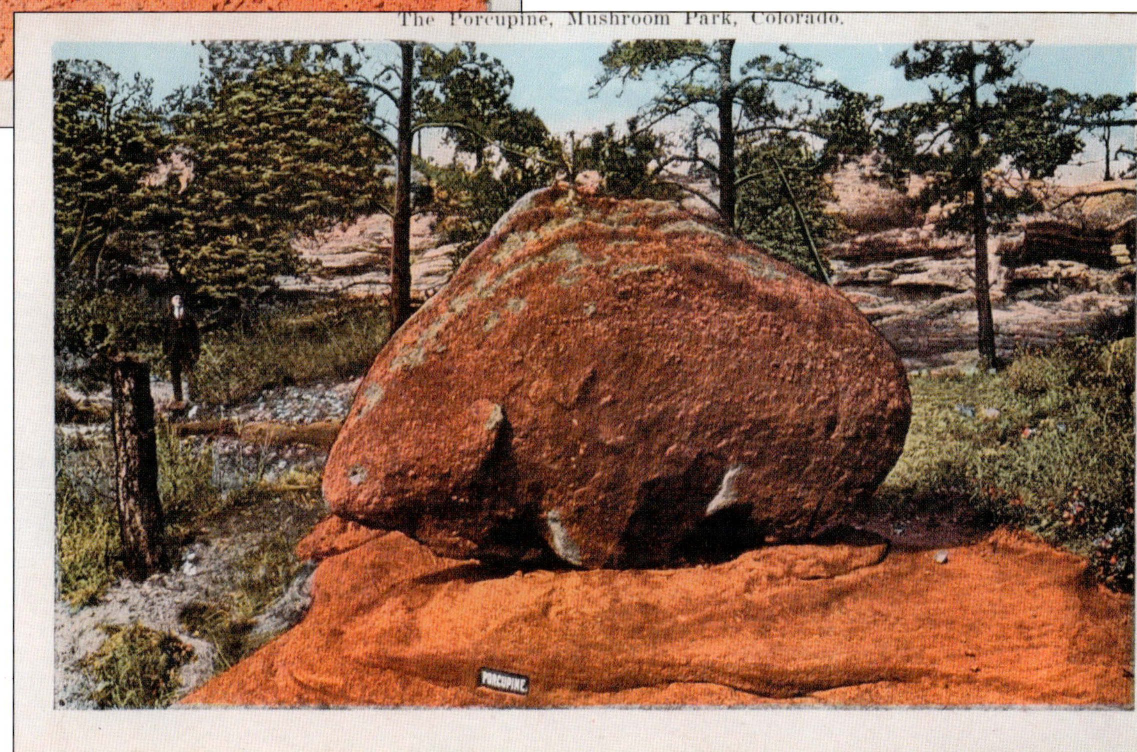

The Porcupine, another of the many unusual formations found in the Garden of the Gods.

Circa 1920s, $4-6

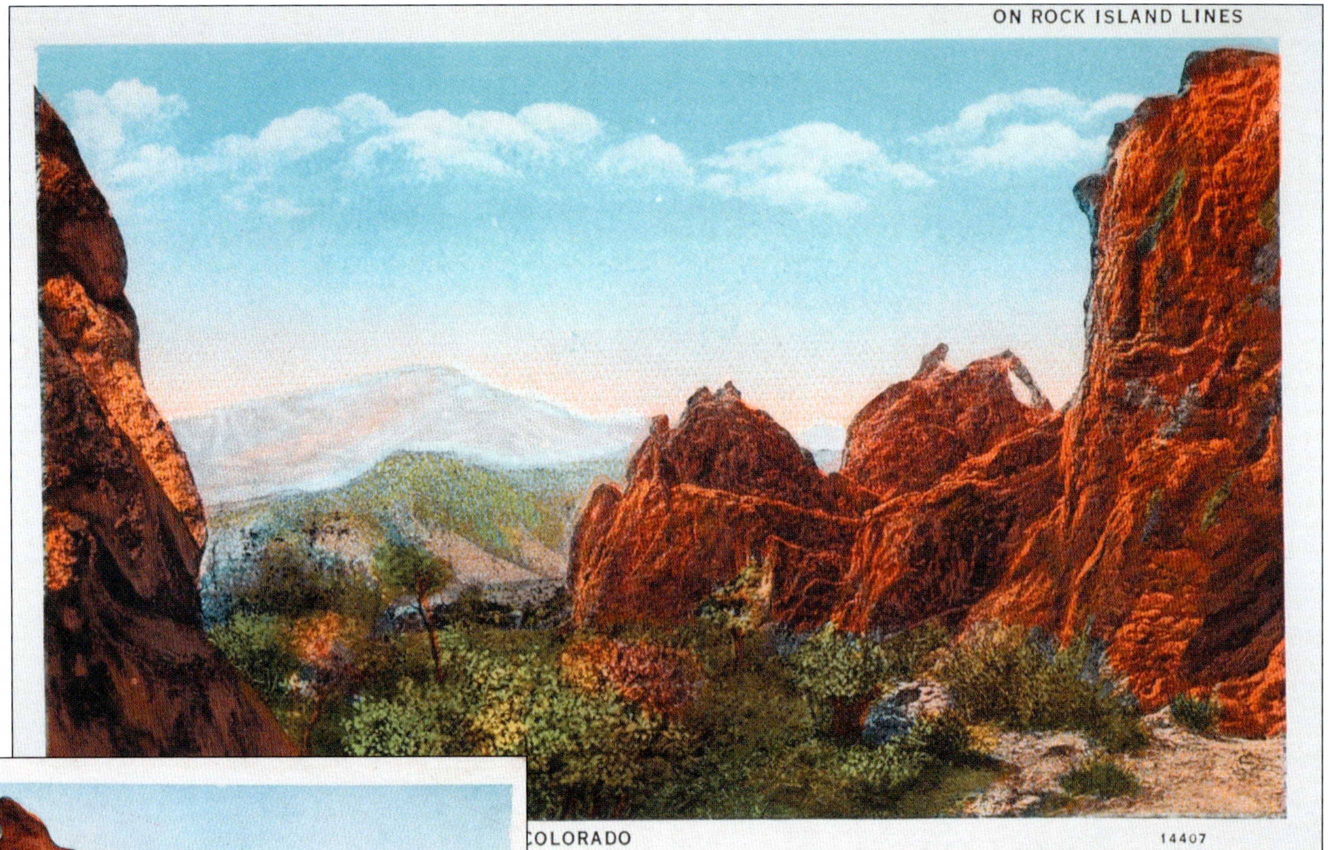

The Seal and the Bear.

Circa 1920s, $4-6

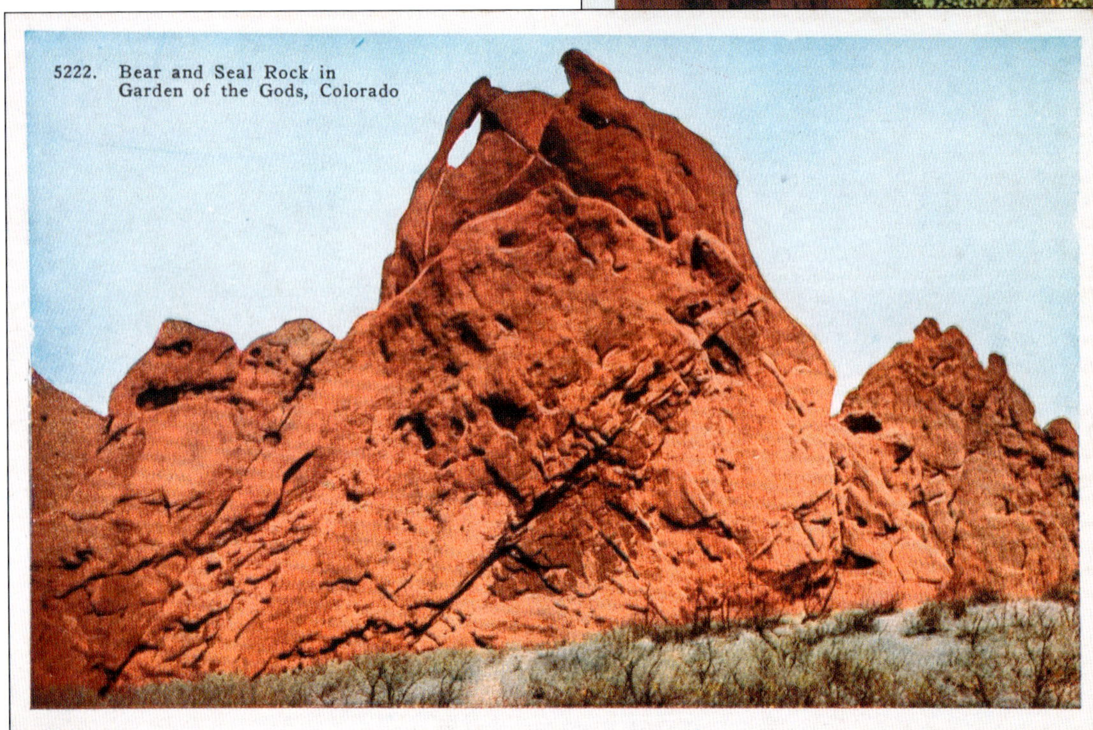

Many of the formations in the Garden of the Gods so closely resembled their namesakes that it was speculated that they were sculpted instead of naturally formed.

Circa 1920s, $4-6

Glen Eyrie

When he settled in Colorado Springs, General Palmer set aside 2,225 acres in a valley near the Garden of the Gods for his personal estate. The first building built on the estate was a carriage house, which he and his family lived in while the main house was being built. A twenty-two room frame house, it was remodeled in 1881, with a tower and additional rooms added on.

General Palmer, his wife Queen, and their three daughters, Elsie, Dorothy, and Marjorie, lived in Glen Eyrie until 1880 when Queen Palmer suffered a heart attack. Her doctors advised her to move to a lower altitude, which she did, relocating, with her daughters, to the East Coast and eventually to England. General Palmer remained at his estate, visiting his family as often as he could. He continued to live at Glen Eyrie until his death on March 13, 1909, at the age of seventy-two.

The estate was eventually bought by George W. Strake in 1938 for $350,000. He then sold 1,140 acres, which included the house, to the Navigators, an Evangelical Christian group who are Glen Eyrie's present owners.

The estate was named *Glen Eyrie*, which means "Valley of the Eagle's Nest" in Scots Gaelic, by John Blair a Scottish landscape architect while he was surveying the estate's grounds with General Palmer and his wife after seeing an eagle's nest in the cleft of a nearby rock. Both General and Mrs. Palmer liked the description and adopted it as the estate's official name.

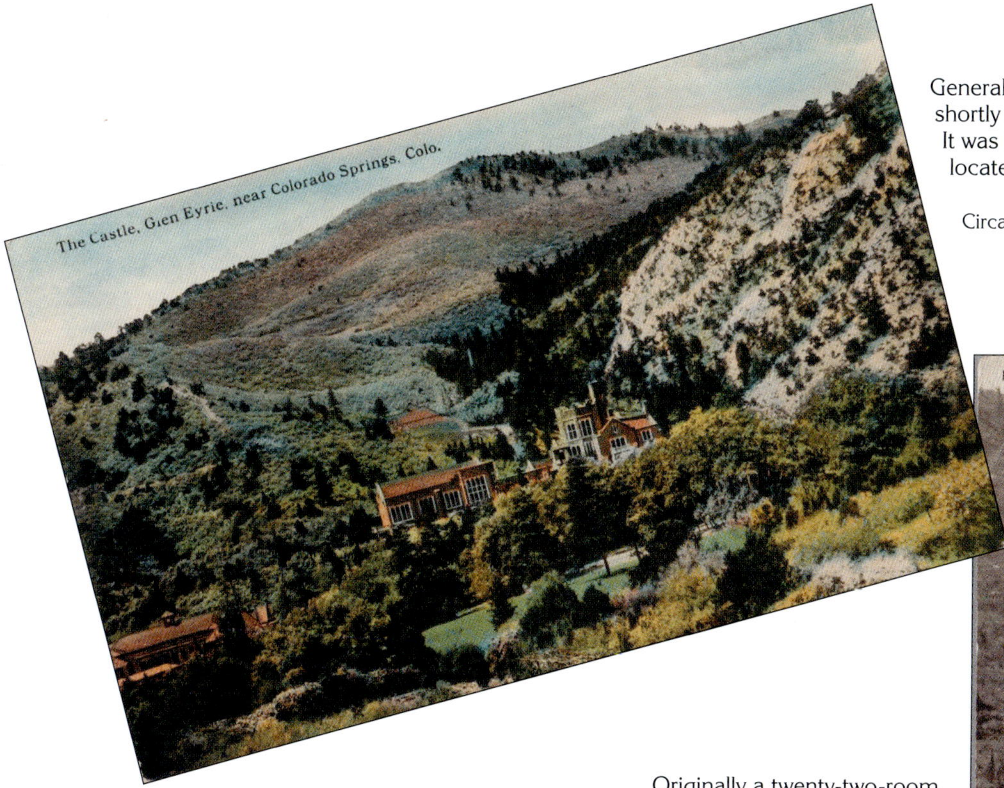

General William Jackson Palmer built Glen Eyrie shortly after he founded Colorado Springs in 1871. It was intended to be his dream home and is located near the Garden of the Gods.

Circa 1910s, $4-6

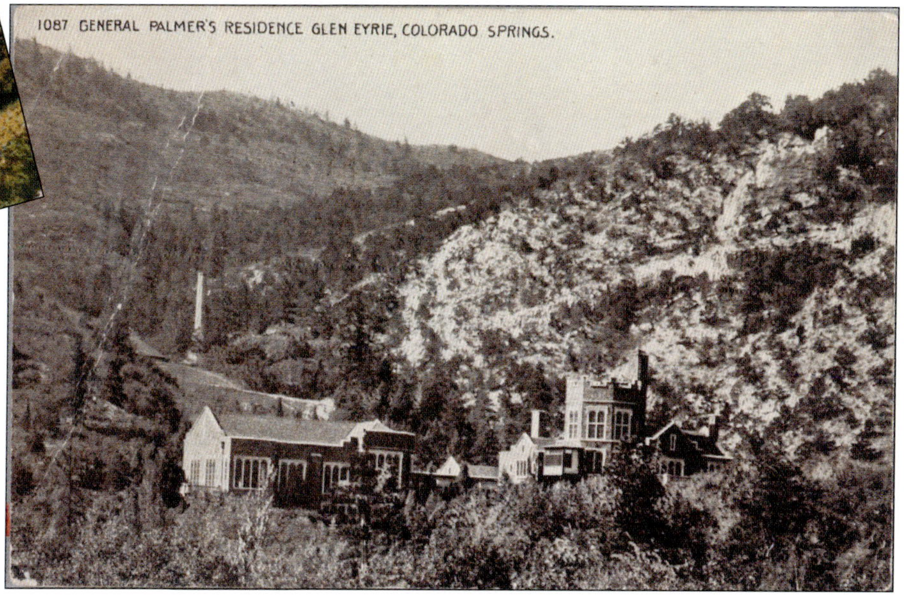

Originally a twenty-two-room frame house, Glen Eyrie was remodeled in 1881 with additional rooms and a tower added on.

Circa 1920s, $4-6

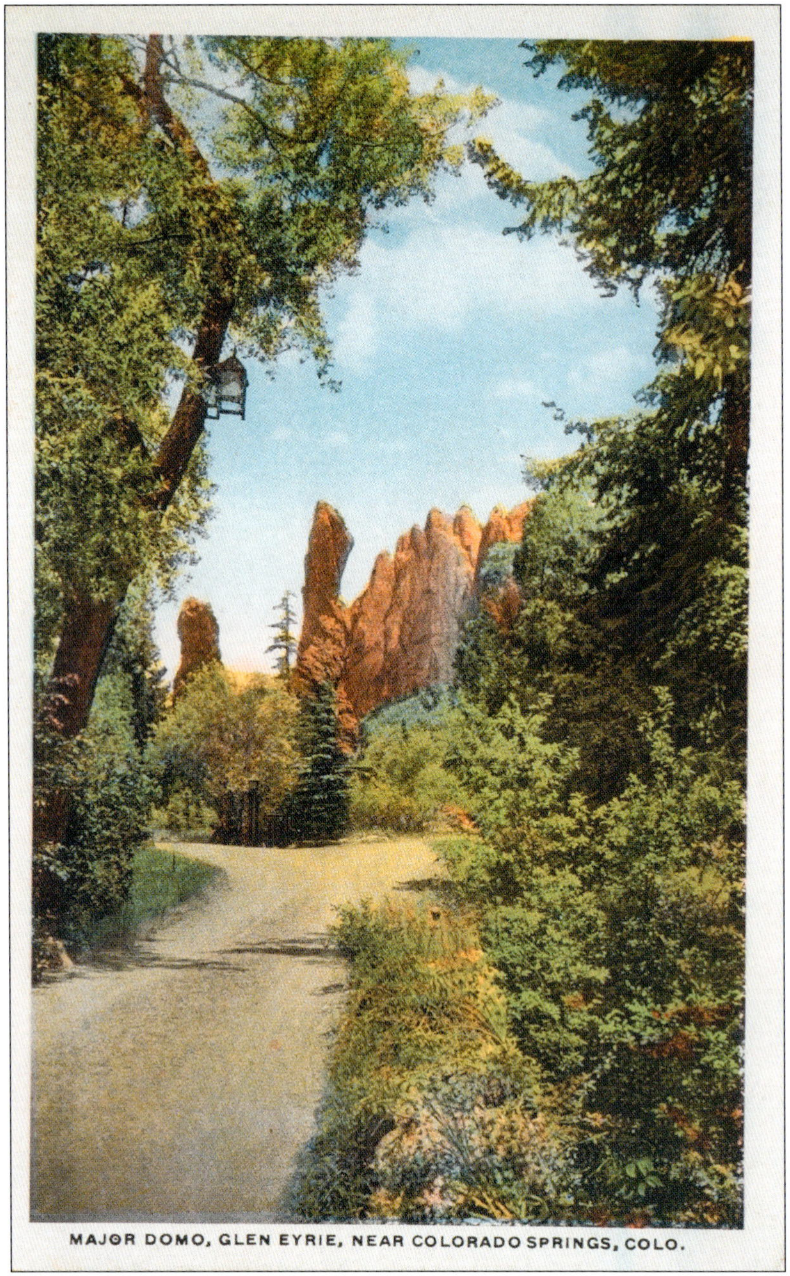

Like its neighbor, the Glen Eyrie Estate was home to a number of unusual sandstone formations and was often referred to as the "Little Garden of the Gods."

Circa 1920s, $4-6

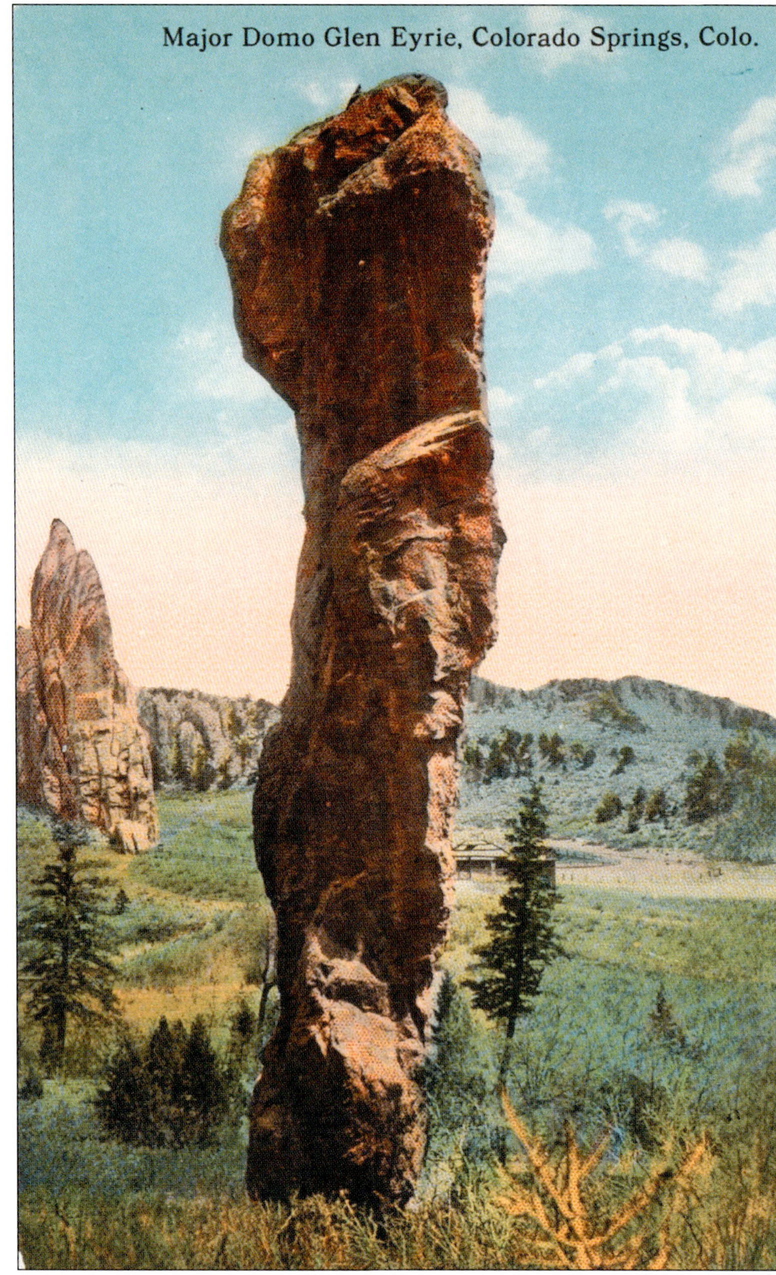

Major Domo, one of the formations found in the "Little Garden of the Gods."

Circa 1910s, $4-6

Highways and Drives

While Colorado Springs was home to a large number of natural curiosities and tourist attractions, very few of them were located inside the city itself. To help visitors get to these destinations the city, along with the private individuals who owned the attractions, financed and built roads leading from the attractions to Colorado Springs. Most of them, like the High Drive and the Crystal Park Auto Road, led to attractions like Bear Creek Regional Park and Crystal Park. Others like the Phantom Cañon and the Corley Mountain Highway were part of larger circuits that led from Colorado Springs to places like Canyon City and the Cripple Creek Mining District. On their way, the highways and drives passed by or through much of the surrounding countryside's best scenery. Eventually they became as much of a tourist attraction as their destinations.

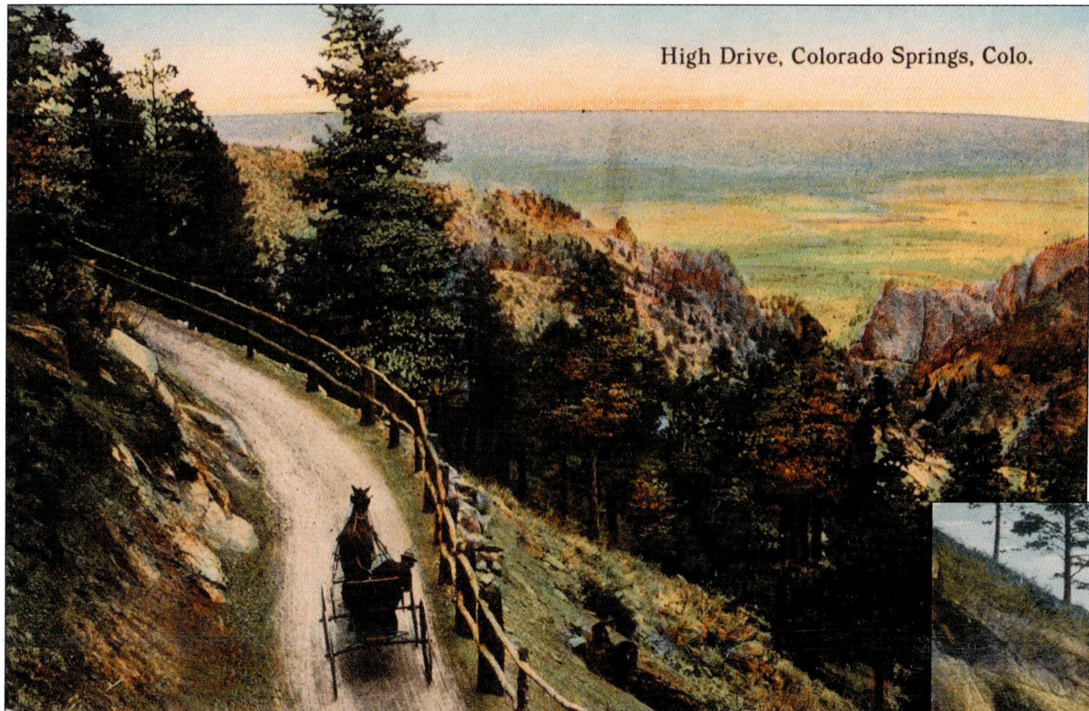

The High Drive runs along the lip of North Cheyenne Cañon and is one the ways to reach the Cañon from Colorado Springs.

Circa 1910s, $4-6

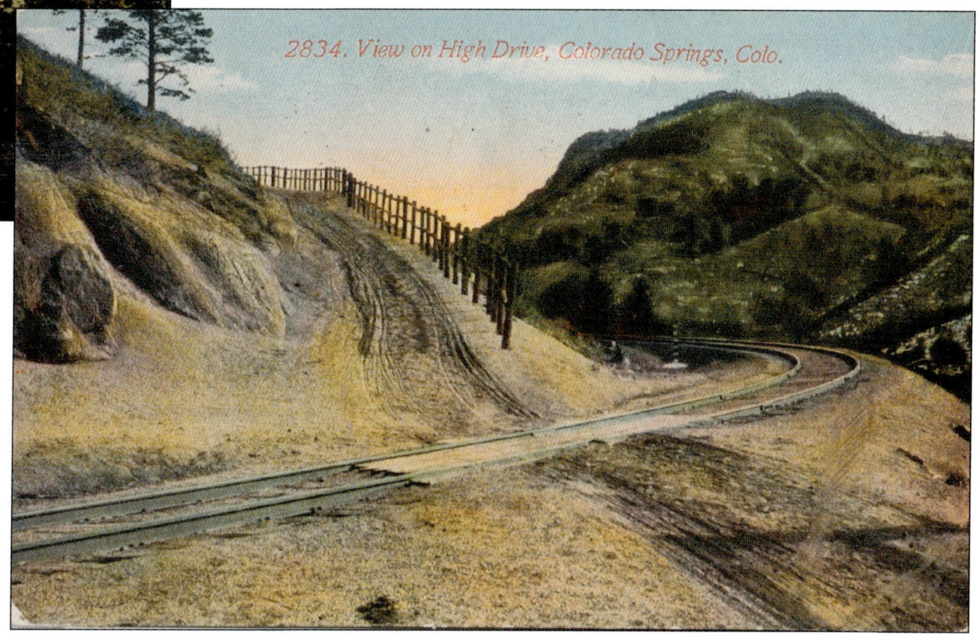

Another view of the High Drive, showing where the road crosses the tracks of the Denver & Rio Grande Railroad.

Cancelled 1912, $5-7

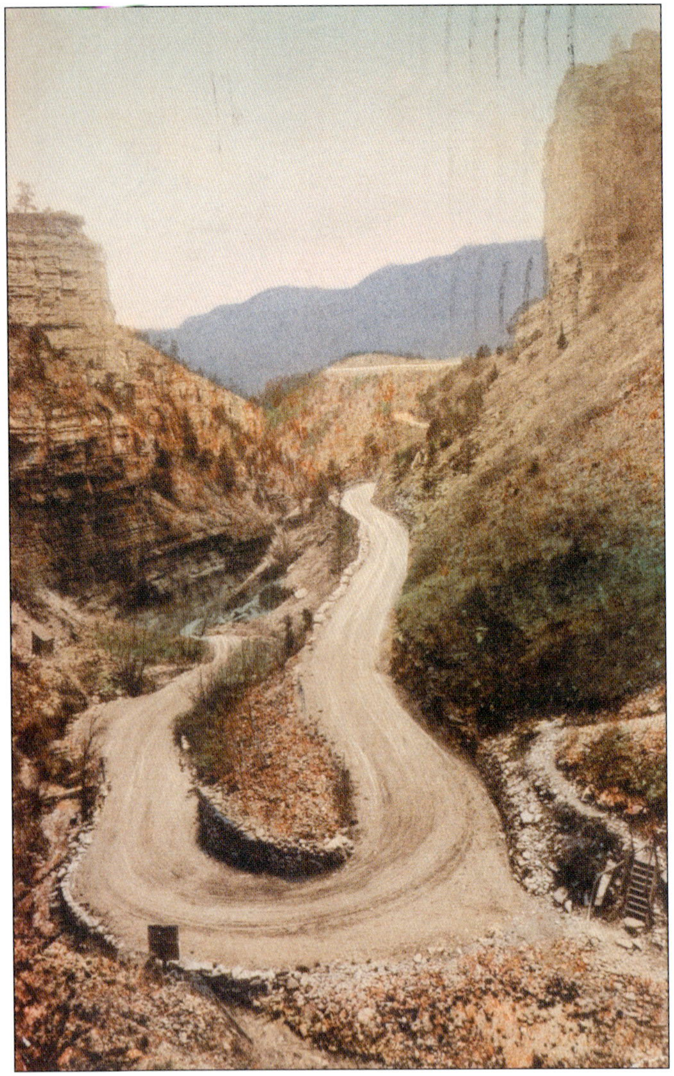

Horseshoe Curve, part of the drive that leads to the Cave of the Winds.

Circa 1928, $4-6

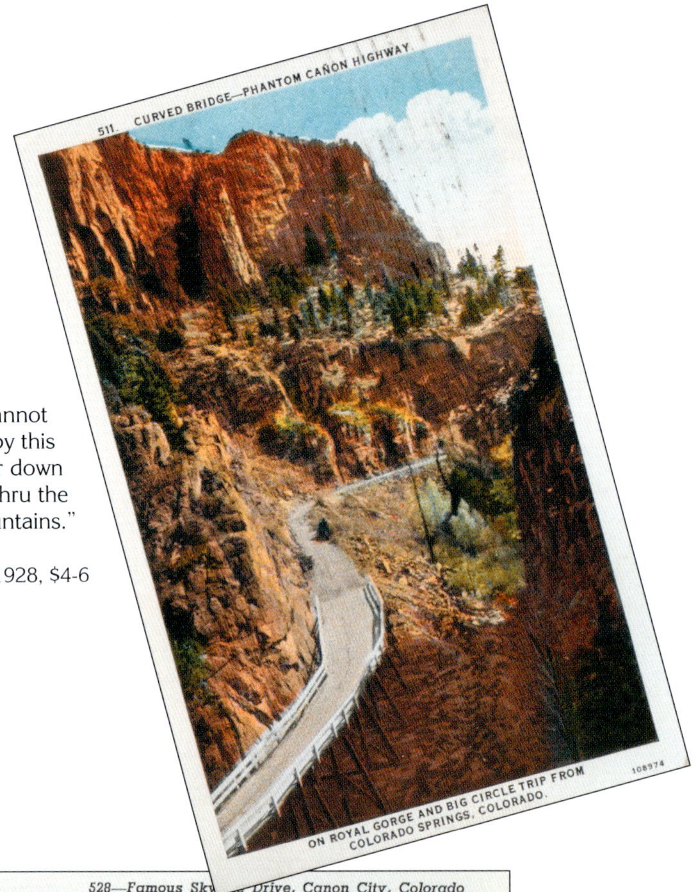

From the back: "One cannot help but be thrilled by this road cutting its way far down tremendous depths, thru the heart of the mountains."

Cancelled 1928, $4-6

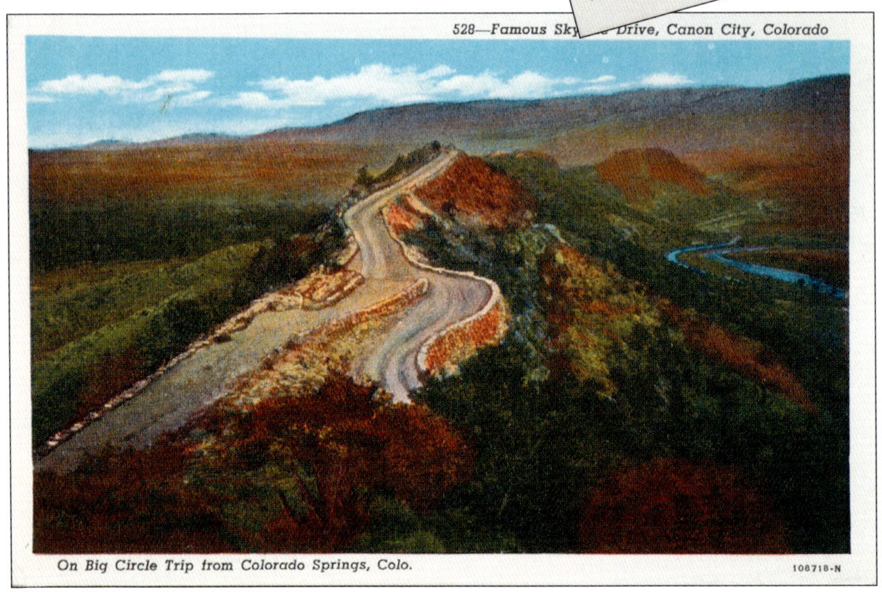

The Skyline Drive leads from Canyon City to Colorado Springs.

Circa 1940s, $4-6

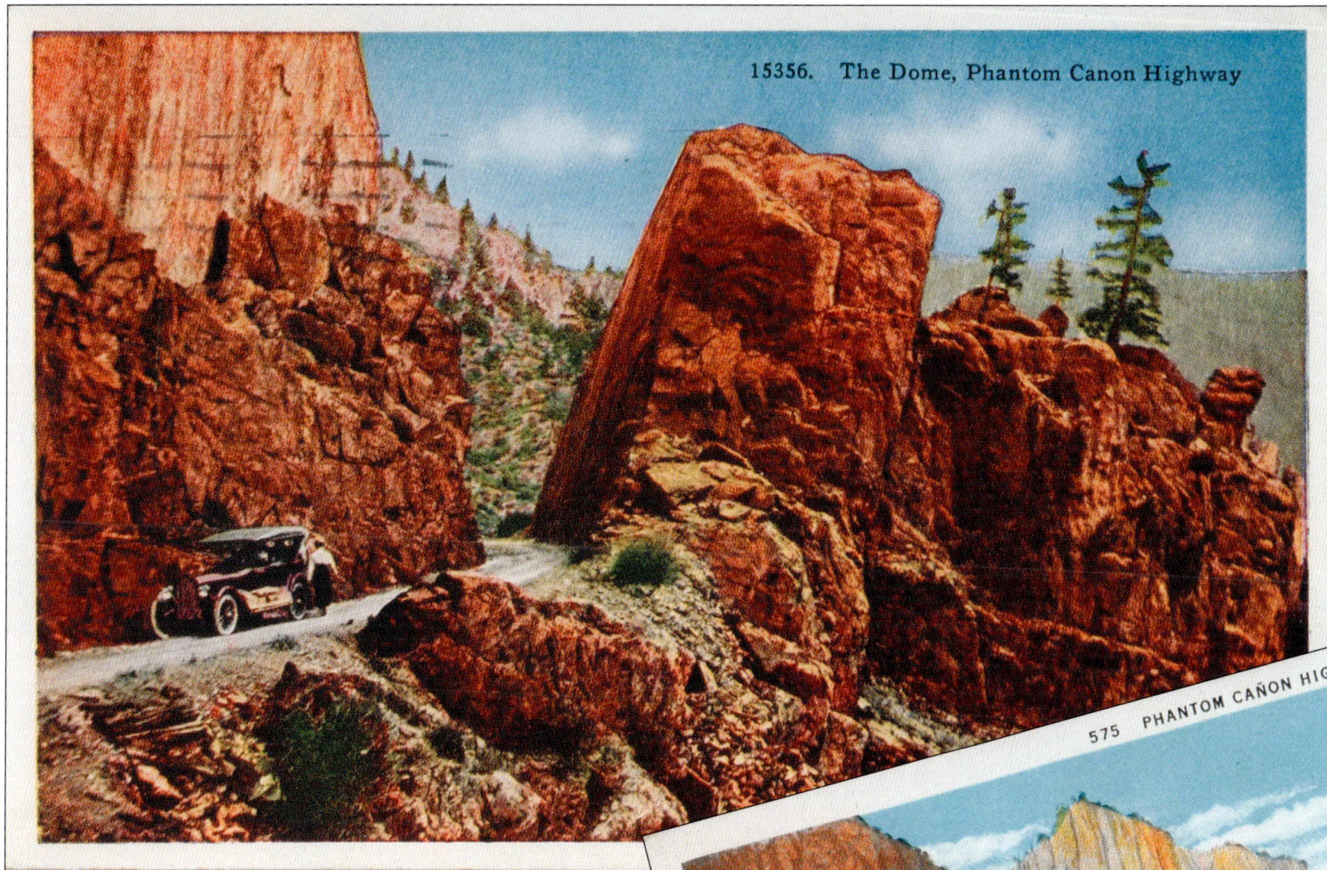

The Dome, a rock formation along the Phantom Cañon Highway.
Cancelled 1928, $4-6

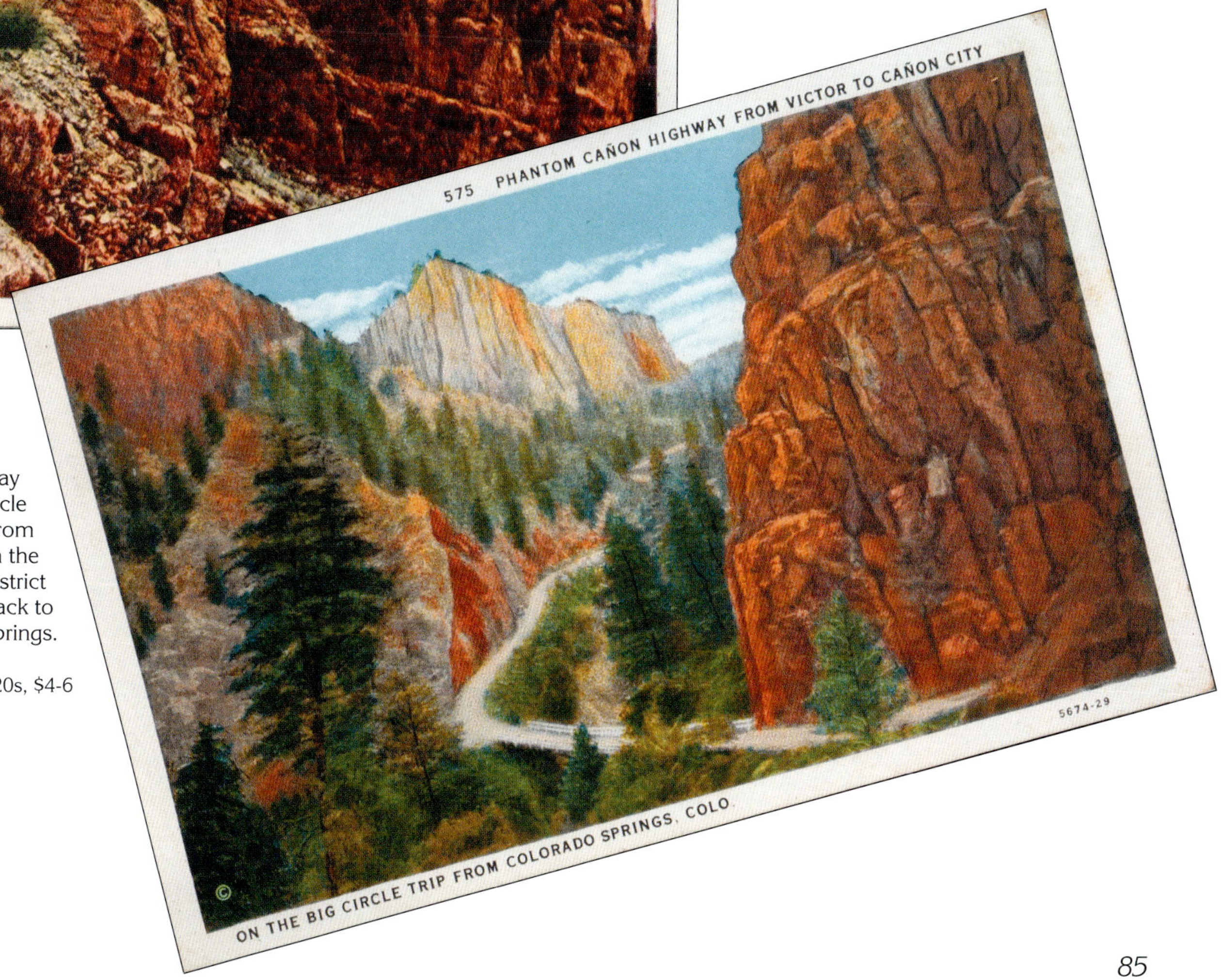

Phantom Cañon Highway was part of the Big Circle Trip, a highway route from Colorado Springs through the Cripple Creek Mining District and Canyon City and back to Colorado Springs.

Circa 1920s, $4-6

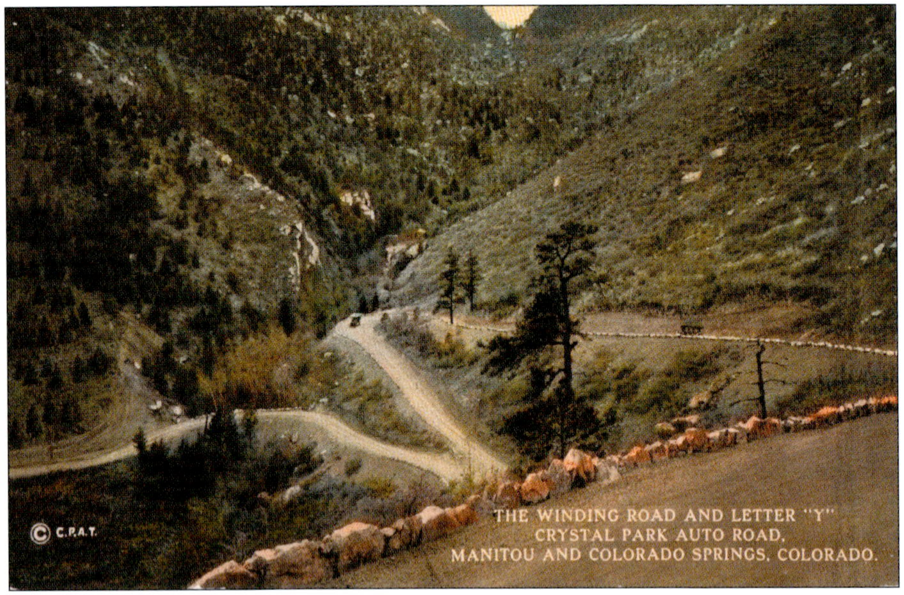

The Winding Road and the Letter "Y," part of the Crystal Park Auto Road from Manitou Springs to Colorado Springs.

Circa 1910s, $4-6

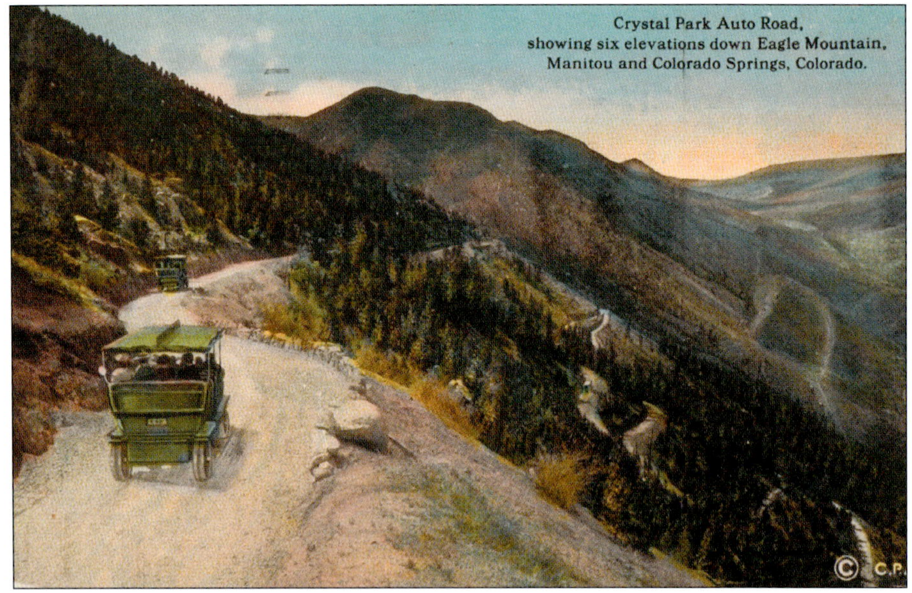

View showing the elevations of the Crystal Park Auto Road as it travels down the slope of Eagle Mountain.

Cancelled 1915, $4-6

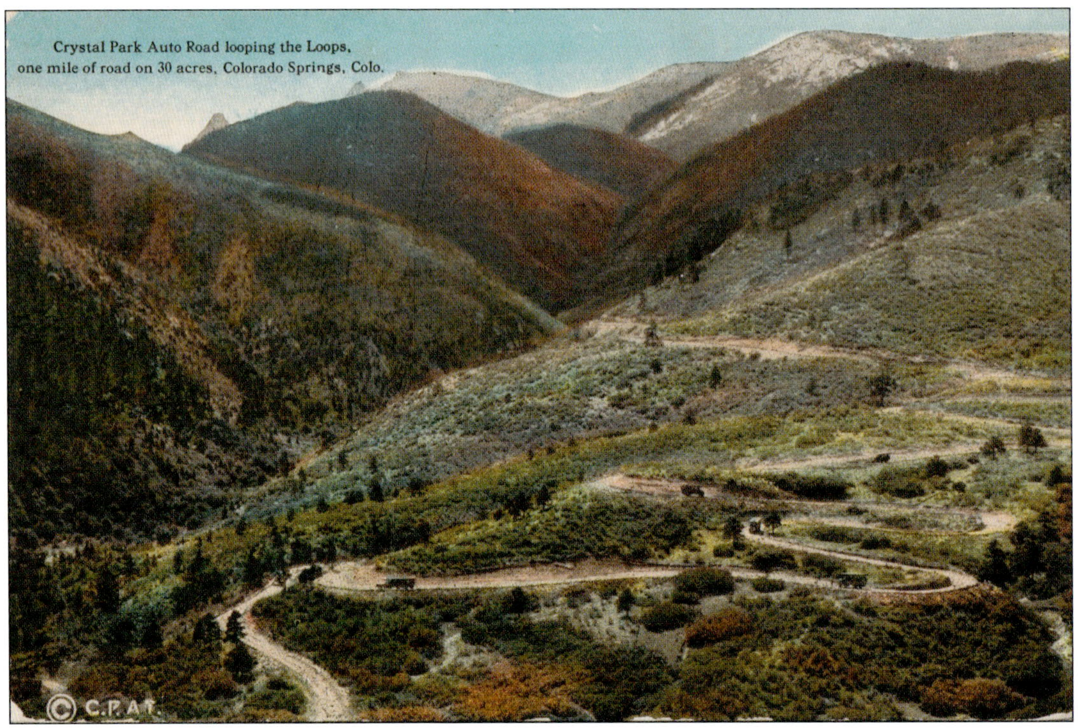

From the back: "The Crystal Park Auto Trip is now one of the foremost sightseeing trips that can be taken from Manitou and Colorado Springs. It is said to be the most wonderful and delightful sightseeing trip in Colorado and the panoramic view had at all points along the route are unexcelled. The scenery is grand and sublime."

Circa 1910s, $4-6

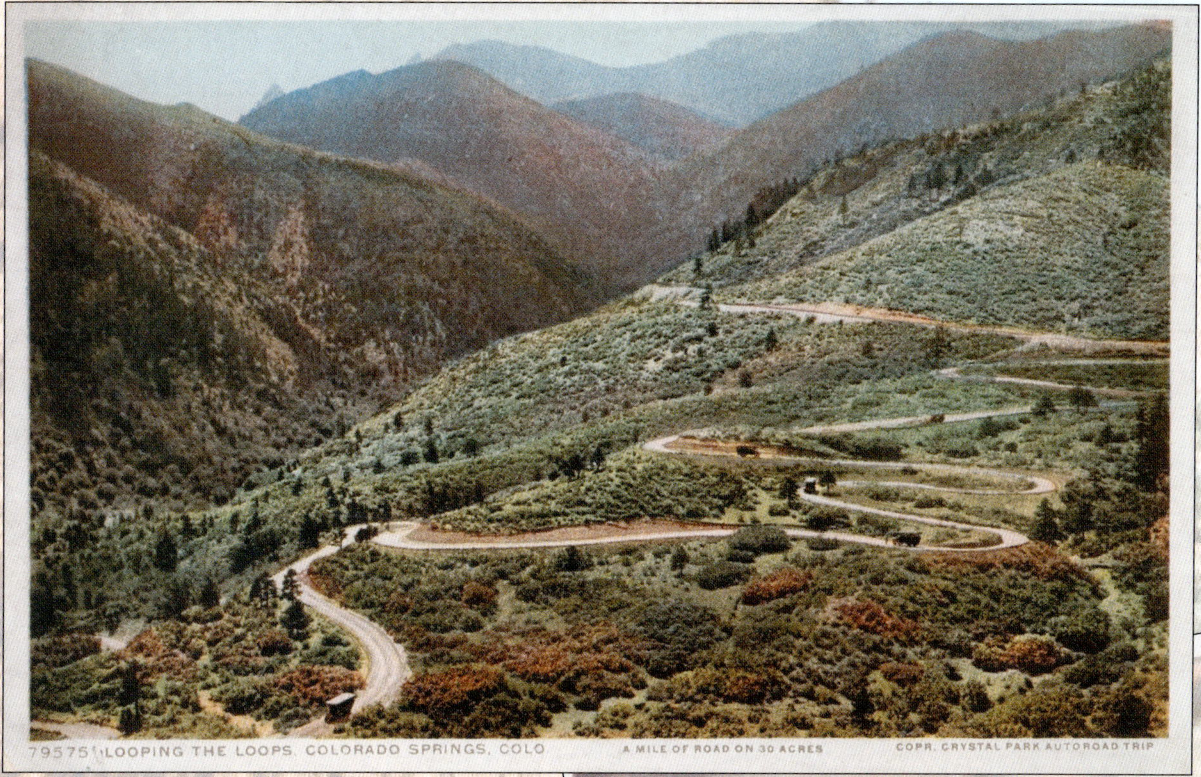

Looping the loops along the Crystal Park Auto Road.

Circa 1920s, $4-6

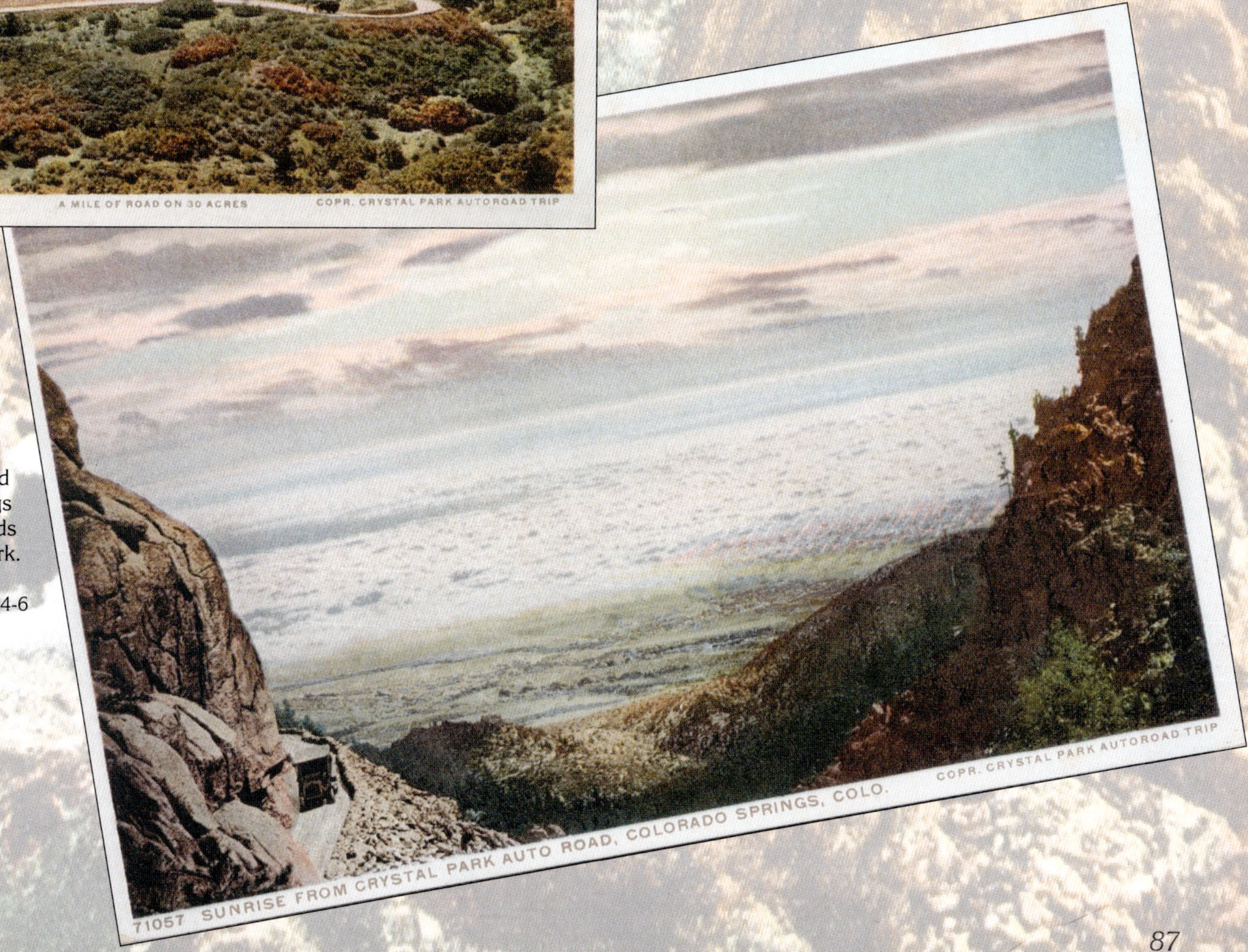

The Crystal Park Auto Road starts at Colorado Springs and Manitou Springs and ends at Crystal Park.

Circa 1920s, $4-6

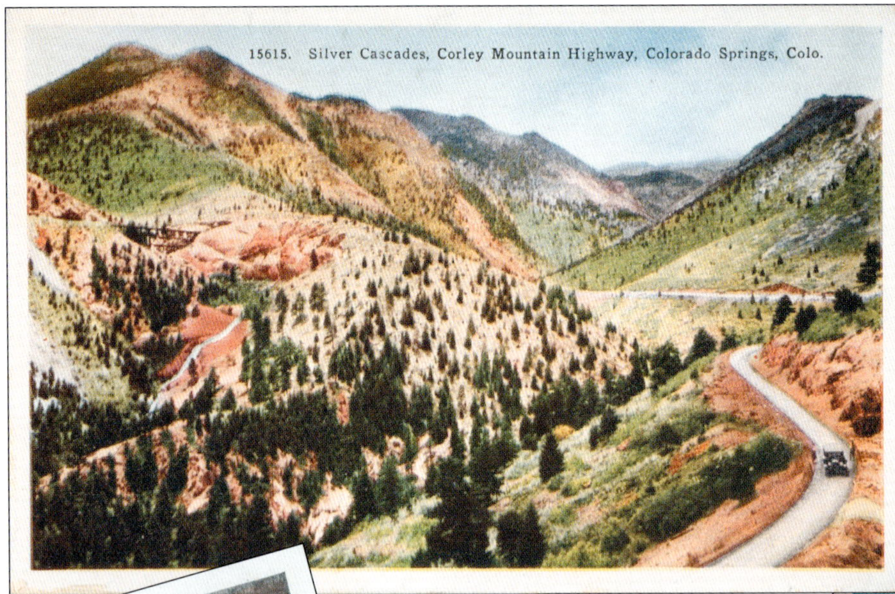

Situated at the head of North Cheyenne Cañon, the Silver Cascades can be seen from the Corley Mountain Highway.

Circa 1920s, $4-6

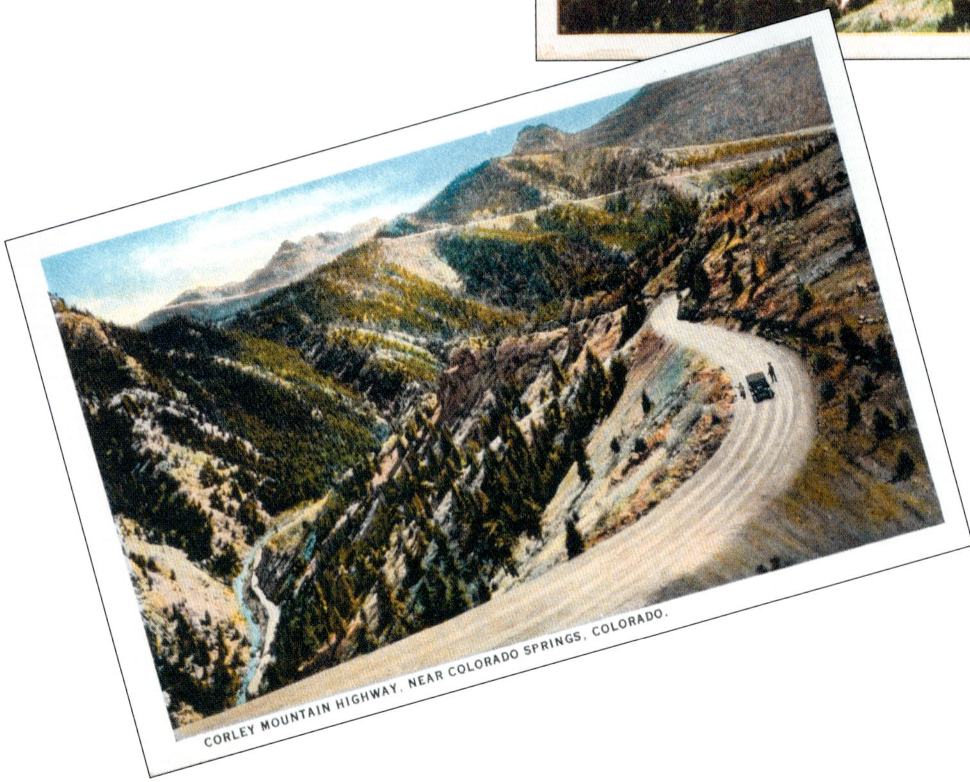

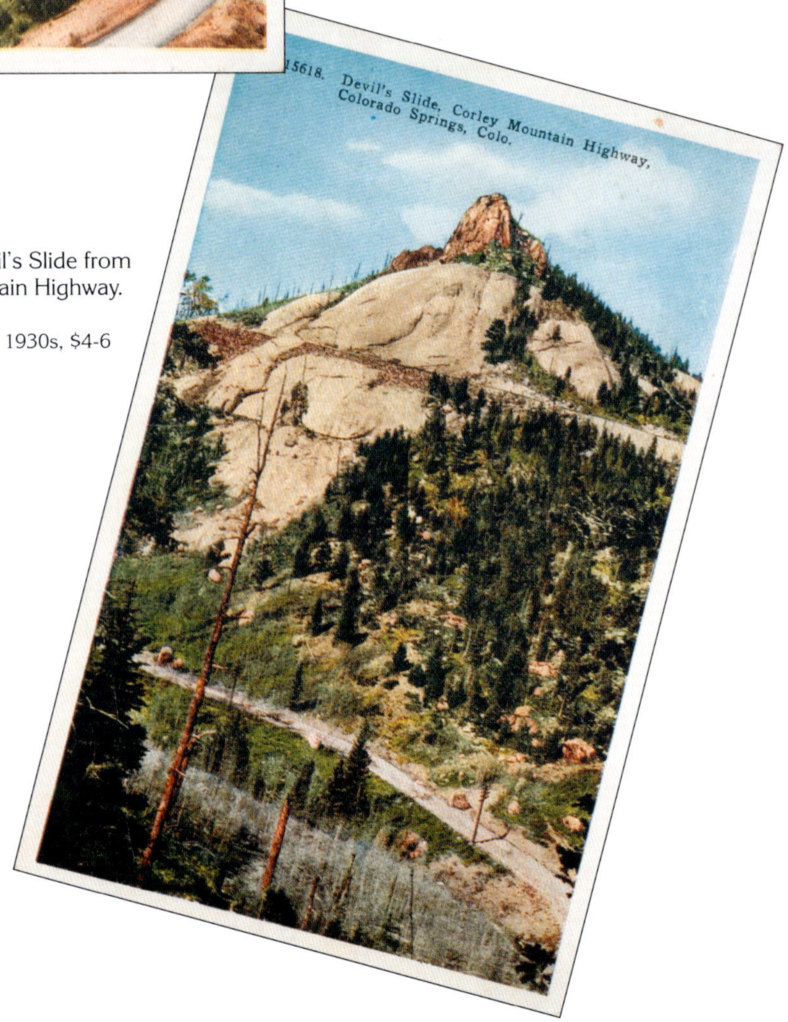

View of the Devil's Slide from the Corley Mountain Highway.

Circa 1930s, $4-6

Also known as Gold Camp Road, the Corley Mountain Highway was designed by and named after W.D. Corley of the Colorado Springs and Cripple Creek Railroad.

Circa 1920s, $4-6

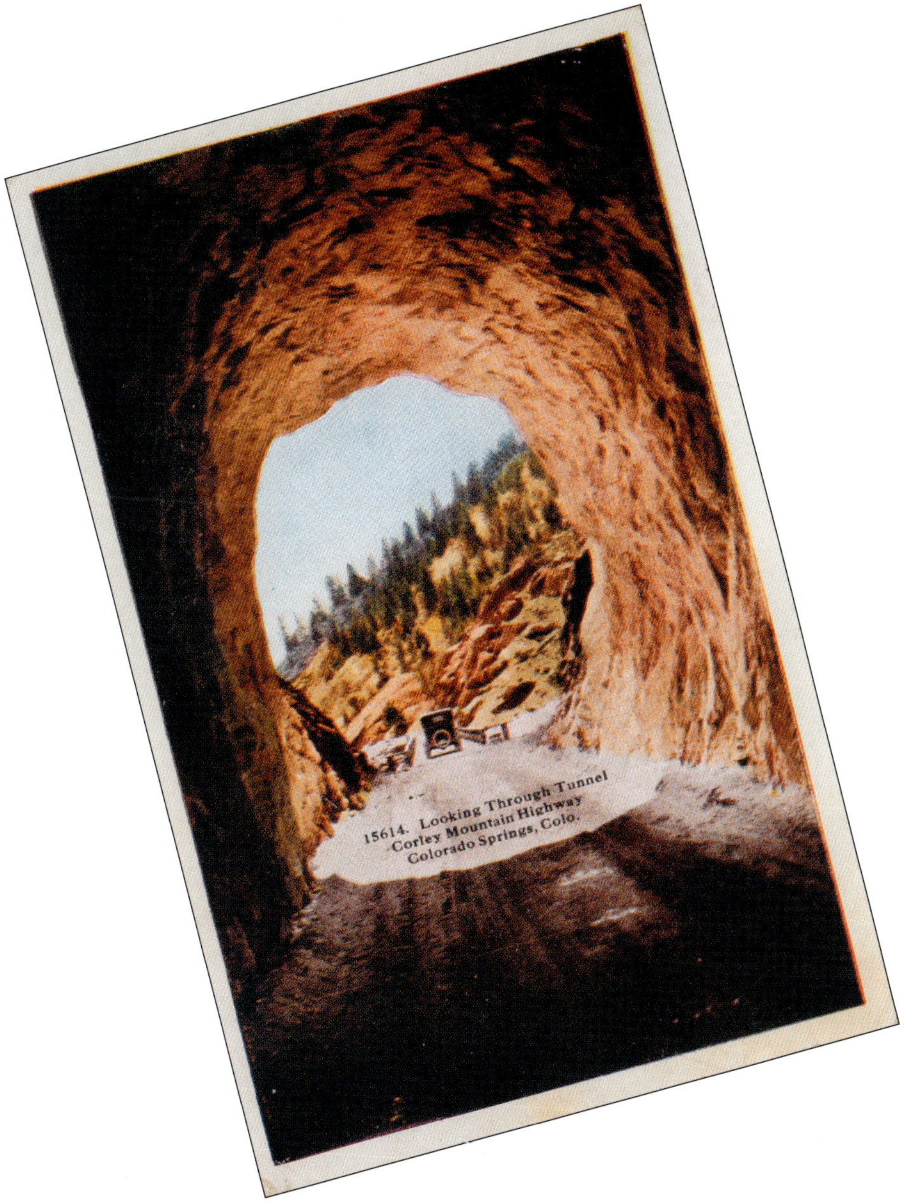

Stretching twenty-four miles, the Corley Mountain Highway connects Colorado Springs with the famous Gold Rush town, Cripple Creek. The highway was often used by tourists staying in Colorado Springs to visit the nearby community.

Circa 1930s, $4-6

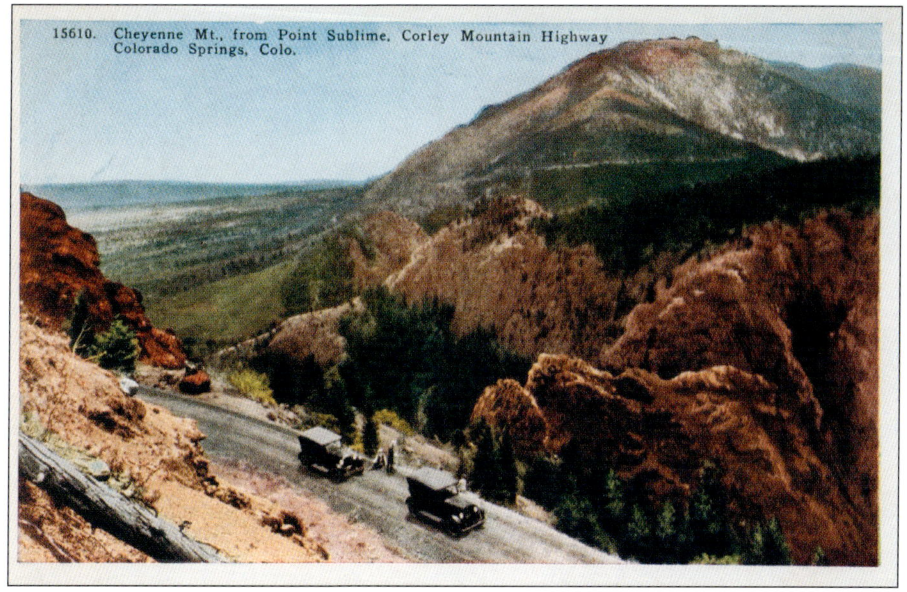

View of Cheyenne Mountain from Corley Mountain Highway.

Circa 1930s, $4-6

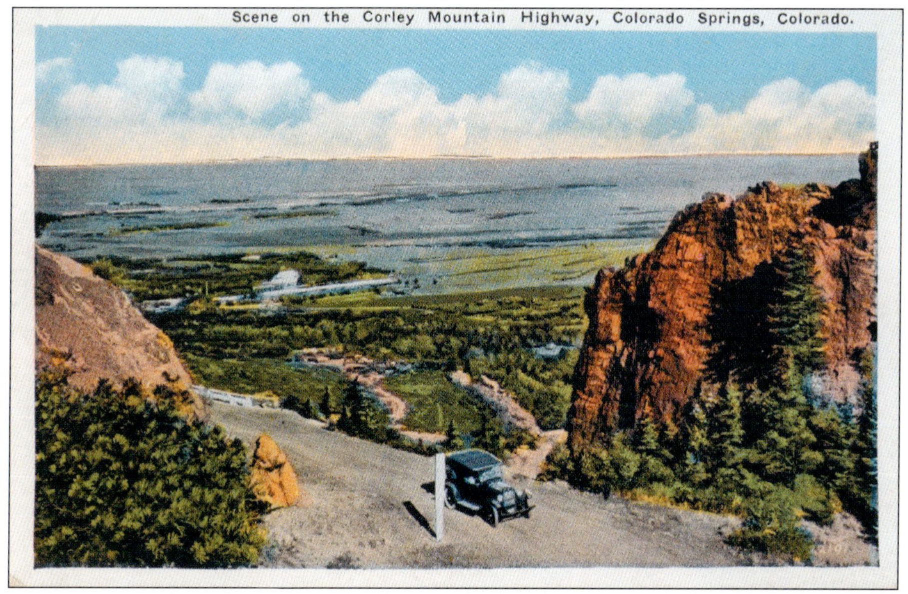

Built in the early 1900s, the Corley Mountain Highway was added to the National Register of Historic Places in 1999.

Circa 1930s, $4-6

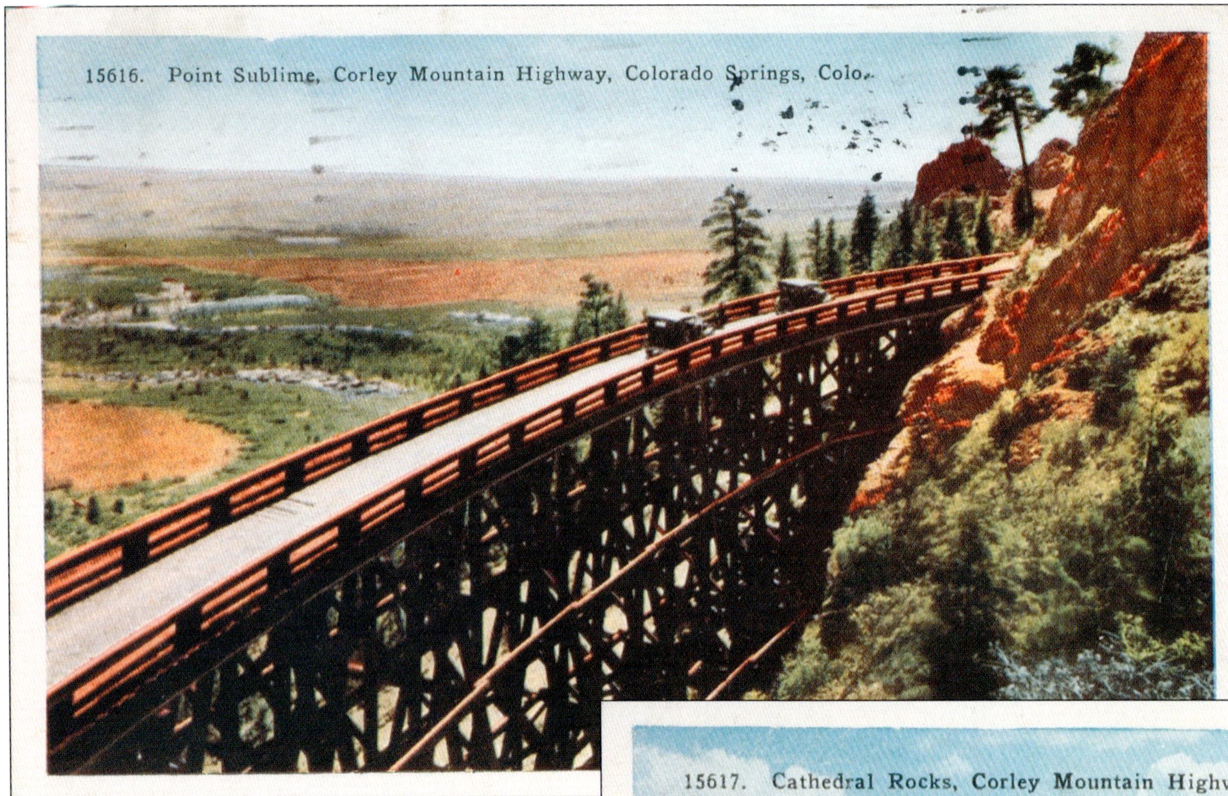

Passing Point Sublime on the Corley Mountain Highway.

Cancelled 1926, $4-6

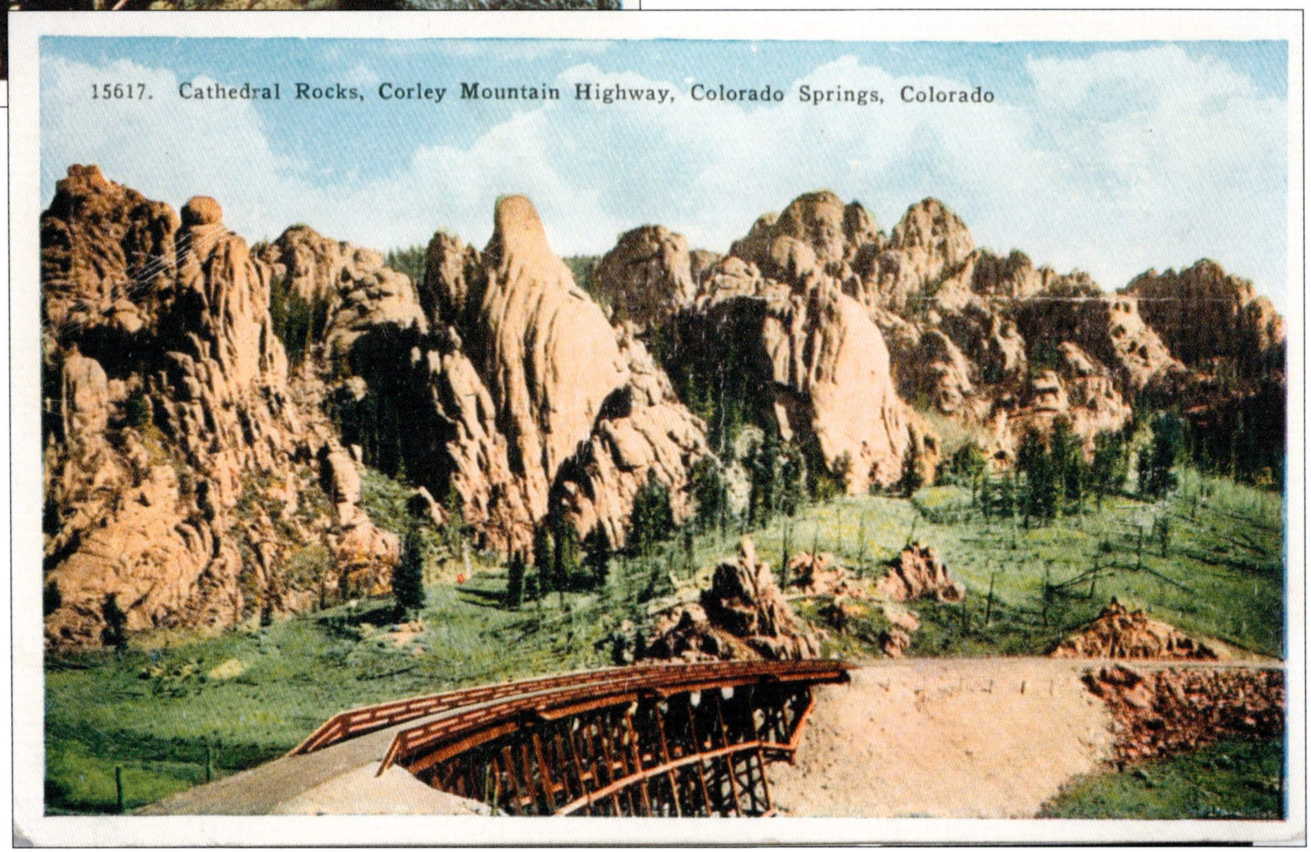

The rock formations at Cathedral Park: One of the many sights to see along the Highway.

Circa 1930s, $4-6

Cheyenne Mountain

When her soon-to-be husband William Sharpless Jackson bought their house on the corner of Weber and Kiowa Streets, Helen Hunt Jackson was in favor of selling the property again as it had no view of Cheyenne Mountain. Instead, the couple spent two years renovating the house until it faced Cheyenne Mountain. The Mountain, along with North and South Cheyenne Cañons, soon became Jackson's favorite spots and were mentioned frequently as sources of inspiration and as subjects for her poems and other literature.

When Spencer Penrose built the Broadmoor Hotel, he too recognized the potential of Cheyenne Mountain. Soon after he finished the Broadmoor, Penrose built a road up the mountain, the Broadmoor-Cheyenne Highway, which allowed automobile tourists to travel quickly and easily to the top. At the top of the Mountain he built the Cheyenne Mountain Zoo, one of the only mountain zoos in the United States in the 1930s. Also in the 1930s, he built the Will Rogers Shrine of the Sun, dedicating it to Will Rogers after hearing of his death in a plane crash in 1935. The shrine remains a popular tourist attraction today, serving as a memorial to Will Rogers and Spencer and Julie Penrose, an architectural curiosity, and a museum dedicated to the history of the Pikes Peak Region.

In 1963, the North American Aerospace Defense Command (NORAD) built its primary technical facility in Cheyenne Mountain, contributing to the city's thriving military boom.

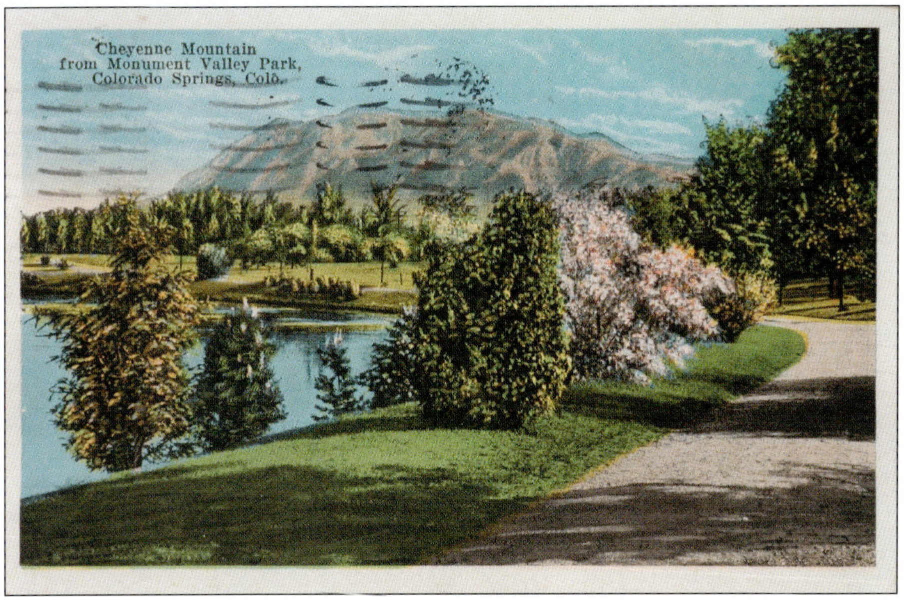

Cheyenne Mountain was named after the people of the Cheyenne Nation, which was made up of ten bands who lived in the territory ranging from the Black Hills in South Dakota to southern Colorado.

Cancelled 1928, $4-6

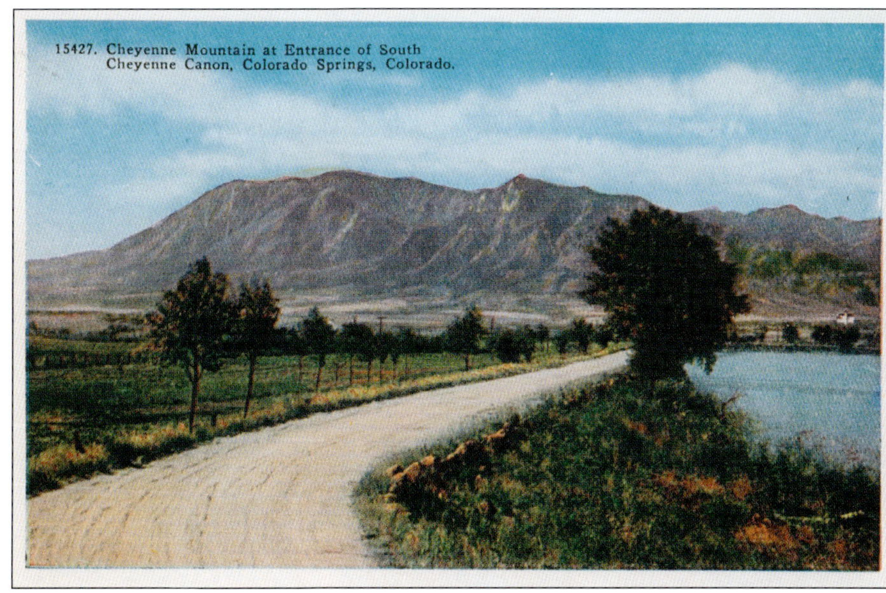

Cheyennes, Arapaho, Utes, and other Native Americans would often visit Cheyenne Mountain as it was considered an excellent place to gather teepee poles.

Circa 1930s, $4-6

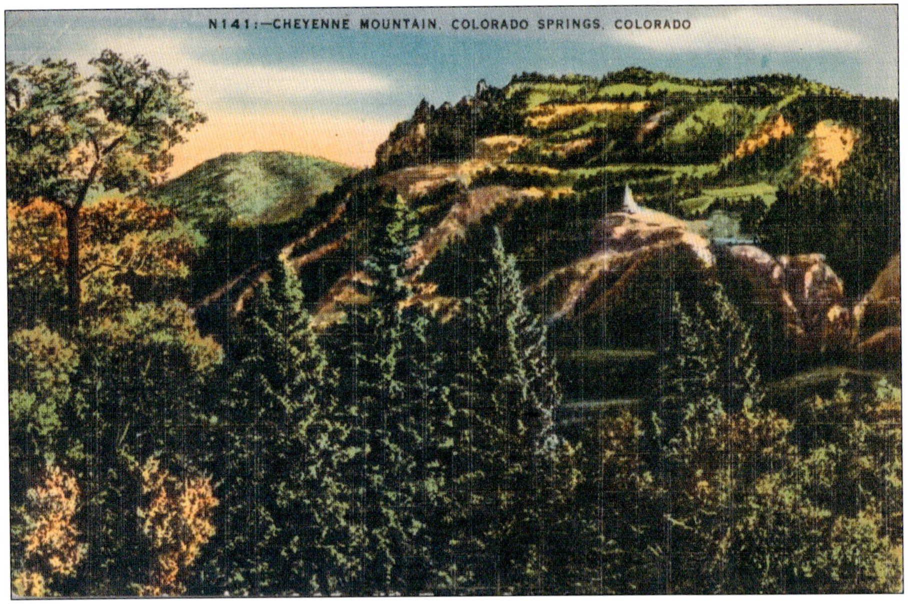

View of Cheyenne Mountain with Will Rogers Shrine to the Sun in the distance.

Circa 1940s, $4-6

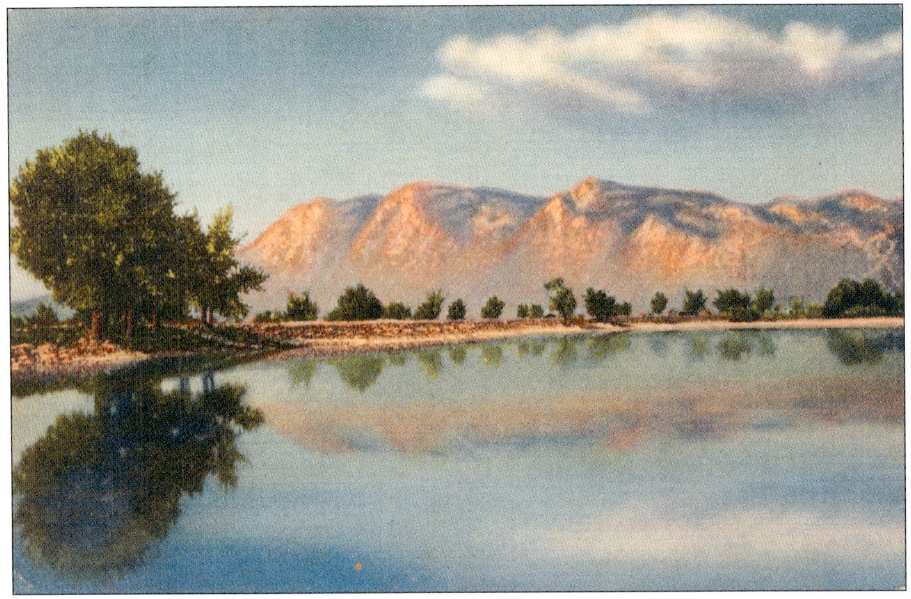

Cheyenne Mountain is currently home to a major United States military command base, the Cheyenne Mountain Operation Center. The facility is home to four commands, the North American Aerospace Defense Command, the United States Northern Command, the United States Strategic Command, and the Air Force Space Command.

Circa 1940s, $4-6

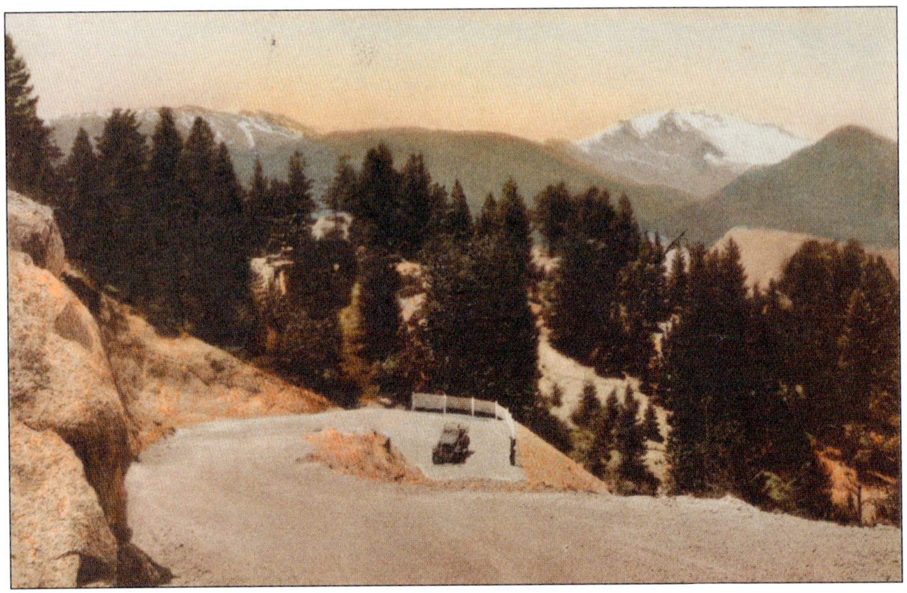

A view of Pikes Peak from the Broadmoor-Cheyenne Mountain Highway.

Circa 1930s, $4-6

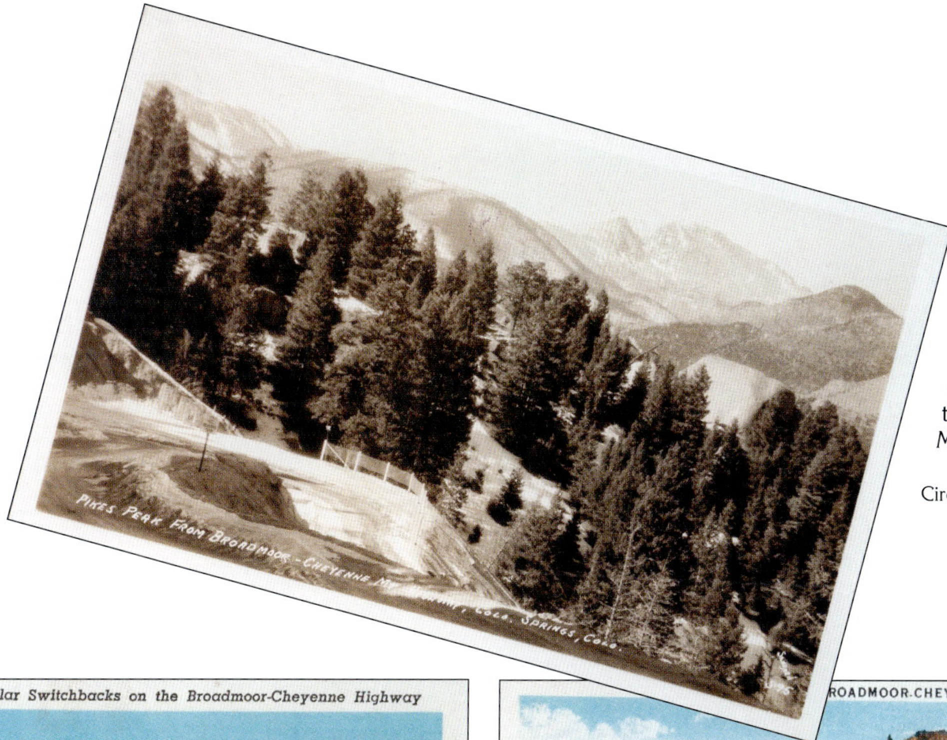

The Grande Swing, one of the many curves on the Broadmoor-Cheyenne Mountain Highway.

Circa 1930s, $4-6

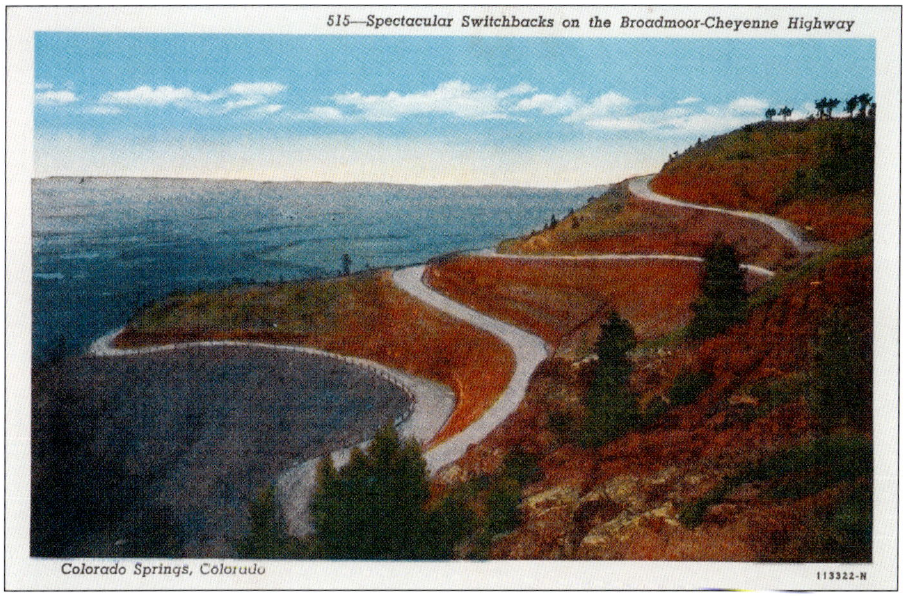

The Broadmoor-Cheyenne Mountain Highway was built by Spence Penrose in 1924. Originally stopping at the Mountain's summit, it has since been expanded and leads to the Cheyenne Mountain Zoo and the Will Rogers Shrine of the Sun.

Circa 1930s, $4-6

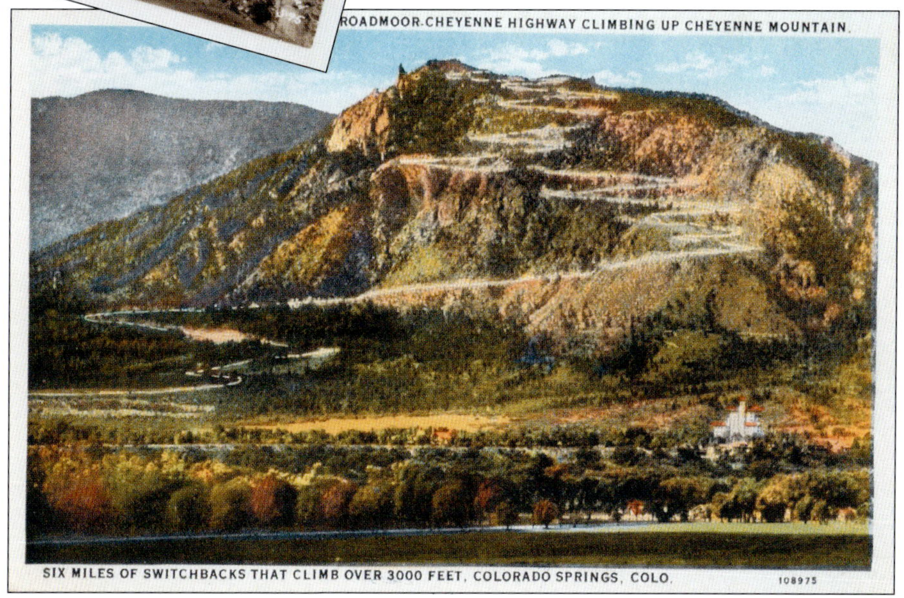

View of Cheyenne Mountain showing the Broadmoor-Cheyenne Mountain Highway and the Broadmoor Hotel.

Circa 1920s, $4-6

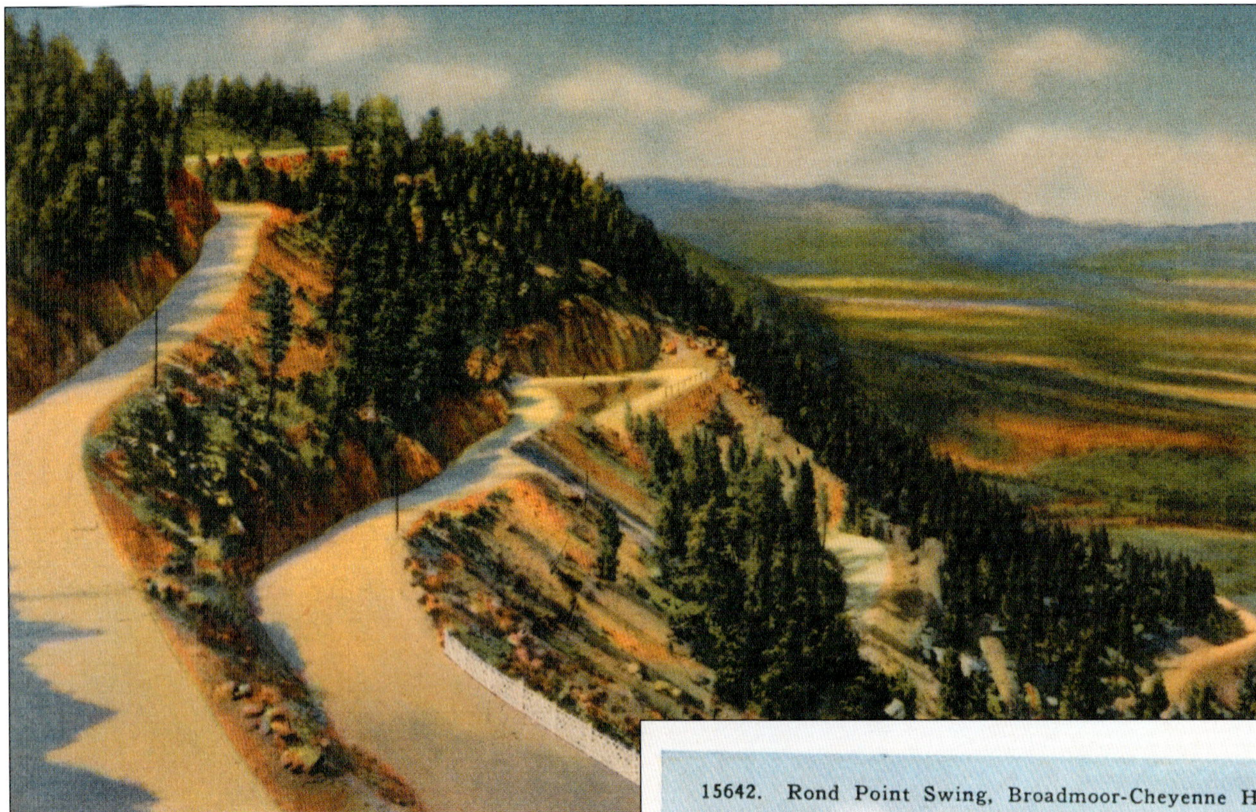

The Broadmoor-Cheyenne Mountain Highway stretched for six miles from the Broadmoor Hotel to the top of Cheyenne Mountain. The highway was largely made up of switchbacks offering spectacular views of the valley below.

Circa 1940s, $4-6

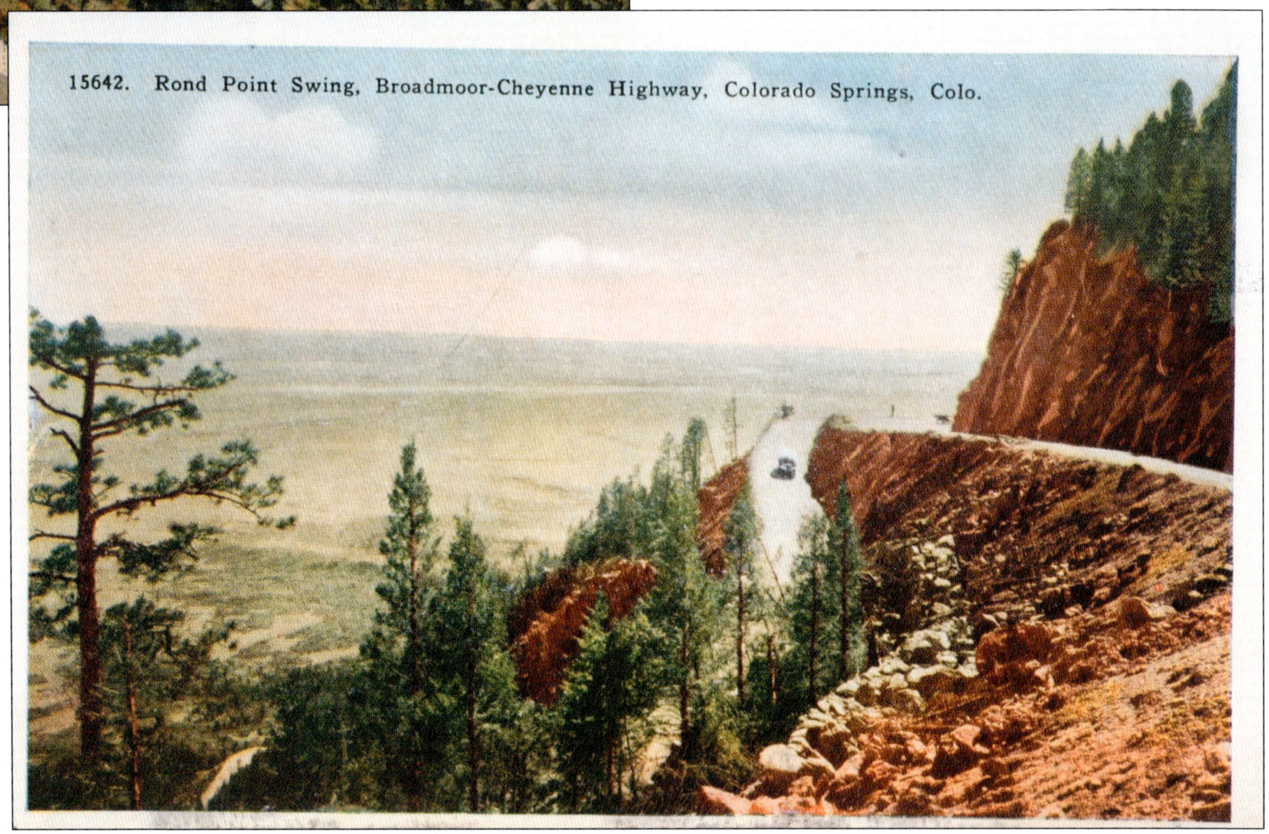

Because of its amazing construction, the Highway was also known as "the Wonder Road."

Circa 1930s, $4-6

The original terminus of the Broadmoor-Cheyenne Mountain Highway was the Cheyenne Lodge located at the summit of the Mountain.

Circa 1930s, $4-6

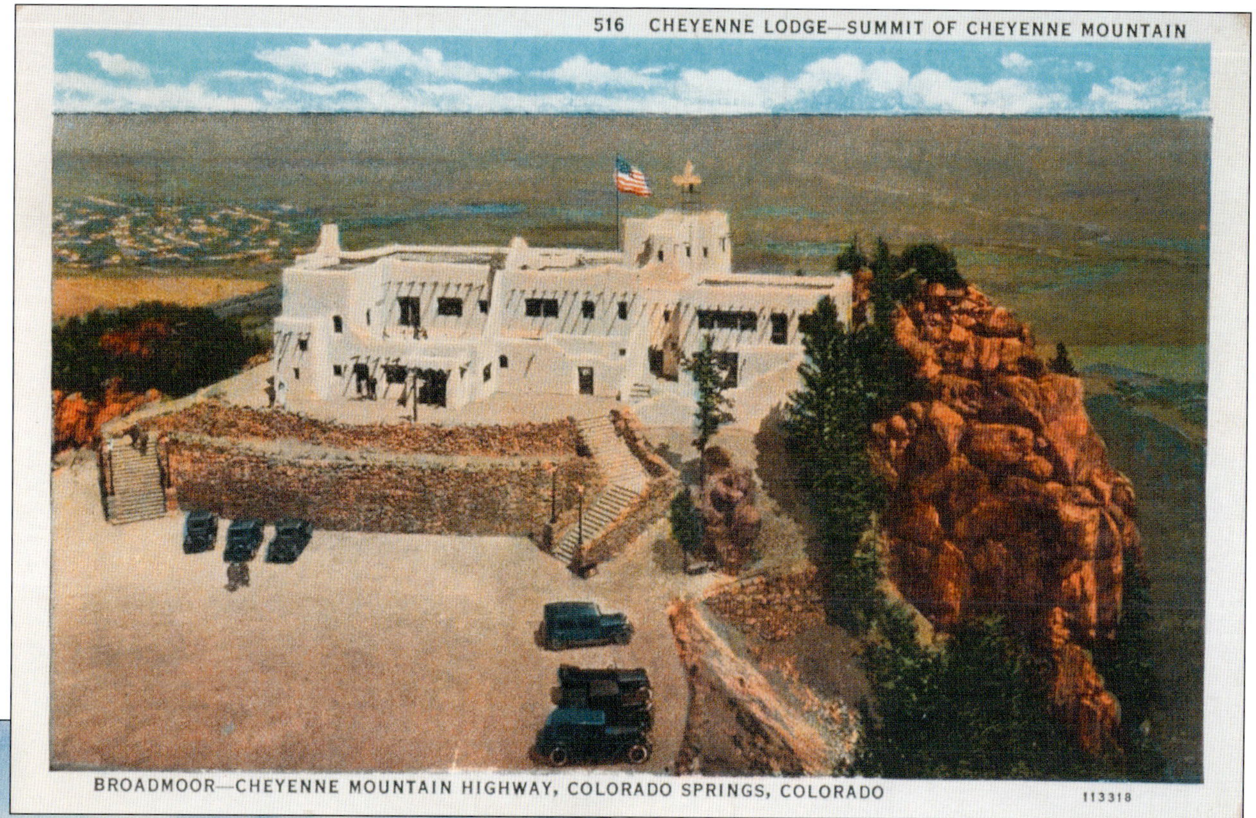

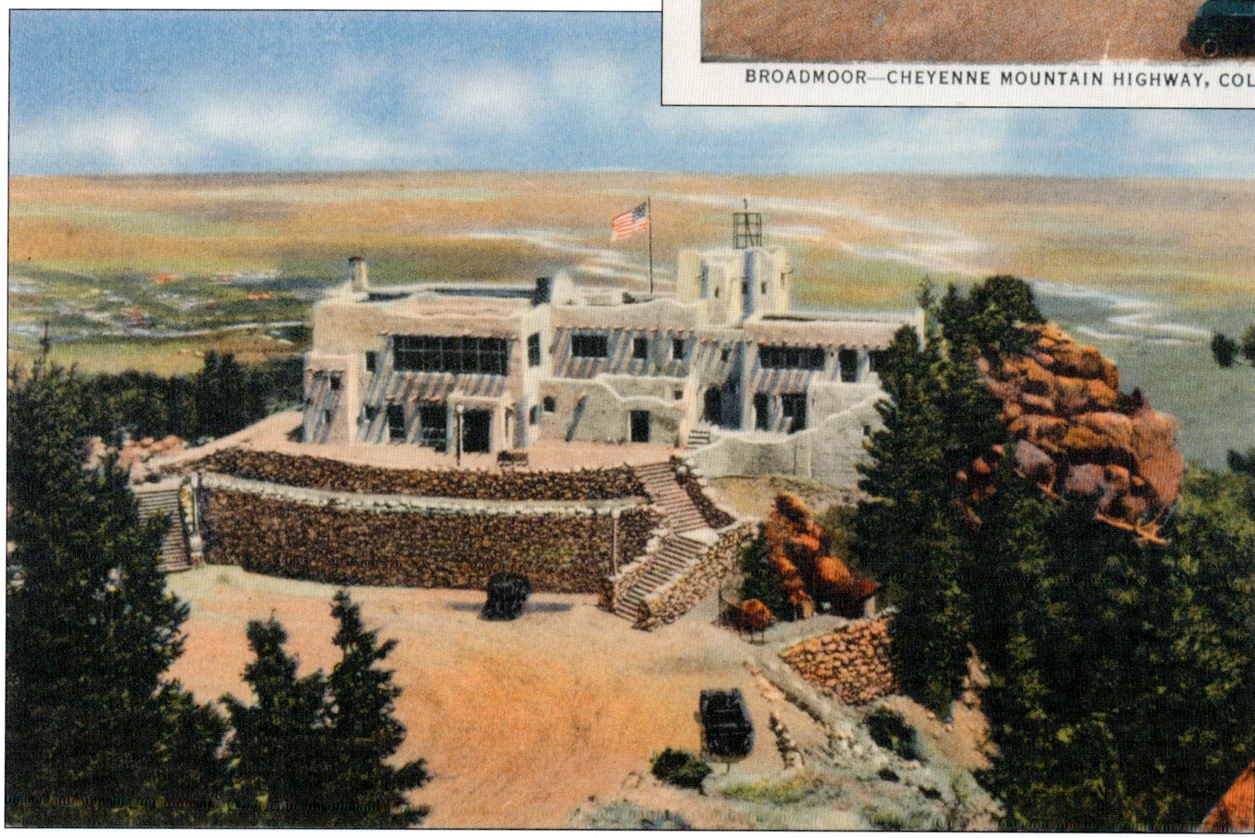

At an altitude of 9,500 feet, the Cheyenne Lodge featured some of the finest views in the region.

Circa 1940s, $5-7

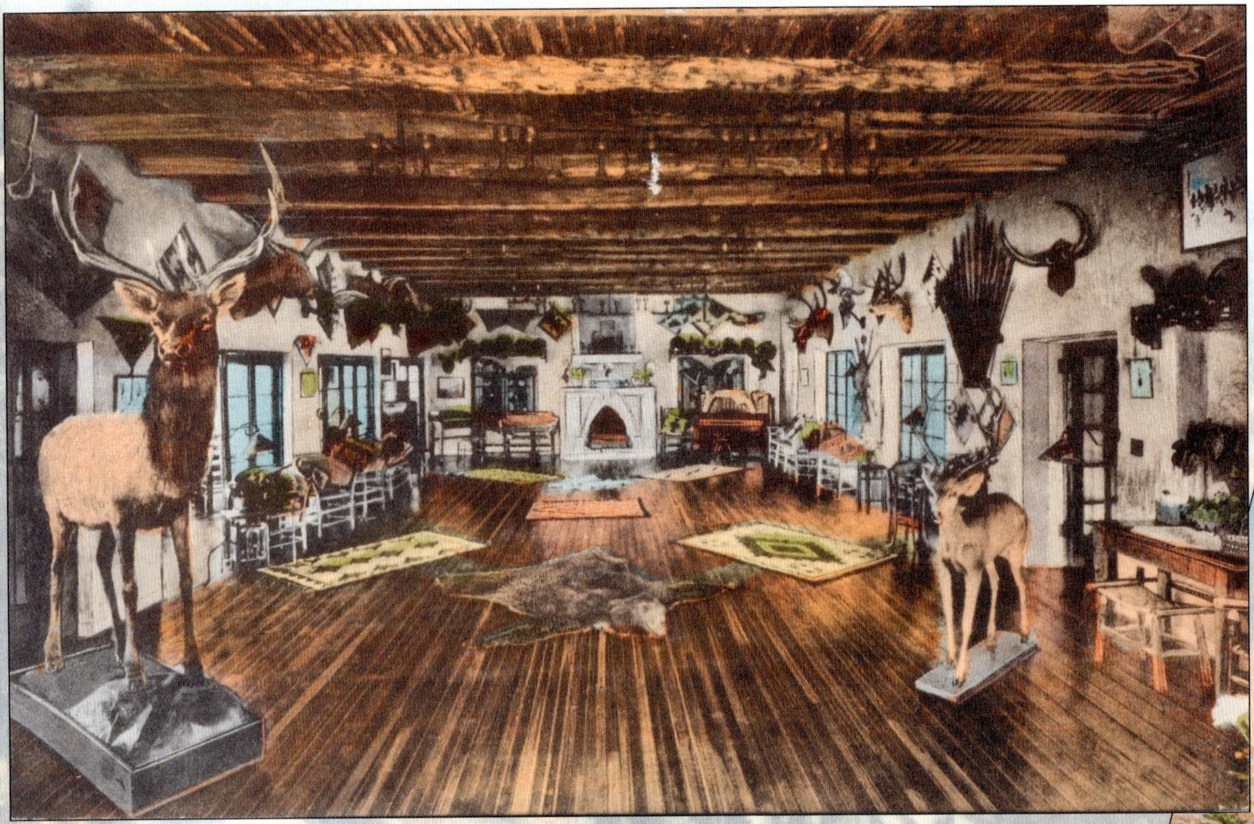

The recreation room at the Cheyenne Lodge.

Circa 1930s, $4-6

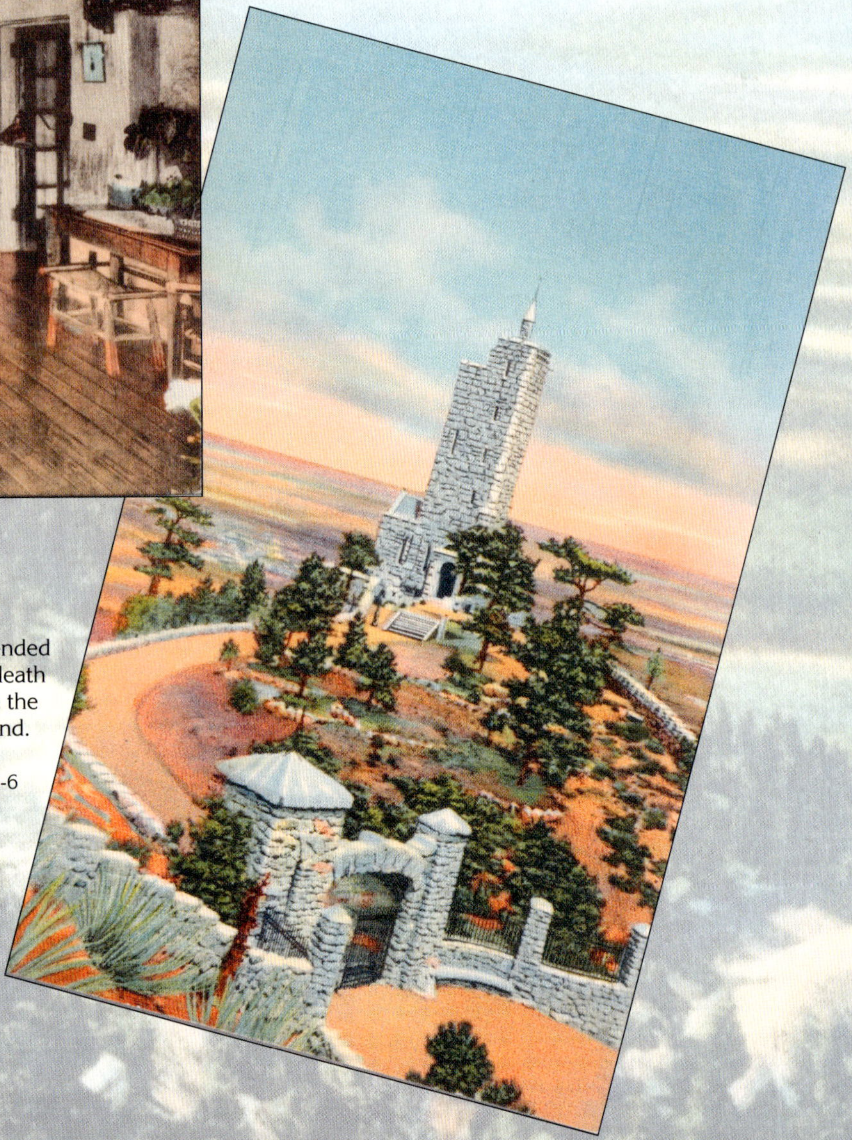

The Will Rogers Shrine of the Sun was originally intended to be Spencer Penrose's tomb. After hearing of the death of Will Rogers in 1935, Penrose decided to rededicate the Shrine to honor the memory of his friend.

Circa 1940s, $4-6

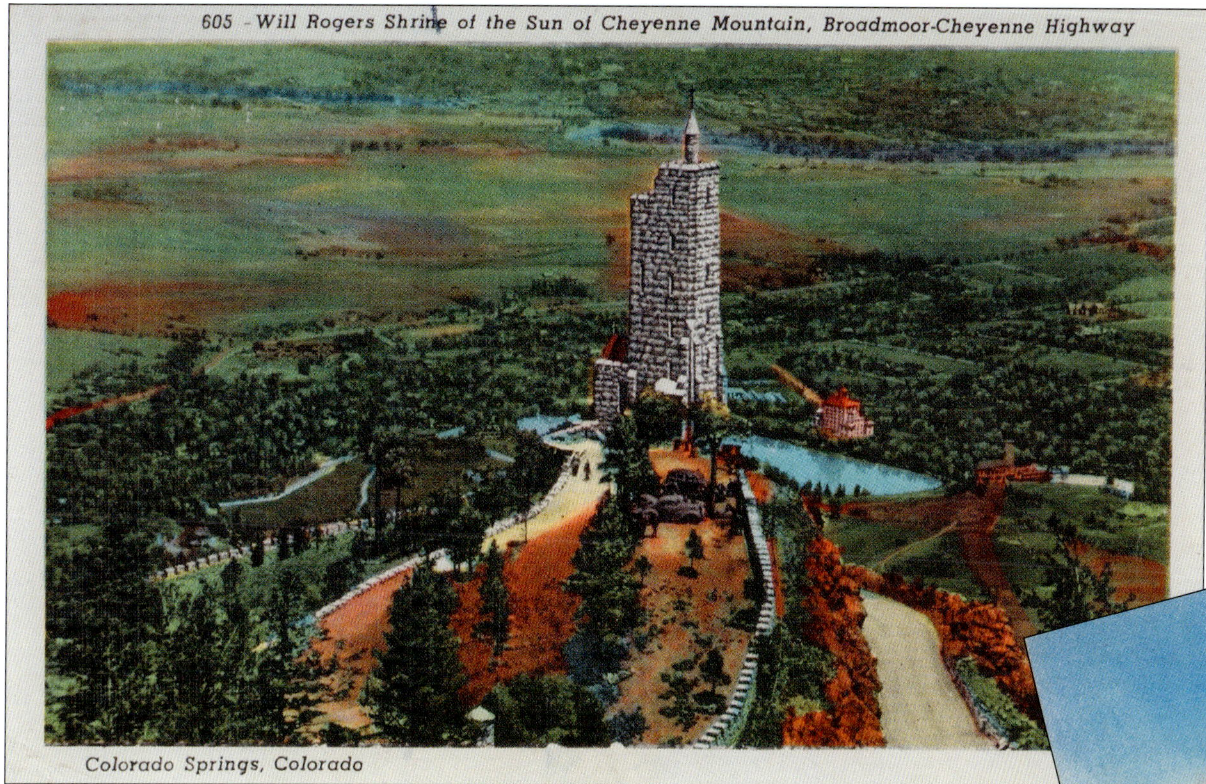

Construction on the Shrine began in 1934 and was finished three years later. It was dedicated in a nationally broadcast radio ceremony on September 6, 1937.

Cancelled 1949, $4-6

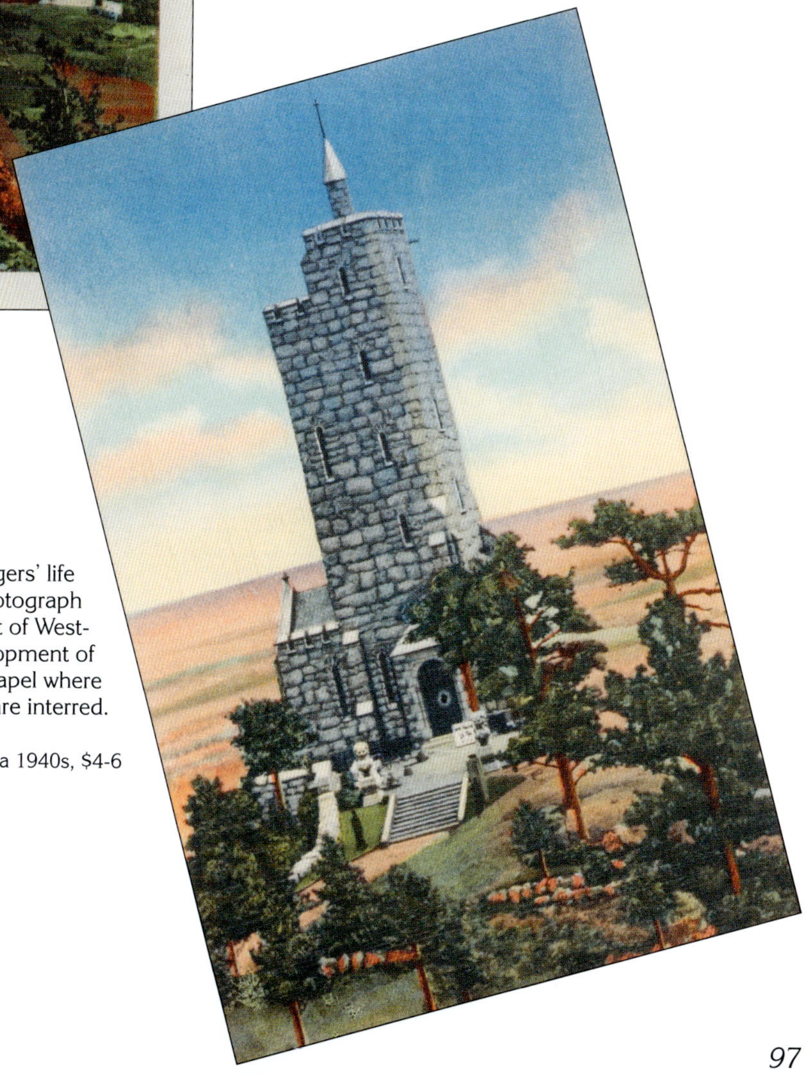

The Shrine houses a photographic history of Will Rogers' life from his early childhood in Oklahoma to the final photograph taken before his death. The shrine also houses a set of Westminster Chimes, a series of murals showing the development of Colorado Springs and the Pikes Peak Region, and a chapel where the ashes of Spencer Penrose and his wife Julie are interred.

Circa 1940s, $4-6

North Cheyenne Cañon

North Cheyenne Cañon became part of Colorado Springs in 1885 when the citizens of the city voted to buy 640 acres of the Cañon from Colorado College for use as a public park. Several years later, in 1907, General Palmer and another well-to-do Colorado Springs citizen donated an additional 480 acres to the park, which included the High Drive and Silver Cascade and Helen Hunt Falls.

The Cañon itself is known for its rock formations, hiking paths, plentiful and diverse flora, and its waterfalls. So many people visited the Cañon that the city's Park Commission called it, "The grandest and most popular of all the beautiful canons near the city." Today it remains extremely popular with hikers, rock climbers, picnickers, and nature enthusiasts, with close to 7,000 people visiting the Cañon each year. The park itself encompasses 1,626 acres, which includes the Stratton Open Space.

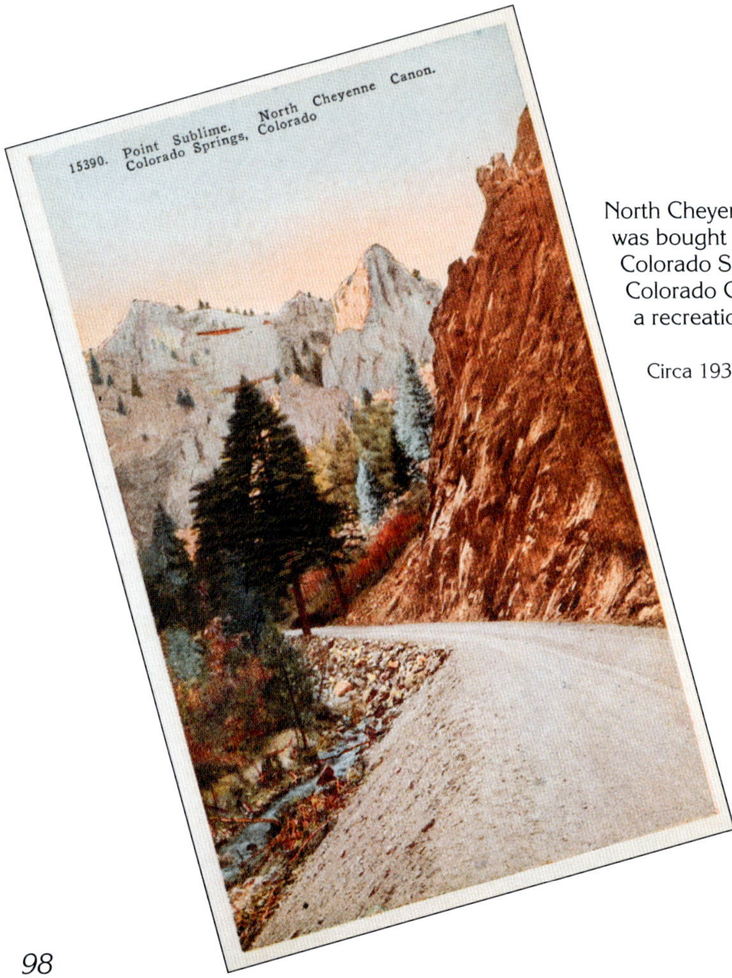

North Cheyenne Cañon Park was bought by the city of Colorado Springs from Colorado College for use as a recreational area in 1885.

Circa 1930s, $4-6

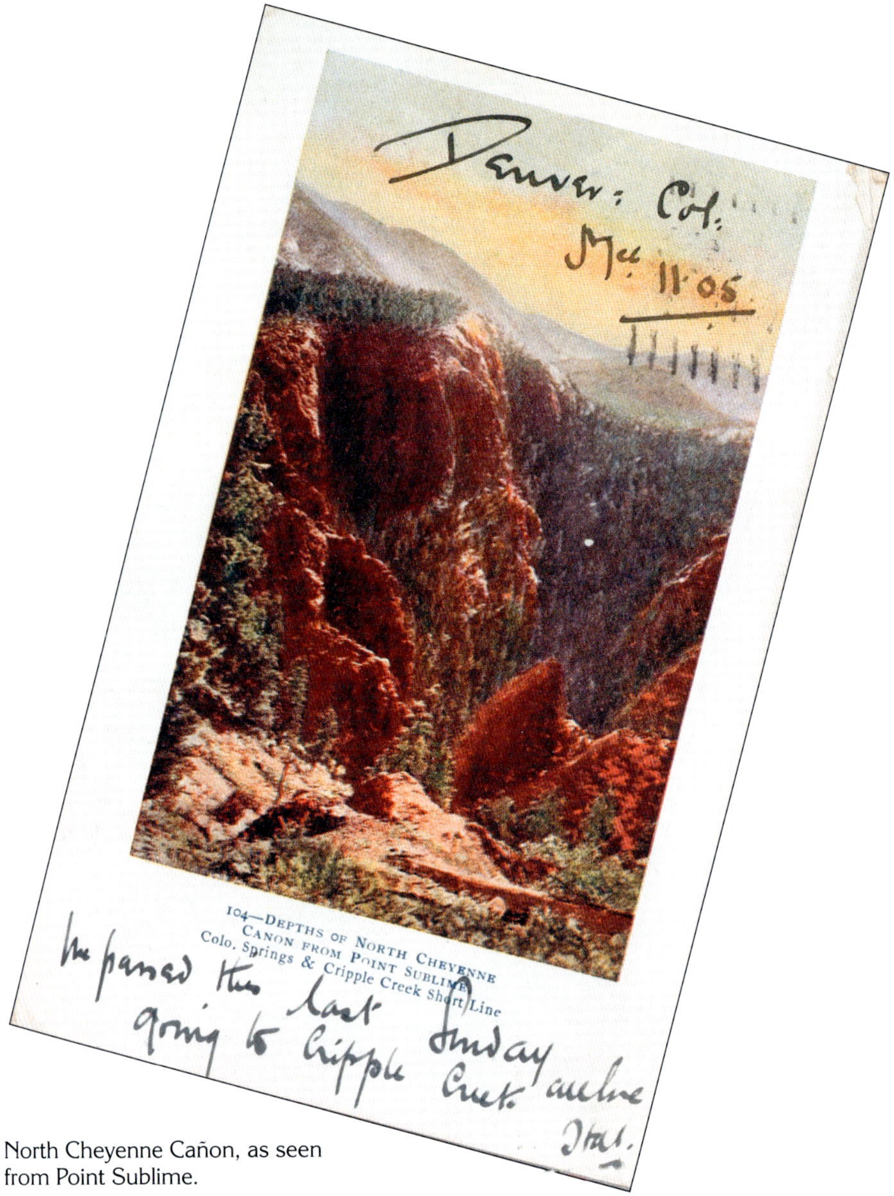

North Cheyenne Cañon, as seen from Point Sublime.

Cancelled 1905, $4-6

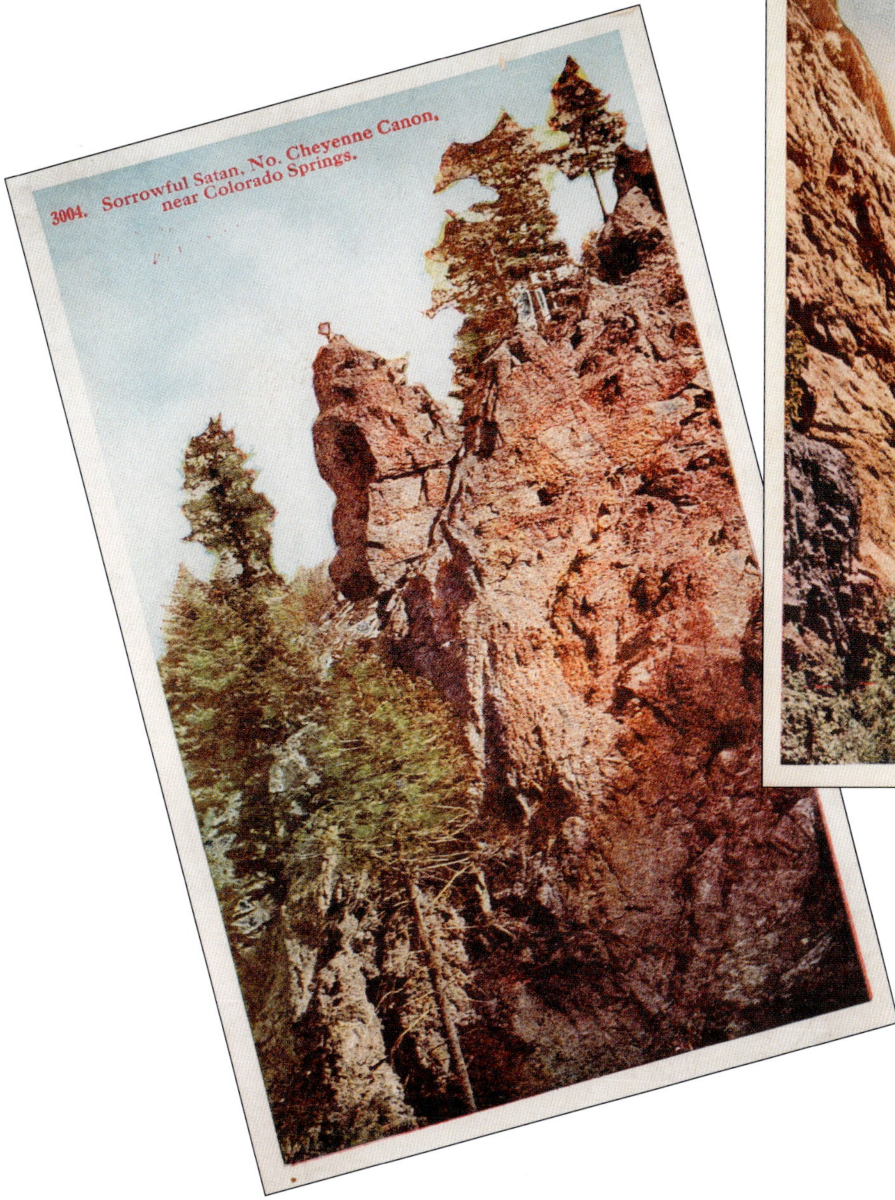

Two of Colorado Spring's leading citizens, General William Jackson Palmer and Fred Chamberlain, each donated land in 1907, adding to the original purchase of 640 acres.

Circa 1930s, $4-6

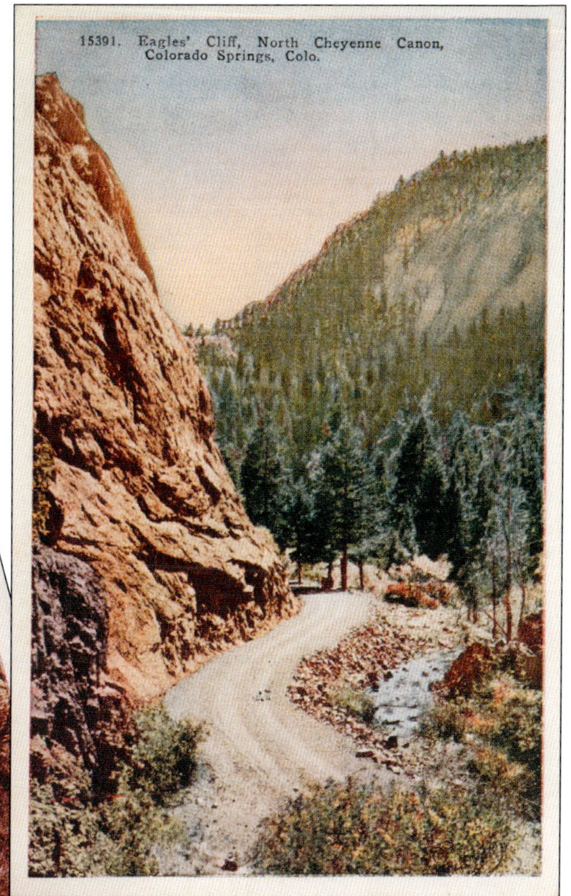

Today North Cheyenne Cañon Park consists of 1,600 acres and is visited by around 70,000 people a year.

Circa 1930s, $4-6

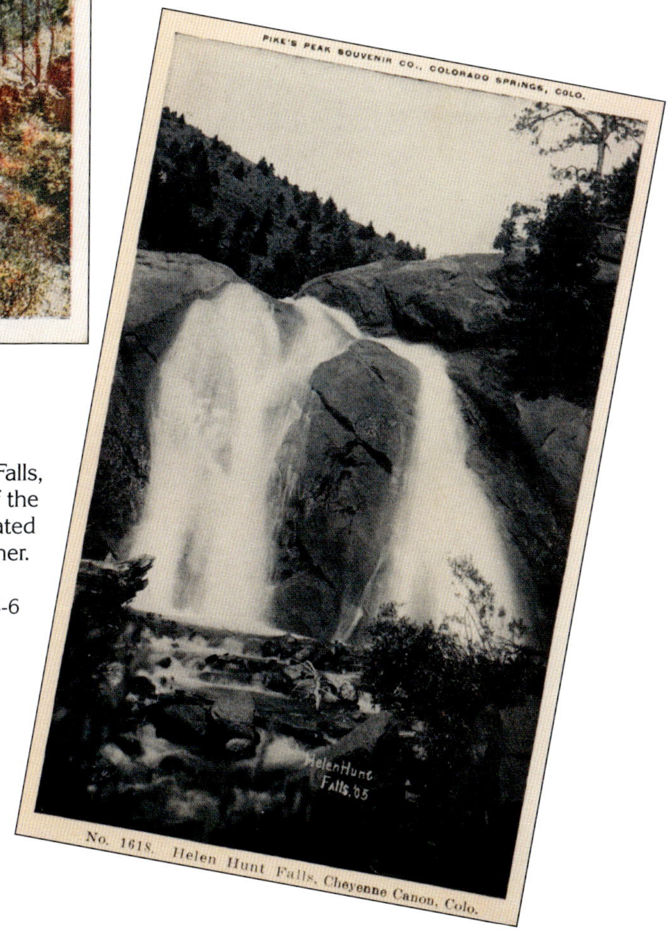

Along with Silver Cascade Falls, Helen Hunt Falls was part of the 480 acres in the Cañon donated by General Palmer.

Circa 1910s, $4-6

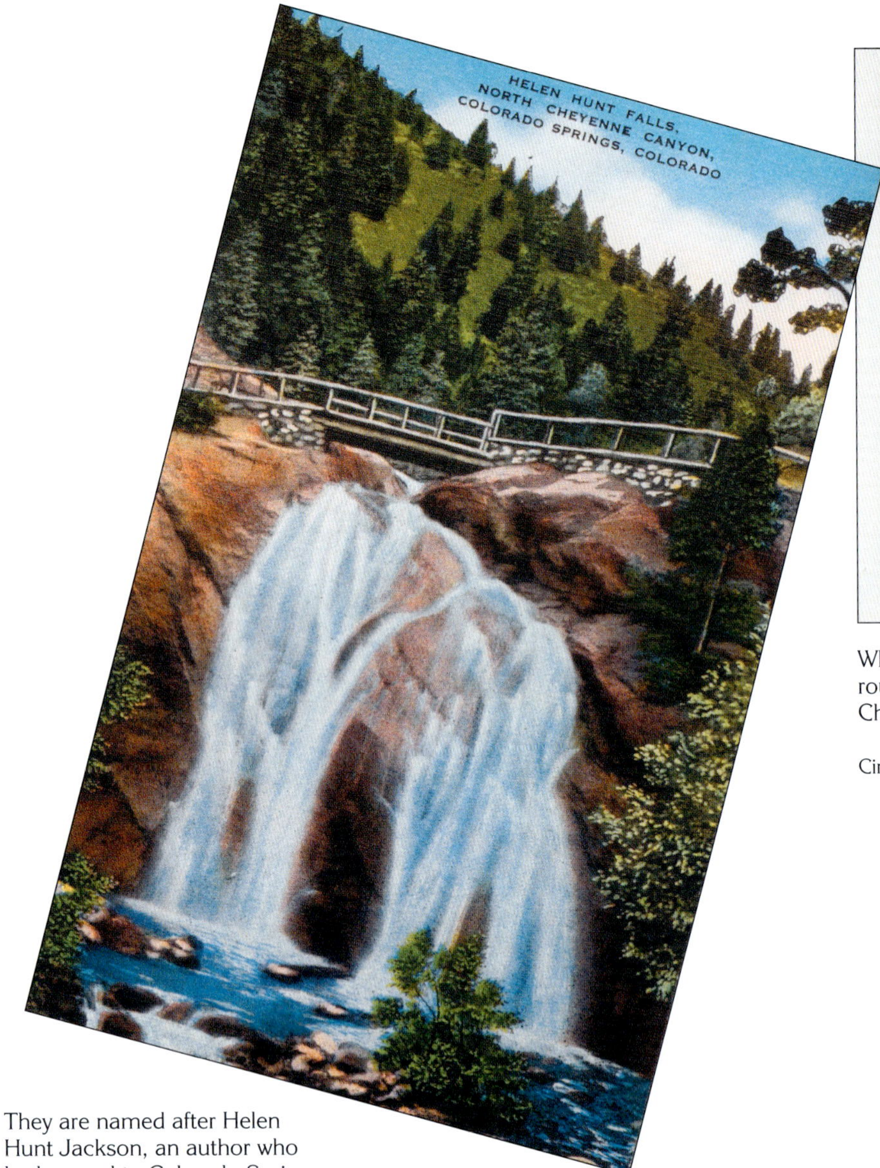

They are named after Helen Hunt Jackson, an author who had moved to Colorado Springs for her health. She stayed and married William Sharpless Jackson, one of the founders of Colorado College.

Circa 1940s, $4-6

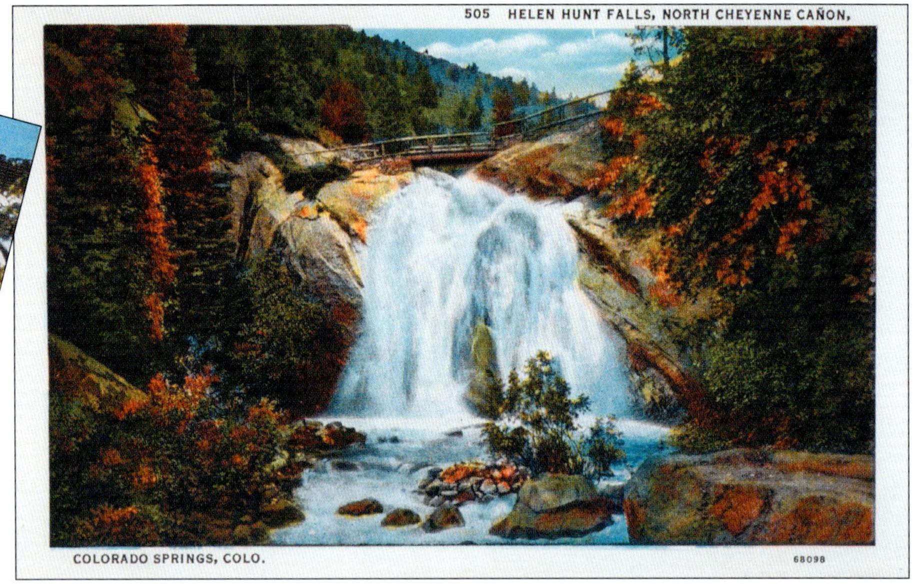

When she first moved to Colorado Springs, Helen Hunt Jackson initially disliked the surrounding landscape. However, she eventually grew to love the countryside, in particular Cheyenne Mountain and Canyon, writing about them in her book, *Bits of Travel at Home*.

Circa 1940s, $4-6

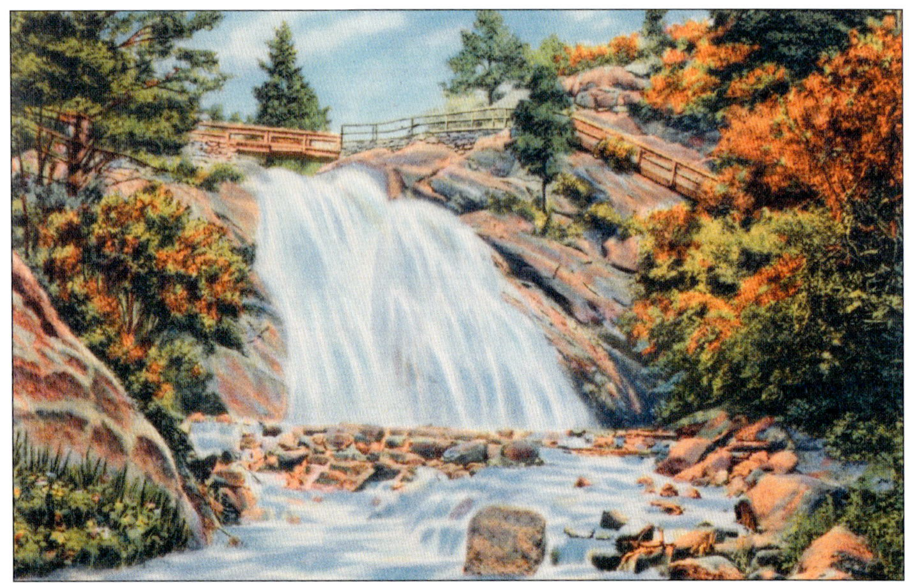

Visitors who wanted to reach Helen Hunt Falls would often take the Columbine Trail, which began at the mouth of the Cañon three miles away.

Cancelled 1941, $4-6

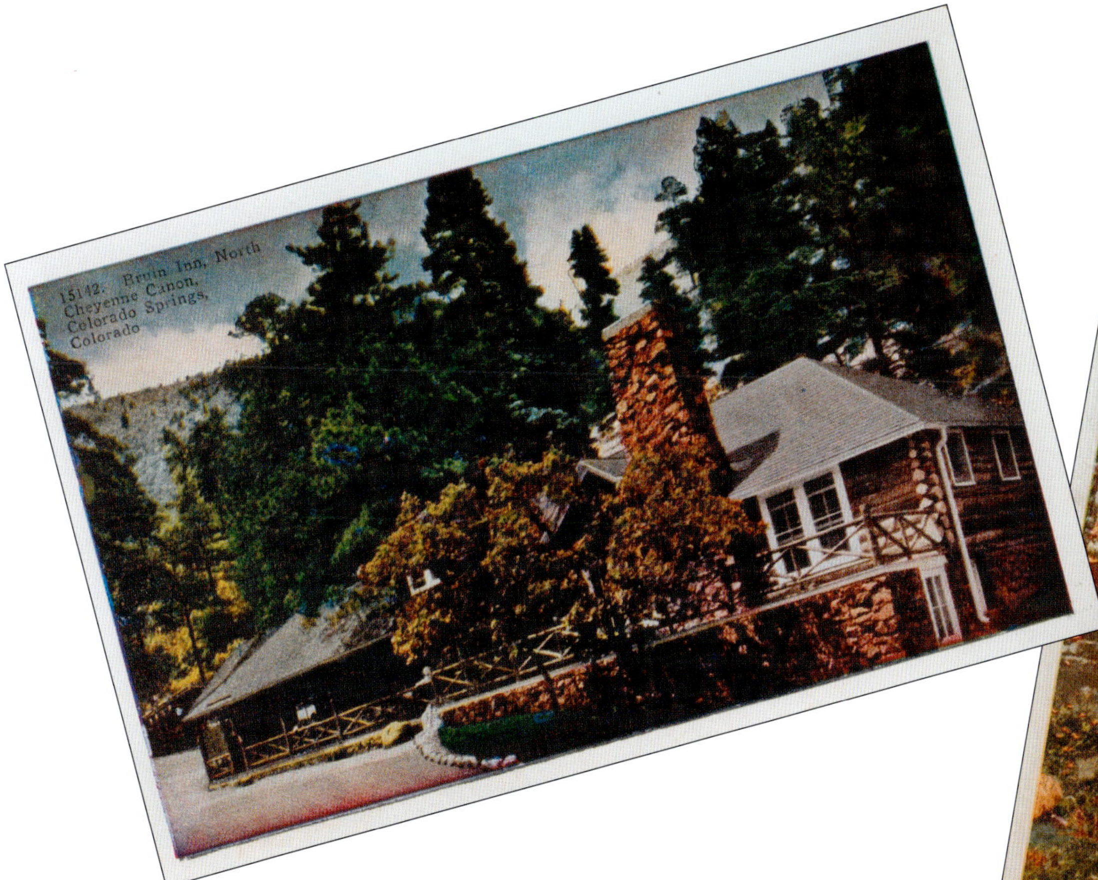

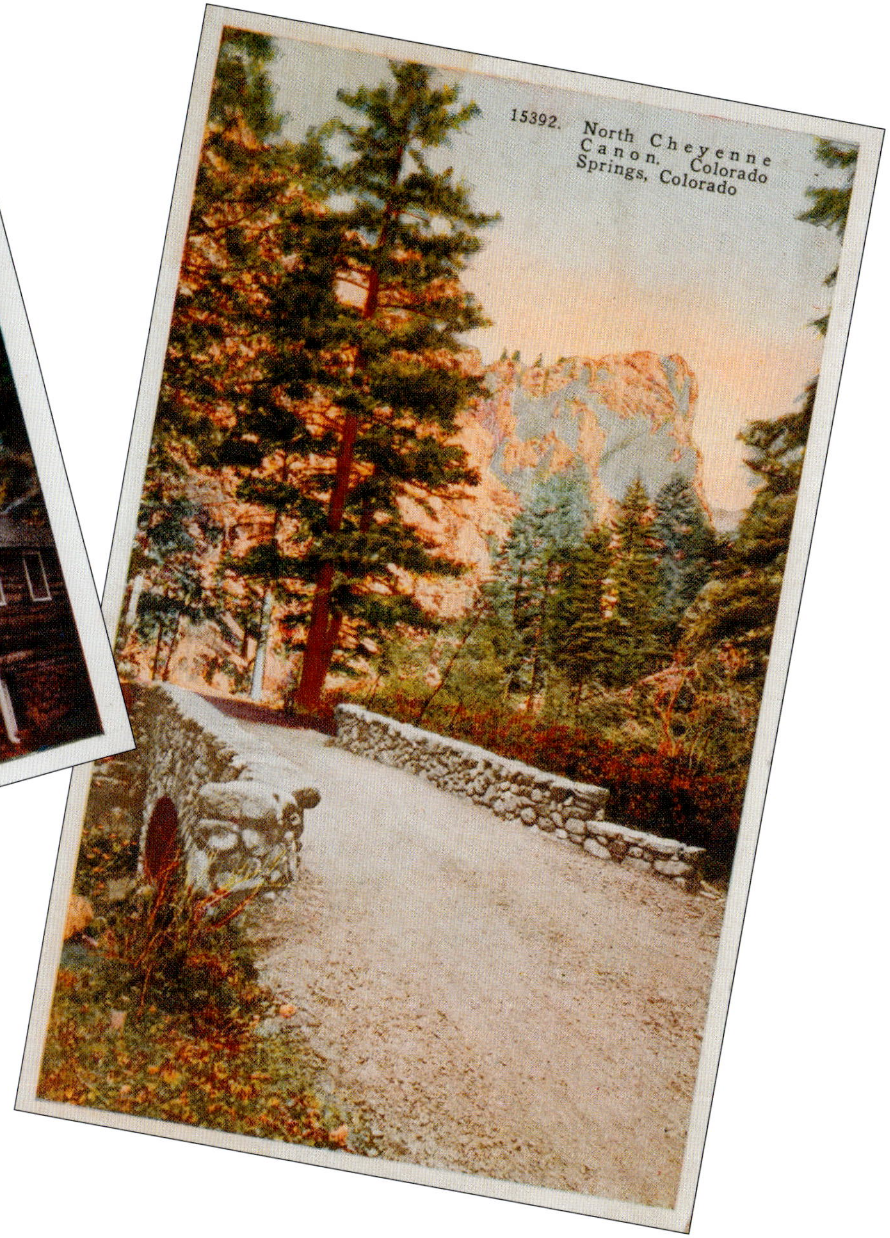

Located near the Falls, the Bruin Inn was once the home of Mr. and Mrs. Hatch, who were friends of Helen Hunt Jackson.

Circa 1930s, $4-6

North Cheyenne Cañon was also a favorite camping ground for Native Americans, particularly the Ute tribes who lived in the area.

Cancelled 1924, $4-6

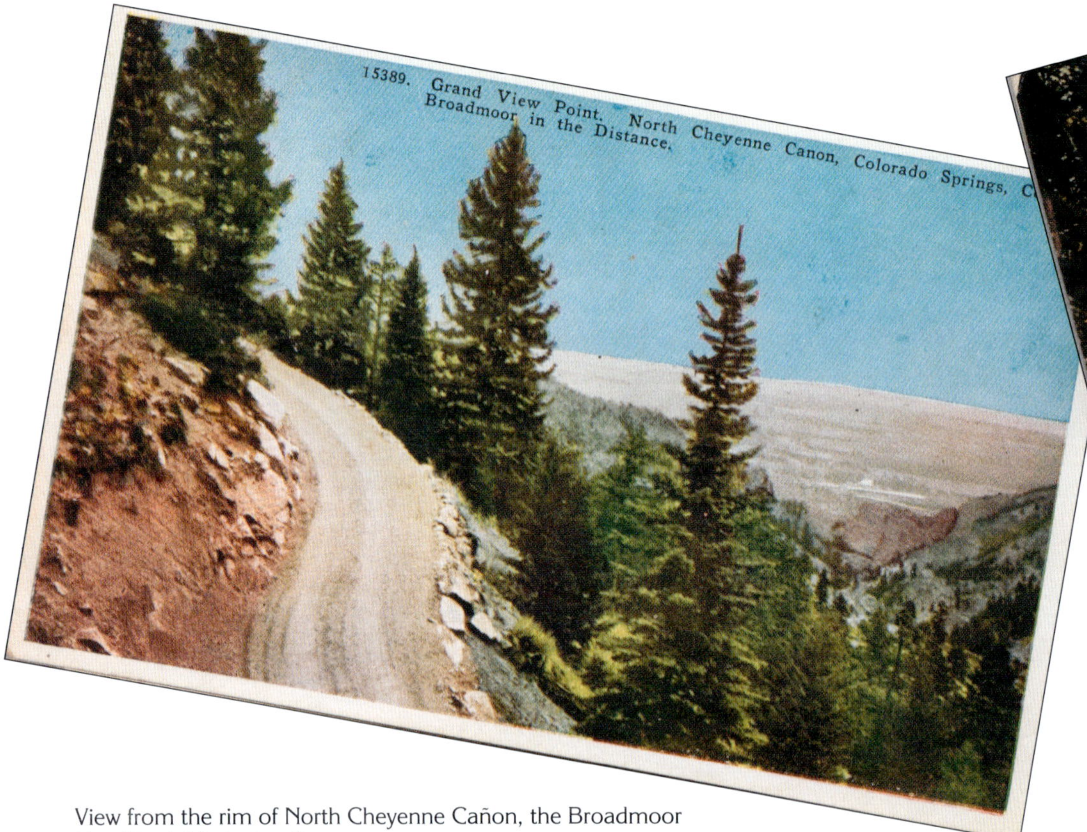

View from the rim of North Cheyenne Cañon, the Broadmoor Hotel is visible in the distance.

Circa 1920s, $4-6

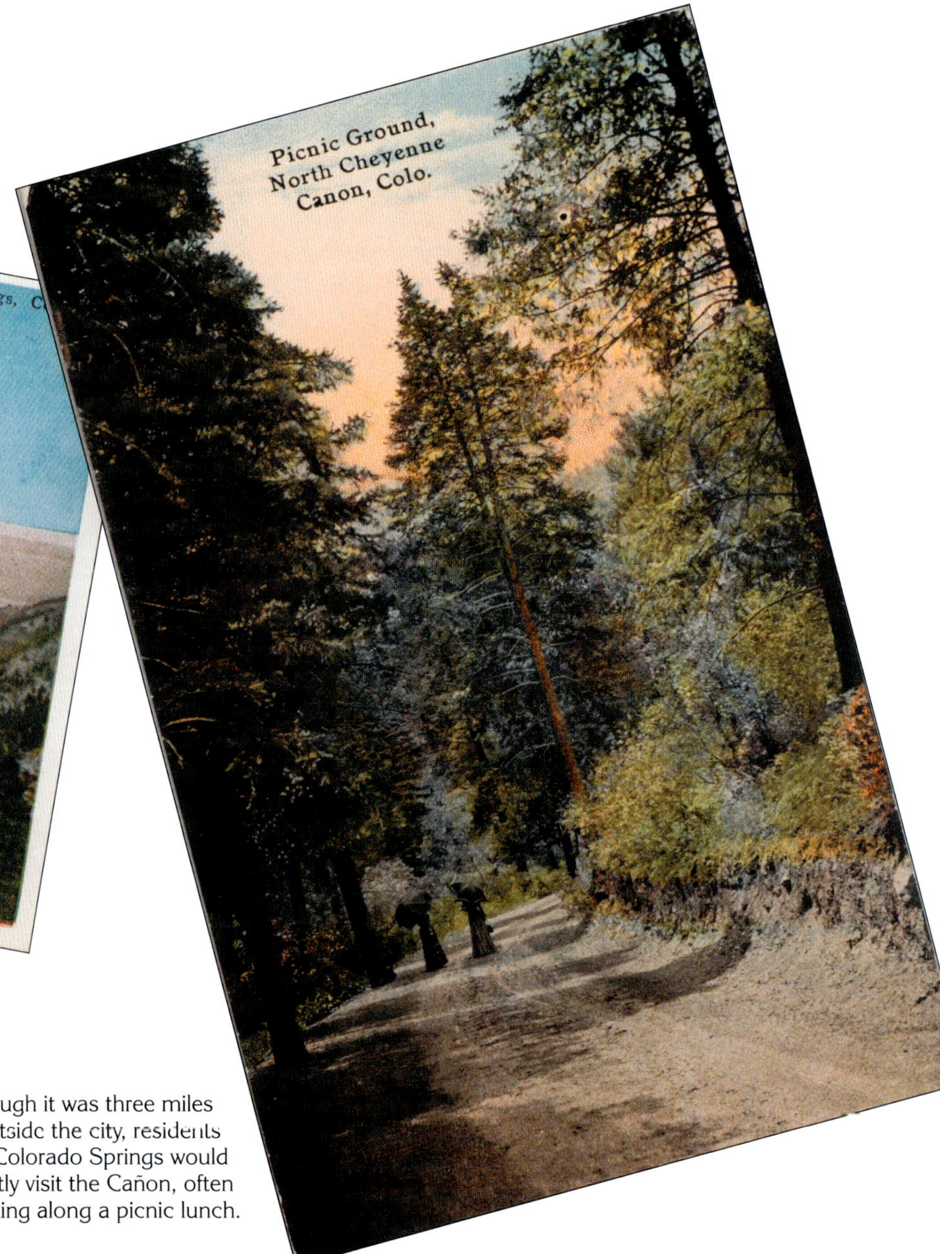

Though it was three miles outside the city, residents of Colorado Springs would frequently visit the Cañon, often taking along a picnic lunch.

Circa 1910s, $4-6

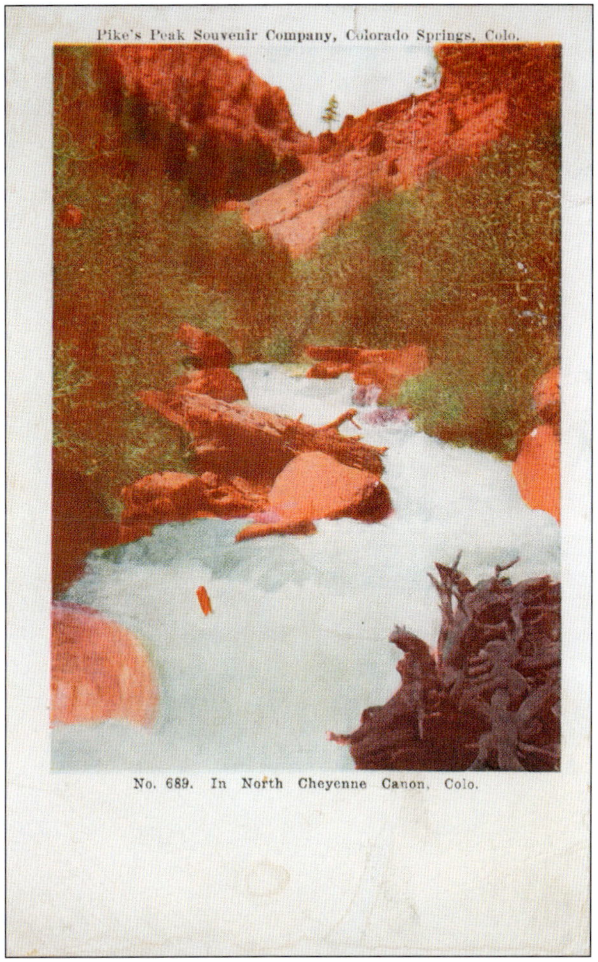

North Cheyenne Creek begins at the Stratton Reservoir at Mount Almagre; it flows into the Canyon over Helen Hunt Falls and continues on until it meets South Cheyenne Creek. The waters of the creek flow very strong and very fast. Visitors to North Cheyenne Cañon are warned not to go into the creek.

Cancelled 1909, $4-6

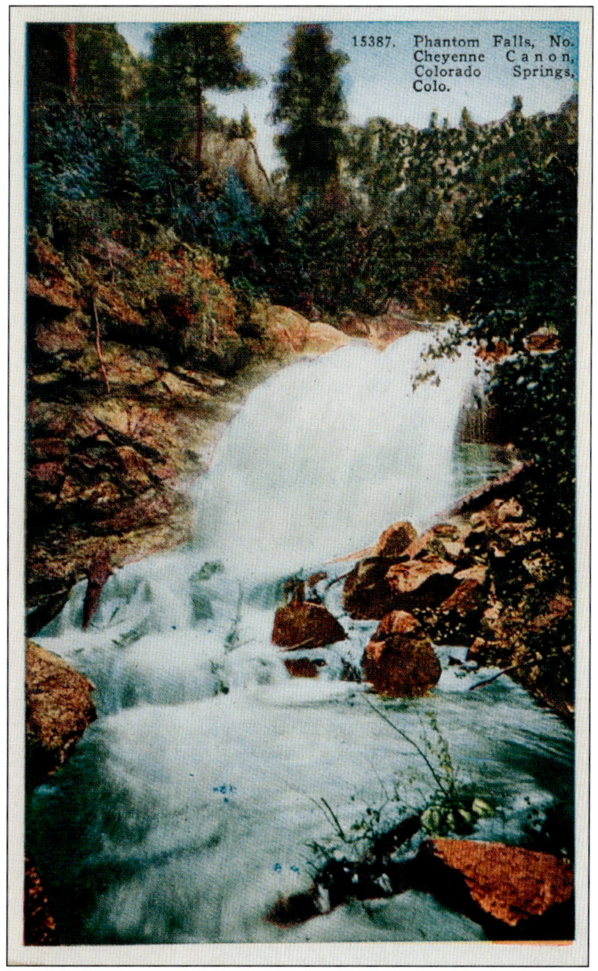

In its trip through North Cheyenne Cañon, North Cheyenne Creek flows over several waterfalls like Phantom Falls pictured here.

Circa 1920s, $4-6

Bridal Veil Falls was named for the water that flows down the falls like the graceful and delicate veil of a bride before the altar.

Circa 1930s, $4-6

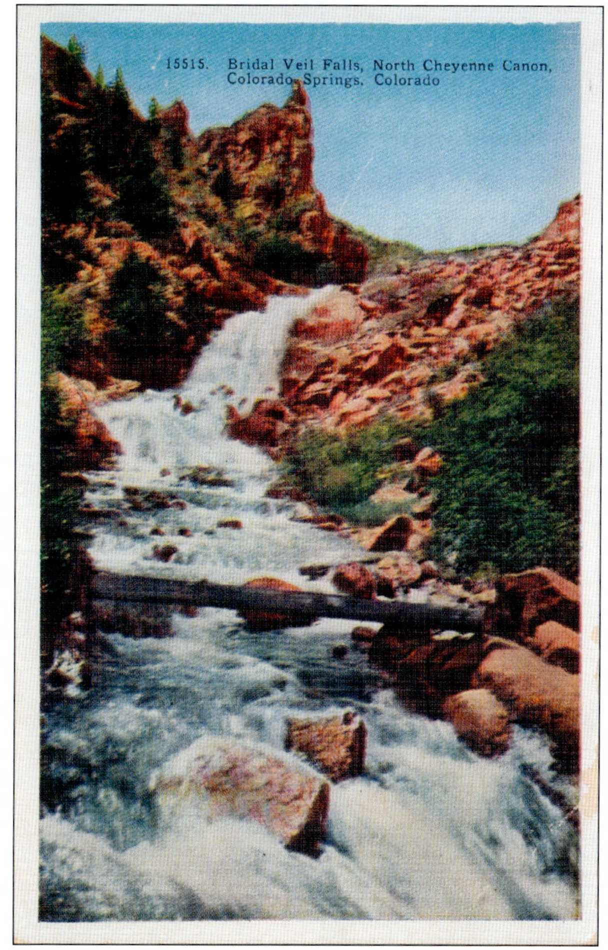

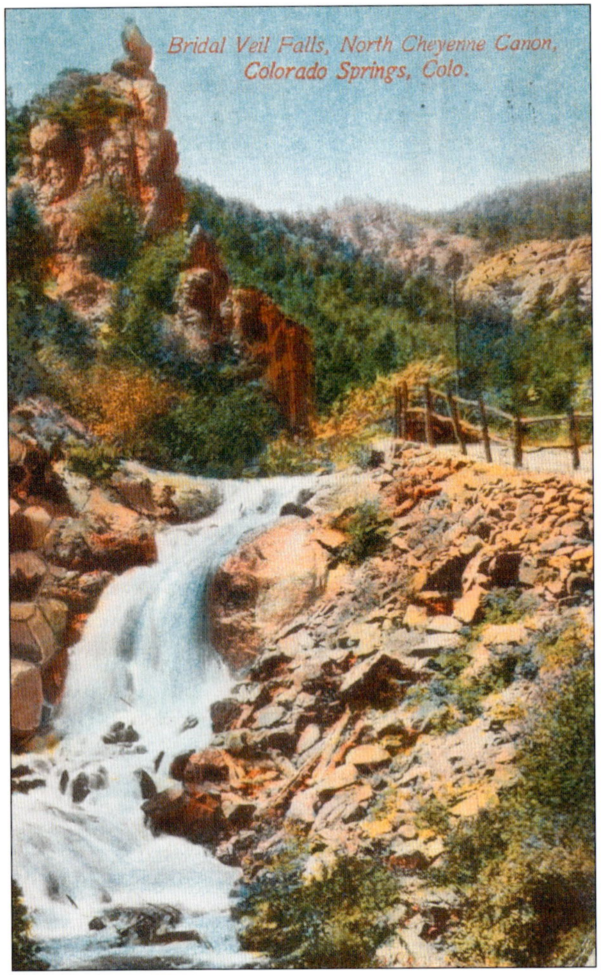

Young couples who crossed over Bridal Veil Falls were said to be "crossing the Rubicon of Love," committing themselves wholeheartedly to the risky venture of love.

Cancelled 1914, $4-6

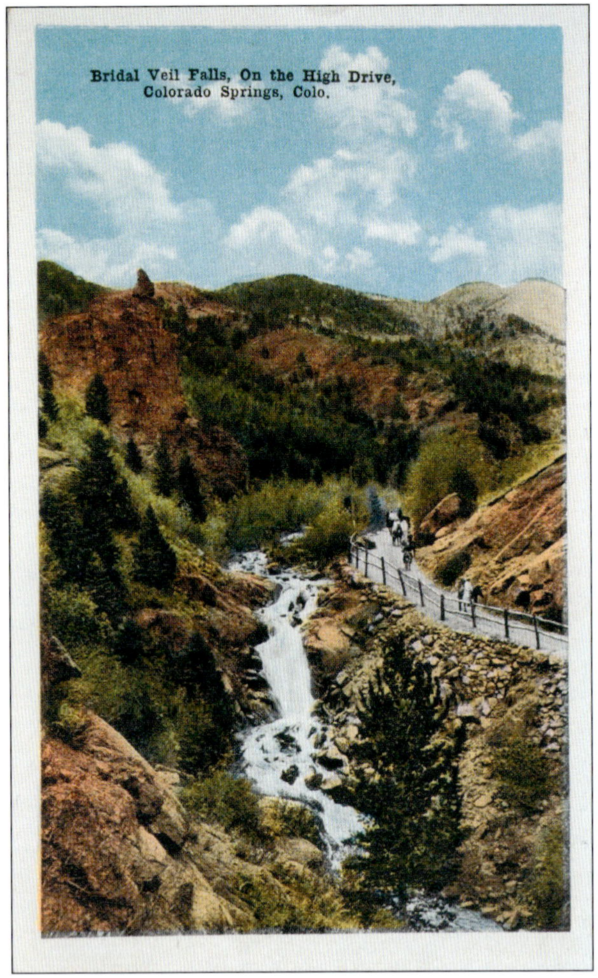

Bridal Veil Falls as seen from the High Drive.

Circa 1910s, $4-6

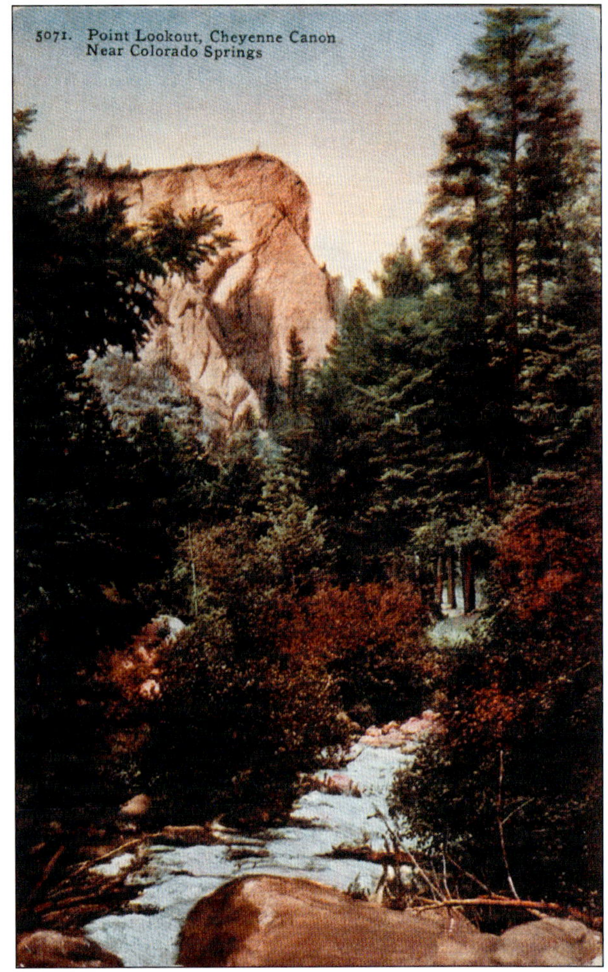

Point Lookout, from there visitors had a splendid view of the Cañon and beyond.

Circa 1930s, $4-6

South Cheyenne Cañon and Seven Falls

South Cheyenne Cañon's first owner was a homesteader, Nathaniel Colby, who obtained the land in 1872. He did not stay long. Nine months later, Colby sold the land to the Colorado Springs Land Company. The property passed from one owner to another until James Hull purchased it in 1882. A naturalist, Hull had bought the property largely in order to keep local logging companies from felling any more of the Cañon's trees. Believing others might share his appreciation for South Cheyenne Cañon's scenic beauty, James Hull began advertising his property as a scenic resort, setting up a tollbooth at the Cañon's mouth and charging visitors admission to enter. Hull and his son after him managed the property until C.D. Weimer purchased it in 1905. Weimer owned the property until it was bought in 1946 by Albert Galatyn Hill.

The Cañon is home to a number of interesting features, including the Pillars of Hercules – which stand 790 and 740 feet tall and forty-one feet apart at their narrowest point – and the former gravesite of Helen Hunt Jackson. Jackson spent a great deal of her time in Colorado Springs visiting the Cañon and, as her final wish, wanted to be buried on a point overlooking South Cheyenne Cañon and Cheyenne Mountain. At the end of the Cañon stands its most famous feature, Seven Falls. Measuring 181 feet tall, water from the stream above the Cañon falls down the walls in seven cascades before reaching the bottom.

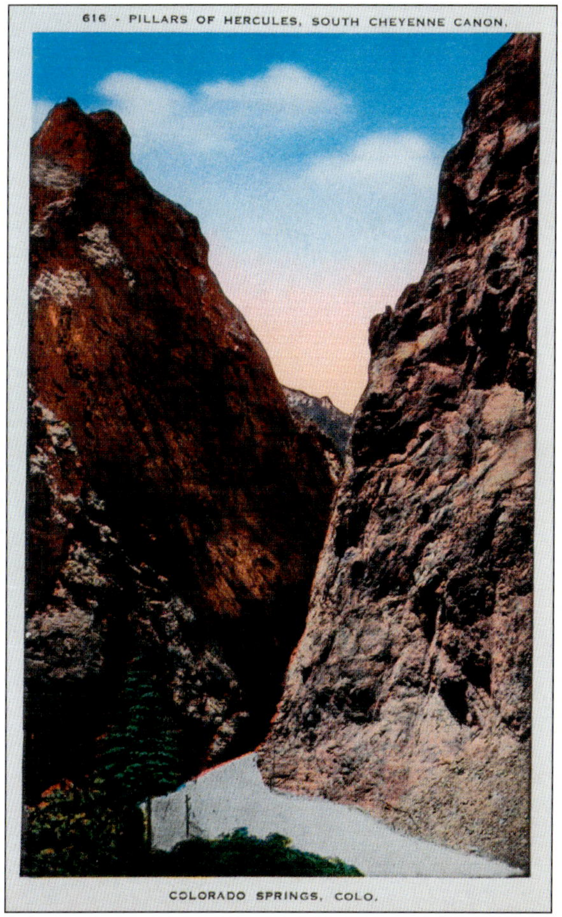

The Pillars of Hercules, the entrance to South Cheyenne Cañon.

Circa 1930s, $4-6

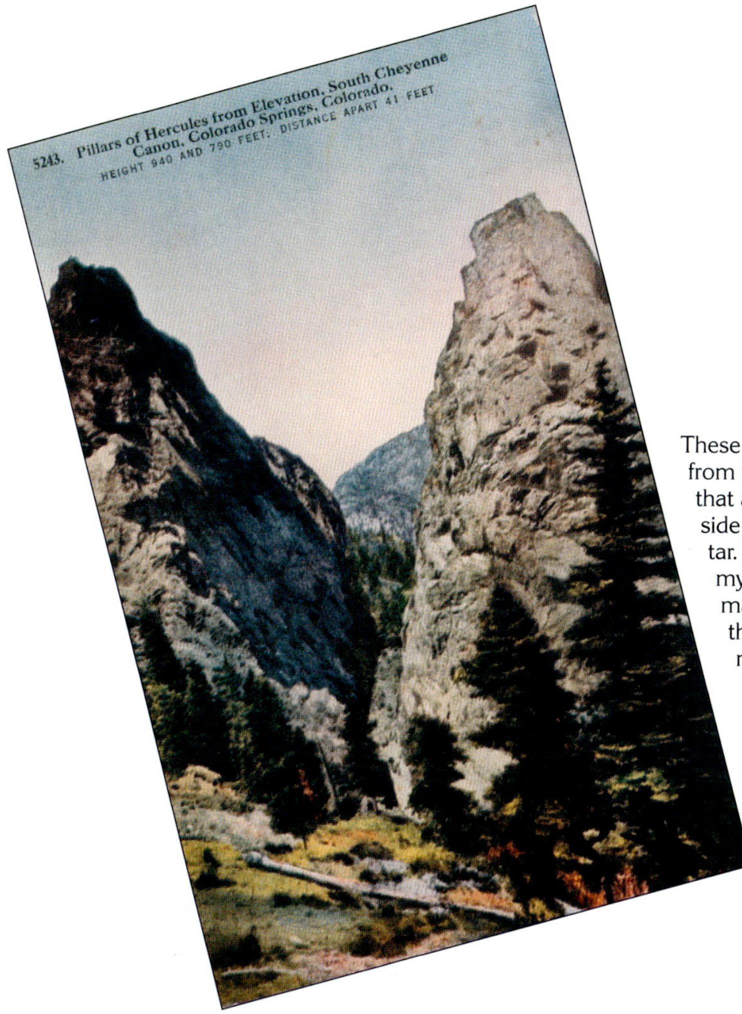

These Pillars take their name from the Pillars of Hercules that are located on either side of the Strait of Gibraltar. According to Greek myth, the hero Hercules made the Pillars and the Strait by splitting a mountain in half.

Circa 1930s, $4-6

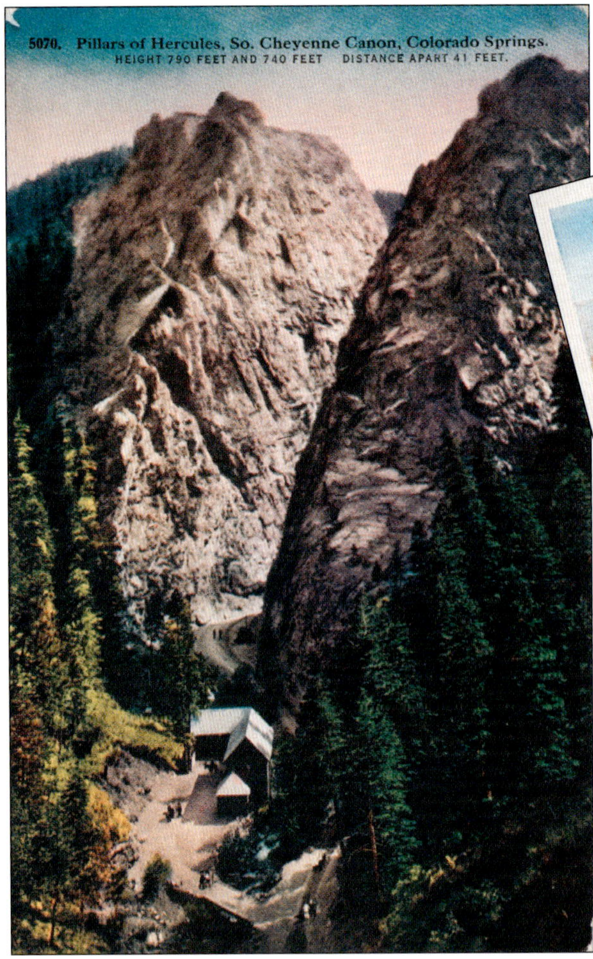

In South Cheyenne Cañon the Pillars are 790 and 740 feet high, but only forty-one feet apart at their narrowest point.

Circa 1910s, $4-6

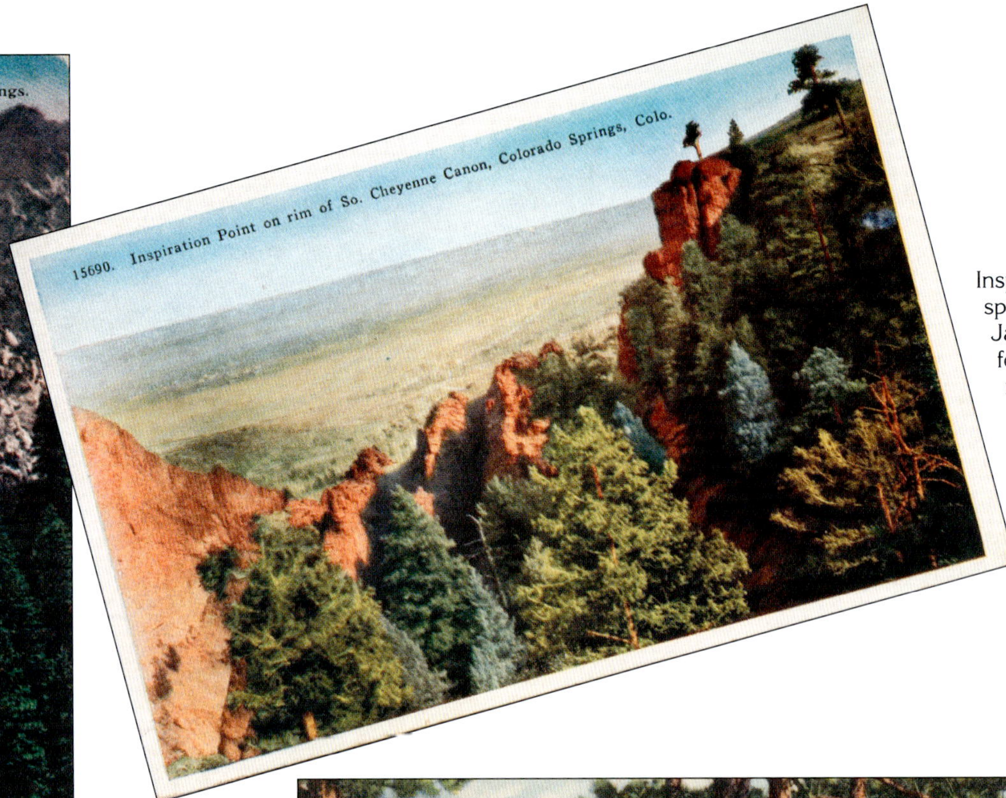

Inspiration Point was the favorite spot of author Helen Hunt Jackson. It was there that she found the inspiration to write many of her poems.

Circa 1930s, $4-6

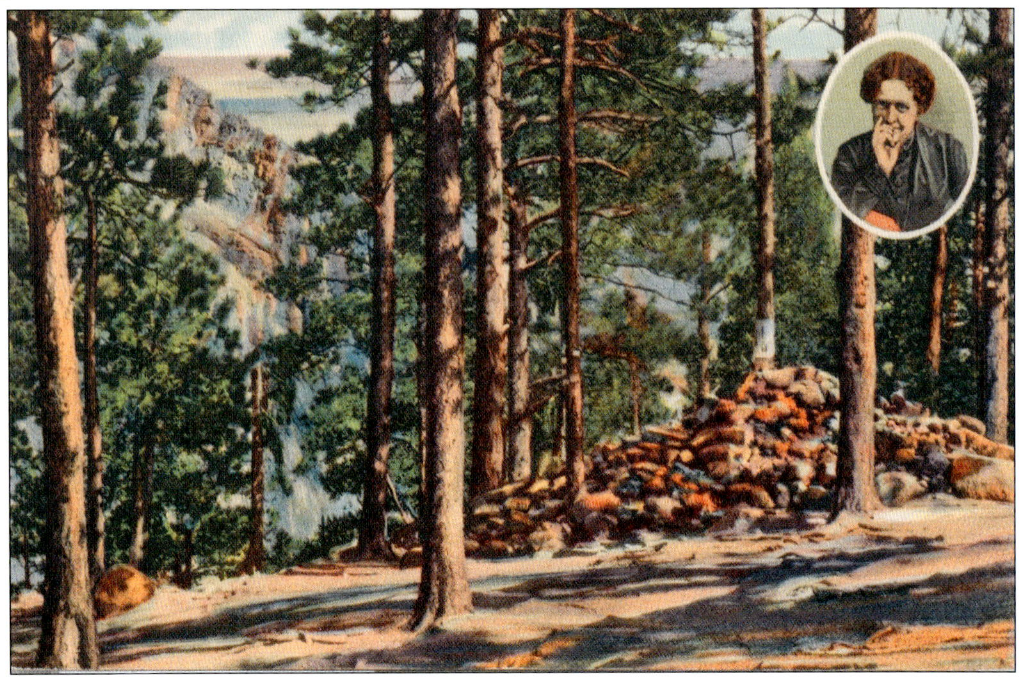

Helen Hunt Jackson died of cancer in San Francisco in 1885. It was her final wish that she be buried in a spot overlooking Cheyenne Cañon and Colorado Springs, two of the places she loved so well.

Cancelled 1938, $8-10

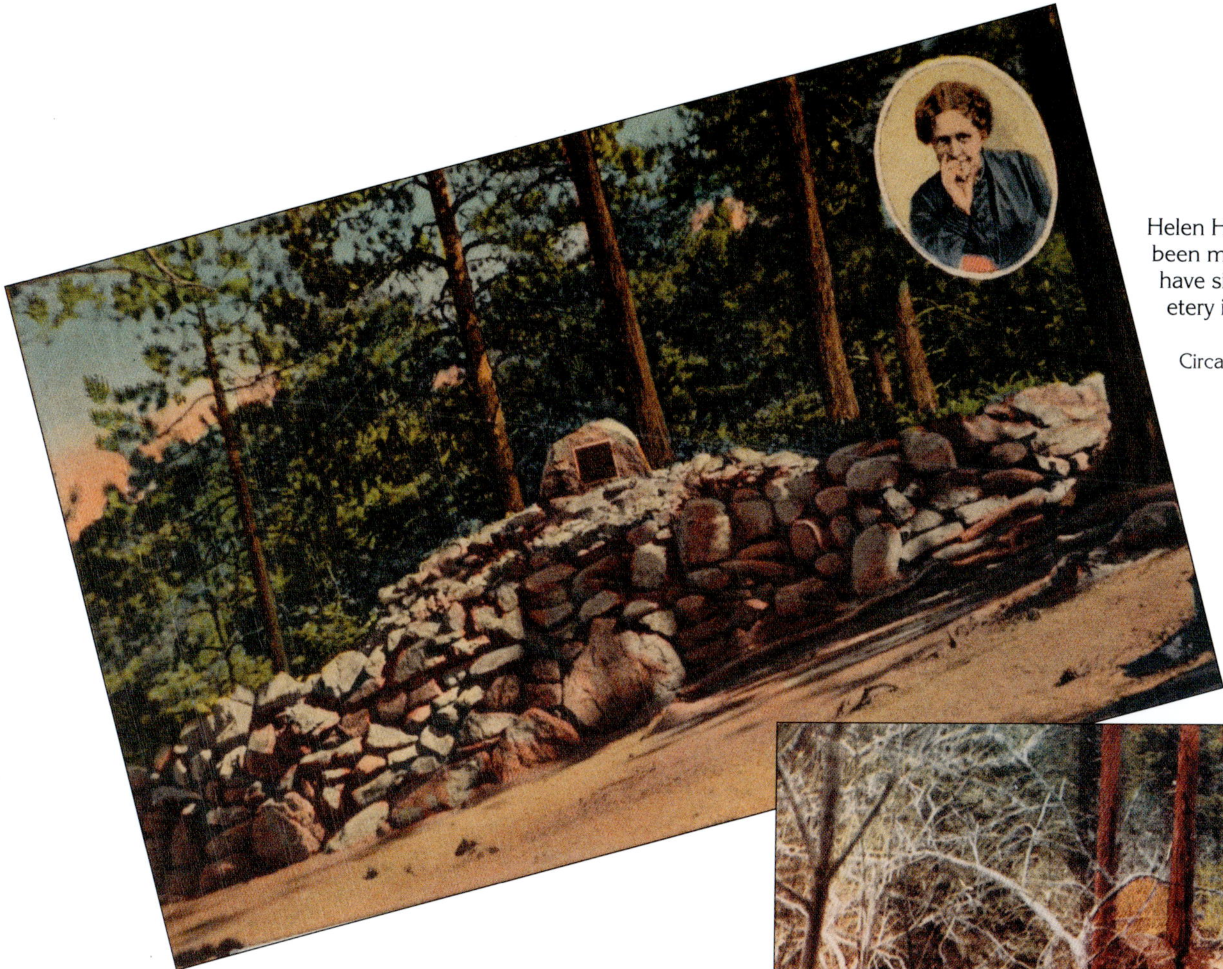

Helen Hunt Jackson's original gravesite has been marked with a plaque and her remains have since been relocated to Evergreen Cemetery in Colorado Springs.

Circa 1940s, $8-10

Like North Cheyenne Creek, the waters of South Cheyenne Creek flowed very fast over a number of rapids and waterfalls.

Circa 1930s, $4-6

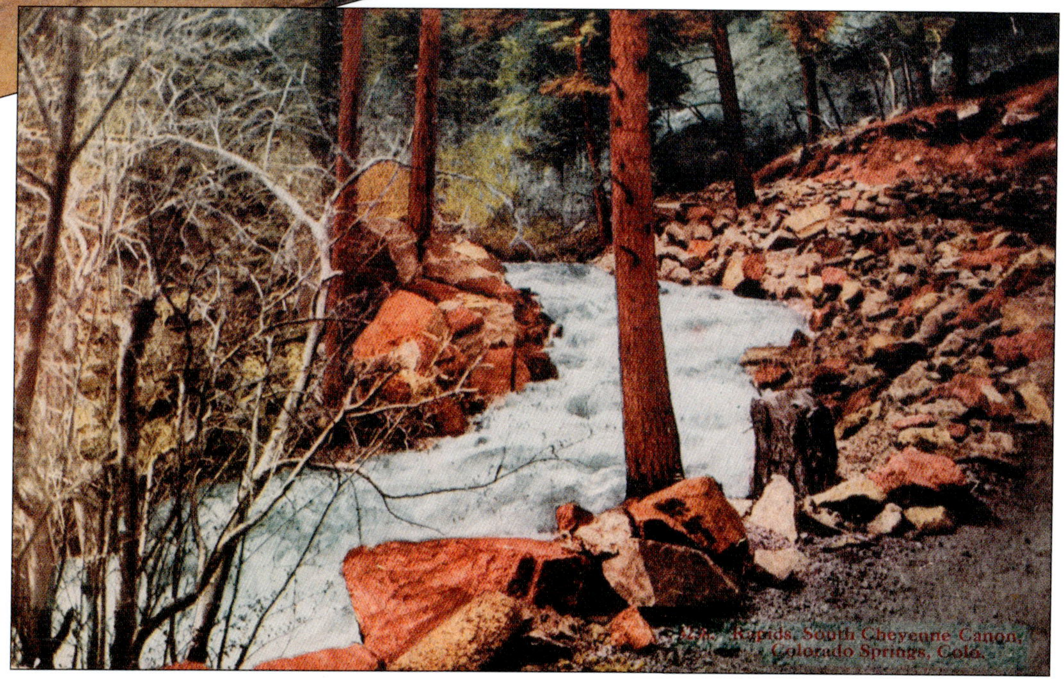

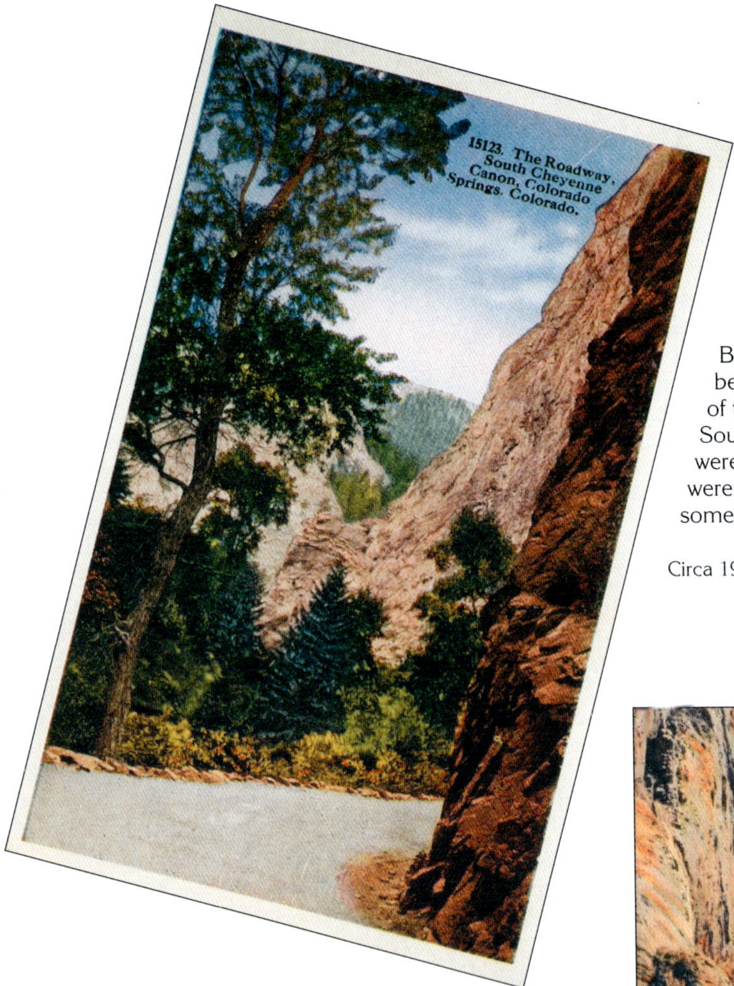

Before the automobile became popular, most of the roads and trails in South Cheyenne Cañon were made of dirt and were not paved over until some years later.

Circa 1930s, $4-6

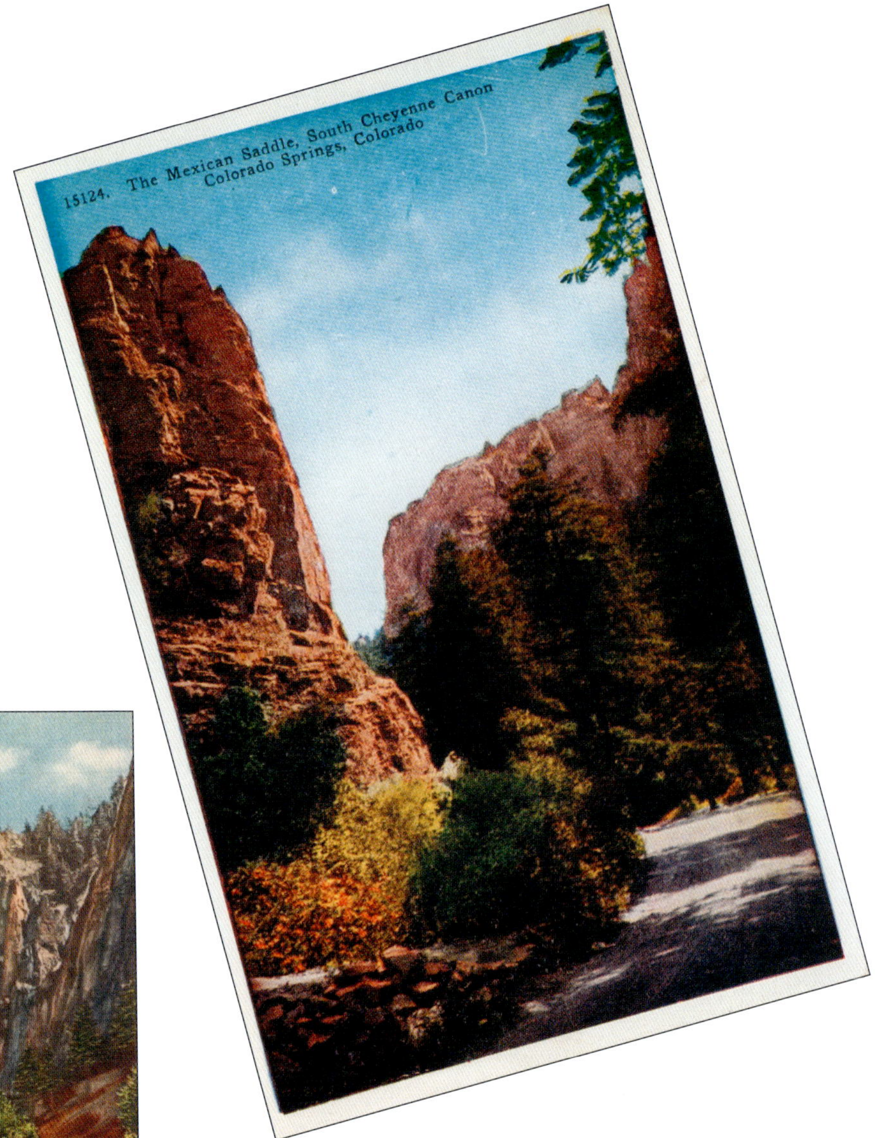

From the back: "Of all the wonderful scenic attractions in Colorado, none excel South Cheyenne Cañon in its combination of idyllic romance and magnificent scenery."

Circa 1930s, $4-6

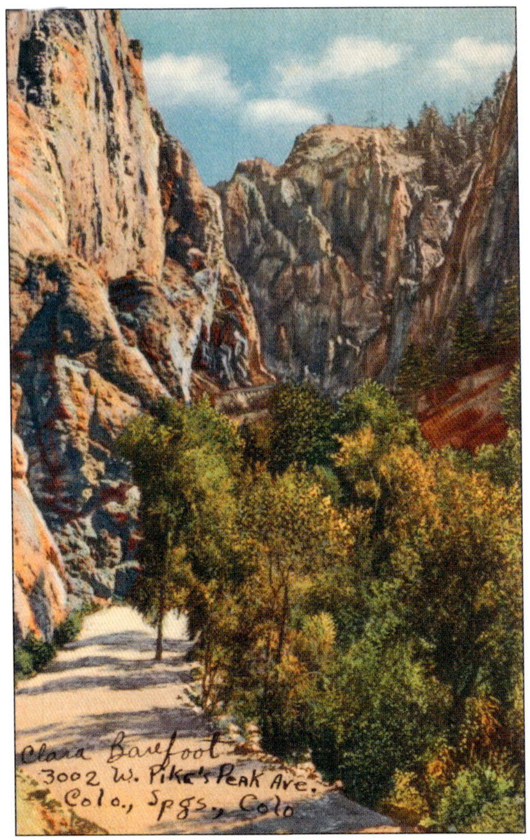

A typical example of the crags that line the walls of South Cheyenne Cañon.

Cancelled 1937, $4-6

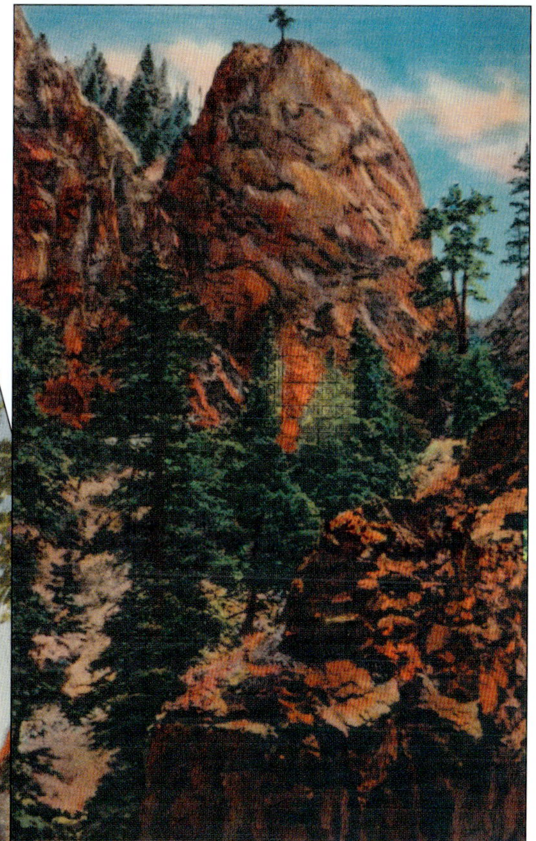

Forty feet tall and eighteen inches around, the Lonesome Pine stands alone on the slopes of South Cheyenne Cañon.

Circa 1940s, $4-6

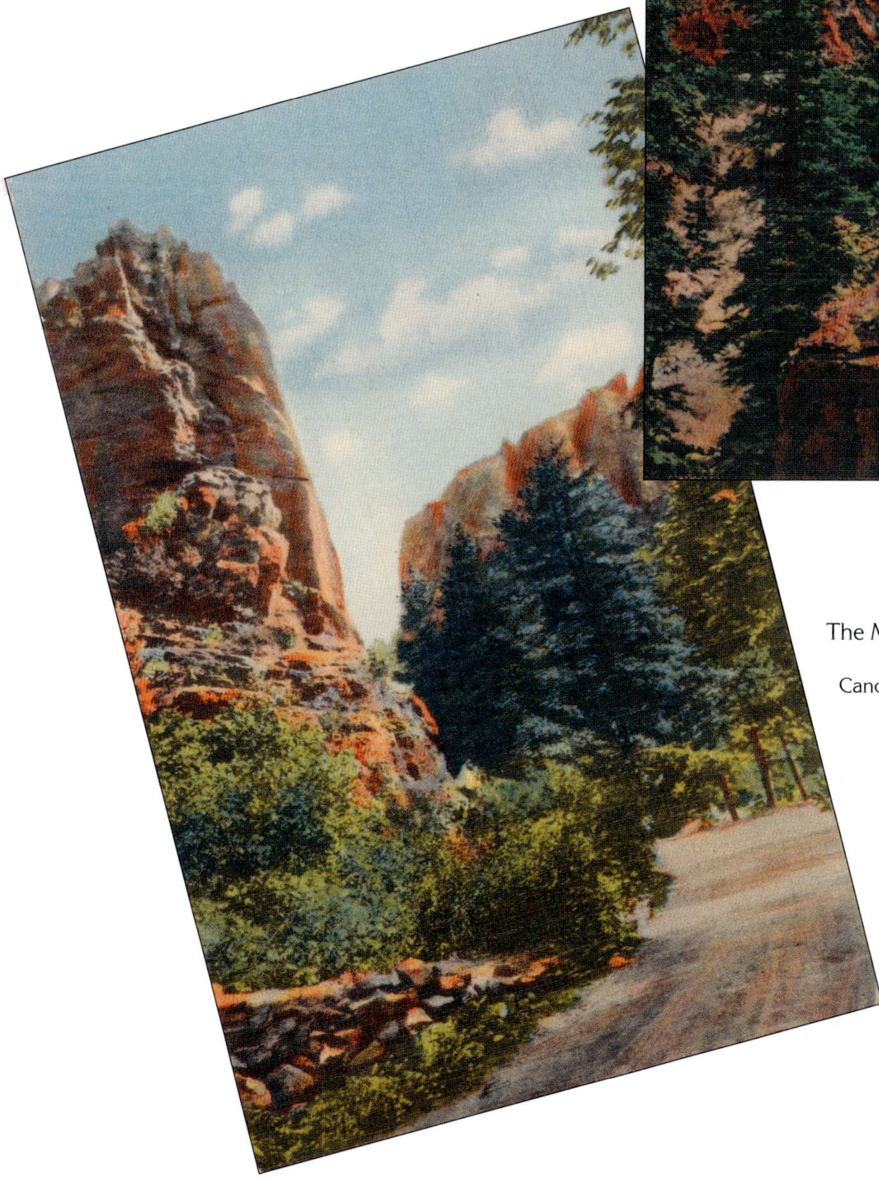

The Mexican Saddle.

Cancelled 1943, $4-6

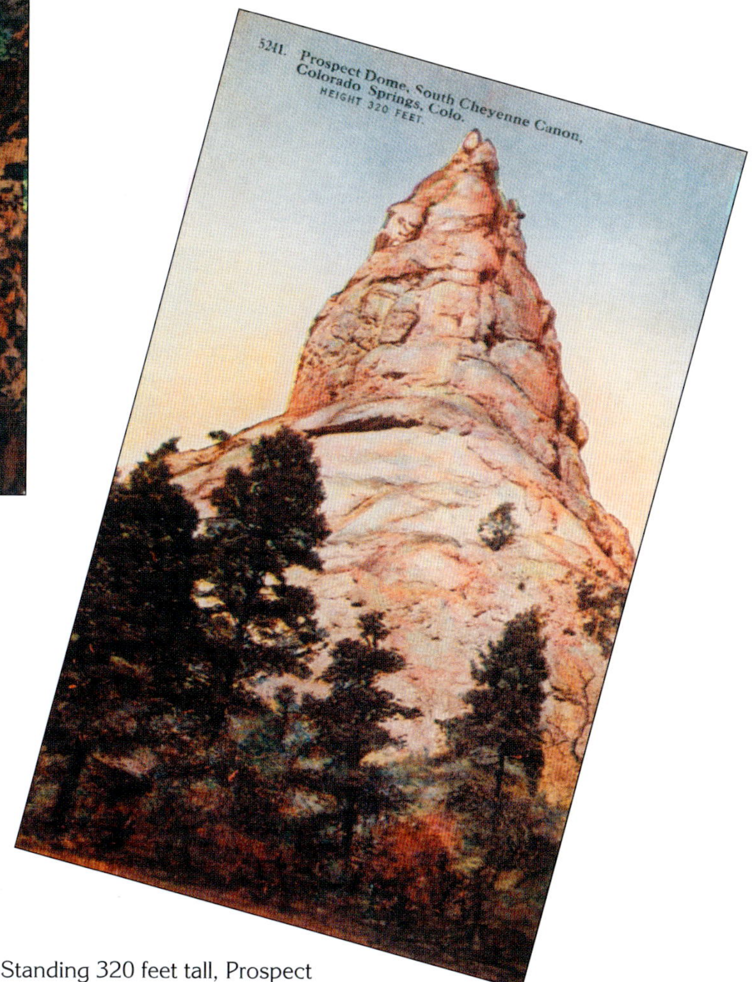

Standing 320 feet tall, Prospect Dome is visible from inside and outside the Cañon.

Circa 1930s, $4-6

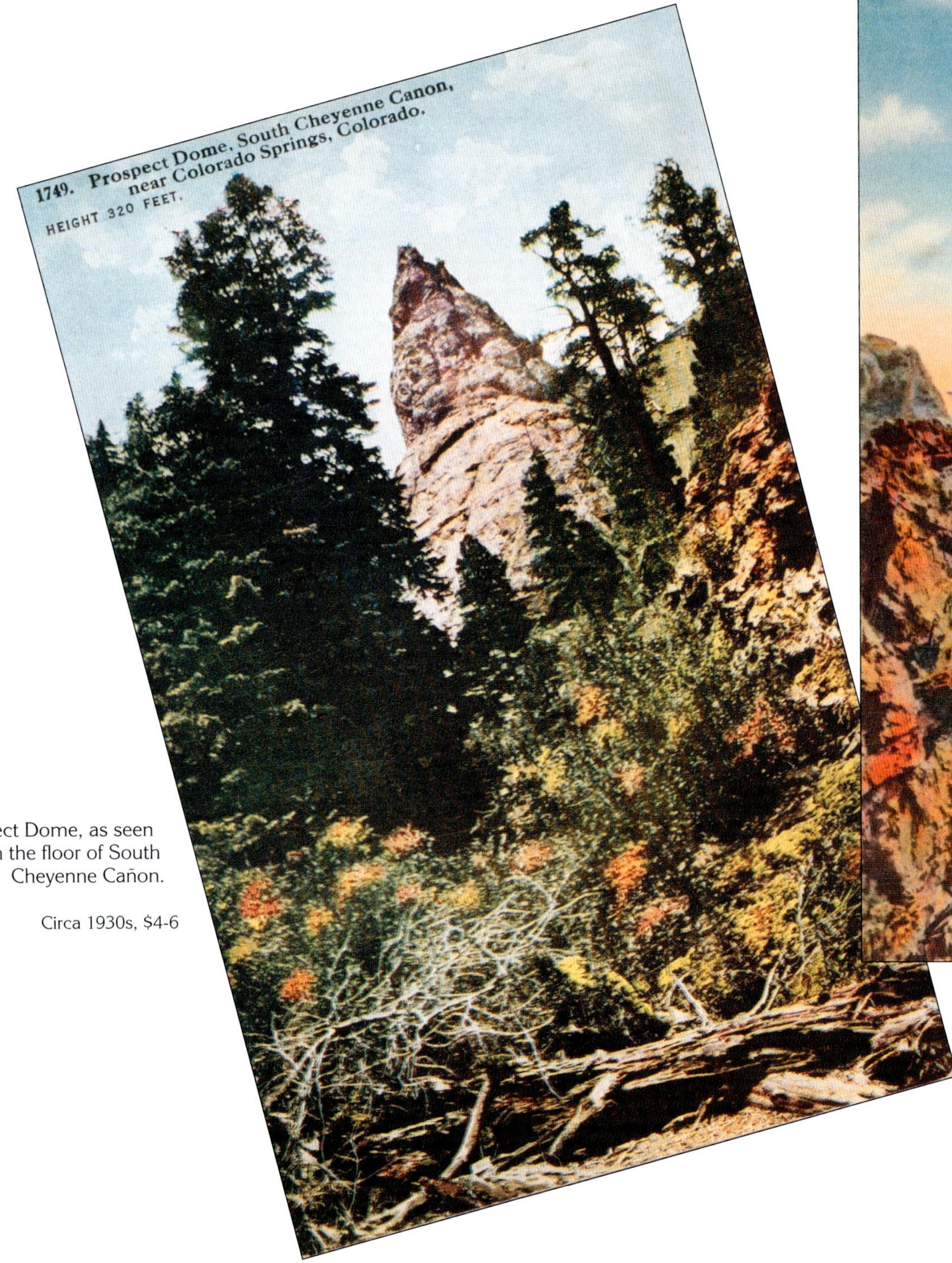

Prospect Dome, as seen from the floor of South Cheyenne Cañon.

Circa 1930s, $4-6

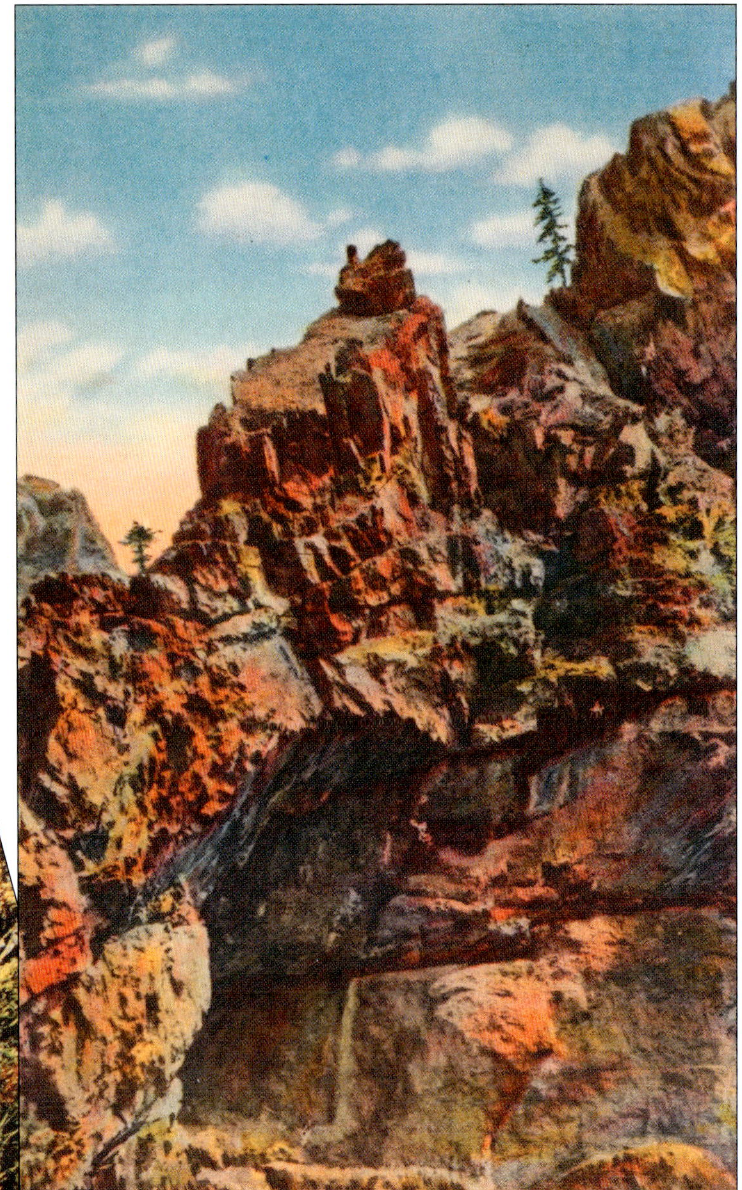

When viewed from the right angle, the rock formation pictured here resembles a sitting turkey.

Circa 1940s, $4-6

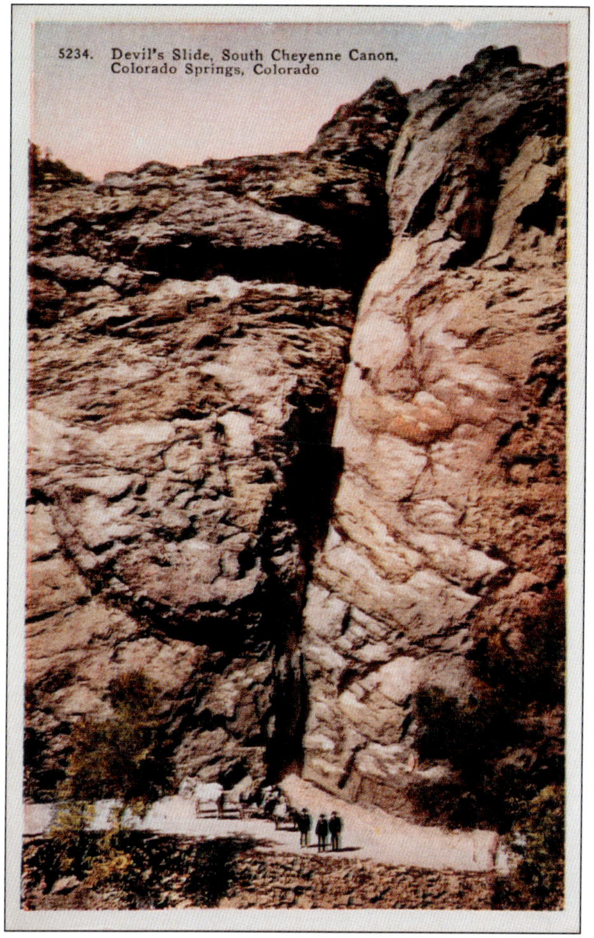

The Devil's Slide, one of the most impressive sights in South Cheyenne Cañon.

Circa 1930s, $4-6

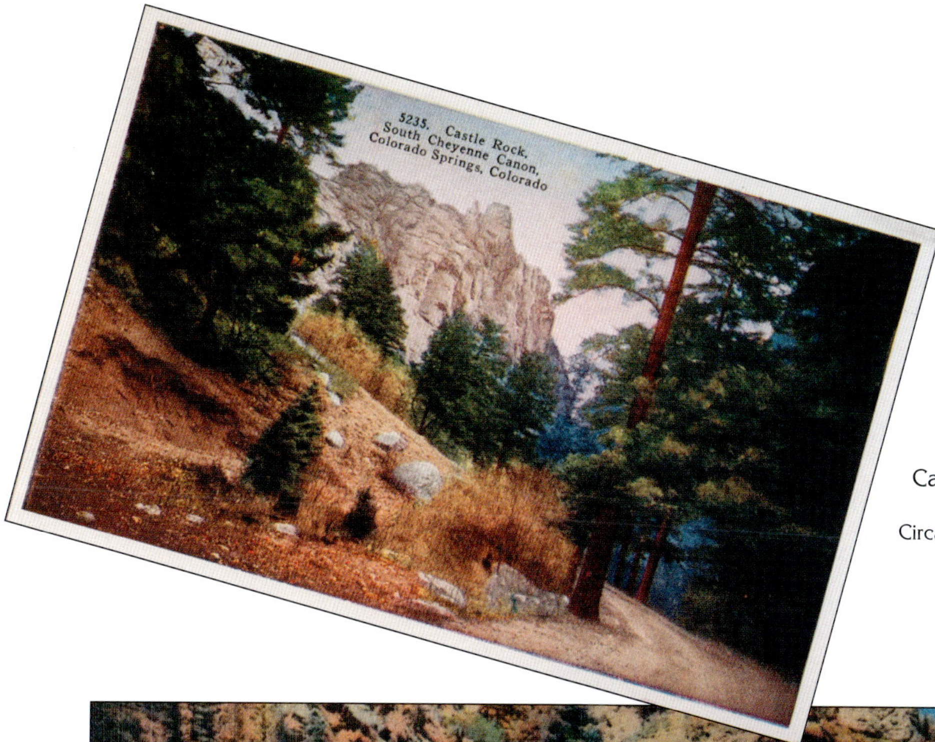

Castle Rock.

Circa 1930s, $4-6

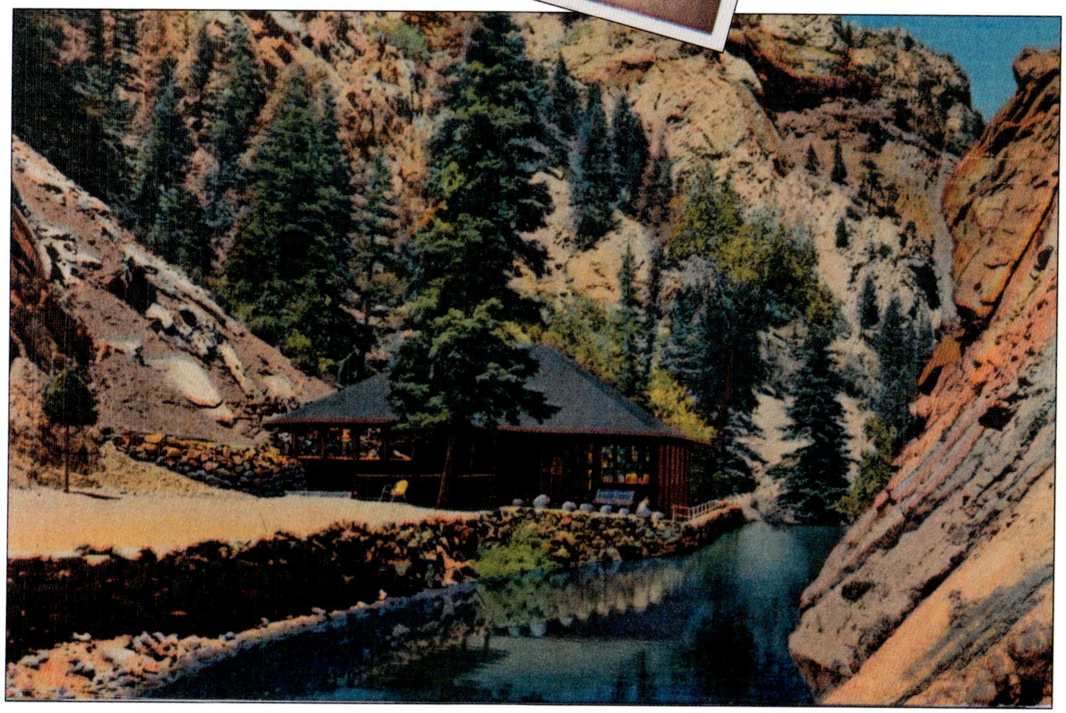

Trout Pool and Pavilion at the bottom of Seven Falls.

Circa 1940s, $4-6

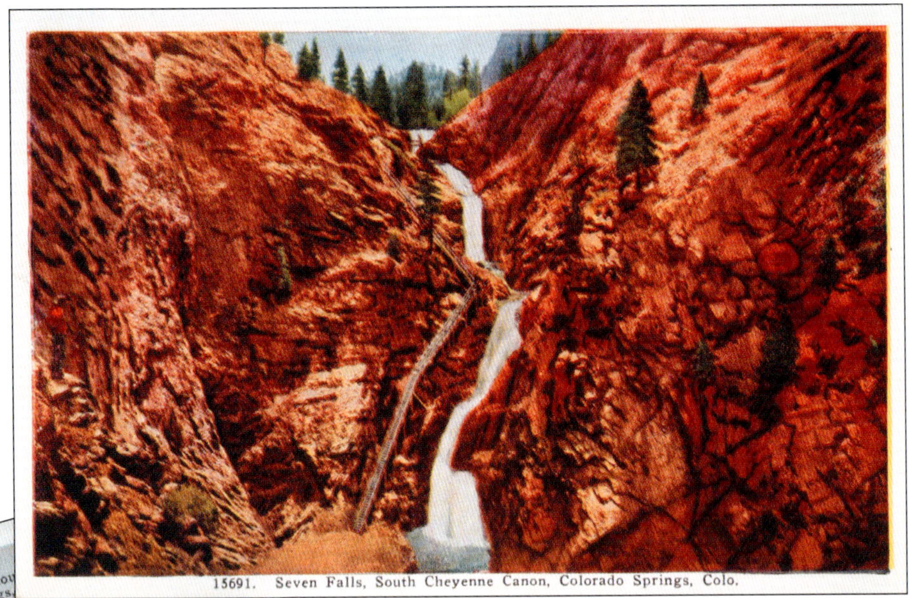

Located at the end of South Cheyenne Cañon, Seven Falls is considered to be one of the most famous attractions in the Pikes Peak Region.

Circa 1930s, $4-6

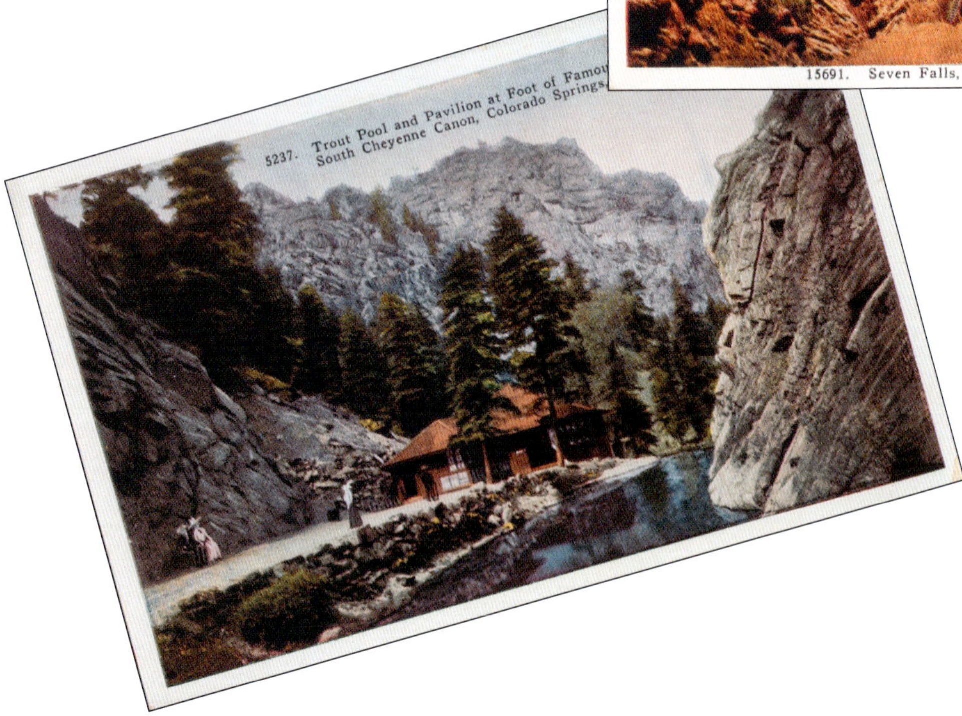

Here visitors could rest and find refreshment before climbing up the stairs to Seven Falls.

Circa 1920s, $4-6

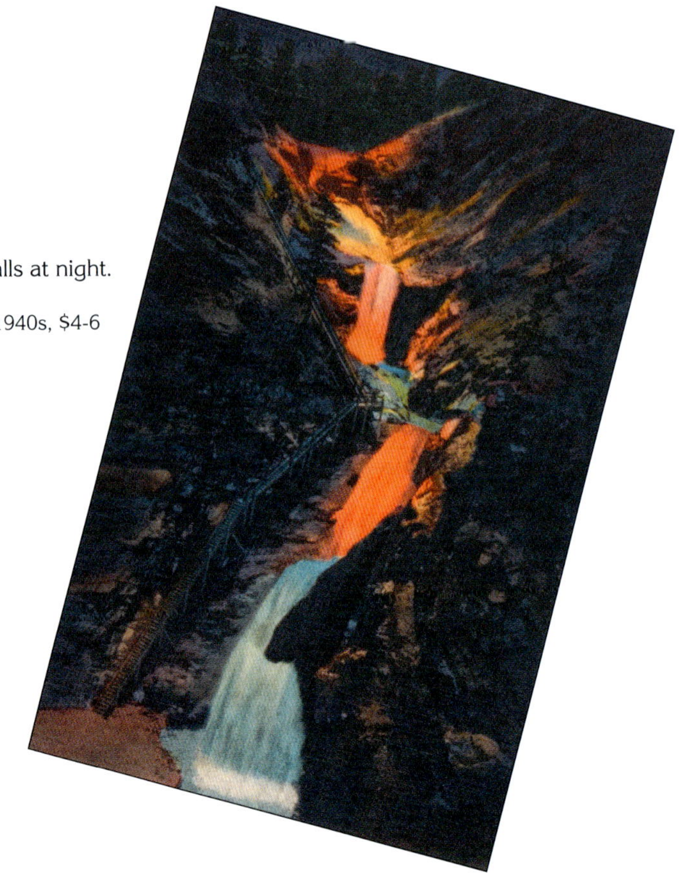

Seven Falls at night.

Circa 1940s, $4-6

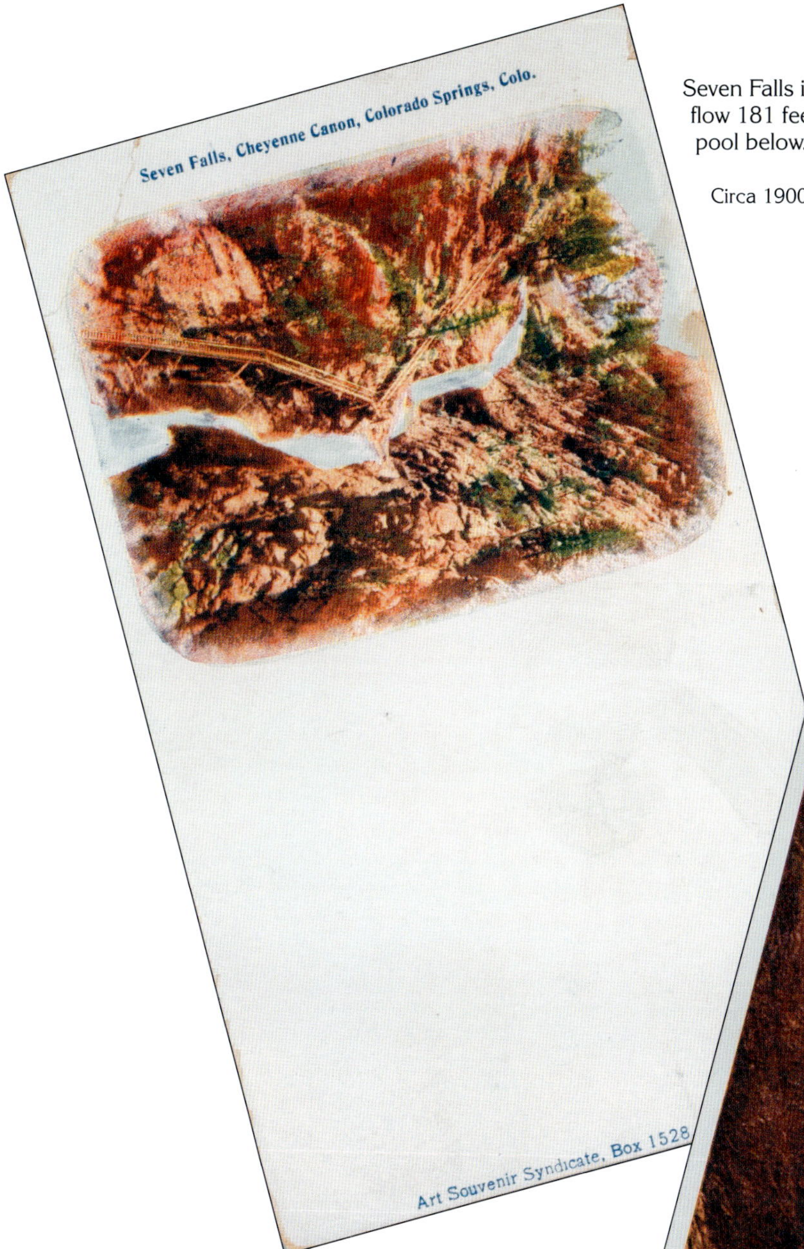

Seven Falls is made up of seven cascades which flow 181 feet down the side of the Cañon into a pool below.

Circa 1900s, $4-6

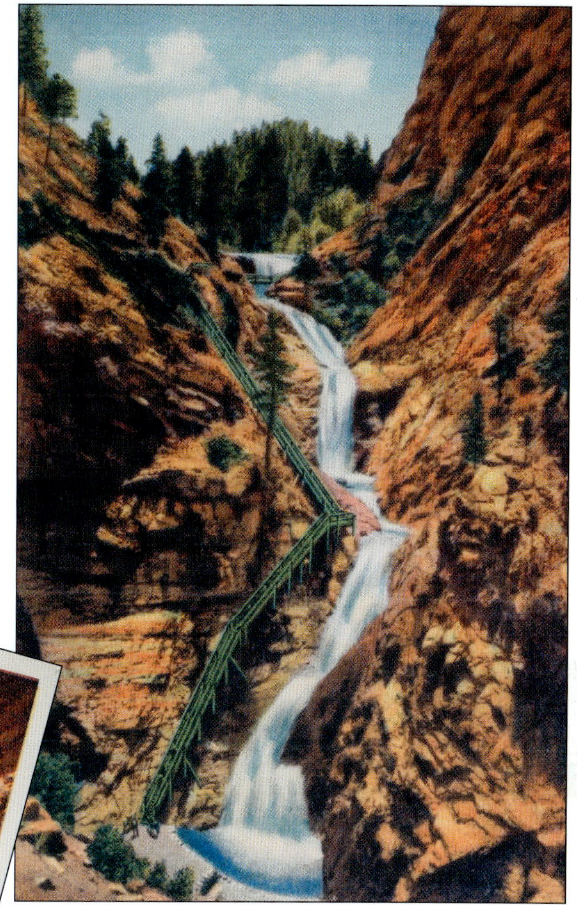

The stairs beside the Falls are 224 steps high and were built by James Hull, who purchased the Seven Falls and South Cheyenne Cañon in 1882.

Circa 1940s, $4-6

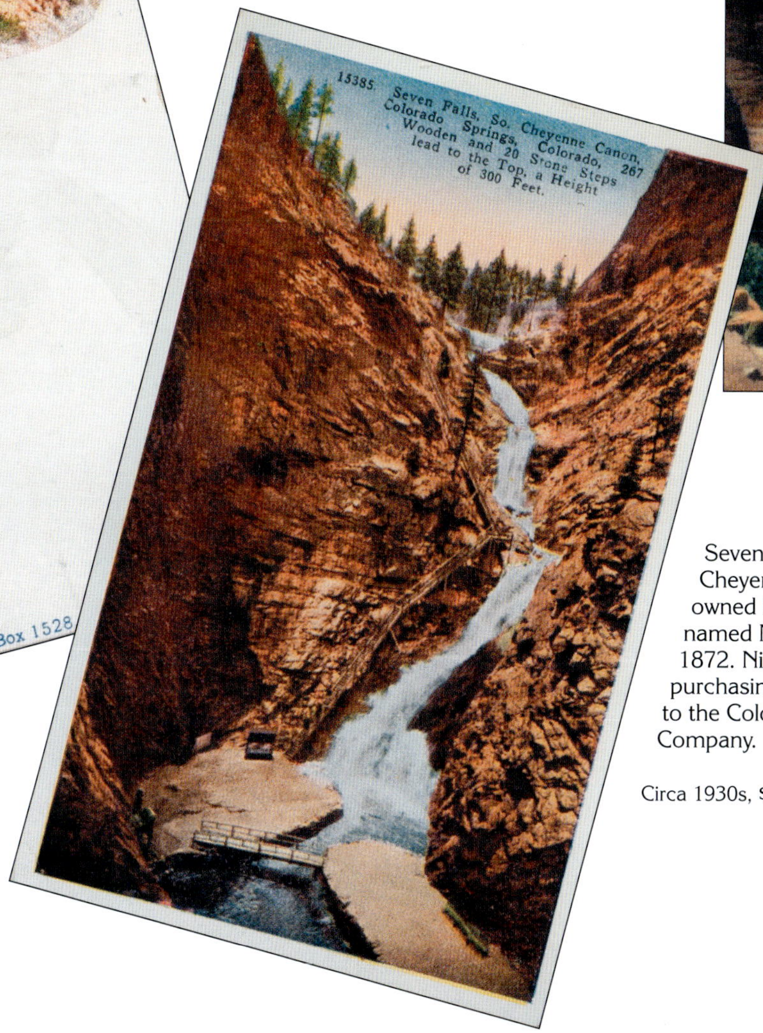

Seven Falls and South Cheyenne Cañon were first owned by a homesteader named Nathaniel Colby in 1872. Nine months after purchasing the land, he sold it to the Colorado Springs Land Company.

Circa 1930s, $4-6

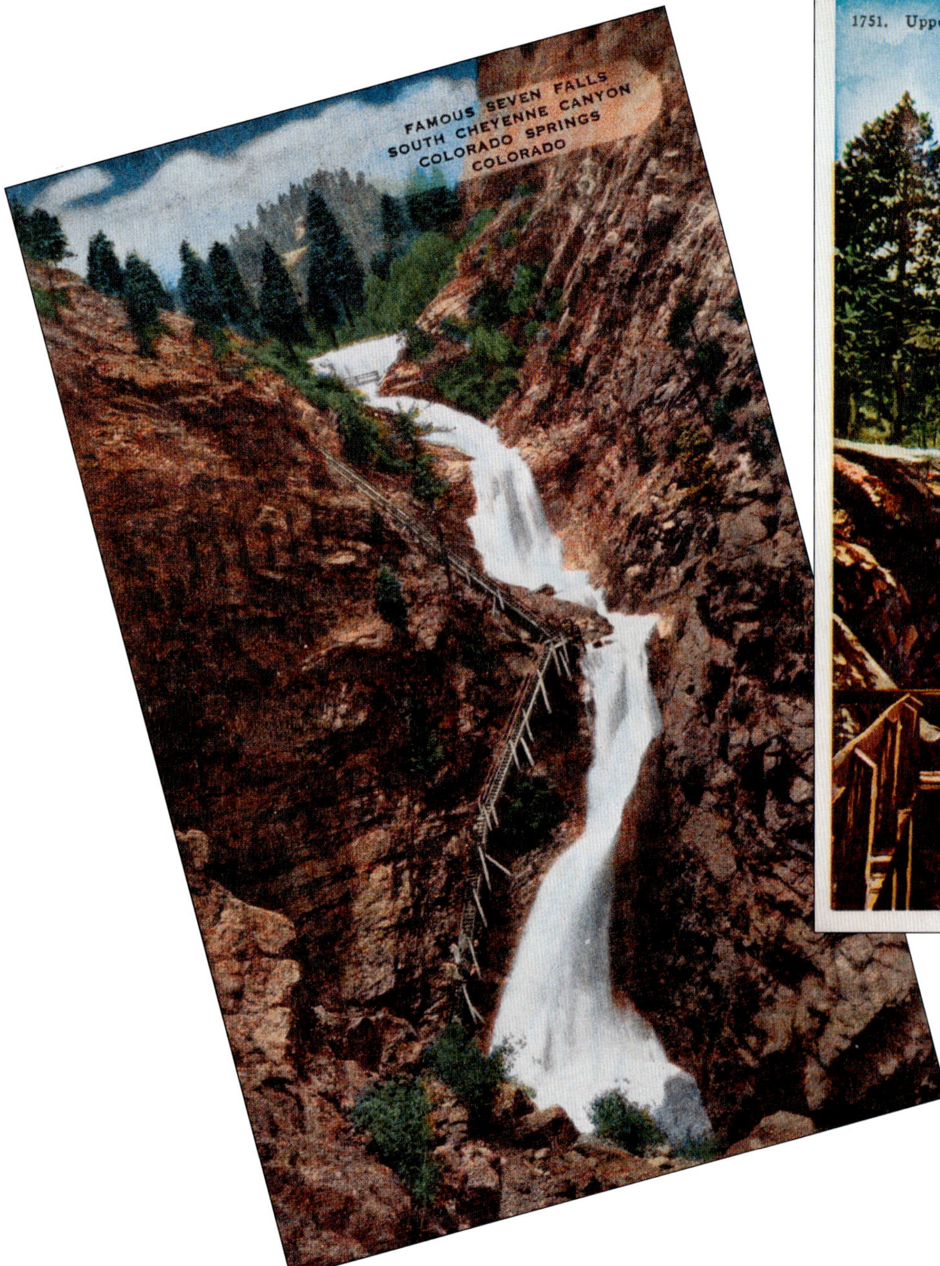

Recognizing the value of his purchase, Hull installed a tollgate at the mouth of the Cañon and started advertising the Cañon and the Falls as a scenic resort.

Cancelled 1957, $4-6

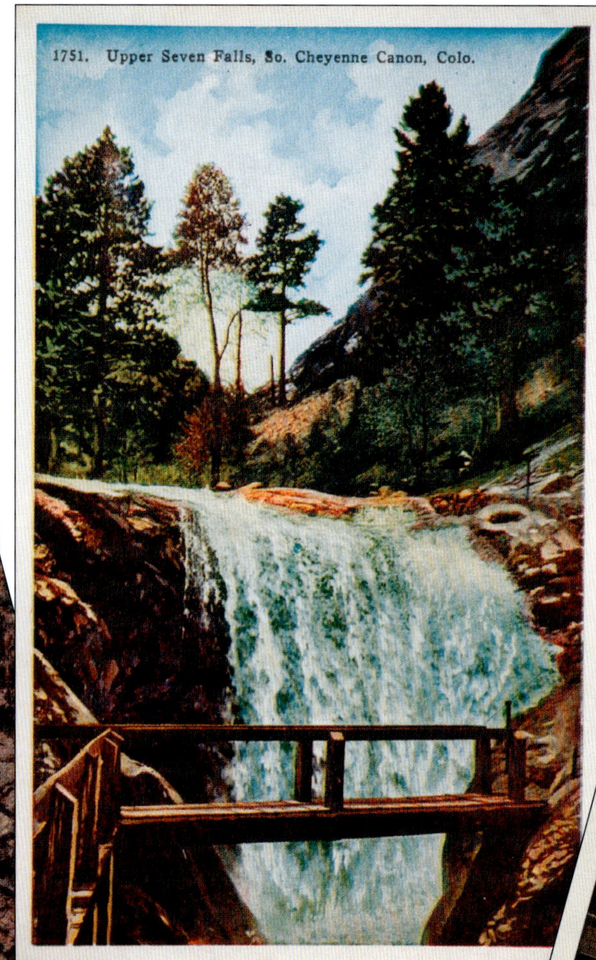

The top of Seven Falls.

Circa 1930s, $4-6

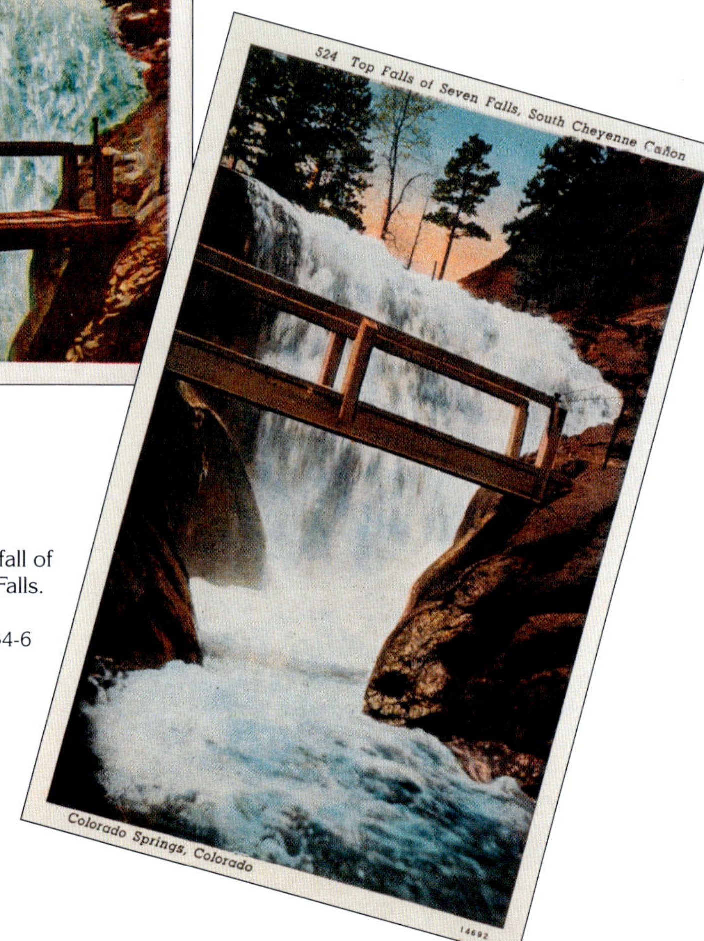

The first waterfall of Seven Falls.

Circa 1930s, $4-6

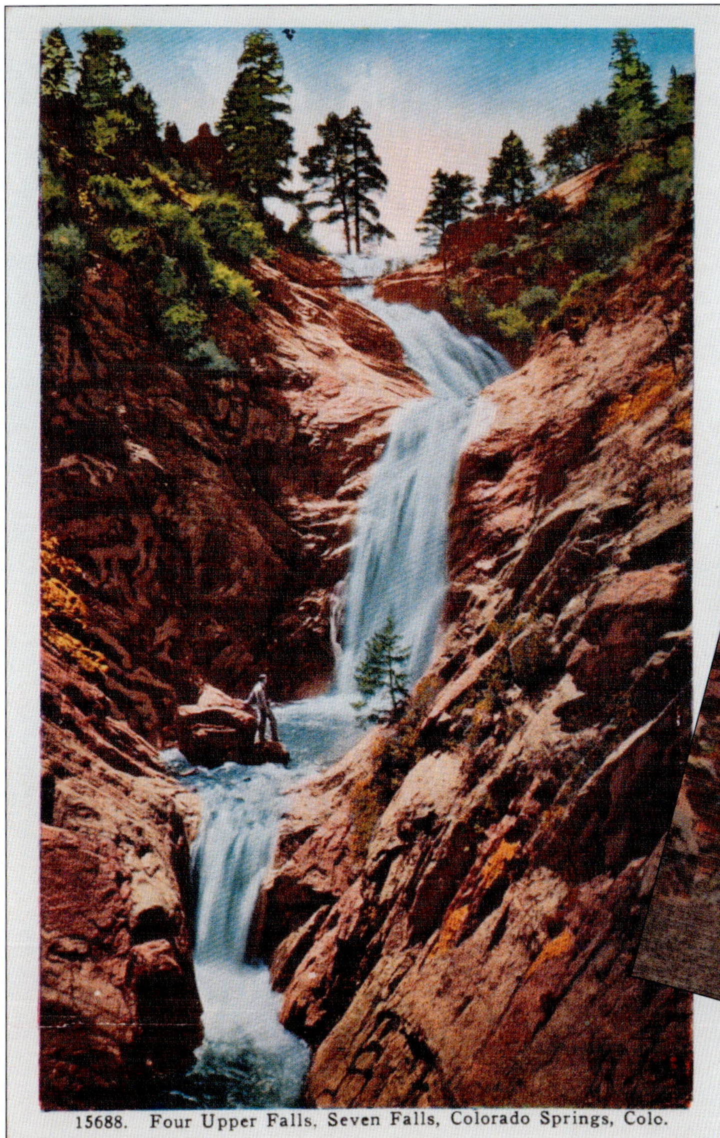

A curious tourist gets a closer look at Seven Falls.

Circa 1930s, $4-6

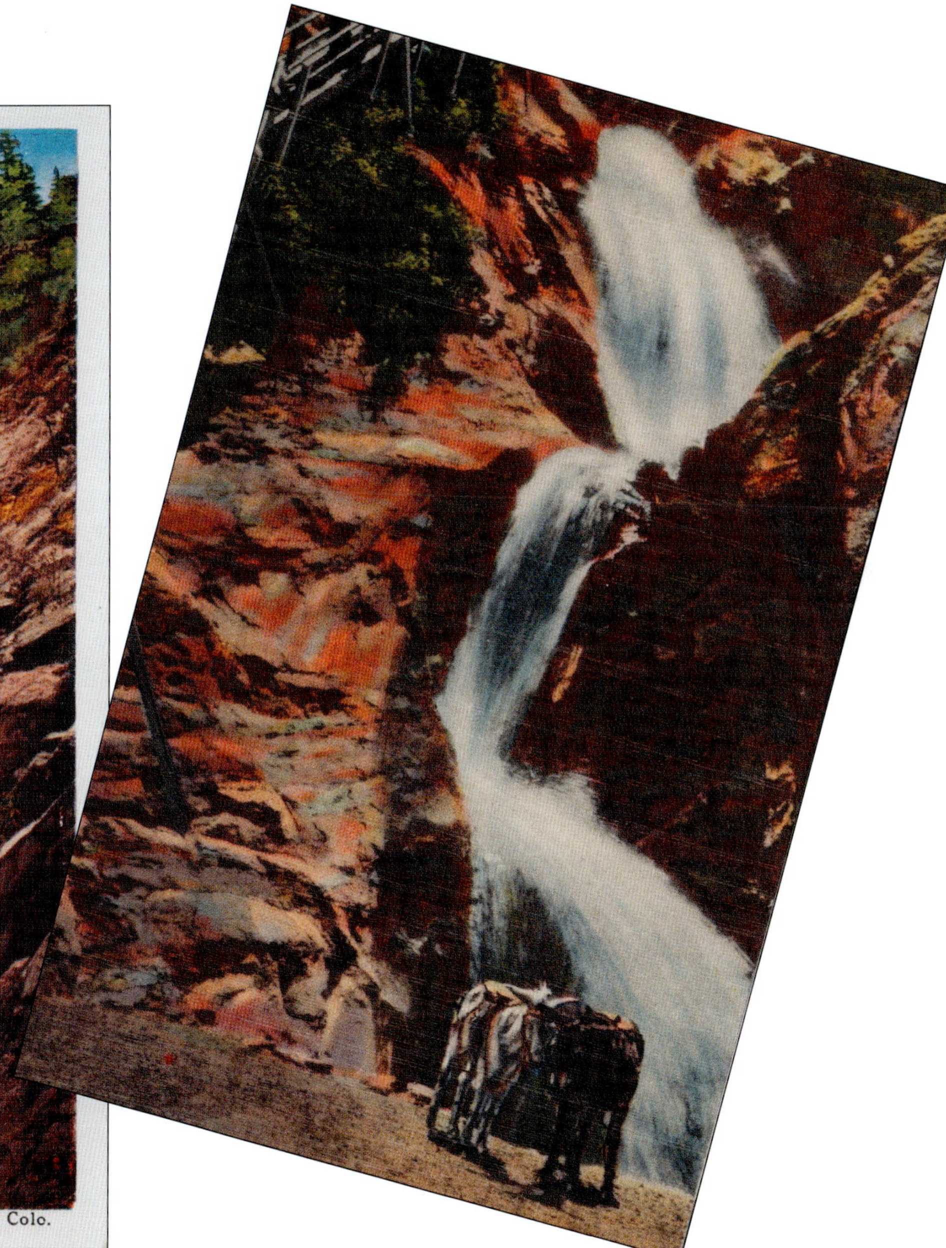

The lower three cascades of Seven Falls.

Circa 1940s, $4-6

Pikes Peak

On November 15, 1806, Zebulon Pike first laid eyes upon a distant mountain which he called the "Grand Peak." Upon reaching the Peak, he and members of his expedition attempted to climb the mountain. Unfortunately, Pike and his men were not prepared for the inhospitable conditions found on the mountain's slope and were forced to retreat and abandon their climb.

Dr. Edwin James, the first person in recorded history to reach the top of Pikes Peak did so in 1820, fourteen years after Pike's attempt. A recent graduate of Vermont's Middlebury College, he had signed on as a relief botanist with the Long Expedition, an expedition lead by Stephen Harriman Long which conducted the first scientific exploration of the Platte River.

While the majority of the expedition remained camped on the plains below, James and two other men climbed to the summit of Pikes Peak, reaching the top in two days.

When it came to naming the mountain, opinion was divided. During the period when Colorado was still being explored, the mountain was called "Pike's Peak" after Zebulon Pike. After Edwin James' accomplishment became well known, some said that it should be called "James' Peak" after the first man to climb to the top. The debate went back and forth until "Pike's Peak" was eventually decided on. The United States Board on Geographic names officially discouraged the use of apostrophes, so the mountain became known as "Pikes Peak," though both spellings were used. In 1978, the Colorado State Legislature passed a legislation making "Pikes Peak" the official spelling.

When he founded Colorado Springs, General Palmer recognized the value of Pikes Peak and used it to promote both the town and to encourage travel west on the Denver & Rio Grande Railroad. The plan worked and soon people were coming to Colorado Springs and Pikes Peak from all over the eastern United States and Europe.

At first the best way to reach the summit was to travel by horse and carriage halfway up the mountain, then continue the rest of the way by mule. The trip was long, difficult, and often took two days. After making such a trip in the late 1880s, Zalmon Simmons, owner of the Simmons Mattress Company, decided that there must be an easier way to get to the top. In 1889, Simmons founded the Manitou and Pike's Railway Company and built a cog railway, a railway which uses a special toothed rack situated between the rails on the track and a cog mounted on the undercarriage of the engine in order to ascend steep slopes, which ran from nearby Manitou Springs to the top of Pikes Peak and back. In 1915, Spencer Penrose also improved the methods of reaching the top and built the Pikes Peak Auto Highway. To promote his new highway, Penrose sponsored the first Pikes Peak Hill Climb Race, a race that is still held to this day.

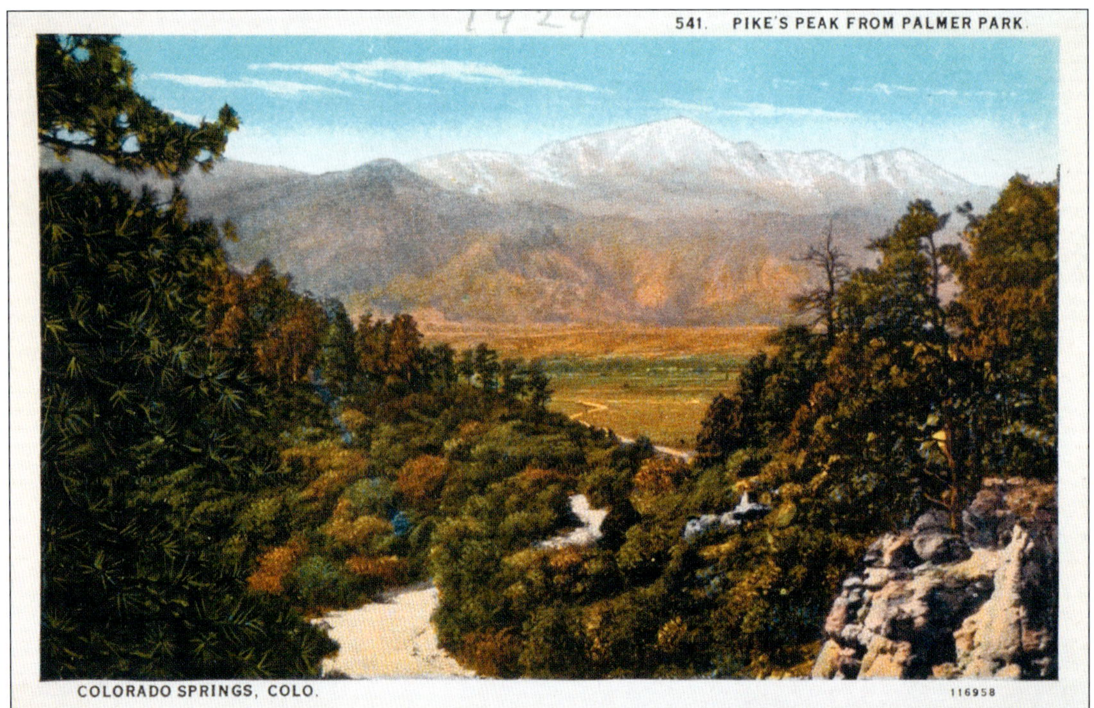

Only ten miles from Colorado Springs, Pikes Peak is, perhaps, the most famous mountain in the state of Colorado and has been named a National Historic Landmark.

Circa 1920s, $4-6

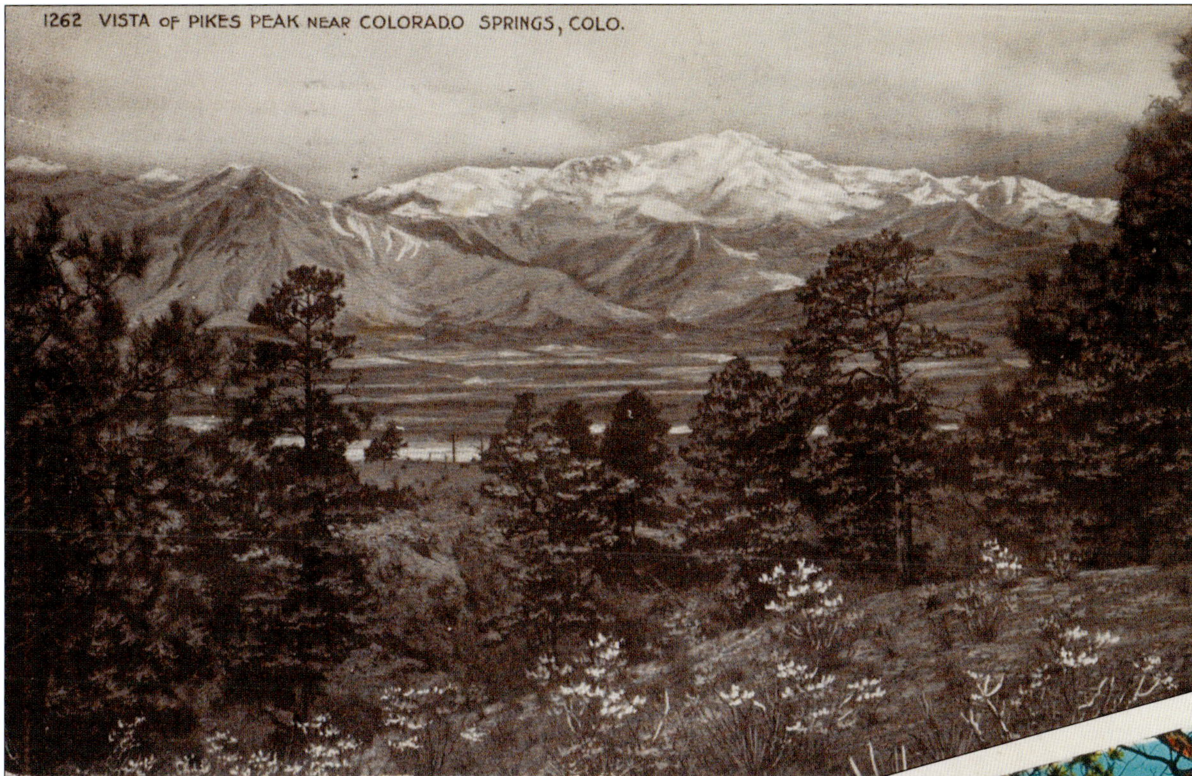

Pikes Peak is 14,110 feet tall and is one of Colorado's fifty-four "fourteeners," a mountain that is over 14,000 feet tall.

Cancelled 1914, $4-6

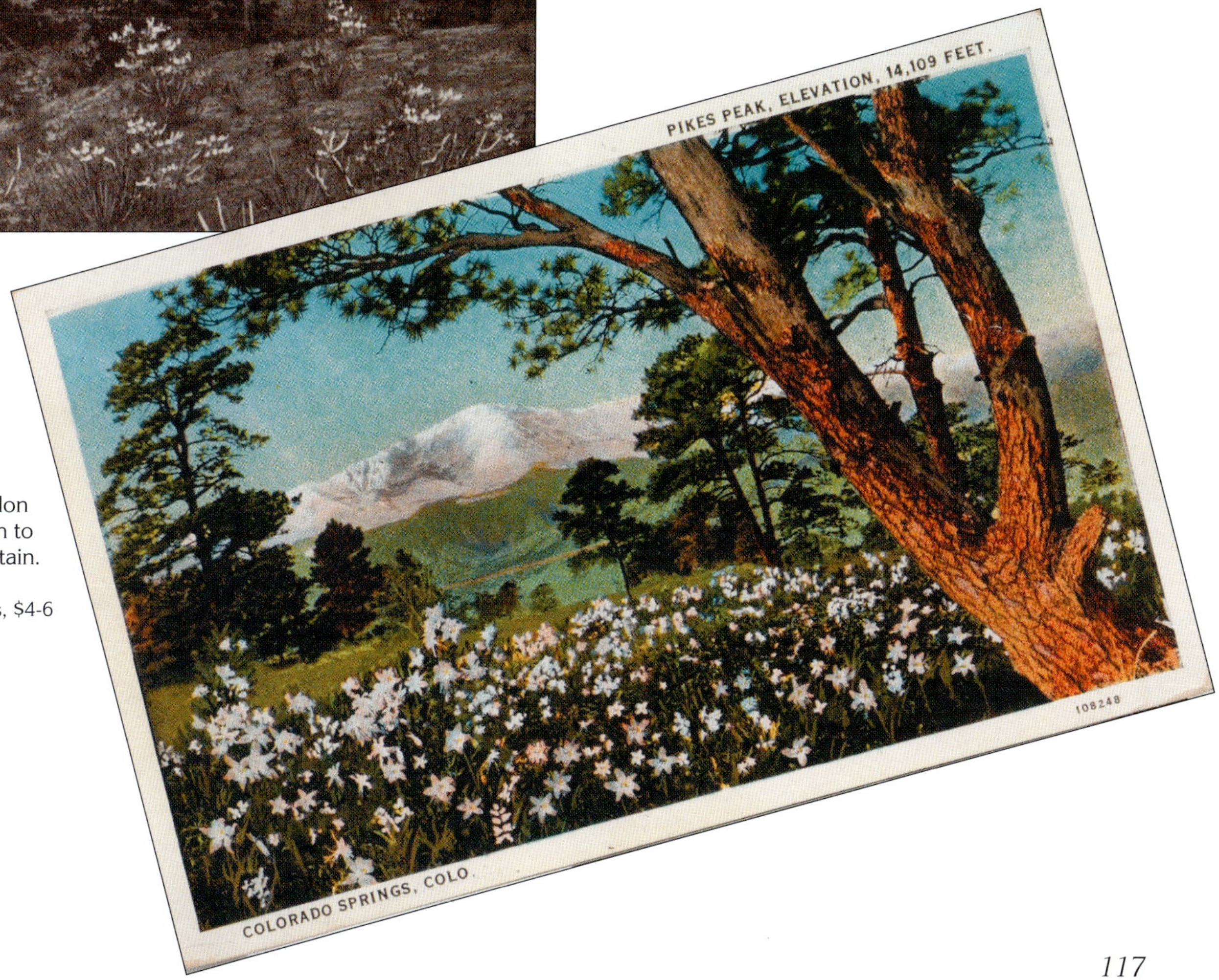

Pikes Peak is named after Zebulon Pike, the first non-Native American to see the mountain.

Circa 1940s, $4-6

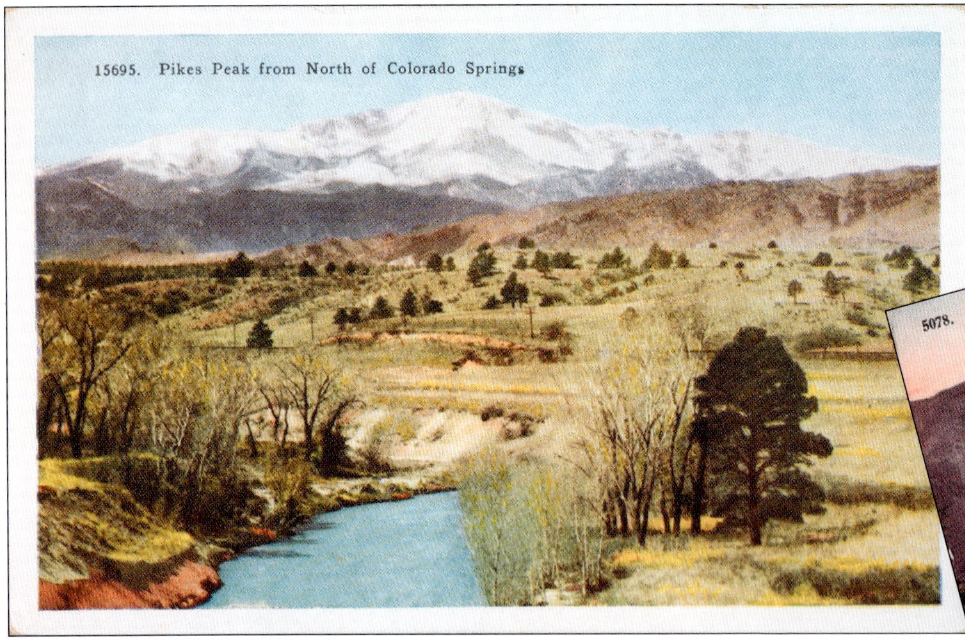

In November of 1806, Pike and his expedition attempted to climb Pikes Peak. The attempt failed because Pike and his men were not adequately prepared for the conditions found on the mountain.

Circa 1930s, $4-6

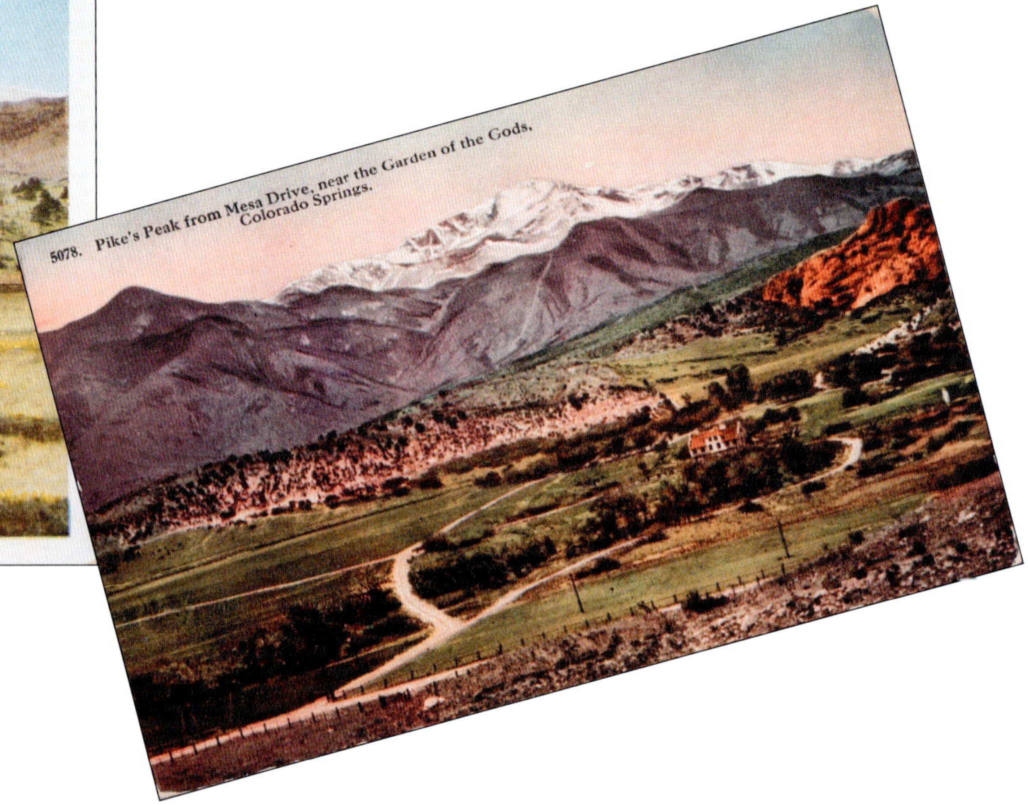

During the Colorado Gold Rush, the saying "Pikes Peak or Bust!" became the unofficial motto of the miners who traveled in droves to Colorado since it was the first landmark visible upon entering Colorado.

Circa 1910s, $4-6

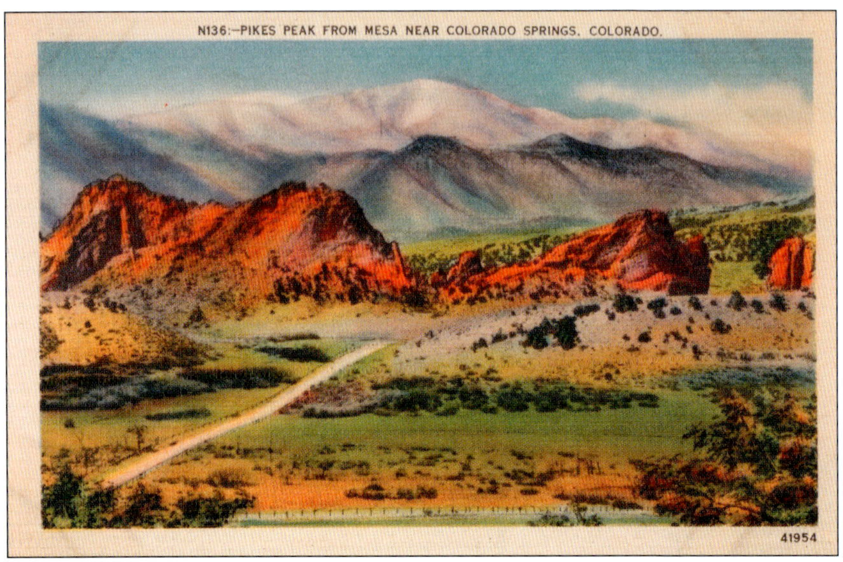

Gold was discovered on Pikes Peak in 1893. This led to the last great gold rush in the lower forty-eight states and established the fortunes of Colorado Springs benefactors, Winfield Scott Stratton and Spencer Penrose.

Circa 1940s, $4-6

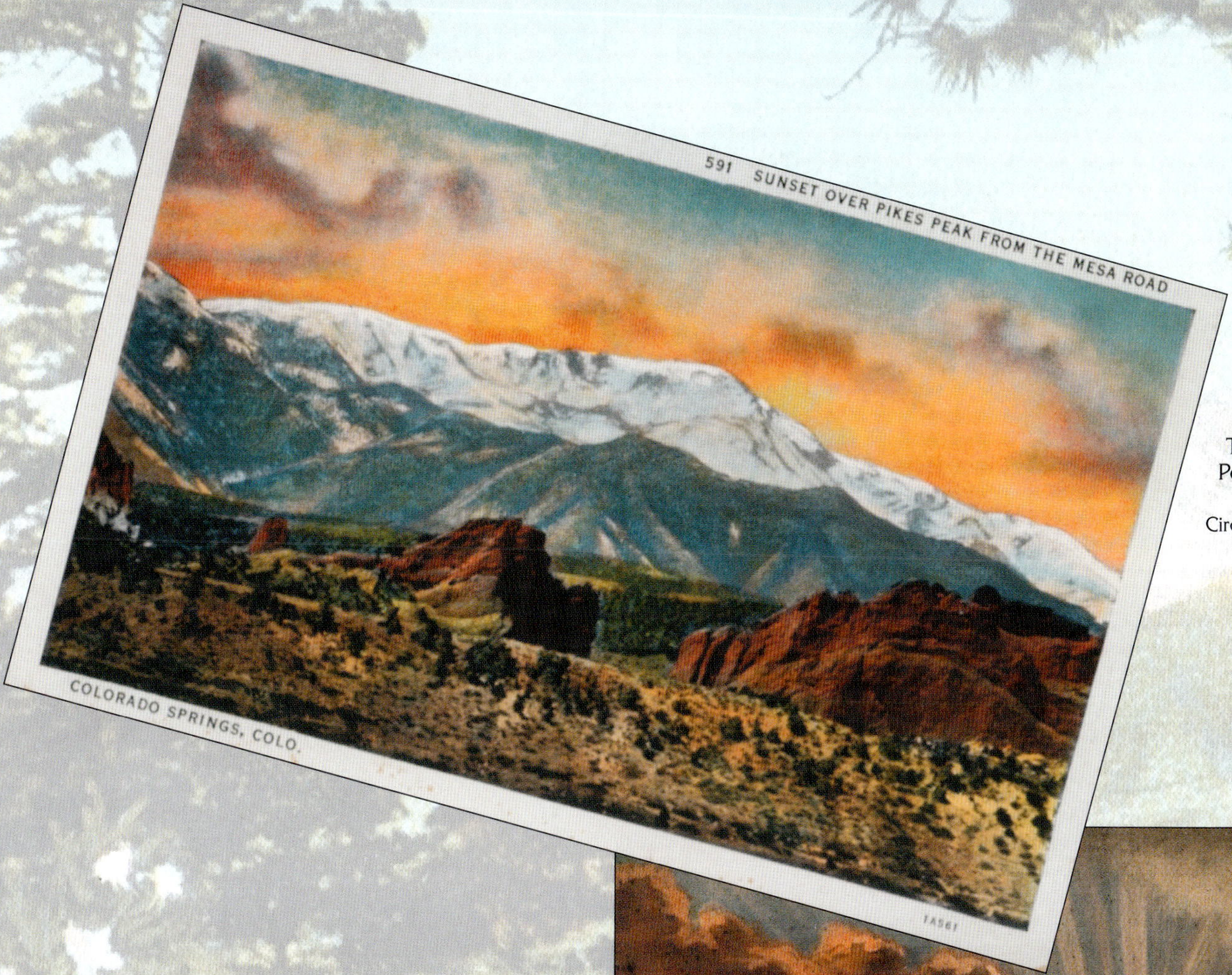

The first woman to ever climb Pikes Peak was Julie Holmes in 1858.

Circa 1930s, $4-6

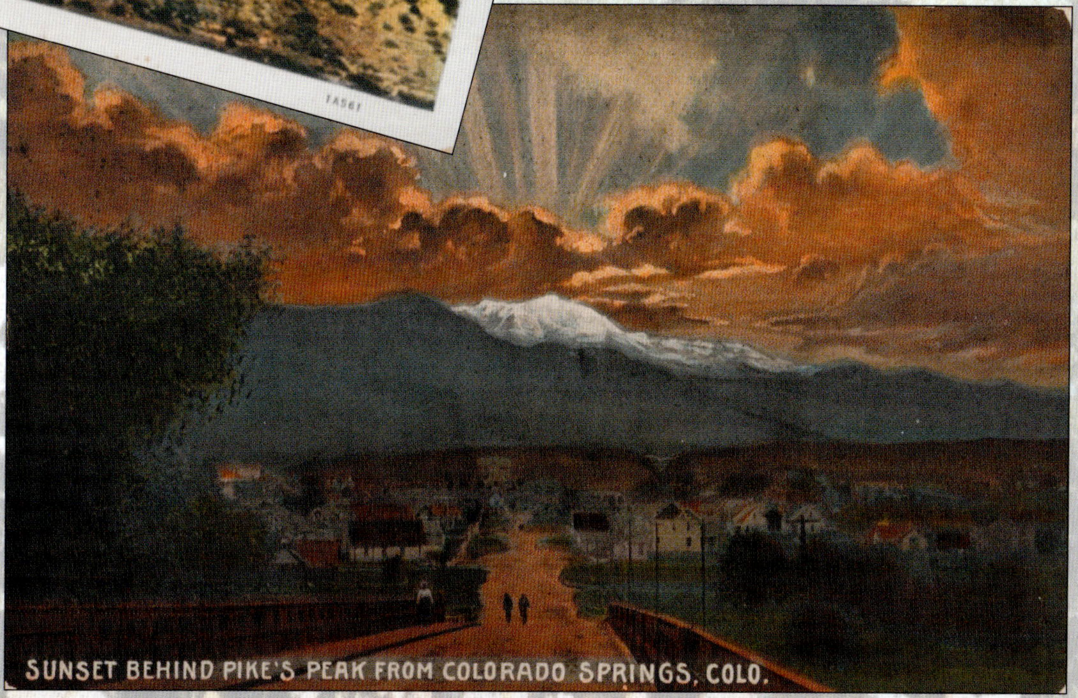

In order to acquire ceremonial feathers, Ute Indians would often scale Pikes Peak to set eagle traps at the summit.

Cancelled 1913, $4-6

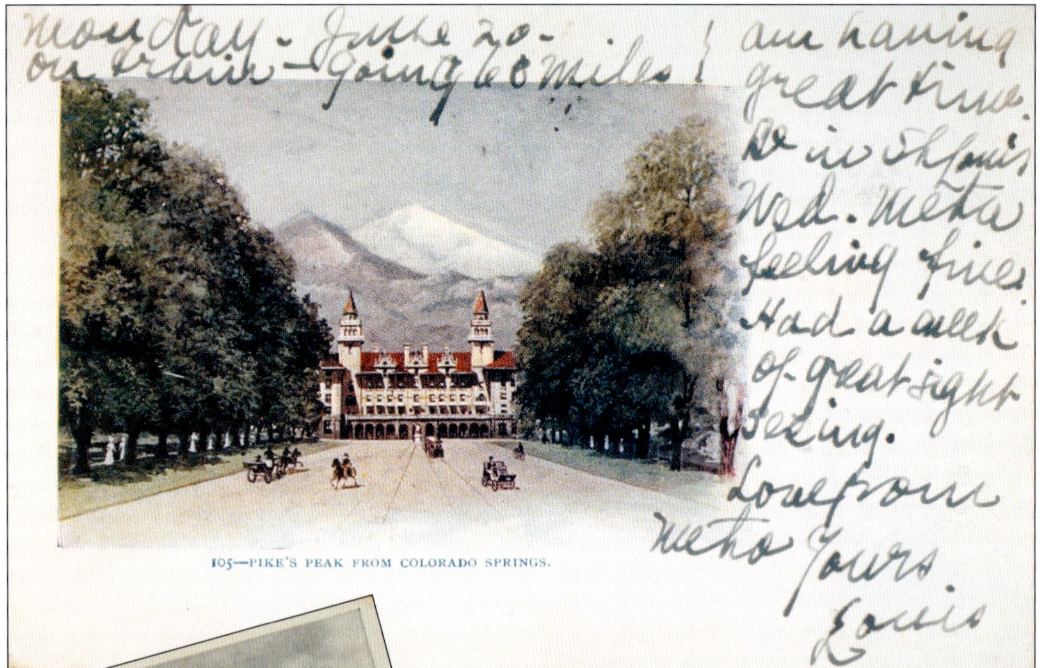

Pikes Peak as seen from Pikes Peak Avenue in front of the Antlers Hotel.

Cancelled 1904, $4-6

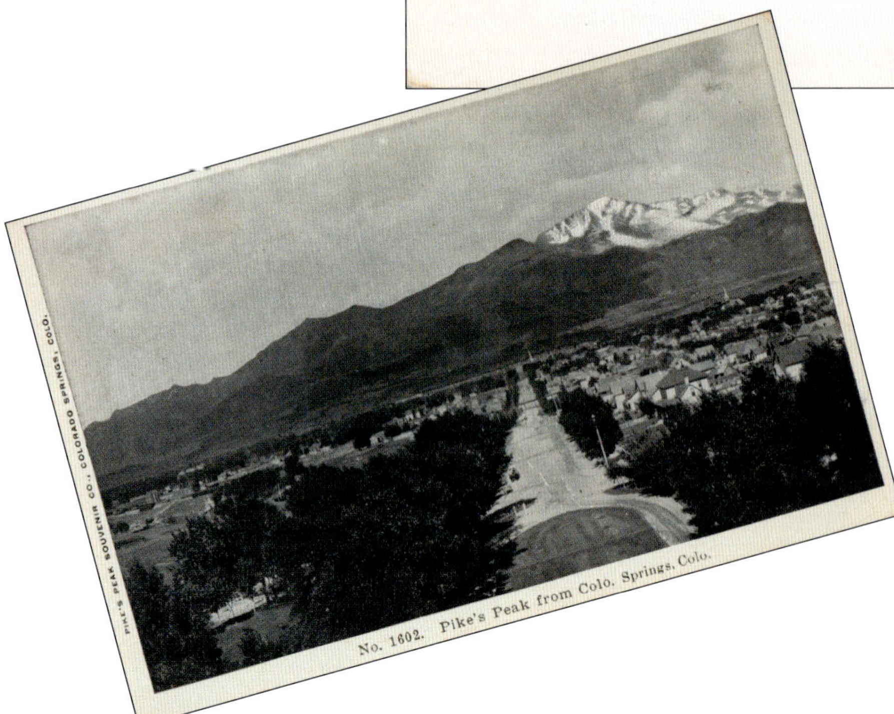

It was after a trip to the summit of Pikes Peak that Katherine Lee Bates was inspired to write the poem that would eventually become the song, "America the Beautiful."

Circa 1910s, $4-6

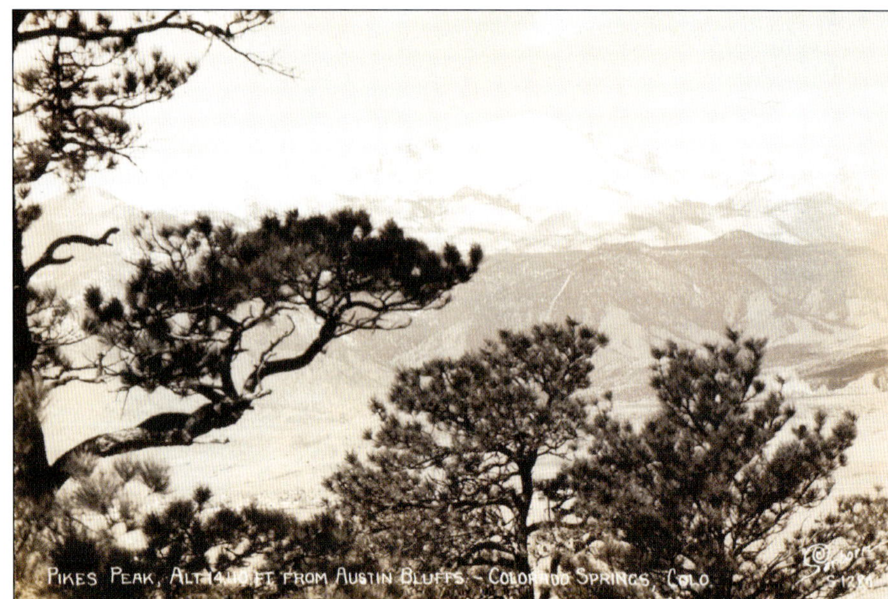

Pikes Peak is part of the Front Range, a mountain range that runs from the Wyoming-Colorado Border to south-central Colorado.

Circa 1930s, $5-7

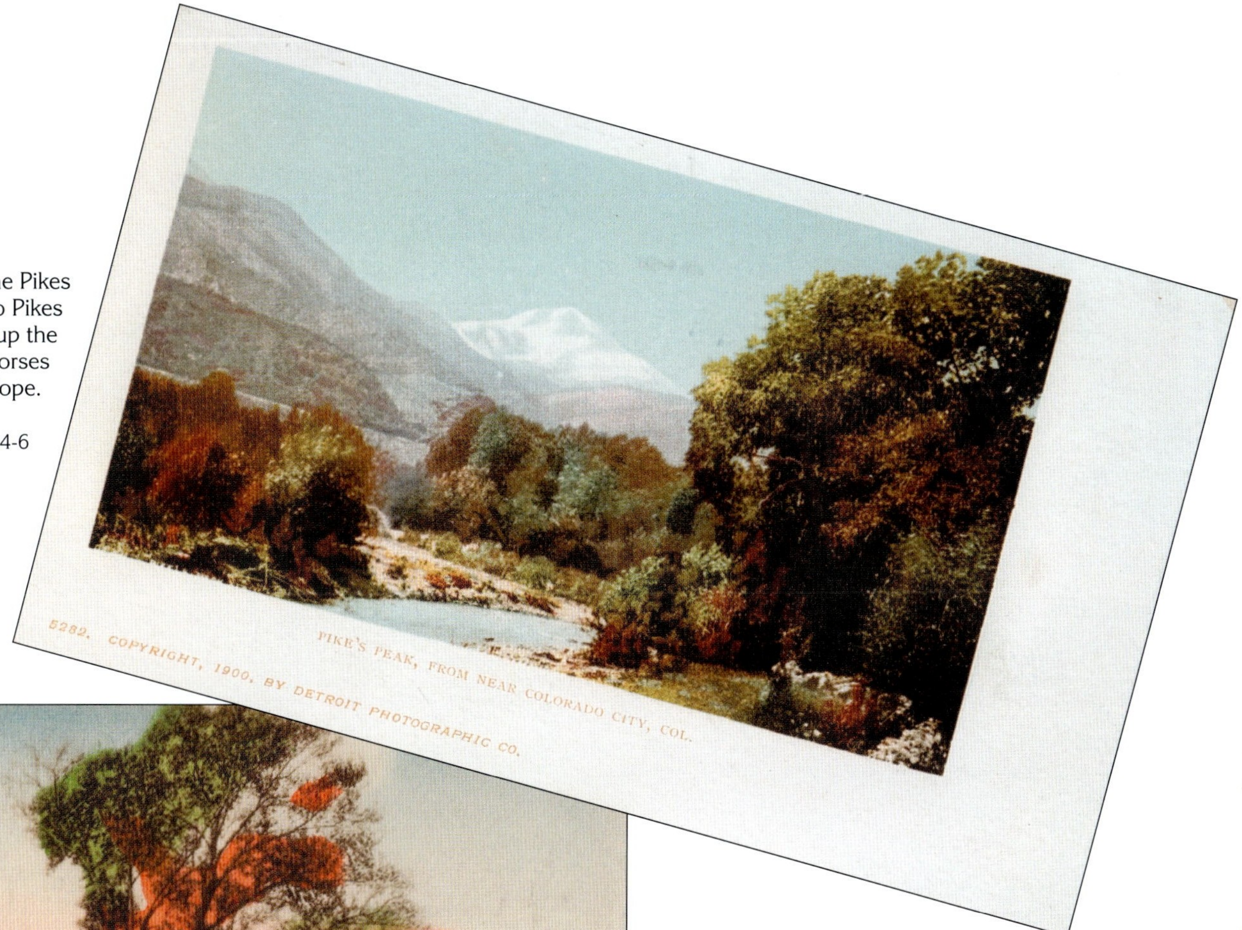

Before the building of the Pikes Peak Auto Highway, visitors to Pikes Peak would take carriages up the mountain, exchanging the horses for mules halfway up the slope.

Circa 1900s, $4-6

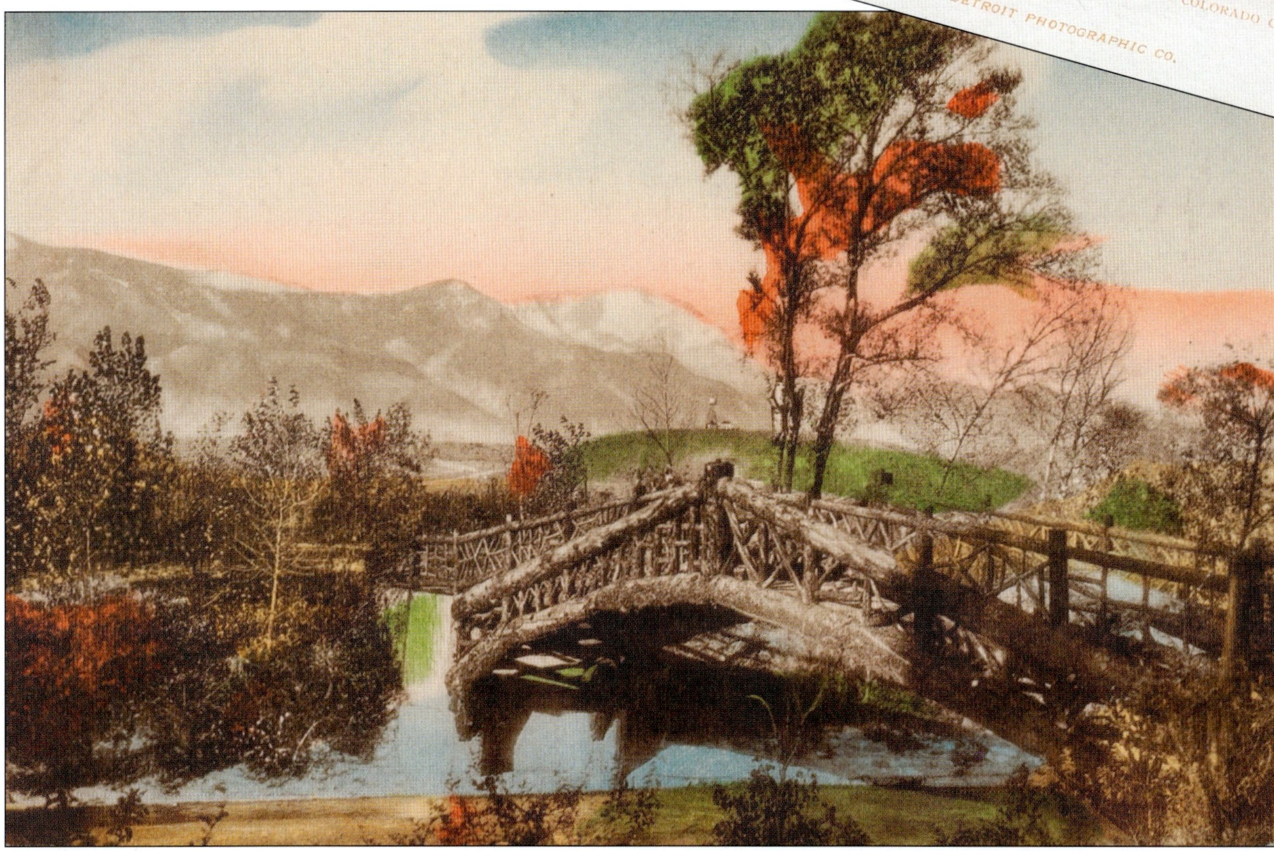

When choosing the location for his resort community, General Palmer saw the potential in building close to Pikes Peak. After he founded Colorado Springs, he used the mountain to promote both Colorado Springs and travel on the Denver & Rio Grande Railroad.

Circa 1930s, $4-6

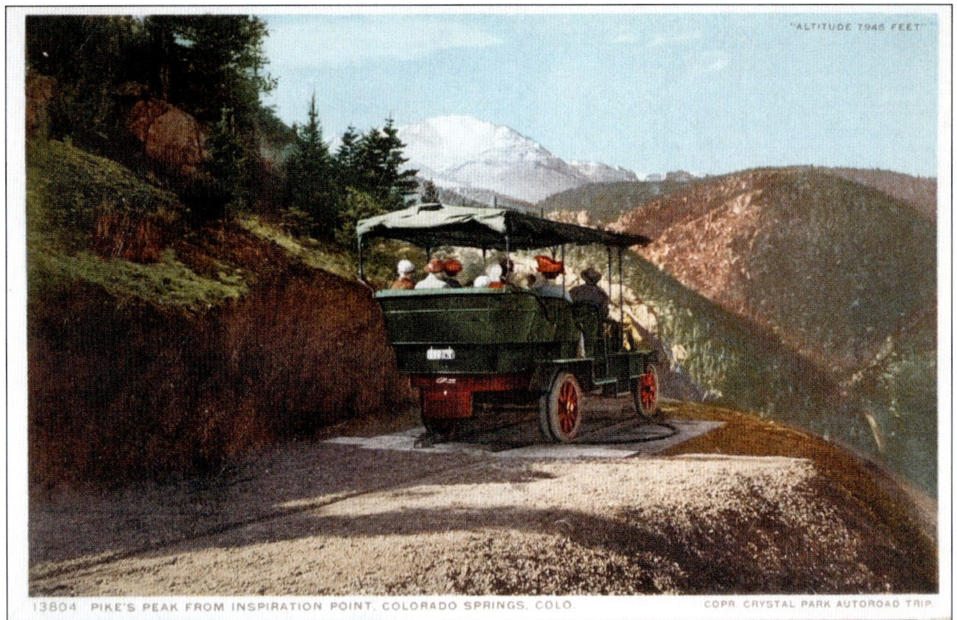

Tourists take a look at Pikes Peak from Inspiration Point in South Cheyenne Canyon.

Circa 1910s, $4-6

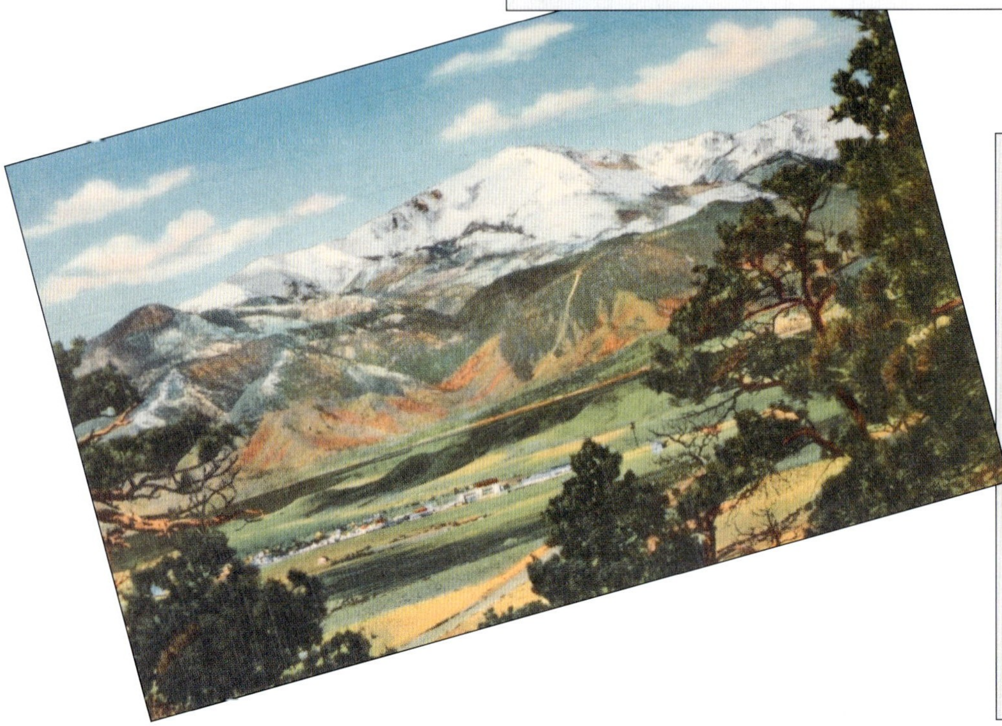

Postcard photo showing Pikes Peak in relation to Colorado Springs.

Circa 1940s, $4-6

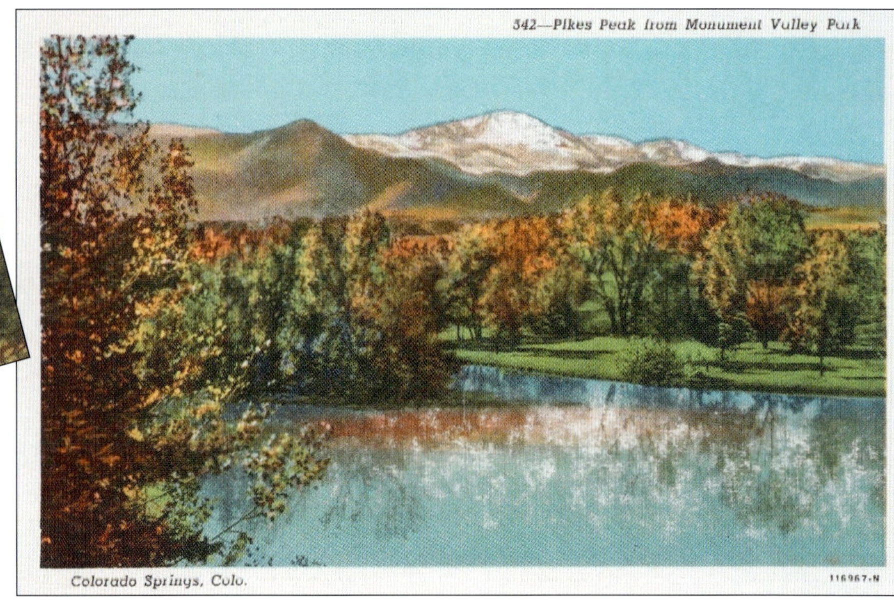

Pikes Peak as seen from Monument Valley Park.

Circa 1930s, $4-6

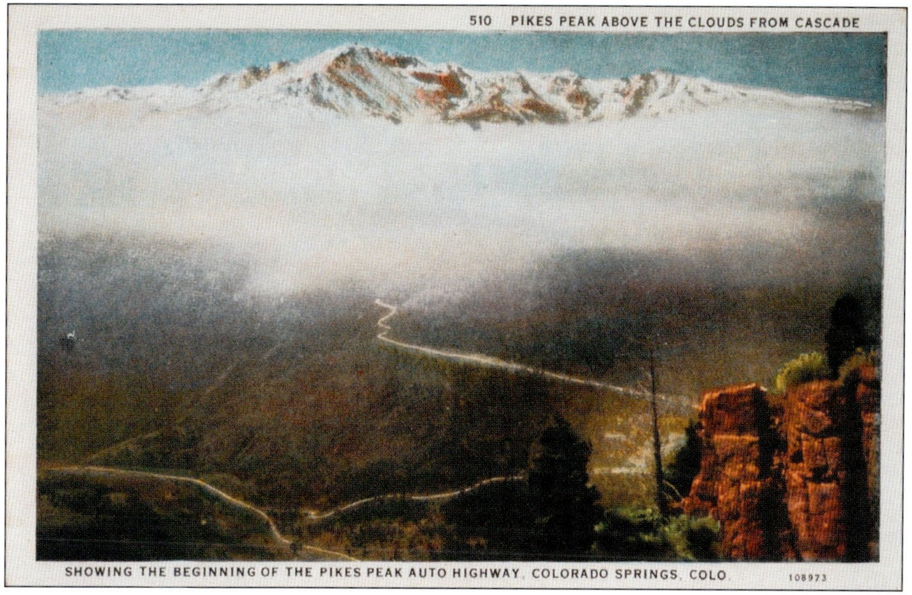

During the summer, thunderstorms are very common around the summit of Pikes Peak.

Circa 1920s, $4-6

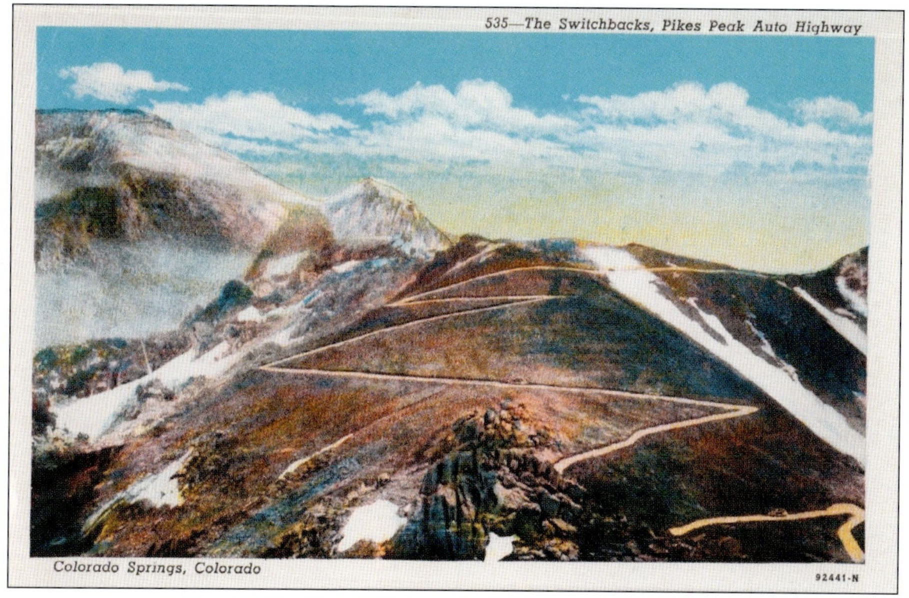

Beginning at Cascade in Ute Pass, the Pikes Peak Auto Highway runs for nineteen miles to the top of Pikes Peak.

Cancelled 1955, $4-6

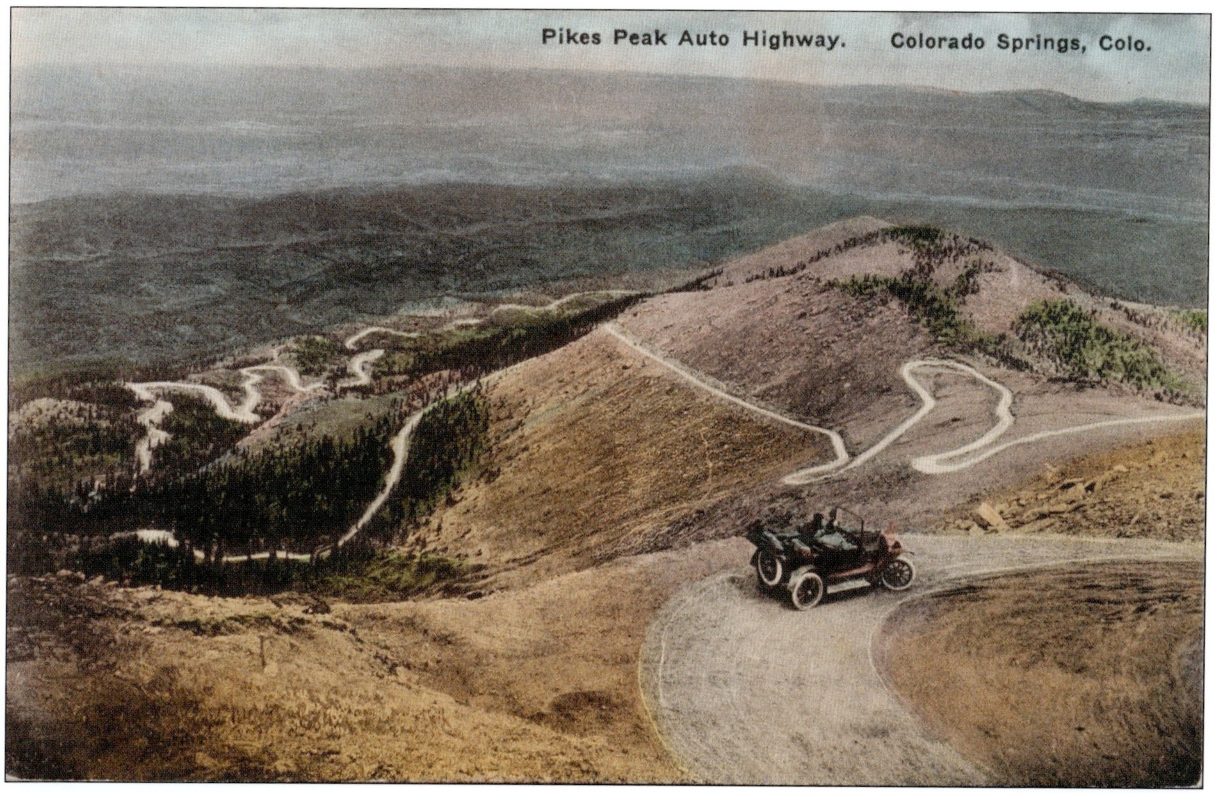

Since 1916 the Pikes Peak Auto Highway has been part of the annual Pikes International Hillclimb, a car and motorcycle race to the top of Pikes Peak.

Cancelled 1935, $4-6

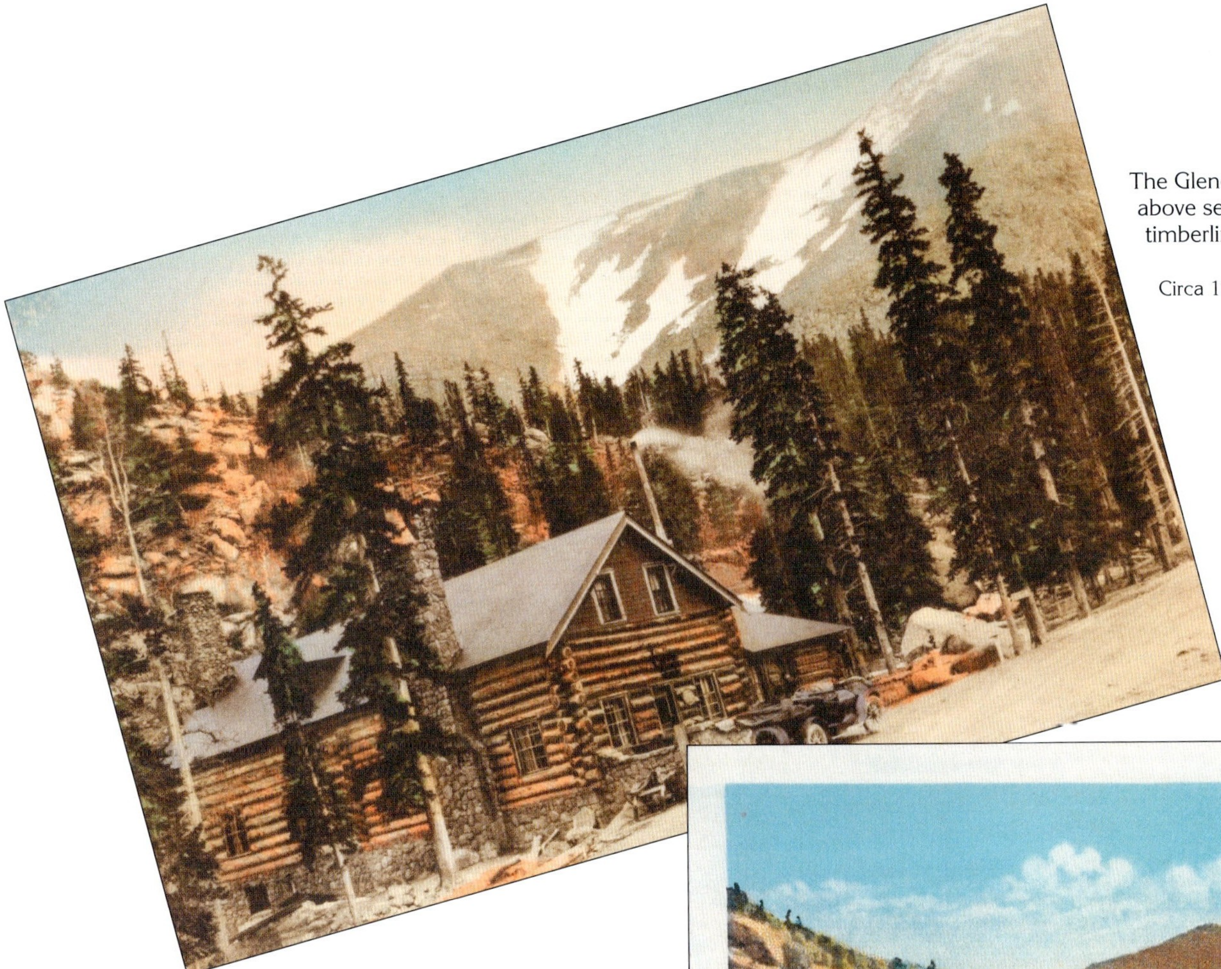

The Glencoe Inn located 11,425 feet above sea level at the Pikes Peak timberline.

Circa 1930s, $4-6

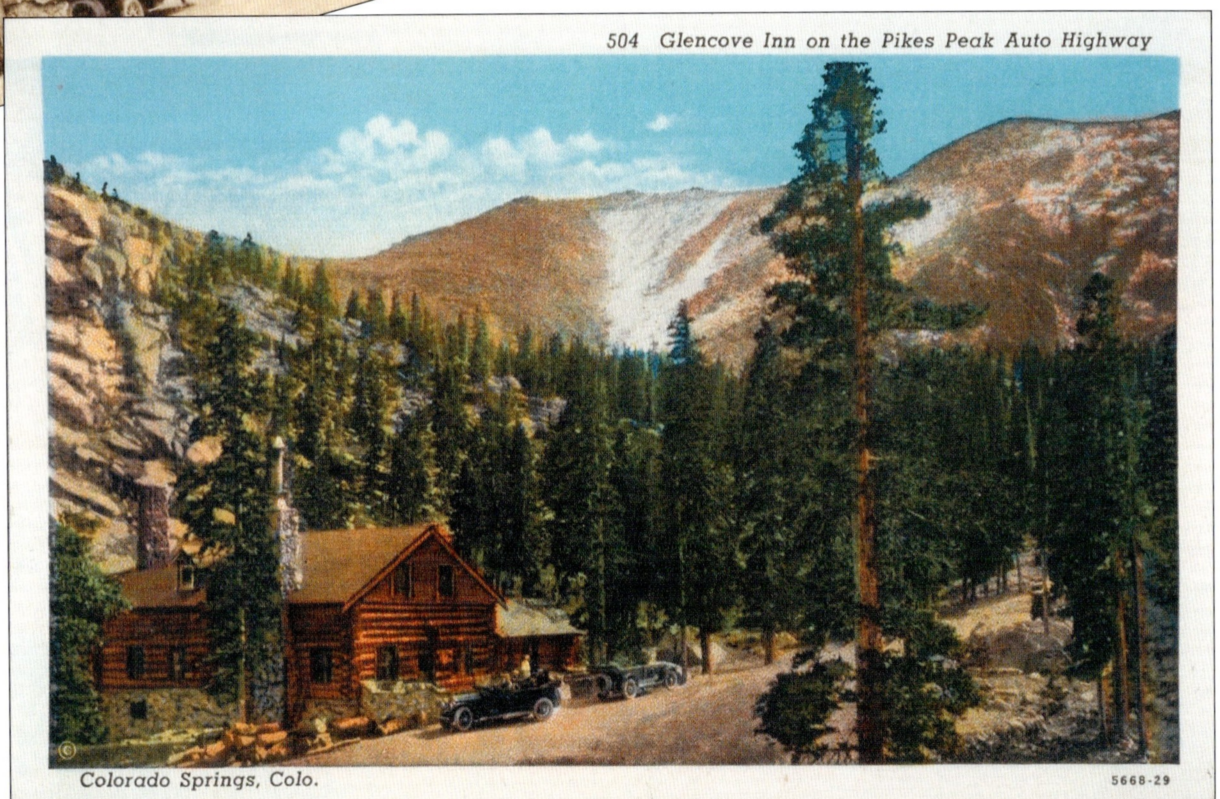

Built to accommodate travelers, the Glencoe Inn was the main stopping point along the Pikes Peak Auto Highway.

Circa 1930s, $4-6

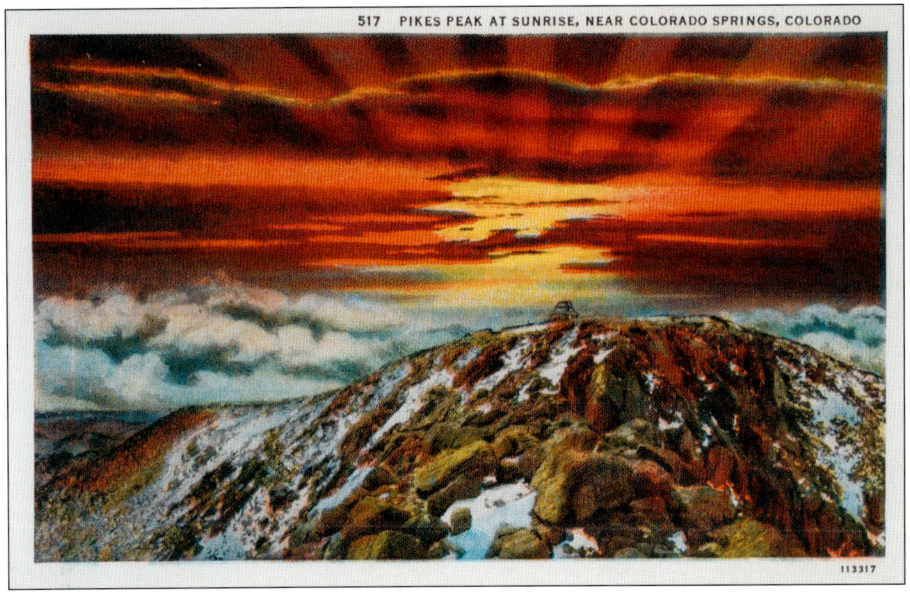

The Utes called Pikes Peak *Tavakiev*, which means "Sun Mountain," as it is the first of the Colorado peaks to greet the sun as it rises in the morning.

Circa 1920s, $4-6

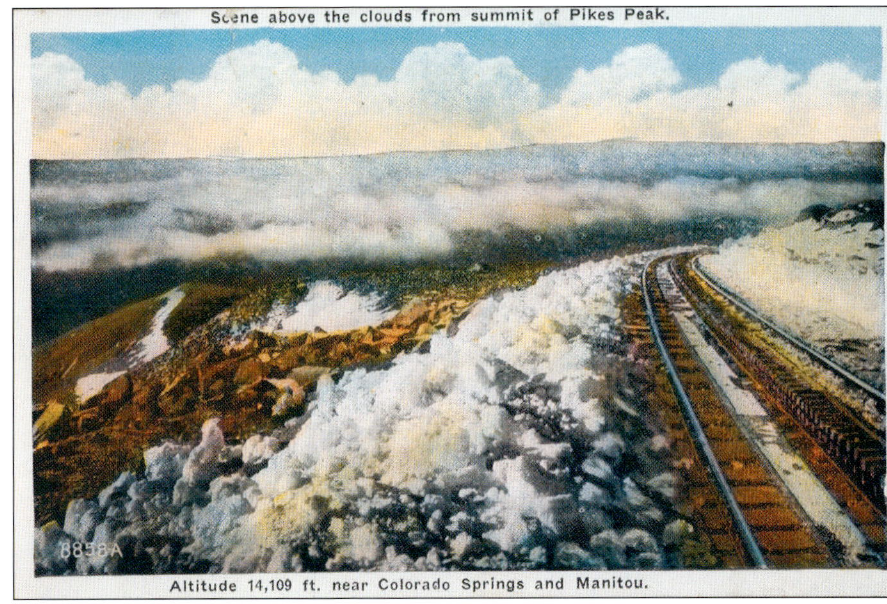

The tracks of the Manitou and Pike's Peak Railway. The Railway runs from Manitou Springs to the summit of Pikes Peak from April to December and is the highest cog railroad in the world.

Cancelled 1934, $4-6

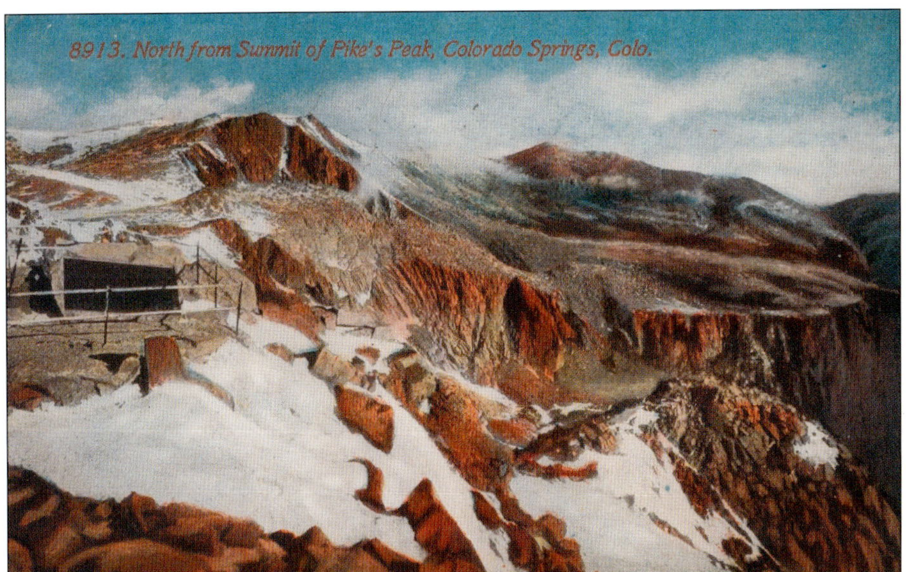

Snowfall was very common at the summit of Pikes Peak, and could happen at anytime throughout the year.

Cancelled 1913, $4-6

Members of the AdAmAn Club of Colorado Springs would hike to the summit of Pikes Peak in the dead of winter to initiate one new member. The club would also set off a fireworks display from the summit on New Years Eve.

Circa 1930s, $4-6

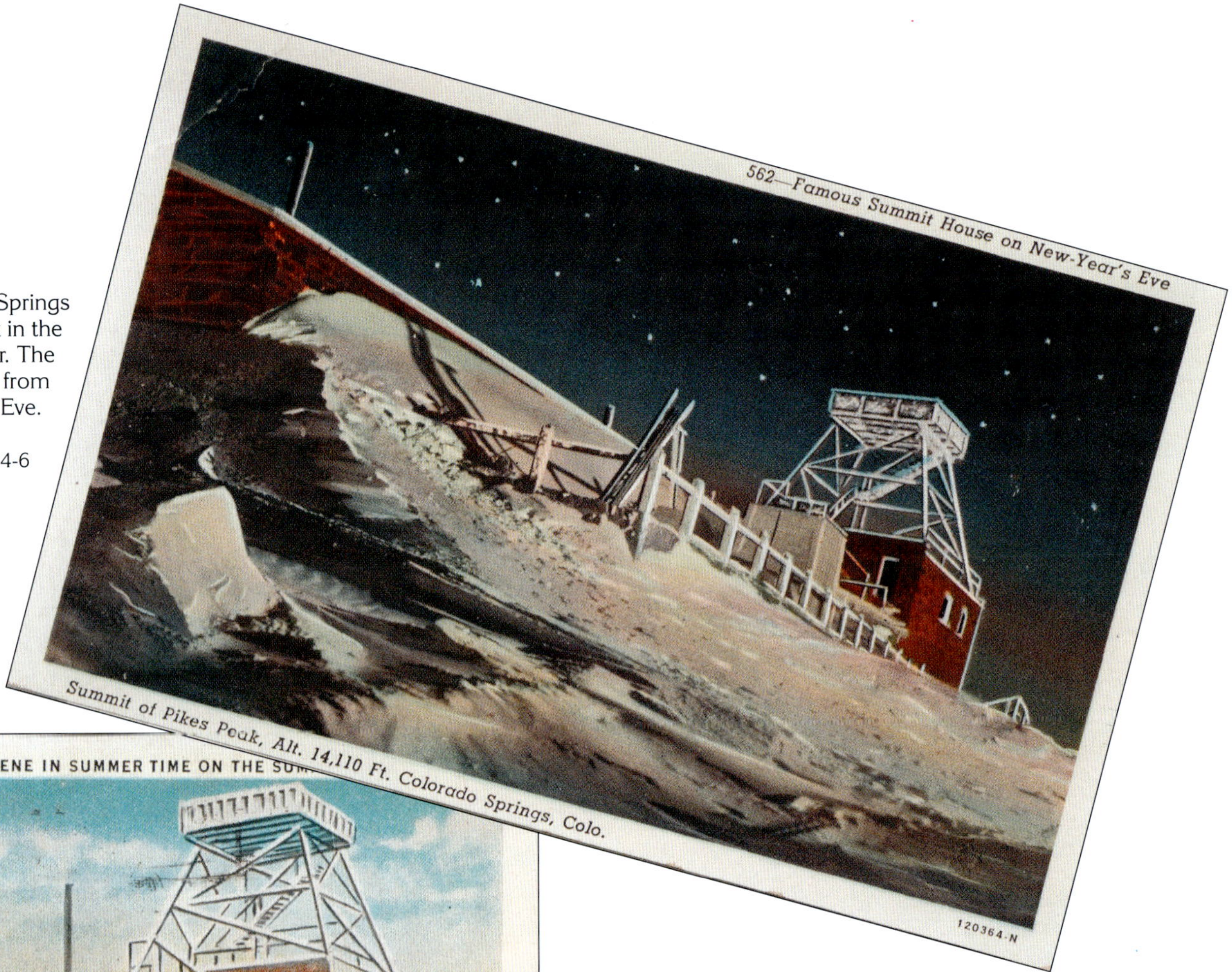

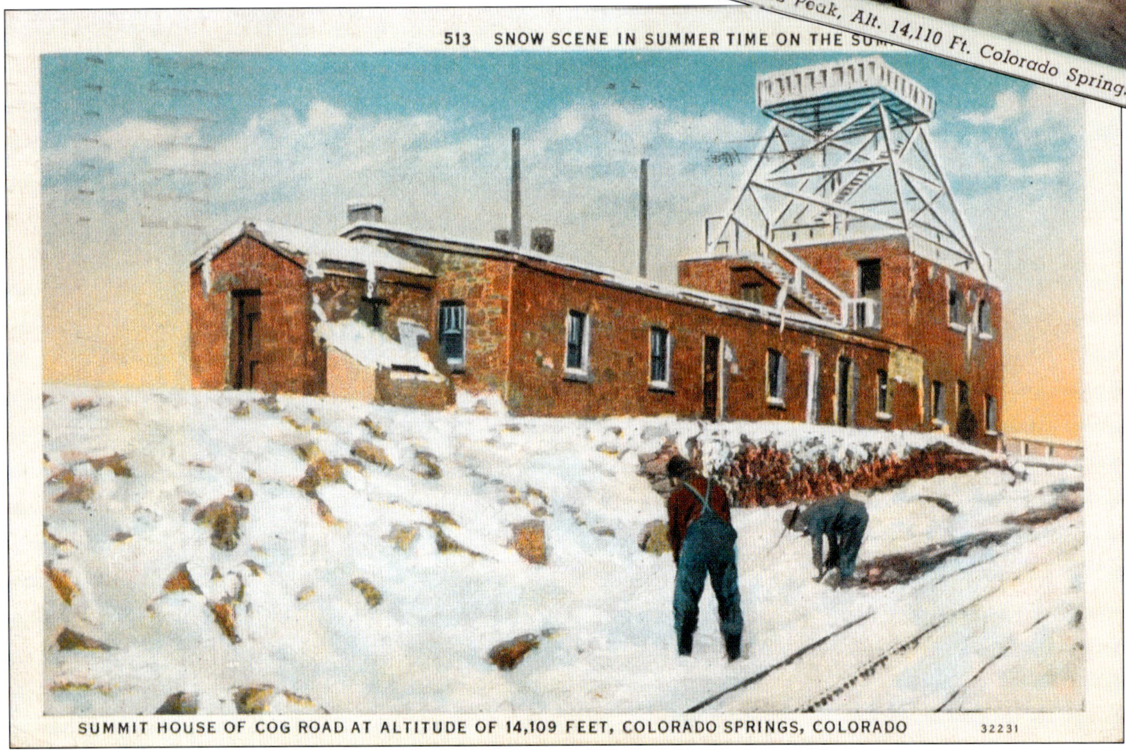

In 1873 the United States Signal Service built a telegraph station at the summit of Pikes Peak in order to monitor the weather.

Cancelled 1936, $4-6

Bibliography

AAA. Colorado & Utah. Heathrow: AAA Publishing, 2002.

"A Brief History of Grace Church." Grace Church & St. Stephen's. http://www.graceandststephens.org/history.html. 5/31/06.

"A Brief History of the Famous Seven Falls and South Cheyenne Cañon." Seven Falls, The Grandest Mile of Scenery in Colorado. http://www.sevenfalls.com/history.htm.

"About Pikes Peak." Pike's Peak Cog Railway. http://www.cograilway.com/aboutpikespeak.htm. 6/7/06.

"Broadmoor Story." The Broadmoor, Colorado Springs. http://www.broadmoor.com/page.asp?id=broad moor_story. 5/31/06.

"Cheyenne Mountain." Wikipedia. http://en.wikipedia. org/wiki/Cheyenne_Mountain. 6/2/06.

"Colorado Springs, Colorado." Wikipedia. http://en.wikipedia.org/wiki/Colorado_Springs. 5/29/06.

"Garden of the Gods Facts." Springsgov.com. http://www.springsgov.com/Page.asp?NavID=989. 6/1/02.

"General Palmer: 1836-1903." The Navigators Glen Eyrie Group. http://navigators.gospelcom.net/gleneyrie/index2.php?option=com_content&task=view&id=80&Itermid=125. 6/5/06.

"Helen Hunt Jackson: American Author, Colorado Springs Resident." Springsgov.com. http://www.springsgov.com/Page.asp?NavID=6253. 6/1/06.

"Historic Ownership of Garden of the Gods." Springs gov.com. http://www.springsgov.com/Page.asp? NavID=992. 6/1/06.

"Historic Parks of Colorado Springs, Colorado." Springsgov.com. http://www.springsgov.com/Page.asp?NavID=945. 6/1/06.

"History." Antlers Hilton Colorado Springs, Colorado. http://www.web.archive.org/web/20041010082935/www.antlers.com/history.htm. 6/8/06.

Jackson, Helen Hunt. *Bits of Travel at Home* (1878). Yosemite Online Library. http://www.yosemite. ca.us/library/bits_of_travel_at_home/colorado. html. 6/6/06.

Lamb, Susan. *The Smithsonian Guides to Natural America: The Southern Rockies*. Washington D.C.: Smithsonian Books, 1995.

"Penrose House." El Pomar Foundation. http://www.elpomar.org/page.asp?pageid=016151&id= 01penrose_house. 6/1/06.

"Pikes Peak." Wikipedia. http://en.wikipedia.org/wiki/Pikes_Peak. 5/29/06.

Sprague, Marshall. *Greetings from Colorado*. Portland: Graphic Arts Center Publishing, 1988.

"The First People of the Cañon and the Pikes Peak Region." Springsgov.com. http://www.springsgov.com/Page.asp?NavID=3069. 6/1/06.

"Will Rogers Shrine of the Sun." Cheyenne Mountain Zoo. http://www.cmzoo.org/shrine.html. 6/2/06.

Index